G W IRVIN

Trade Liberalization Under Imperfect Competition

An analysis of the European Union's market for banana imports

A thesis submitted by

Claudius Preville
(St. Lucia)

in fulfilment of the requirements for the degree of
DOCTOR OF PHILOSOPHY IN DEVELOPMENT STUDIES
of the Institute of Social Studies,
The Hague, The Netherlands.
August 2002.

Thesis Committee

Promotores:

Professor Dr. J. B. (Hans) Opschoor
Rector, Institute of Social Studies

Professor Dr. M. P. van Dijk
Erasmus University Rotterdam

Dr. G. W. Irvin
Associate Professor, Institute of Social Studies

Examiners:

Dr. R. Read
University of Lancaster

Professor Dr. G. Junne
University of Amsterdam

Professor Dr. R. P. Vos
Institute of Social Studies

This dissertation is part of the research programme of CERES, Research School for Resource Studies for Development

Funded by the Netherlands Fellowship Programme (NFP)

Printed in The Netherlands.

ISBN 90-423-0207-0

Shaker Publishing BV., St. Maartenslaan 26, 6221 AX Maastricht
Tel.: 043-3500424   Fax: 043-3255090   http:// www.shaker.nl

Acknowledgements

When I embarked upon this Ph.D. research in January 1999, I knew it would be a challenging and demanding project. What I did not know then was the extent of that challenge, the depth of that demand and the loneliness I would have to endure before completing it. In that connection, a number of persons have contributed in various ways to making this dream a reality and I would like to publicly acknowledge their input.

First of all, my promoters, the intellectual guardians of this project, Prof. Dr J. B. (Hans) Opschoor, Prof. Dr M. P. Van Dijk and Dr G. W. Irvin have all provided tremendous motivation, assistance and support. Let me say a few things about them individually.

Prof. Dr. Opschoor joined the project at a very late and crucial stage. An advanced manuscript of the thesis already existed and my original promoter with first responsibility, Prof. Dr S. A. R. Sideri, had been ill for a prolonged period following his retirement (he had been professor of international trade) to his native Italy. Internal rules of the Ph.D. programme require that the promoter with first responsibility must be from the Institute, and so I approached Prof. Dr Opschoor to consider taking on that responsibility. He willingly read my manuscript and agreed to assume the responsibility of promoter with first responsibility for its completion, while Prof. Dr Van Dijk and Dr Irvin retained substantive technical responsibility for the finishing touches. Therefore, although this work has benefited tremendously from Prof. Dr Sideri's input (especially on the theoretical framework) and I hope he is well enough to read the final product, I must acknowledge Prof. Dr Opschoor's input into Chapter 9 in particular, and his wisdom, diplomacy and humility in seeing this work to a smooth completion.

Prof. Dr Van Dijk has made a sterling contribution to this work and I thank him for his generosity. Despite his full agenda (professor at Erasmus University Rotterdam and recently professor at IHE Delft), he took an intimate interest in my work right from the first year, when he served as external discussant at my thesis seminar. Since then he has read every chapter of this thesis several times and watched this work evolve, intervening only when he thinks it necessary. I particularly acknowledge his advice on WTO issues, the concept of the commodity chain and much of the discussion on the division of wealth among nations.

Dr Irvin's contribution to this work has been just as important. In fact, it was he who originally tempted me with the idea of doing a Ph.D., having provided excellent supervision of my MA research paper in 1997 (which was awarded a distinction). He has read every one of my chapters several times, right from the start, and has provided very practical and helpful comments at all stages. Dr Irvin has a penchant for structure and logic, which is so crucial for undertaking such a task. I credit Dr Irvin with, among other things, guiding the econometric work that has been done in this thesis.

Given that this study is transnational in nature, the field work has been challenging, since I had to visit several strategic locations in different countries in order to acquire the relevant data. That meant rapidly establishing contact with a number of key organizations and individuals, and I owe a huge debt of gratitude to them. I am particularly grateful for the assistance I received from the following Commission officials in Brussels: Christian Simon, Alexia Divisson, and Isabel Maltby. Other helpful people in Brussels were Philippe Binard, Alvaro Gonzalez De Cossio, Gérald Harte, HE Edwin Laurent and Patricia Auguste. In Antwerp, I am extremely grateful to industry official Luc Hellebuyck, who provided me with a wealth of original information as well as regular updates on developments in the field through e-mail.

In Geneva, I am grateful to WTO officials Peter van den Bossche, Nicolas Lockhart, Werner Zdouc, Petina Gappah, Barthel Rosa, Catherine Hennis-Pierre, Judy Cowell, Joelle Vuille Memot and Arif Hussain for interviews, discussions and assistance provided during my visit to the WTO. I am also grateful for assistance received from Gabriel Kholer, Mary McGee, Djidiack Faye, John Gara and Allessandra Velluci of UNCTAD for the assistance they provided. Other helpful people in Geneva were Cristian Espinosa, Kathy Ann Brown, Ramiro Recinos-Trejo and Anna Rodriguez and family, who extended several courtesies to me. In Luxembourg, I am particularly grateful for the support and assistance which I received from a good friend, Mehran Kafai, who arranged my meetings with EUROSTAT officials and my visits to the European Court of Justice. The data from EUROSTAT's Comext database and NewCronos were extremely useful for econometric modelling and exploratory data analysis. Other helpful people in Luxembourg were Philip Corman, Christine Alberti and Bjarne Meyer.

At FAO in Rome, a number of officials of the Commodities and Trade Division were extremely helpful in providing most of the data that have been used for econometric and exploratory data analysis. I am especially grateful to Paul Pilkauskas and his secretary Daniela Piergentili, who sat with me for several days while processing my data requests. Other helpful people at FAO were Daniela Margheriti, Pascal Lui, Mario Castejon, Terri Raney and Orio Tampieri. In connection with FAO, I am also grateful to Prof. Dr A. Saith for providing me with the name of an initial contact.

During the writing of the thesis, I benefited tremendously from contact with a number of staff and MA participants. In that regard the Economic Research Seminar series at the ISS has been invaluable. I am grateful for the comments and suggestions that I received from Prof. Dr G. Pyatt, Dr H. Nicholas, Prof. Dr R. Vos, Dr K. Jansen, Dr A. Bedi, Dr P. de Valk, J. Alarcon, J. van Heemst and N. de Jong. I am particularly grateful to Prof. Dr R. Vos, who discussed my final seminar paper and provided some useful comments. Dr K. Arts, Dr M. Spoor, Dr D. Gasper and Dr C. Kay have all been helpful, providing me with journals and news clippings from time to time. Prof. Dr J. Bjorkman, Prof. Dr M. Salih, Prof. Dr M. Doornbos, Dr A. Ahmed, Dr R. Tangri and Dr F. Schiphorst have all been supportive in various ways.

However, in order to write a Ph.D. thesis, in addition to the mentors and data that are required, one also needs an extremely efficient and reliable support service base and I have found this at the Institute. I am particularly grateful to Dita Dirks, Maureen Koster, Ank van den Berg, Lenneke Warnars, Gitta Wijnvoord, Avril Digby, Karin Hirdes, Marja Zubli, Annet van Geen, Willy Hooymans, John Sinjorgo and Sylvia Cattermole for their administrative efficiency and friendship. The computer department staff have all helped generously at various stages: John Steenwinkel, Ton Rimmelzwaan, Henri Robbemond, Jeff Glasgow and Harold van der Linden have all be very helpful. The library staff, Eef van Os, Mila Wiersma-Uriate, Riet Eijnsbergen and Joy Misa, have all been generously supportive and accommodating and I thank them sincerely. I would also like to thank Amin Kassam for the commitment and efficiency with which he has edited my thesis and formatted it for publication.

One of the privileges I enjoyed while doing my Ph.D. was the opportunity to co-lecture with a number of Institute faculty members, whom I have got to know a little better, and I have benefited tremendously from their teaching experience. I fondly recall designing a web site for the economics staff group, the idea for which was pioneered by Dr Irvin and Dr Nicholas. I also fondly recall teaching introductory statistical concepts with Prof. Dr M. Wuyts and J. Van Heemst, both of whom I enjoyed working with. My opportunity to co-lecture in the Institute's general course in development studies was an enriching experience and allowed me to interact more closely with Dr P Mihyo, Dr C Kay and over one hundred MA students. Over the years I have also co-lectured in the international economic law course with Dr J. Busuttil and Dr W. Hout, with whom I have shared ideas and learned a lot. Finally, using a computer model developed by the Open University, I have led several simulation courses on Structural

Adjustment, which brought me into contact with Prof. Dr M Wuyts, Dr R. Kurian and L. Keysers.

Loneliness, which I abhor, is systemic within the Ph.D. process and I am thankful for having made so many friends over the years. I am especially grateful to my good friend and office mate for three years, Omu Kakujaha-Matundu, with whom I have had intellectual exchanges and participated in numerous social activities. Marco Sanchez, my other office mate for one year and good friend, has motivated me and we have spent lots of time socializing. A number of other Ph.D. friends and colleagues have contributed to making my experience a rich one. I note especially Anne Karanja, Imani Tafari Ama, Stefania Abakerli, Sarah Gammage, Nicholas Awortwi, Grace Fisiy, Ngo Men, Mahmoud Hamid, Jun Borras, Le Thi Van Hue, Nguyen Manh Cuong, Nguyen Do Anh Tuan, Hannington Odame, Nicky Pouw, Mathew Kurian, Daniel Chavez, Sharada Srinivasan, Immaculate Mogotsi, Marleen Dekker, Anouka van Eerdewijk, Woldeab Teshome, Merra Tegegne and Gerhard Anders. I also treasure the support of some Ph.D. participants who have since graduated, Roodal Moonilal, Philomen Harrison, Takawira Mumvuma, Gabriel Rugalema, Getnet Alemu and Godfrey Asiimwe.

I have been blessed to have found an international Roman Catholic church in The Hague, where I attended Mass as often as possible. The parishoners have all been extremely supportive, but I recognize Fr Sjaak de Boer (Ph.D.) as both friend and mentor. At challenging points in the programme, he was always supportive and provided inspiration to persevere. Serge Jean has been especially helpful and I cherish his friendship. I am also grateful to Mayte Gonzalez, Karoll Kock, Sue Day, and Mandy Beasley-Suffolk for their friendship. My discovery of a small Caribbean Community in the Netherlands has enriched my study experience tremendously. I would like to mention in particular Deems Warner, June, Adian La Roche, Duncan, Sealey, Gomes, McKenzie, Linda, Naomi and Greg, all of whom have contributed to enriching my social life.

Over the years I have also come into contact with a number of people, some of whom have left bigger footprints than others in my life. I fondly recall Veronica Bayangos, Arlene Williams, Elvis James, Claudine Petgrave, Moipone Letsie, Madhuri Supersad, Nchimunya Nkombo, Venecia Cook, Maureen Minjo, Scholastica Williams, Gail Young, Suzanne Burke, Elizabeth Solomon, Reem and Eisa Abdelgalil, Leslie Ann Thomas, Alize Akat, Ingrid Hagen and Jacco Knotnerus, Paula Bownas, Anna Marie and Wim Lepelaars, Ank van Willems, Yetty Haning, Angela Agbomson, Billy Allwood, John Vigman, Melonie Carrol, Michael Sharpe, Natalie Rande, Frank Patterson and Katrin Riecke.

One of the biggest sacrifices of doing a Ph.D. away from home is the loss of regular contact with family members and close friends. I would like to extend heartfelt love and affection to my mother Pamela, my father Milton Joseph, my brothers Leo Titus and Urban, and my sisters Clarita, Militina, Lorna and Lindsay. I also extend my love and affection to their families. Lifelong friends like Augustin Antoine, Suzy Hall, Thomas Alexander, Peter Louis, Desmond Henry, Carlisle George and Paul Francis have all been supportive.

My son Ronell Vaughan and his mother Angela have paid the huge social cost of my absence from their lives for most of the time I have spent on this project. I would like to extend my deepest love and affection to them, especially Ronell who is only two. It is my hope that we can spend more time together now that this project is over.

Finally, I could not have done this work without the daily health, strength and blessing I continue to receive from the one and only Almighty God.

Claudius Preville
August 2002

Contents

Tables, Figures and Appendices

Tables

Figures

Appendices

Appendix 3   **322**

Acronyms

ACP	African, Caribbean and Pacific countries that are parties to the Lomé Conventions, now renegotiated as the Cotonou Agreement.
ADF	Augmented Dickey-Fuller (used with test statistics).
c.i.f.	Cost, insurance and freight.
CARICOM	Caribbean Community and Common Market.
CET	Common External Tariff.
DEM	Deutsche Mark.
DOM	Départment d'Outre Mer (Overseas Territory of an EU member-state).
DSB	Dispute Settlement Body (of the WTO).
DSU	Dispute Settlement Understanding (of the WTO).
DW	Durbin-Watson statistic (used for testing for serial correlation).
ECD	Eastern Caribbean Dollar
ECU	European Currency Unit (forerunner of the Euro)
EU	European Union.
EUR	Euro.
f.o.b.	Free on board.
f.o.r.	Free on rail.
f.o.t.	Free on truck.
FAO	Food and Agricultural Organization of the United Nations.
FDI	Foreign Direct Investment.
FFR	French Franc.
GATS	General Agreement on Trade in Services (of the WTO).
GATT	General Agreement on Trade and Tariffs (predecessor of the WTO).
GBP	Great Britain (United Kingdom) Pound.
HO	Heckscher Ohlin theory of international trade.
HOS	Heckscher Ohlin Samuelson theory of international trade.
IQR	Inter Quartile Range.
MFN	Most Favoured Nation.
NBR	New Banana Regime of the EU (implemented in July 1993).
NEIO	New Empirical Industrial Organization.
NTT	New Trade Theory.
OECS	Organization of Eastern Caribbean States
SCP	Structure Conduct Performance.

SE	Standard Error.
SEM	Single European Market.
TNC	Transnational Corporation.
TON	Metric Ton.
TRIMS	Trade Related Investment Measures (of the WTO).
TRIPS	Trade Related Intellectual Property Rights (of the WTO).
UK	United Kingdom.
US	United States.
USD	United States Dollar.
USTR	United States Trade Representative.
WIBDECO	Windward Islands Banana Development and Export Company.
WTO	World Trade Organization.

1   Introduction to the Study

1.1   Introduction

Neo-classical economists typically assume that markets are competitive and contestable; and that the liberalization of trade policy, as advocated by the World Trade Organization (WTO), is self evidently desirable.[1] The European Union (EU)'s banana trade is perhaps the most prominent and topical example of liberalization being advocated by economists from the World Bank to academia,[2] and the WTO, propelled by an acrimonious trade fight between the United States (US) and the EU, ruling against the EU. Yet, even a casual examination of the evidence suggests that both the above assumptions are likely to be incorrect and so there are implications for the magnitude and possibly direction, of the overall welfare effect of liberalization of the EU's banana trade.

The objectives of this study are twofold. First, to simulate the welfare effects of EU banana trade liberalization under imperfect competition,[3] – taking into consideration the nature of the commodity and how it is actually traded, the observed structure of the market and the strategic actions of transnational corporations (TNCs). We achieve this objective by constructing an oligopoly model in which TNCs are assumed to be engaged in Cournot-Nash behaviour for setting quantities of output, while each TNC enjoys some degree of strong monopoly pricing power due to branding and oligopolistic interdependence is strong.[4] The second objective is to analyse how the revenue and surplus (wealth) created in the transnational EU banana trade is divided among nations and discuss how liberalization is likely to impact upon such division of wealth. In order to achieve this objective we employ the concept of a commodity chain to trace the flow of bananas from their point of production to consumption. Theories of the TNC are used to explain the process, while exploratory data analysis is utilized for establishing the division of wealth.[5]

The remainder of this chapter is organized as follows. Section 1.2 presents the research problem and discusses the context in which it relevant and in which it is analysed, followed by the hypotheses that are explored in this work. Section 1.3 discusses the methodological approaches that are utilized in this study, both for the collection of data and their analysis in subsequent chapters. Section 1.4 discusses the basis on which cases have been chosen for analysis of the division of revenue and surplus. Section 1.5 discusses the relevance of the study to both theory and policy. Finally, the chapter concludes in Section 1.6 with a brief discussion of the organization of the remaining chapters of the thesis.

1.2   Research problem

In May 1997, a WTO Panel ruled that certain aspects of the EU's banana regime which was introduced under regulation 404/93, were not compliant with existing world trade rules (WTO, 1997a). Therefore, the EU was directed to bring its banana import policy into compliance with WTO rules, or risk facing applicable sanctions.[6] Like all other WTO Panel rulings, this ruling was the outcome of a legal process; and so the decision of the Panel was based simply on whether or not any of the covered agreements had been violated by the EU. Yet, the ruling found comfortable accommodation within academia, particularly economics, and, because most of the empirical work on the EU's banana import policy have been inspired by a neo-classical methodology, which assumes a single retail price, results typically suggest that liberalizing trade will significantly increase economic efficiency and welfare, so any losers can be adequately compensated by the gainers and remain better off than before.[7]

How accurately has such empirical work captured the complexity of the problem and what are the policy implications? Indeed, if the neo-classical assumptions about the structure of the EU banana market and the nature of trade in the commodity are correct, consumers will reap windfall gains; however, if these assumptions are not correct, consumers might well suffer colossal losses at the expense of worsening the division of wealth among nations. Let us briefly discuss some empirical evidence about the EU banana trade and contrast that evidence with the above neo-classical assumptions. First, economists following the neo-classical approach assume that if trade was liberalized EU-wide, there would be a single retail price for bananas in all member states, since they treat the commodity as homogeneous. However, the empirical evidence shows that although the variety of bananas marketed in the EU (cavendish) is fairly standardized, TNCs undertake extensive product differentiation (notably branding) and advertising, which results in bananas being sold at different prices in local markets as well as from one member-state to the next (Chapter 3).[8]

Second, economists following the neo-classical approach assume that the EU banana market is contestable, so any agent should be able to enter and exit the market costlessly at will.[9] However, the empirical evidence paints a very different picture. This shows that the EU banana trade as a whole is best described as a transnational oligopoly in which there exists strong interdependence, and the three firm concentration in the industry has grown over time from 47 per cent in the 1960s to over 60 per cent in the 1990s (Chapter 3). Moreover, the transnational oligopolistic structure dominating the EU banana trade also dominates world banana trade in general, and particularly trade in bananas in the other major importing countries – the US and Japan. The non-contestability of the market arises from the fact that the banana industry is characterized by substantial capitalization costs of high asset-specificity, which has resulted in a stable oligopoly comprising three US-based TNCs – Chiquita Brands International (Chiquita), Dole Food Company (Dole) and Fresh Del Monte Produce (Del Monte).[10]

Third, economists following the neo-classical approach do not consider the nature of the banana as a commodity, and the complex sequence of stages it goes through from its original country of production to the country of consumption, as important factors in explaining trade. Far from being a finished product ready for consumption after being harvested, bananas are subjected to major stages of service value-addition, which continuously transforms and/or becomes embodied within them before they appear at the retail level. Given the fragility of the commodity, it could be easily damaged through inappropriate handling and/or storage conditions, so the efficacy with which each stage of the chain is handled is crucial and the *timing* between stages is of paramount importance. Thus, the nature of the commodity lends itself to natural monopoly for efficient and profitable trade and it has resulted in TNCs adopting vertically integrated structures throughout the commodity chain. Vertical integration allows TNCs to exploit *economies of scale* at all stages of the commodity chain in order to minimize costs; and *economies of common governance* in order to minimize risk and maximize profit (Hymer, 1970; Teece, 1993).

With the preceding in mind, this study seeks to address two questions. First, whether or not the structure of the EU banana market and the nature of the commodity are significant factors for explaining trade in bananas and predicting the welfare effects under liberalization. Second, whether or not liberalization is likely to result in a more (or less) progressive division and distribution of wealth between the EU member-states and those of their trading partners that survive. The answers to these questions require the formulation of the following hypotheses, which are explored and tested in the succeeding chapters of the thesis.

First, the EU banana market is typified by a transnational oligopolistic interdependence structure in which individual TNCs are capable of exercising some degree of monopoly power through which super-normal profits are appropriated.[11] Second, due to the persistence of oligopolistic interdependence, and given the nature of trade in bananas, liberalization is likely to widen the wealth gap between the producers that survive and individual EU member-states.

1.3   Methodology and sources of data

This study uses diverse methods for exploring and testing hypotheses because each of the questions that have been posed requires distinctive analytical techniques for arriving at the answers. First, a method for conceptualizing transnational trade in bananas is needed, which treats the commodity as an intermediate good being subjected to continuous value-addition at various stages, between its point of production and its point of consumption. Second, a method is needed for exploring the elements of market structure, which also provides for estimating the degree of market power and isolating the importance of oligopolistic interdependence in the trade of the commodity. Third, a method is needed for explaining the division and distribution of revenue and surplus between the exporting countries and EU member-states. Finally, a method is needed for simulating the welfare effects of trade liberalization under imperfect competition. We briefly discuss elements of these methodologies below.

The search for an alternative way of thinking about transnational trade in bananas led the author to the concept of a commodity chain. A commodity chain is defined as a transactionally linked sequence of functions in which each stage adds value to the process of production of goods or services (Gereffi, 1999; Dicken, 1998). Different authors use different variations of this concept in the literature, including "production chain" and "value-added chain" (see Chapter 4). This study uses the term "commodity chain" in order not to confuse the reader, who might otherwise think we are only discussing the banana production process or are only concerned with value-addition. With the commodity chain concept, we can identify distinct stages in the banana trade: production, ocean transportation (shipping), importation, ripening and consumption. At each of these stages, bananas are subjected to continuous service value-addition, which transforms and/or becomes embodied within the commodity. Thus, we can best think of the traded banana as a physical good embodied within a 'vector' of services, the value of which continuously changes over space and time. This approach to conceptualizing trade in the commodity is compelling, not only because it better captures what happens to traded bananas in reality, but also because one element of the WTO ruling against the EU banana regime was discrimination under the General Agreement on Trade in Services [GATS] (WTO, 1997a: paras. 9.1-9.2). Since the GATS discrimination, in this context, is only applicable after bananas have entered an EU member-state, its effect is to treat the banana as a physical commodity embodied within a 'vector' of services. This methodology is developed further in Chapters 4 and 5, and it is applied together with exploratory data analysis in Chapters 6 and 7 to demonstrate the division and distribution of revenue and surplus, respectively.

Next, this study uses exploratory data analysis, particularly box plots, to present and analyse the data used for empirical work.[12] Exploratory data analysis has the strength of visually revealing patterns in the data, which serve as entry points for exploring and testing hypotheses (Mukherjee et al., 1998). In particular, that method is used in Chapter 3, where the empirical evidence of the structure of the EU banana trade and the conduct of firms in it are analysed, and Chapters 6 and 7, where the commodity chain is decomposed and the division and distribution of revenue and surplus along it analysed. Exploratory data analysis also helps us to visually identify where a correlation might exist between certain variables, which are subsequently used for identification of market power in Chapter 8.

In order to empirically measure the degree of market power in the EU banana trade, this study uses a structural econometric model based on the works of Deodhar and Sheldon (1995), and Buschena and Perloff (1991), in which it is assumed that the behaviour of firms in an oligopolistic market can be captured by their conjectural variations parameters. A conjectural variations parameter is best thought of as the reaction beliefs of one firm about the outputs set by others in the market (McMillan, 2001). However, the above econometric method is extended by formally treating the problem of non-stationarity of time series data using co-integration analysis techniques following the Johansen (1995, 1991) method. Co-integration analysis has the advantages of providing more robust coefficients for a model estimates, coping with the problem of multi-collinearity and capturing long run dynamics in the interaction of all model variables.

This study conceptualizes TNC oligopolists as engaging in Cournot-Nash type of behaviour while being capable of enjoying monopoly power due to product differentiation. The relevant literature on Cournot and Bertrand models of oligopoly is reviewed in Chapter 4 and the specifications actually used are refined and applied in Chapter 8. Finally, a three-period *sequential* oligopoly 'game' is used to simulate the welfare effects of trade liberalization under imperfect competition in Chapter 9.

One of the biggest challenges encountered in conducting this study was the acquisition of the relevant data during field-work in 2000. The author originally hoped to conduct a detailed firm-level analysis of the EU banana trade, but from a very early stage the prospects of achieving such a feat were daunting. The major reason for this is that although the WTO had ruled against the EU's banana regime since 1997, the process did not end there.[13] In fact, as discussed in detail in Chapters 3 and 5, subsequent to the WTO Panel and Appellate Body rulings the EU requested a reasonable time period for compliance, which lasted nearly two years.[14] Even after the EU had made substantive changes to its banana regime, difficulties in achieving consensus among the main parties concerned led to further delays in implementation. It was only in February 2002 that the EU and the US finally agreed to an alternative to the original EU banana import policy, which was implemented under Council Regulation 404/93.[15]

Therefore, while the banana dispute was still a major agenda item in the WTO and the world press, it was impossible to get the representatives of firms and exporting countries to provide detailed information about their activities in the industry. These actors were overtly cautious, and conscious of the possibility that their opinions if expressed publicly, could compromise the final outcome of what was an already protracted process. At best, some firms made available their annual and other periodic reports. Although detailed information on corporate strategy, costs of production, and profitability of individual stages of the commodity chain are mandatory publications since most producers are publicly liable TNCs, these details were not readily divulged. In fact some of the TNCs in the EU banana business went to great length to argue that their operations were not profitable and that the new regime was simply exacerbating a bad situation.

Notwithstanding these challenges and constraints, the author was able to collect a reasonably comprehensive set of data, which have been used to construct a *database* from which this thesis has been written.[16] Our connections with some of the major organizations involved in compilation of world banana trade data were invaluable in that regard. The most reliable sources of primary data for this research were officials who were interviewed at the WTO in Geneva and the European Commission in Brussels.[17] WTO officials commented on the dispute settlement and arbitration processes, thus presenting a clearer picture of the complexity of the banana dispute and the positions that were taken by individual actors throughout the deliberations. Commission officials provided internal memoranda, letters and draft legislation of their intended changes to the banana regime. They also provided internally monitored data on banana import, wholesale and retail prices for a limited period since the implementation of Regulation 404/93.

Detailed time series data, which are used for both exploratory data analysis and econometric modeling, were obtained from two reliable sources, the FAO and EUROSTAT. Given that our study is both multi-country and multi-region in nature, standardization of data sources for the sake of comparability is extremely important, which is why these international sources were chosen. The author visited the FAO during 2000 and spent one week with both administrative and professional officials involved in the compilation of data on the world banana trade, who provided an assortment of unpublished data, covering the 1970-99 period. In addition, they provided recent FAO policy papers presented at Ministerial meetings and proposals on diversification. Similar visits were made to EUROSTAT and the European Court of Justice in 2000. Officials at EUROSTAT were extremely helpful and provided unpublished data on the EU banana trade covering the 1976-99 period. Access was also provided to internal computer databases, which are normally accessible only to officials of the Commission. At the European Court of Justice, the author obtained detailed data on the legal issues in the EU banana trade since the 1960s, including the judgements of the Court, opinions of the Advocate-General, and the arguments presented by various actors against the EU banana regime.

1.4   Selection of cases

One methodological challenge in this study has been to compare representative EU banana commodity chains, which reflect the patterns of trade and trade policy, between EU member-states and their exporting partners in the pre-SEM period.[18] Since the neo-classical consensus is that implementing free trade EU-wide will significantly increase economic efficiency and welfare, this study seeks to test whether or not the commodity chain for bananas into a free market was more efficient than that into a protected and/or mixed market in the pre-SEM period. Therefore, it analyses the EU banana commodity chain for the flow of bananas from the exporting countries into Germany, France and the United Kingdom (UK), which are reasonably representative of the different trade policies in EU member states during the pre-SEM period (Chapter 3). For simplicity, and given that several producing countries export to each of these EU member-states, the study will refer to these banana commodity chains as the German, French and British commodity chains, respectively. However, the welfare effects of liberalization under imperfect competition are simulated for the EU as a whole and its trading partners, treating different trading partners as different categories of TNCs.

In addition to capturing the type of trade policy that a particular EU member state implemented in the pre-SEM period, the choice of cases also reflects the governance structure of these chains (Gereffi, 1999; Dicken,

1998). The German commodity chain is characterized by extreme vertical integration, with individual TNCs and their affiliates controlling all stages of the chain, from plantation production to ocean transportation, importation, ripening and distribution. In contrast, the French and British commodity chains are characterized by distinct operators engaged in the various stages. Contractual arrangements exist for the purchase of bananas from producers in the latter chains, and the bananas are produced on small-scale individually owned farms. Additionally, once the bananas have been imported into France and Britain they are distributed to several independent ripeners and retailers (see Chapter 3).

1.5   Relevance and purpose

The study seeks to make a contribution to the explanation of the welfare effects of trade liberalization under imperfect competition, how trade liberalization is likely to affect the various banana-producing countries in general, and whether or not it results in widening revenue and surplus gaps between the producers that survive liberalization and EU member-states. Its relevance and purpose are therefore readily apparent.

As briefly discussed earlier, although there is widespread confidence among economists following the neo-classical approach that trade liberalization is likely to result in increases in economic efficiency and welfare, given their assumptions about the market, empirical evidence typically does not support such assumptions. In fact welfare gains to EU consumers previously assumed significantly positive are here shown to be negligible, relative to losses due to imperfect competition. Moreover, the Bretton Woods international financial institutions, which were strong advocates of trade liberalization in the 1980s and 1990s, have recently taken somewhat different positions. The World Bank seems to have conceded the need to rethink the process in light of continuing contradictions between theoretical expectations and observed outcomes (Wolfensohn, 1999).[19] However, the IMF seems to have adopted the more mainstream view of simple causality – that trade leads to growth, which in turn results in poverty reduction (Camdessus, 1999).[20]

Therefore, the relevance and purpose of this study embraces both theory and policy. From the theoretical perspective, it seeks to contribute to the literature on the conceptualization of international trade in commodities in light of the following facts: (i) that transnationals play a central role in controlling all value-addition activities along the commodity chain; and (ii) that the WTO's ruling in the case of the EU banana regime has effectively called for a redefinition of the concept of a commodity. The approach that is used here for conceptualizing the EU banana trade could be applied for conceptualizing trade in other primary commodities that are subjected to similar value-adding (transforming) processes along their commodity chains. From the policy perspective, since the study will demonstrate that liberalization of trade in the commodity is likely to lead to greater impoverishment (and not wealth) for the exporting countries that survive, there seems to be no reason why it is self-evidently desirable. The findings will also be interpreted in the context of the EU's own development policy objectives for the developing countries, which its member states trade and otherwise co-operate with.[21] However, since this study has been only of the EU banana trade, further research needs to be conducted in other commodity sectors to determine the desirability for liberalization in each case. The study suggests some of these sectors in Chapter 10.

1.6   Organization of the thesis

The thesis is organized as follows. Chapter 2 begins with the theoretical arguments that have been advanced for liberalization of the banana trade in the EU, all of which assume perfect competition and contestability, and empirical estimates of the welfare effects.[22] It then shows that, by making simple changes to the major assumptions of these studies about the price transmission mechanism, both the magnitude and direction of the welfare effects become questionable. Chapter 3 discusses and analyses the structure and organization of world banana trade in general, with specific emphasis on the EU banana trade. The purpose is to develop the evidence about the oligopolistic structure of the EU banana market and to demonstrate the persistent behaviour of firms in re-inventing oligopoly over time. The chapter then briefly looks at the issues which led to a WTO ruling against the EU banana policy and relates the significance of this ruling to the persistence of oligopoly in the trade of the commodity.

Having developed the importance of oligopoly and its likely perverse effect on trade liberalization in Chapter 3, in Chapter 4 the thesis explores various strands of literature that are used for developing a framework for explaining and analysing the EU's banana trade. Theories of international trade, transnational firms, industrial organization and the concept of the commodity chain are discussed in some detail and applied to the EU's banana business. Chapter 5 examines the importance of lobbies in influencing world trade policy. It analyses the various stages of the WTO banana dispute in the context of the severity of political action taken by the US in the WTO and political contributions made to the Republican and Democratic parties by Chiquita. The findings in that chapter point to the possibility of perverse conduct by Chiquita if it were allowed to operate freely in a liberalized EU banana market. In Chapter 6 the commodity chain concept is applied, using exploratory data analysis to demonstrate how revenue is divided and distributed between individual exporting countries and EU member-states. The division and distribution of revenue is shown to be most progressive between the exporting countries who previously enjoyed some protection from an EU member-state and that member-state.

Chapter 7 applies a similar methodology to that of Chapter 6 to demonstrate how the surplus is divided and distributed between EU member-states and their respective banana-exporting partners. It argues that, like the division and distribution of revenue, the division and distribution of surplus is most progressive between exporting countries that previously enjoyed some form of protection from an EU member-state and that member-state. Chapter 8 uses a structural econometric model to estimate the degree of market power in the EU banana business both prior to and after the implementation of the SEM. It argues that despite the system of protection that existed in France and free trade that existed in Germany in the pre-SEM period, firms in both these countries exercised comparable degrees of market power. Chapter 9 uses the knowledge of strategic quantity setting behaviour by TNCs from Chapter 8 and a three-period *sequential* oligopoly 'game' to estimate the welfare effects of trade liberalization under imperfect competition. Finally, the conclusions and policy recommendations are presented in Chapter 10.

Notes

[1] However, the origins of the idea of liberalization of trade policy, also known as *laissez-faire* in the literature, pre-date neo-classical economists. It was Adam Smith who first advanced the theory that free trade could be advantageous to all nations if each nation engaged in the production and trade of the good in which it had an absolute advantage (Smith, 1776:401-3). Recent empirical work on trade liberalization includes the agriculture sector and perspectives from developing countries (Ingco and Winters 2001); its revenue implications (Ebrill et al., 1999); its linkage with industrial development (Dijkstra, 1997) and its impact on export growth (Shafaeddin, 1994), among others.

[2] Exponents of the neo-classical approach to analysing the potential welfare effects of liberalized EU banana trade include Borrell (1996, 1994), Borrell and Yang (1990, 1992), Borrell and Cuthbertson (1991).

[3] The theory of imperfect competition, which has its origins in the seminal work of Joan Robinson in 1933, arose out of her desire to reconstruct Alfred Marshall's theory of value, taking into account the existence of monopolies. It is in her work that the concept of marginal revenue was first introduced. See J. V. Robinson (1933) *The Economics of Imperfect Competition*. London: Macmillan.

[4] A Cournot-Nash equilibrium is one in which, while competing in quantities, each agent does the best that he can given what other agents are doing. As McMillan (2001:9) puts it, in a Nash equilibrium "No agent can do better than play his Nash strategy given that all the other agents are playing their Nash strategies". The Nash equilibrium concept was first formalized by the mathematician John Nash in 1951. For an introduction to Nash's seminal work see: John Nash (1951) "Non-Cooperative Games", *Annals of Mathematics*; and John Nash (1950) "The Bargaining Problem", *Econometrica*.

[5] Hymer (1970, 1976)'s works on the theory of the TNC are extremely useful in this regard. In particular his argument that the major objective of TNCs "is to gain control over marketing facilities in order to facilitate the spread of their products" (Hymer, 1970:445) is highly applicable for explaining the global and EU banana trade.

[6] Specifically, in its ruling against the EU's banana regime the Panel concluded that certain aspects of the EU's banana regime were inconsistent with its obligations under Articles I:1, III:4, X:3 and XIII:1 of the GATT; Article 1.2 of the Licensing Agreement; and Articles II and XVII of the GATS (WTO, 1997a: paras. 9.1–9.2).

[7] Compensation is defined here in terms of the Kaldor-Hicks-Scitovsky criterion. See Nath (1969) for a detailed discussion of the subject, but particularly pp. 95-6.

[8] Four distinct price classes for banana brands are identified in this work. "Chiquita" branded bananas occupy the first price category and command a price up to 44 per cent higher than that of fourth-class brands; 38 per cent higher than that of third-class brands; and 17 per cent higher than that of second-class brands.

[9] Contestability is defined along the lines of Baumol (1982) and Baumol et al. (1982). Put simply, a market is contestable if an agent can enter it costlessly, enjoy some profits, and costlessly exit the market if adverse conditions set in.

[10] Interestingly, none of the numerous neo-classical works on the EU banana trade of Borrell et al., notably Borrell (1994, 1996), Borrell and Yang (1990, 1992), Borrell and Cuthbertson (1991), has even a passing reference to the structure of the transnational banana trade, despite the fact that attention was drawn to this important aspect prior to the publication of these works (see Litvak and Maule, 1977; Casson, 1986; Read 1986; among others).

[11] It is widely accepted in the literature that firms generally earn a normal economic profit, which is the opportunity cost for investing their capital. Where the firm can exercise some degree of market power, it can earn profits over and beyond a normal return. The term "super-normal profit" is borrowed from Marshall (1920).

[12] The use of box plots is particularly helpful when working with non-stationary data. Box plots simultaneously display the median of a sample (as opposed to the mean), its inter-quartile range (which is really the height of the box), and the smallest and largest values within 1.5 times the inter-quartile range. Outliers are defined as observations within 1.5 and 3 times the inter-quartile range of the body of data, while extreme values are observations at distances beyond 3 times the inter-quartile range. See Mukherjee et al. (1998:83-97) for a detailed explanation and examples.

[13] In fact, even after the ruling in 1997, the banana featured prominently in practically all the major international media. See, for example, "Trade War Set to Escalate", *News.bbc.co.uk* (13 July 2000); "WTO Panel Rules for U.S. Over EU in Banana Fight", *The Wall Street Journal* (19 March 1997); "EU/US – Commission Mulls Banana Reform Options", *Reuters* (26 May 1999); "EU Appeals at WTO over Ruling on Bananas", *Reuters* (11 June 1997); and "EU/Bananas – In Geneva, All Banana Supplier Countries Dispute EU's New Import Regime", *Agence Europe* (8 February 2001).

[14] Specifically, the reasonable period of time granted to the EU for implementation of the rulings of the Panel and Appellate Body expired on 1 January 1999.

[15] Specifically, at a meeting of the WTO Dispute Settlement Body (DSB) of 1 February 2002, the EU made a request to officially remove its dispute with Ecuador and the US over its banana import policy from the DSB's agenda. The dispute had been settled in December 2001 when EU Ministers of Agriculture adopted a new banana regime that had been agreed to by the US and Ecuador in October 2001. See also "EU Agriculture Council Adopts Proposal", *Tradewatch* (16 January 2002).

[16] The comprehensive listing of the materials used for constructing the *database* appears after the list of *references* used in the thesis.

[17] Attempts to reach the US Embassy to the European Union proved futile. A letter from the author to HE Richard Louis Morningstar, US Ambassador to the EU, dated 14 March 2000 is yet to be acknowledged.

[18] Details of the banana trade policy of EU member-states in the pre-SEM period, the EU's banana trade policy introduced under Regulation 404/93, subsequent changes as mandated by the WTO, and the pattern of trade between exporting countries and EU member-states, are presented in Chapter 3.

[19] World Bank President James Wolfensohn is quoted saying in his statement to the WTO Ministerial Conference in Seattle, "The state of our knowledge about the practical impact of different patterns of trade liberalization on poverty is still far too limited."

[20] At the same Seattle WTO Ministerial Conference, the IMF's Managing Director, Michel Camdessus is quoted as saying that the "growth of trade has been one of the main engines of economic growth in the extraordinary half-century now drawing to

a close – and further growth in trade will help sustain growth and reduce poverty, worldwide."

[21] For a brief overview of the Cotonou Agreement, see, for instance, Karl, K. (2000) "Signing Ceremony in Cotonou. A New Era of Cooperation", *The Courier*, Special Issue (September).

[22] The author draws heavily upon his previous works (Preville, 1999; 1997) for developing the arguments in Chapter 2.

2 Welfare Effects of EU Banana Trade Liberalization Under Perfect Competition

2.1 Introduction

By the mid-1980s the prospects for deepening the economic integration of the EU in 1992, through the formation of a Single European Market (SEM),[1] had drawn attention and interest to the issue of the potential gains (and losses) that might result from trade liberalization in general.[2] This focus included bananas, the most important tropical fruit in international trade in 1995.[3] This chapter discusses the existing literature on the likely welfare- and efficiency-effects of liberalization of trade in the commodity by the EU, under the assumptions of perfect competition. It then offers a slightly modified approach to the standard methodology for estimating these welfare- and efficiency-effects. The welfare effects are analysed by identifying who the gainers and losers from trade liberalization are likely to be, and by how much. Specifically, producers' surplus, consumers' surplus, producers' revenue and EU member-states' tax revenue are calculated individually, from which the overall welfare effects are derived.

In the early 1990s a number of studies were conducted on the pre-SEM banana import systems that existed in EU member-states in order to estimate the potential welfare- and efficiency-gains from liberalized trade. Foremost and most influential of these were the works of Borrell and Yang (1990, 1992).[4] Attempts at measuring the welfare- and efficiency-effects had also been undertaken by Fitzpatrick and Associates (1990), Davenport and Page (1991) and Borrell and Cuthbertson (1991). The implementation of the SEM witnessed a number of additional studies of the possible welfare effects. By the mid-1990s these included Borrell (1994, 1996); Read (1994); Arthur D. Little International (1995); Kersten (1995) and McCorriston and Sheldon (1996). More recently, the welfare effects have again been estimated by Guyomard et al. (1999).

The neo-classical studies conducted in the early 1990s share the major assumption that trade liberalization is likely to lead to a single retail price for bananas in all EU member-states (Borrell and Yang, 1990:19; Borrell and Yang 1992:7). This is because they assume (though not always explicitly) that the EU's banana market is perfectly competitive and/or contestable, and that liberalization of trade would therefore result in significant increases in both market efficiency and the economic welfare of its citizens. The methodological underpinnings of these works are presented in Figure 2.1.[5] In the absence of trade, if EU production was sufficient to match consumption then a total quantity Q_0 of bananas would be consumed at price P_0. By opening up to free trade a total quantity Q_f of bananas could be consumed at a much lower price P_f, of which Q_d would be supplied by EU producers and $Q_f - Q_d$ is imported.

Figure 2.1   Neo-classical conceptualization of the welfare effects of trade liberalization

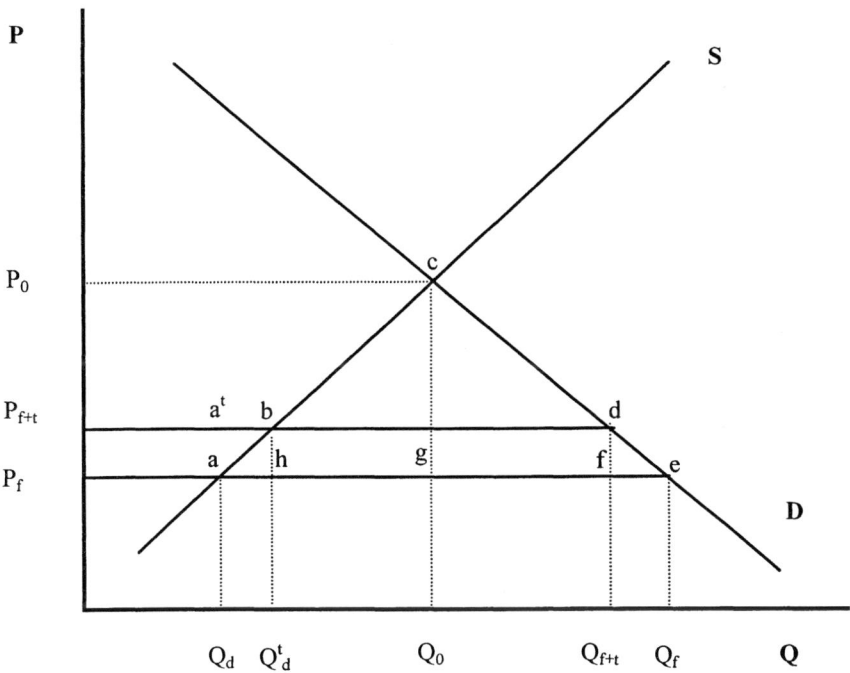

The imposition of a tariff t by the EU causes a reduction in the total quantity of bananas consumed to Q_{f+t} at a higher price P_{f+t}, of which quantity Q'_d is supplied by EU producers and $Q_{f+t} - Q'_d$ is imported. Consequently, consumers lose surplus represented by the area of region $deP_f P_{f+t}$, while EU producers gain surplus given by area $abP_{f+t} P_f$.

Since the results of these studies invariably suggest that trade liberalization is likely to result in considerable increases in consumer welfare,[6] they have strengthened the economic basis for the trade policy stance on bananas that is promoted by the WTO.[7] Although in subsequent studies a few authors have taken issue with the assumptions of perfect competition and/or contestability and their implications for the welfare- and efficiency-effects (Read, 1994),[8] such studies have not presented alternatives, while explicitly acknowledging the difficulties of modelling the welfare effects using oligopoly theory (Guyomard et al., 1999).[9]

This study is based on the belief that the hypotheses of perfect competition and/or contestability are not likely to be applicable to the EU banana trade, and it begins its argument by first demonstrating the fragility of these assumptions – and hence why later the welfare effects are modelled under Cournot oligopoly (Chapters 8 and 9).[10] It argues for the moment that since dominant suppliers in the market possess similar technology and comparable production costs (see Chapter 3), if anything it is the import price of bananas that is likely to be the same throughout the EU after liberalization. Therefore, whether or not liberalization increases global economic welfare depends on the extent to which (i) exporting countries gain revenue; (ii) dominant suppliers reduce the import price; and (iii) reductions in the import price are transmitted to the consumer at the retail level.

The remainder of the chapter is organized as follows. In Section 2.2 a brief background to the trade policies of EU member-states and the pattern of trade in the pre-SEM period is presented. This is followed by an analysis of price margins in Section 2.3. Next, the model used for estimating the welfare effects is developed in Section 2.4. This is followed, in Section 2.5, by an application of the model to generate two sets of simulations, one before and one since the implementation of the SEM. Section 2.6 summarizes the argument, draws some initial conclusions and identifies the questions that will be addressed in subsequent chapters.

2.2   Background – trade policy and the pattern of trade

The EU banana market has had a history of fragmented organization dating at least as far back as the signing of the Treaty of Rome in 1957.[11] Since fairly extensive literature already exists on the history of the banana import policies of individual EU member-states, this aspect is dealt with here only briefly.[12] Since the end of World War II, banana imports into individual EU member-states have fallen into three broad categories, reflecting the historical, political, economic and strategic interests of EU member-states with their sources of supply. Those supplied by individual EU member-state overseas territories or *Départment d'Outre-Mer* (DOMs);[13] those supplied under a preferential trade agreement between an EU member-state and its former colonies or the ACP countries;[14] and those supplied from the dollar-zone countries.[15] Let us examine the characteristics of these sources of supply in greater detail.

2.2.1   Sources of supply

Given the differences in geographic spread, location advantages and market access for bananas, there exists a certain degree of interregional variability in their production technology, costs of production, marketing strategy and quality. In the DOMs bananas are grown on a large number of small farms, most of them less than 5 hectares, but the bulk of production takes place on farms of over 20 hectares (FAO, 1986:29). A combination of strict minimum wage laws; low levels of agricultural inputs; rugged terrain and poor soil quality results in high costs of production and low yields per hectare.[16] The ACP countries face similar constraints in their production processes to those faced by the DOMs, but are marginally more efficient. Cultivation of bananas takes place on small-holder farms, which tend to be characterized by high costs of production and relatively low yields per hectare (FAO, 1986).[17] Conversely, dollar-zone bananas are generally grown using large-scale plantation technology and high levels of agricultural inputs, with resulting high yields per hectare. These conditions, combined with extremely low wages, cause dollar-zone bananas to be the most competitive, globally.[18] But the most distinct feature of banana production in the latter is the extensive involvement of a small number of TNCs (FAO, 1986), with their tendency towards vertical integration within the industry from plantation production to final retail (Read, 1986). By controlling all aspects of the banana commodity chain,[19] these TNCs are likely to enjoy scale economies not only on plantations, but also in ocean transportation[20] and ripening centres in Europe (Read, 1986:321). Consequently, in 1992-93, the cost of production per metric ton of bananas ranged from $162 in Ecuador to $200 in Colombia (Hallam and Peston: 1997:23); and yields ranged from 36.4 to 45.5 metric tons per hectare (Kasteele, 1998:2).[21] These banana supply sources shaped the pattern of trade in the EU.

2.2.2   Pre-SEM pattern of trade

There is widespread consensus that the pre-SEM pattern of trade was based
on the existing sources of supply and the trade policies of individual EU
member-states towards these sources.[22] DOMs' bananas were marketed
almost exclusively in France, Spain, Portugal and Greece, which all
imported them free of duty and taxes. ACP states' bananas were marketed
almost exclusively in France, the UK and Italy, where they enjoyed duty-
and tax-free access. Dollar-zone bananas were marketed primarily in the
other EU member-states, that is, Germany, where they were admitted duty-
and tax-free;[23] and the Netherlands, Belgium, Luxembourg, Ireland and
Scandinavia, where they were subjected to a 20 per cent tariff. Additionally,
dollar-zone bananas were a residual source of supply for markets in the UK,
France and Italy, but were always subjected to a tariff, a quota, and a licence
in some cases.[24]

2.2.3   EC regulation 404/93 under the SEM

The formation of the SEM meant that the EU had to find a new way of
conducting the banana import trade, since bananas did not feature among
commodities dealt with under the EU's Common Agricultural Policy
(CAP). This necessitated the implementation of a New Banana Regime
(NBR) in July 1993,[25] under EEC Regulation 404/93, structured as follows:
(i) a general quota of duty-free entry for 854,000 metric tons of bananas
produced in EU territories', (ii) another general quota of duty-free entry for
857,700 metric tons of bananas produced in ACP countries that were
traditional suppliers to the EU market, and (iii) a general tariff quota of 2
million metric tons for bananas produced in third countries (primarily
dollar-zone) and/or non-traditional quantities of ACP and EU bananas. In
the latter case, bananas originating from an ACP country or an EU producer
territory were admitted free of duty, provided that the quantity fell within
the 2 million- metric-ton quota, otherwise they were subjected to a tariff of
ECU[26] 750 per metric ton. Bananas originating from a third country were
admitted at a duty rate of ECU 100 per metric ton, provided that the
quantities fell within the established general quota of 2 million metric tons.
Additionally, a much higher tariff of ECU 850 per metric ton applied in
respect of all bananas from a third country in excess of the established
general quota of 2 million metric tons (European Council, 1993).[27]

However, since tensions created by the implementation of the NBR
resulted in early attacks against it, as part of the outcome of the Uruguay
Round the EU agreed to increase the tariff quota to 2.1 million metric tons

in 1994 and 2.2 million metric tons in 1995. Additionally, the EU reserved the right to modify the tariff quota, subject to any increases in demand resulting from the enlargement of the Community (European Commission, 1994:5).[28]

But the NBR was not limited to tariffs or quotas; its implementation, particularly with regard to the tariff quota, was subjected to a licensing system based on a system of classification of operators according to three activity functions: purchase and transport, customs clearance and ripening and selling to wholesalers. Thus, 57 per cent of licences were issued to operators that imported bananas, 15 per cent were issued to operators that performed customs clearance and 28 per cent were issued to operators involved in ripening and selling wholesale to retailers. Additionally, provision was made for operators who marketed bananas originating in EU territories and ACP countries that were traditional suppliers to the EU market to access up to 30 per cent of all licences. This meant that they were also able to market 30 per cent of the quota for third party and non-traditional ACP bananas. Effectively, as Hallam (1995:532) put it, traditional dollar-zone operators were disadvantaged since they were limited to 66.5 per cent of the quota in their category, while the remaining 3.5 per cent were available to new market entrants.

From its inception, the implementation of the EU's NBR generated tensions both among member-states on the one hand, and third-countries who argued that the regime discriminated against them on the other (Read, 1994:225-7).[29] In an early row among the member-states, Germany and the Benelux countries took the Commission to Court (Kuilwijk, 1996a; Everling, 1996). However, it was the subsequent attacks on the NBR from outside the EU, notably in the GATT and the WTO, that eventually led to a WTO ruling against it.[30]

We shall return to this discussion in detail in Chapters 3 and 5, but for the moment our focus remains on the welfare effects of trade liberalization under perfect competition, and we continue this by analysing banana price margins.

2.3   Price margins

The changes in the ratios of retail- to import-price (price margins) of bananas in the major EU member-states for 1986-96, are shown in Figure 2.2. The price margins for the United States are included since the market price there has been considered by many of the studies reviewed as the representative world price (see Borrell and Yang, 1990, 1992).[31] Given that the EU's banana import policy has changed since the implementation of the SEM, a distinction is made between the two periods. A quick glance at Figure 2.2 seems to suggest that the effect of the SEM has been to reduce the overall level as well as degree of variability in price margins, Community-wide. However, a somewhat different picture emerges if the Italian trend is excluded: then, both the overall level and degree of variability in price margins are seen to have increased.[32] Let us discuss these trends in greater detail, taking those in the pre-SEM period excluding Italy, the pre-SEM Italian trend and the post-SEM period, in turn.

2.3.1   Pre-SEM period excluding Italy

In the pre-SEM period the extent to which banana average retail prices exceeded import prices was highest in France – 2.6 times; followed by Germany – 2.5 times; and lowest in the UK – 2.4 times (Figure 2.2). That these margins were highest in France can be easily explained with neo-classical theory – the fact that the French market was highly protected conferred a certain degree of monopoly power on firms operating there. More difficult to explain, and in contrast to the expectations of neo-classical theory, are similarly high German margins, since banana imports into the German market were duty- and tax-free. Equally difficult to explain, and again in contradiction to neo-classical theory, is the fact that it is in the UK market that margins were lowest, despite its protectionist import policy.

While our discussion so far is not sufficient to fully explain the preceding trends (nor is it the intention of this chapter to do so), at least one initial conclusion can be suggested. The extent to which consumers' welfare is maximized or not depends on the extent to which retail prices exceed import prices, and free markets might be a necessary but not a sufficient condition to guarantee an optimal solution. After bananas are imported, they are subjected to other value-adding processes including transportation to ripening centres, ripening, transportation to retailers and final preparation for retail sale.[33] The efficiency of all of these stages after importation determines the extent to which consumers' welfare is optimized. Thus, in the context of trade liberalization, whether or not consumers' welfare increases depends on the extent to which removal of the tariff is transmitted to consumers as a reduction in retail price.[34] Interestingly, even United States banana margins were considerably higher than those in France despite the *laissez-faire* system in the former, again contradicting neo-classical expectations. A possible explanation for this is likely to come from analysis of the differences in organization of the commodity chains into the various markets.[35] We shall return to this argument in Chapter 3 where we analyse the market structure and conduct of firms in world banana trade, and further develop the commodity chain concept in Chapter 4.

Figure 2.2   EU banana price margins

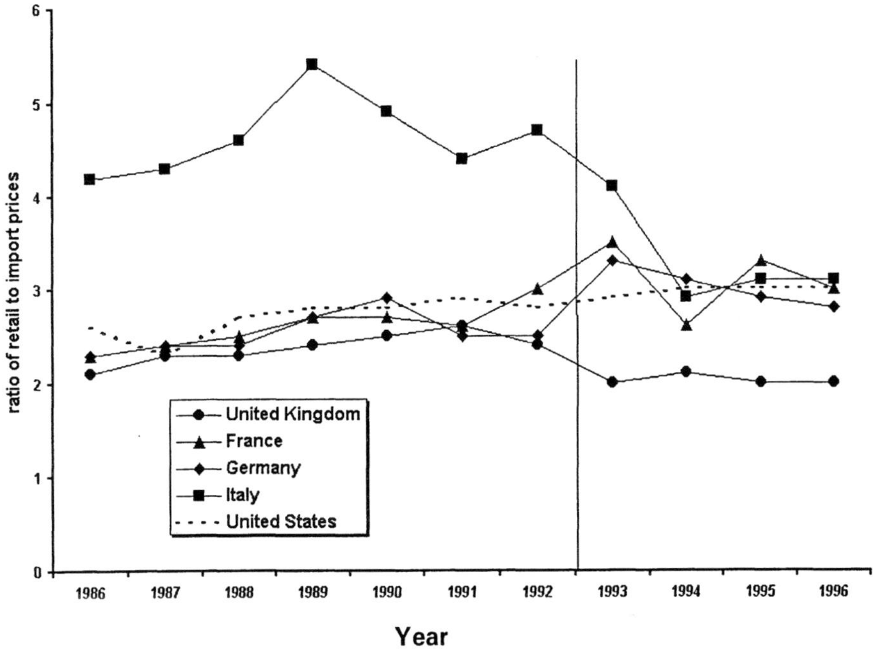

Source: Preville (1999:15).

2.3.2   Italy in the pre-SEM period

During the pre-SEM period, Italy implemented a rather complex system of tariffs, quotas and consumption taxes, which, unlike in France and the UK, did not meet the objective of protection.[36] While protection of the banana markets in France and the UK resulted in significant market shares for their preferential suppliers, Italy's preferential supplier, Somalia, furnished only a marginal share of its demand due to production difficulties. Consequently, despite Italy's protectionist policies most of the bananas consumed there were from dollar-zone sources and were marketed by the same TNCs who operated in Germany and the United States. Therefore, part of the

explanation for high Italian margins seems linked to the explanation for
equally high margins in Germany and the United States, and not exclusively
to the welfare losses due to protection as predicted by neo-classical theory.

2.3.3   Post-SEM period

The overall level of the margins of banana retail-over-import prices in the
EU has increased since the SEM was implemented, except in Italy and the
UK where they have decreased considerably. The decline in the Italian
margin is explained in part by the elimination of its complex system of taxes
in the pre-SEM period. Yet, Italy continues to source most of its banana
imports from the dollar-zone and these margins have stabilized at the levels
of those in the United States and Germany, both of which have increased
since the SEM. This might reflect changes in the corporate strategy of the
major TNCs that are likely to be engaged in oligopolistic interdependence.[37]
Although part of the decline in the UK margin could be explained by its
elimination of licences, the remainder needs further explanation. That
explanation might come from the decreasing market power of TNCs as a
result of vertical disintegration of the British banana commodity chain as
the SEM took effect. This hypothesis will be further developed in Chapters
6 and 7 where the division of revenue and surplus along the banana
commodity chain is discussed and analysed. Finally, the increase in France
might be explained by the increasing monopoly power of firms operating
there, although such increases are in line with those observed in Germany
and the United States.

    The preceding discussion seems to strongly suggest that the mere
existence of free trade in a market – as in Germany in the pre-SEM period,
and the United States – does not guarantee that the welfare of consumers is
being improved, but nor does the absence of free trade – as in Britain in the
pre-SEM period – guarantee that their welfare is being worsened. Other
factors are likely to matter, such as the structure of the market and the
conduct of firms in it. The argument on market structure and firm conduct
will be developed in Chapter 3. However, the remainder of this chapter is
concerned with modelling the welfare effects of trade liberalization under
modified assumptions of price determination.

2.4   Model

Since the purpose is primarily to demonstrate the fragility of the neo-
classical assumption of a single retail price, the model used here is similar in

some respects[38] to that originally introduced in Noich (1985) and applied in the studies of Borrell and Yang (1990, 1992) and Guyomard et al. (1999). However, the model in this chapter differs in other respects. Essentially, it takes into consideration the various banana import policies that existed in EU member-states prior to the implementation of the SEM and the pattern of trade between exporting countries and individual EU member-states. The main changes introduced to the basic model are: (i) use of c.i.f. instead of f.o.b. prices, as the price variables that determine export supply;[39] and (ii) the treatment of the price transmission mechanism from import to retail. The choice of c.i.f. price of bananas in the destination market is superior to f.o.b., because nested within the c.i.f. are the scale economies in ocean transportation, a major factor determining the feasibility of exporting bananas in the first place.[40] Additionally, although most of the previous studies implicitly assume that reductions in the tariff will be fully transmitted to consumers, McCorriston and Sheldon (1996) have argued in the case of the UK that this is not likely to be the case. Therefore, retail-import margins, which capture the internal costs of ripening, transportation and distribution of bananas, are used to determine retail prices.

Conceptually, the model comprises the following equations: a supply function; a demand function; a behavioural relationship between import and retail prices; a market clearing condition, and a behavioural relationship between the EU and world import prices. Each equation is discussed in detail below.

2.4.1   Supply function

Export supply decisions of producer countries are defined as constant elasticity functions of their c.i.f. prices in destination markets.[41]

Let X_j^i be the quantity of bananas exported by country j to country i, ω_j the price elasticity of export supply of country j, P_j^i the c.i.f. price for bananas from country j in country i, and ω_0 the constant parameter of export supply for country j. Then, in linear form the supply function is defined as follows:

$$X_j^i = \omega_0 + \omega_j P_j^i + \varepsilon_1 \qquad (2.1)$$

2.4.2   Demand function

Import demand decisions of consumers in EU member-states are defined as constant elasticity functions of their retail prices, which are c.i.f. prices marked up by a price transmission factor and the EU's tariff, where applicable.

Let M_j^i be the quantity of bananas imported by EU member-state i from country j, λ_i the price elasticity of import demand in EU member-state i, P_r^i the retail price for bananas in EU member-state i, and λ_0 the constant parameter of import demand for EU member-state i. Then, in linear form the demand function is defined as follows:

$$M_j^i = \lambda_0 + \lambda_i P_r^i + \varepsilon_2 \tag{2.2}$$

2.4.3   Relationship between import and retail prices

In linear form, the relationship between the import (P_j^i) and retail (P_r^i) prices of bananas in any EU member-state is specified as follows.

$$P_r^i = \beta_0 + \beta_i P_j^i + \varepsilon_3 \tag{2.3}$$

where P_j^i and P_r^i are as defined in equations 2.1 and 2.2 above, β_0 a constant which reflects the minimum retail price of bananas, and β_i the slope coefficient of the relationship between import and retail prices in EU member-state i.

2.4.4   Market clearing

It is assumed that the quota is binding and that consumers' demand for bananas in the EU is just exhausted.[42] Consequently, after trade liberalization competition takes place primarily in prices. Since demand for bananas in the EU member-states just equals supply, the market clears in accordance with the following equation.

$$\sum M_j^i = \sum X_j^i = Q \tag{2.4}$$

Equations 2.1 to 2.4 constitute a model in which there are four endogenous variables (X_j^i, M_j^i, Q, P_r^i) and two exogenous variables $(P_j^i, cons)$. Since it is possible to construct $3*3$ matrices with non-zero determinants for equations 2.1 to 2.4, they satisfy the rank and order conditions for identification (see Appendix 1).

2.4.5 Relationship between import prices at EU and world levels

Instantiating the model requires some behavioural relationship between the banana import prices at world and EU levels. Most of the earlier studies of the welfare effects have assumed that changes in EU banana prices from implementing free trade would have some impact on the world price, but none have proposed a formulation of that relationship.[43] In the following equations this study proposes and empirically estimates one possible formulation. Suppose a relationship of the following form exists between the import prices of bananas at the EU and world levels:

$$LogW_p = \alpha_0 + \alpha_1 LogEU_p + \varepsilon_4 \qquad (2.5)$$

Where $LogEU_p$ and $LogW_p$ are the natural logarithms of the EU and world import prices respectively, α_0 is a constant, α_1 is the elasticity of the world price with respect to the EU price, and ε_4 an error term, such that $\varepsilon_4 \sim N(\mu, \sigma^2)$. Then, by differentiating both sides of the equation 2.5 we have:

$$\frac{\partial W_p}{W_p} = \alpha_1 \frac{\partial EU_p}{EU_p} \qquad (2.6)$$

Rewriting equation 2.6 and solving for α_1 gives:

$$\alpha_1 = \frac{\left(\dfrac{\partial W_p}{W_p}\right)}{\left(\dfrac{\partial EU_p}{EU_p}\right)} \tag{2.7}$$

The relationship presented in equation 2.5 above was estimated using import price data for the United States and Germany over 1971-92. First, import price indices were created for Germany and the United States, then their logarithms were taken in order to explore the above relationship.[44] We find the elasticity of the world import price with respect to the EU import price to be 0.5, that is, a one per cent increase in EU banana import prices results in approximately a 0.5 per cent increase in that of the US.[45]

2.4.6 Additional assumption

Given the general similarities in costs of production and marketing for bananas from Latin America, the study assumes that the c.i.f. price of dollar-zone bananas becomes the EU's single import price under liberalization. Thus, our model is a multi-country regional model in which we assume that elasticities of supply and demand, and competition are specific to producers and consumers, respectively.

2.5   Data and empirical analysis

2.5.1   Elasticities

The elasticities of demand and supply that are used in this chapter are shown in Table A1.4 (Appendix 1). There has been some debate over the values to be used for elasticities and the possible implications for the welfare effects. In some of the studies, attempts have been made to estimate elasticities of import demand econometrically (Guyomard et al., 1999:113), while others appear to have used values rather arbitrarily. In this chapter the elasticities used are from Borrell and Yang (1990), since, again, our objective is primarily to demonstrate the fragility of the assumption of a single retail price.[46] This does not mean that they are not subject to revision, but rather that it is not the principal focus in this chapter. In fact, the elasticities of demand that are used for simulating the welfare effects under imperfect competition (Chapter 9) will be econometrically estimated.

2.5.2 Data

Data for all the simulations are presented in Tables A1.5 and A1.6 (Appendix 1). The likely welfare effects of implementing free trade in the pre-SEM period are based on data for the year 1991, while 1995 data are used for the simulations since implementation of the SEM. There is a considerable amount of debate on the choice of reference year and its implications for the welfare effects obtained.[47] However, there is widespread consensus among previous studies that 1992 was the year when banana supplies were unusually high, with resulting low prices. The over-supply situation was an outcome of the strategic actions of primarily the US TNCs, which wrongly conjectured that any allocation of tariff quotas by the EU when the NBR was implemented would be done on the basis of most recent supplies of various operators.[48]

2.5.3 Pre-SEM welfare simulations

Although the econometrically estimated value of $\alpha_1 = 0.5$, three simulations were performed: (i) a 1 per cent increase in the EU import price triggers a 1 per cent increase in the world import price; (ii) a 1 per cent increase in the EU import price triggers a 0.5 per cent increase in the world import price; and (iii) a 1 per cent increase in the EU import price triggers a 0.25 per cent increase in the world import price. Details of the first simulation are shown in Table A1.7 (Appendix 1) while the aggregate sensitivity effects on individual welfare categories, and the overall welfare effects are shown in Figure A1.1 (Appendix 1).

These results suggest that had the EU liberalized trade in bananas in the pre-SEM period, consumers' surplus would have increased only if changes in the EU import price had led to a considerable change in the world import price. Interpreting equation 2.7 in the context of the results obtained implies the following. Elastic responses of world import prices to changes in the EU import price are likely to lead progressively to increases in consumer welfare and ultimately to overall welfare gains; while inelasticity is likely to have the opposite effect. This contradicts the predictions of Borrell and Yang (1990) that a small increase in the world price in response to an increase in the EU price leads to positive welfare effects.[49] In the unit elastic case, consumers gain $118 million in surplus; however, all other categories of economic welfare suffer losses. Preferential producers lose $166 million in export revenue, all producers lose surplus of $104 million, and EU member-states lose tax revenue of $388 million, resulting in an overall global welfare loss of $540 million. As the response of the world import price to changes in the EU import price becomes more inelastic, consumers' surplus progressively diminishes, with consequent deterioration in the overall welfare effect, contrary to the findings of Borrell and Yang (1990, 1992). Not only do these findings not agree with those of Borrell and Yang (ibid.) in terms of magnitude, but the *direction* of the overall welfare effect is reversed. This is because their assumptions about the relationship between the EU and world banana import prices are not supported empirically.

2.5.4   Post-SEM welfare simulations

The major difference between the pre- and post-SEM organization of the EU banana market is that Germany did not apply the Community's Common External Tariff (CET) of 20 per cent in the pre-SEM period, but was required to do so after implementation of the SEM. As a result, the import price of bananas into the German market is considerably higher than in other large EU member-states like France and the UK. Therefore, if trade is liberalized in the post-SEM period, the extent to which EU citizens gain economic welfare depends on the extent to which retail prices fall.

This was why three sets of simulations were performed to predict the likely welfare effects of trade liberalization in the post-SEM period. First, a 1 per cent decrease in the EU import price triggers a 1 per cent decrease in the world import price. Second, a 1 per cent decrease in the EU import price triggers a 0.5 per cent decrease in the world import price. Third, a 1 per cent decrease in the EU import price triggers a 0.25 per cent decrease in the world import price. Detailed results of the first simulation are shown in Table A1.8 (Appendix 1) while the aggregate sensitivity effects on individual welfare categories, as well as the overall welfare effects are shown in Figure A1.2 (Appendix 1). We see that for high levels of elasticity of response of world import price to changes in the EU import price, all categories of global welfare are negative. As the elasticity of response of the world import price decreases, some components of global welfare gradually increase, resulting in gains in consumers' surplus when the elasticity of response of the world price is set to 0.5. However, overall global welfare remains negative up to a reduction in EU import price of 34 per cent and turns positive thereafter beyond price reductions of 35 per cent.

So, while we find it *theoretically possible* to achieve an overall welfare gain from implementing free trade in bananas, in practical terms the EU import price is required to fall by over 14 per cent in addition to removal of the tariff. An initial price fall of 5 per cent would place dollar-zone suppliers' price just below that of Jamaica and the Eastern Caribbean.[50] Further price falls of up to 10 per cent would place dollar-zone suppliers' price well below the prices of all competing suppliers except Cameroon, Côte d'Ivoire and Somalia.[51] At that point there would be little incentive for TNCs to further reduce prices, since this would lead to further losses in producer surplus and profits. However, net global welfare would remain negative after a 10 per cent price fall. Moreover, even if US TNCs reduced their price further in order to undercut suppliers of Cameroon and Côte d'Ivoire, net global welfare would remain significantly negative up to price falls of just less than 15 per cent.[52]

2.5.5   Sensitivity analysis

In performing the simulations in this chapter we utilized a behavioural relationship between the EU and world banana import prices. Although previous works had assumed that such a relationship might exist, none had attempted to formalize it. So, in order to determine how susceptible the welfare effects would be to that restriction, two sets of sensitivity analysis tests were undertaken. The first sought to determine how the elasticity of response of the world price to changes in the EU price affects the welfare effects, in particular whether decreases in EU import price result in significant decreases in the world import price.[53] We find that the more elastic the response of the world price to the EU price, the larger would be the required decrease in EU import price to make global welfare become positive. In the second set of sensitivity analysis tests, the required price reductions are estimated assuming that the post-SEM margins of retail over import prices are maintained after dismantling the NBR. We find that price falls in the vicinity of *30 per cent* would be required to make global welfare positive.

2.6   Conclusion

The objective in this chapter has been to simulate how, using comparative equilibrium static analysis, the liberalization of trade in bananas by the EU is likely to impact on global economic welfare. Unlike previous studies, by using c.i.f. instead of f.o.b. prices the study has attempted to take into consideration economies of scale in shipping, price transmission through margins, and dominant firm behaviour in setting the import price in the model. In this way, the oligopolistic market structure is brought into the model.[54] Additionally, while prior works considered only the pre-SEM period, this study has performed simulations for both the pre- and post-SEM periods.

While we find that the liberalization of the EU's banana trade could result in overall global welfare gains, more importantly we find that the *magnitude* of such gains has been overestimated by previous studies and that the likelihood of achieving such gains remains at best, *questionable*. Specifically, we find that in the post-SEM period consumers' surplus increases only for low elasticities of response of world import prices to changes in the EU import prices. Moreover, for the post-SEM period we estimated that EU banana import prices would need to fall by at least 15 per cent to make global welfare positive.[55] It was argued, however, that a 10 per cent fall in import price from dollar-zone sources would undercut most preferential competitors, leaving very little incentive for further reductions in price.

The implications of these findings are that, while the implementation of freer trade in bananas might be desirable, it could well result in a paradoxical outcome unless the Commission intervenes to ensure that the benefits of liberalization accrue to final consumers and producers. Otherwise, most of the gains from liberalization of the banana trade might well be appropriated as profits instead of contributing to consumer welfare, while the Commission would not be in a position to compensate the losers, most of whom are its present preferential suppliers. Moreover, Commission intervention would be particularly necessary because of the absence of a global antitrust policy within the WTO, given the history of anti-competitive conduct of dominant firms in the market.[56]

Finally, liberalization of the EU banana trade is likely to be a test case for trade liberalization in other commodity sectors and industries in the years ahead. Despite the standard neo-classical assumptions of perfect competition that dominate trade policy modelling, it is well known that most of world trade takes place in markets that are, at best, oligopolistic. In the remainder of this work therefore, the objective is to first demonstrate that the assumption of perfect competition over-simplifies the conceptualization of the EU banana market, to the extent that the very basis of the WTO ruling is being brought into question. Since models of the type suggested by Krugman (1994) – and others which consider imperfect competition explicitly – might be a useful point of entry, some of these will be explored in Chapter 4 and applied to simulate the welfare effects of trade liberalization under imperfect competition in Chapter 9.

Notes

[1] The power for creation of the SEM was derived from the Single European Act of 1986, which became effective on 1 January 1993 (See *Official Journal of the European Communities*, L169, 26 June 1987).

[2] Trade liberalization in this thesis means the removal of all tariffs, quotas, licences and other similar barriers to the entry of bananas into the EU. See, for instance, Smith and Venables (1988) for an analysis of the potential gains from EU trade liberalization in ten industries.

[3] In 1995 world banana trade was valued at $5.3 billion or 10.6 million metric tons (FAO, 1997a), and in the last decade of the twentieth century bananas have consistently occupied at least third position in the international tropical fruits trade (Author's *database*).

[4] These works of Borrell and Yang have been rather influential for two reasons. First, they were published at a time when very little had been written on the subject. Second, and more importantly, they emerged under the auspices of the World Bank and were published as working papers of that institution. Consequently, practically every study that has been conducted on the possible welfare and efficiency effects of EU banana trade liberalization has adopted these works as its point of entry.

[5] The methodology used in most of these studies is that of comparative equilibrium static analysis, originally introduced in the work of Noich (1985).

[6] There is also a considerable amount of variation in the magnitude of consumer surplus that is likely to result from liberalization, ranging from $505 million (Fitzpatrick and Associates, 1990) to $1.6 billion (Borrell and Yang, 1992). However, most of the studies suggest a consumer surplus in the vicinity of $600 million.

[7] Although the original GATT rules of the WTO were based on the assumption of perfect competition in the 1940s when the GATT was created.

[8] Read (1994:224) argues that while Borrell and Yang (1990, 1992) assume that quotas and licences generate monopoly power, which will automatically be eliminated by implementing free trade; the oligopolistic structure of the market suggests that even if free trade prevailed, it would not be accompanied by perfect competition. We shall return to Read's proposition in Chapter 3.

[9] For instance, Guyomard et al. (1999:119) argue that all the models of the world banana market have assumed perfect competition, essentially due to tractability of this hypothesis, and that incorporating imperfect competition into international trade models remains a formidable challenge.

[10] In a Cournot oligopoly firms compete by setting output quantities, and the resulting equilibrium is a Cournot-Nash equilibrium – every agent is doing the best he can, given what the others are doing. The concept will be defined formally in Chapter 4.

[11] Article 115 of the Treaty of Rome provides the authority for any EU member-state to implement a trade measure consistent with its national interest. Specifically, Article 115 provides that "the Commission shall authorise Member States to take the necessary protective measures, the conditions and details of which it shall determine." (Treaty of Rome, 1957).

[12] For a general background to the EU banana trade, the supply sources and destination markets, and banana import policies prior to the SEM, see Milner and Read (2002:Chapter 11); Guyomard et al. (1999:105-8); Hallam and Peston (1997:5-6); Stevens (1996:327-9), Read (1994:220-3), Deodhar and Sheldon (1995:337-9) and McInerney and Peston (1992:29-32).

[13] Included among these are Martinique, Guadeloupe, Crete, the Canary Islands and Madeira. Production in the DOMs tends to be dominated by small-holder farms, which are 5 hectares or less on average.

[14] Included among the banana-exporting ACP countries are: Jamaica, St. Lucia, St. Vincent, Grenada, Dominica, Suriname, Belize, Cameroon, Côte d'Ivoire and Somalia. As in the DOMs, production is dominated by individual farmers with holdings of less than 5 hectares on the average. Preferential EU market access for ACP bananas was originally arranged under Protocol 5 of the Lomé Convention, subsequently re-negotiated as the Cotonou Agreement.

[15] Included among the dollar-zone countries are: Ecuador, Panama, Colombia, Honduras, Costa Rica, the Dominican Republic, Nicaragua, Guatemala and Mexico. Unlike the DOMs and ACP countries, production takes place on large plantations primarily under the control of a few US transnational corporations (Chiquita, Dole and Del Monte), except in Ecuador.

[16] According to the FAO (1986:29), in the French DOMs – Martinique and Guadeloupe, there are 1100 and 1500 farms below 5 and 3 hectares, respectively; with yields of 10-12 metric tons per hectare. Additionally, in 1984 the f.o.b. cost for one metric ton of bananas was $334.10 (FAO, 1986:30).

[17] Although, the ACP countries are not homogeneous and there is a tendency for growing differences in their production techniques and yields per hectare. For instance, it is estimated that the cost of production in Dominica in 1992-93 was $515 per metric ton while it was only $440 per metric ton in Cameroon (Hallam and Peston, 1997:23). This difference in cost of production is explained in part by the introduction of large-scale plantation technology in some African countries by US transnational firms (Kasteele, 1998:10).

[18] On the subject of low wages, the illicit practices of the US TNCs in Central America are well known. Whereas a worker on a farm in Martinique can make more than $1,800 per month, it is common for a worker on a Central American plantation to make only 10 to 25 per cent of that amount. The Campaign for Labor Rights (1998) found that among other practices used by Chiquita to keep wages low, the firm uses "computerized hiring logs in Honduras that alert Chiquita-

controlled farms when to rotate some workers at supposedly independent companies before they can receive state-mandated salary and health benefits".

This view is also supported in the recent work of Frank (2002), who argues that because workers are typically hired on a temporary basis through sub-contracting, many of them are never officially recorded as employees of a corporation – and thus are locked out of state-mandated health, pension and other benefits.

[19] According to the FAO (1986:17), the major banana TNCs – Chiquita, Dole and Del Monte – actually own land in most Latin American countries. A notable exception is Ecuador, where the land is owned by independent farmers, who nevertheless market most of their bananas through contracts with domestic and foreign TNCs.

[20] The vertical integration of TNCs allows them to exploit economies of scale in shipping by matching the output size of each plantation with the size and frequency of the reefer ships. Vertical integration facilitates TNCs' maximization of the utilization of costly refrigeration space (Read, 1986:321), and hence minimization of per unit cost.

[21] It is noteworthy that on the most modern plantations of Costa Rica, yields of up to 67.34 metric tons per hectare are quite common (Kasteele, 1998:2).

[22] See, for instance, Preville (1999, 1997), Read (1994), Borrell and Yang (1992, 1990) and McInerney and Peston (1992).

[23] Germany's right to import bananas duty- and tax-free from Latin America, or any other source, was granted under a special dispensation under the Treaty of Rome (Hallam and Peston, 1997:6).

[24] While in France the licence was only granted when import prices exceeded a certain level, in the UK a licence minimum level of 30,000 metric tons had been required since 1989. However, the granting of additional licences was subjected to the recommendations of the Banana Trade Advisory Committee (Borrell and Yang, 1990:7, 10).

[25] Details of the European Commission's original proposal for setting up the internal banana market were compiled by a Commission Working Group, in Commission Working Document SEC (92) 940 final. See European Commission (1992) for details.

[26] The reader should note that the ECU was the forerunner of the EUR, the notes for which only came into circulation in twelve EU member-states in January 2002. Since the ECU was the currency in force when the NBR was introduced, it is used in this work to maintain consistency with original documents from the Commission and the Council.

[27] Specifically, Article 12 declares the size of the production quota and its breakdown among EU territories; Article 15 sets out the size of the quota for imports from ACP countries that were traditional suppliers to the EU market, as well as the amount allocated to each country; and, Article 18 specifies the size of

the third-country tariff quota and the applicable tariffs with respect to different sources of supply (European Council, 1993).

[28] In fact, since the implementation of regulation 404/93 the EU has permanently increased its tariff quota from 2.2 to 2.553 million metric tons to take into account the inclusion of Sweden, Austria and Finland as members in 1995.

[29] As noted by Read (1994:225), the Belgian and Dutch ministers of agriculture joined their German counterpart in opposing the proposed regulation. Additionally, the Economic and Social Committee of the Community also opposed the proposed regulation on the grounds that it conflicted with the objectives of market-oriented trade policy.

[30] At least five external formal complaints have been made against the EU's NBR since its implementation. The first two were made before GATT Panels in 1993 and 1994, respectively; the third was a threat by the US to invoke its Section 301 procedure in 1994 at the request of one of its TNCs, Chiquita; the fourth was an "own initiative" of the US Trade Secretary, Michael Kantor, in January 1995 under the section 301 procedure; and the fifth was the request for the establishment of a WTO Panel in 1996, which ruled against the NBR. Subsequent appeals and arbitration procedures pursued by the EU did not succeed in reversing the original Panel rulings. We shall discuss these in detail in Chapters 3 and 5.

[31] This is also considered to be important since the US banana market is only slightly smaller than the EU, and both markets tend to be characterized by similar industrial organization. Hence, observable trends in the EU banana market might have implications for the US, and *vice versa*. This point is elaborated in Chapter 3.

[32] Volatility in the margins between the pre- and post-SEM periods is evident from Figure 2.2, as measured by the mean, although the number of observations is small.

[33] In fact, as Read (1994:231) suggests, banana prices in the EU are likely to vary for a number of reasons, including differences in quality, competition, demand conditions and transport.

[34] McCorriston and Sheldon (1996) address the question of the extent to which reductions in tariffs are likely to be transmitted to consumers in the case of the UK's banana imports. They argue that both the number of vertical stages and the degree of imperfect competition at any specific stage can affect the degree of tariff pass-through, and hence consumer welfare (McCorriston and Sheldon, 1996:664).

[35] A commodity chain is defined as a transactionally linked sequence of functions in which each stage adds value to the process of production of goods or services (Dicken, 1998:7). The commodity chains into France and the UK are not as vertically integrated as those into the United States and Germany. The fact that vertical integration confers efficiency advantages on firms in co-ordination and monitoring of all stages of the banana commodity chain, which is of strategic importance when dealing with the highly perishable banana (Read, 1994:220)

suggests that this might play a crucial role in predicting consumer welfare. This concept will be developed further in Chapter 4 and applied in Chapters 6 and 7.

[36] Although bananas imported into Italy from EU producer territories and ACP countries had not been subjected to tax or quota restrictions since 1974, imports from other countries were subjected to the EC's common external tariff of 20 per cent and a quota which ranged from 205,000 to 265,000 metric tons during 1974-77. Additionally, Italy charged a *consumption tax* of $270 per metric ton in 1982 (FAO, 1986:47).

[37] Data from the FAO suggest, that more than 80 per cent of bananas sold in the United Sates and Germany are under the control of similar transnational firms and their affiliates (FAO, 1986:81). Thus, the general increase in US margins might be a reflection of changes in the strategy of transnational firms.

[38] The similarity lies in the factual issues surrounding the EU banana trade, that is, a system of preferences existed for some countries and not others, which largely influenced the pattern of trade; and that we are using comparative equilibrium static analysis.

[39] In this study, c.i.f. is the cost plus insurance plus freight applied to bananas when they arrive at a port of entry into Europe, while f.o.b. is the cost of bananas when they have been loaded onto a vessel and are ready for shipment from the supplying country. To the best of the author's knowledge, all the previous studies that have been conducted on the welfare effects have used the f.o.b. price as the determinant of export supply.

[40] In fact, Casson (1986:52) suggests that scale economies in the shipping of bananas are possibly of greater strategic importance than scale economies on plantations, making it more cost effective and desirable to use large ships on few voyages, as opposed to small ships on many voyages.

[41] The *natural* gestation period for bananas is nine months. This implies that in the short run the response of a supplier to changes in price is restricted to available capacity. A constant elasticity function captures this.

[42] In practice, this is a reasonable assumption for both the pre- and post-SEM periods. In the pre-SEM period, the objective of quotas and licences was to ensure that only a controlled quantity of bananas from specified sources entered respective markets. The same objective is achieved in the post-SEM period by imposing very high tariffs on out-of-quota quantities. See sub-section 2.2.3 for details.

[43] The basic assumption of the models used by Borrell and Yang (1990, 1992) is that some relationship exists between banana import prices in the US and the EU, and the import price of bananas in Germany in the pre-SEM period has been taken as a proxy for the import price of bananas into the EU under free trade.

[44] Exploration of these data revealed that they were not stationary in levels and first differences. However, they were stationary at second differences and so the latter were used in the final econometric estimations.

[45] Specifically, the elasticity $\alpha_1 = 0.497$, $R^2 = 0.40$, and the t-statistic was 3.597. Additionally, the Durbin-Watson (DW) statistic was 2.72, indicating the absence of auto-correlation. Moreover, results of the Granger causality test performed on these data suggest there might be *weak* reverse causality.

[46] The author is aware of the widespread criticism of the elasticities used by Borrell and Yang and their implications, which has been properly documented by the McInerney and Peston (1992:37-40), among others.

[47] For instance, See Hallam and Peston (1997) for a summary of these.

[48] Instead, the EU allocated its tariff-quota on the basis of the best-ever export levels of all countries within the prior decade (1980-89).

[49] Moreover, while Borrell and Yang (1990, 1992) arbitrarily assumed that a relationship exists between the EU and world banana prices, they did not empirically demonstrate this to be so.

[50] It is important to note that for the post-SEM simulations, the prices being compared here are those that presently exist with those that are likely to result after removal of the CET Community-wide. The disparity between dollar-zone banana import prices and those of the Caribbean, for instance, becomes more obvious when it is considered that German banana prices increased by 48 per cent between 1992 and 1994, in response to implementation of the CET of 20 per cent. See Chapter 3 for a detailed discussion.

[51] Somalia's banana industry would be the least of threats to the trade at this time. Whereas the banana industry was restructured as part of a structural adjustment package in 1981, the reforms did not improve development, since, over 75 per cent of the earnings were realized by overseas interests. Additionally, the collapse of the Somali military regime in 1991 destroyed its banana industry (Samatar, 1993:40-1).

[52] Our basic proposition here is that dominant firms operating in these countries are likely to reduce their prices only to the extent to which they undercut the competition. Since price reductions generally imply smaller profits, especially where demand is inelastic, there seems to be no rationale for profit-driven firms to voluntarily accept a lower level of profit than necessary.

[53] In other words, the tests sought to determine the direction and magnitude of the welfare effects if $\alpha_1 \to 0$, and if $\alpha_1 \to \infty$, respectively, where

$$\alpha_1 = \frac{\left(\dfrac{\partial W_p}{W_p}\right)}{\left(\dfrac{\partial EU_p}{EU_p}\right)} \text{ as defined in equation 2.7.}$$

[54] However, neither the familiar Cournot or Bertrand models of oligopoly, nor any of their derivatives are presented here; these models will be discussed in Chapter 4 and applied in Chapter 9 to estimate the welfare effects under imperfect competition.

[55] Note that the price reduction here is in addition to the elimination of the CET Community-wide, which would effectively imply a 35 per cent reduction in import prices.

[56] This argument will be developed further in Chapter 3.

3 Market Structure, Firm Conduct, Trade Policy and the Pattern of the Banana Trade in the EU

3.1 Introduction

Chapter 2 used a simple empirical model to demonstrate that liberalization of the EU banana trade could lead to perverse welfare effects if the assumptions of perfect competition and/or contestability are not reasonably satisfied. Specifically, it argued that in addition to elimination of the tariff, if firms do not reduce import prices by at least 15 per cent, overall welfare might decrease after liberalization.[1] It further argued that banana c.i.f. prices are preferred to f.o.b. for predicting welfare effects of trade liberalization because they capture economies of scale that are likely to exist at the shipping stage of the commodity chain.

With the preceding in mind, this chapter has two objectives. First, to present and discuss the empirical evidence about the structure of the EU banana market, the pattern of EU banana trade, the conduct of firms in the market and the various banana import policies that have existed in the EU. The central proposition of this thesis is that the structure of the EU banana market and the conduct of firms have major implications for its performance, which include the likely welfare effects, if trade in the commodity is liberalized. The second objective is to set the stage for the empirical analysis in Chapters 5 to 9 of the thesis. Therefore, this chapter begins with a descriptive analysis of the world banana trade in general and the EU banana trade in particular, in Section 3.2. Then in Section 3.3 the structures of the world and EU banana markets are described and analysed, identifying the major actors in the banana trade along its commodity chain. Next, Section 3.4 discusses the conduct of major firms in the world and EU banana trade. Section 3.5 analyses the price formation process along the banana commodity chain and attempts to determine whether or not certain actors have been more influential than others. Section 3.6 then examines the trade policies that dominated the EU banana market in the pre-SEM period, the banana import policy that was implemented under the SEM, and why the new banana import policy was challenged in the GATT and the WTO. Finally, Section 3.7 presents some concluding remarks.

3.2   Pattern of world and EU banana export trade

Although world banana exports have doubled during the last 25 years of the twentieth century, increasing from 6.0 million metric tons in 1973 to 12.1 million metric tons in 1997, most of this growth took place in the 1987-97 period (Figure 3.1). In fact, while the 1973-86 period was characterized by stagnation, exports grew at 7.7 per cent per annum on the average during the 1987-97 period.

Figure 3.1   World banana exports ('000 tons)

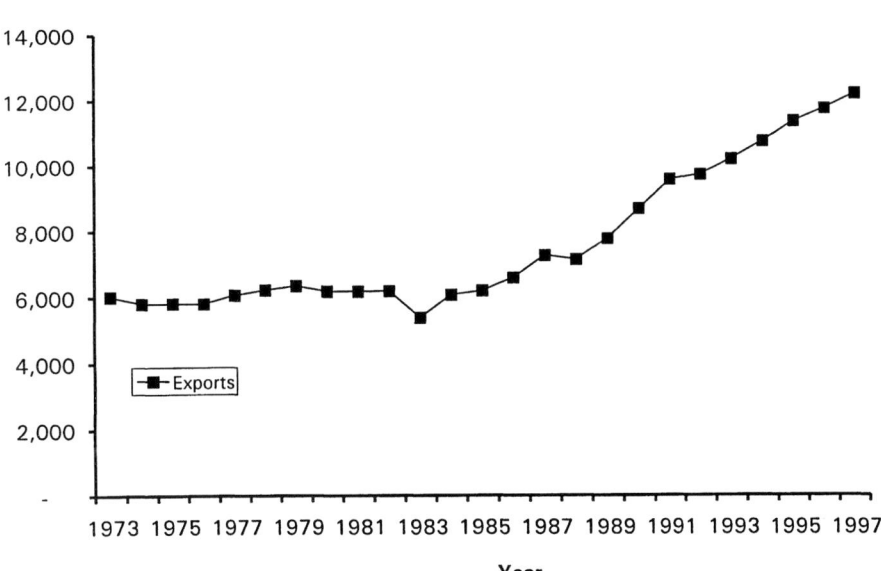

Source: Author's database.

Within the trend of increasing growth in world banana exports during the 1987-97 period, there are variations in the performance of major supplying regions. The trend of world banana exports is explained largely by the Latin American export trend, with regional trends of the Far East, the Caribbean and Africa contributing very little to the overall explanation.

Of the 7.2 million metric tons of bananas entering the world export trade in 1987, 5.9 million came from Latin America, 0.9 million from the Far East, 0.3 million from the Caribbean and 0.2 million from Africa. This relative distribution of shares among banana-exporting regions changed very little in 1997: of the 12.1 million metric tons of bananas exported that year, 10.2 million came from Latin America, 1.3 million from the Far East, 0.4 million from Africa and 0.2 million from the Caribbean (Figure 3.2).

Effectively, the tendency in world banana exports has been for an increase in the degree of monopoly control by countries in Latin America, whose regional market share increased from 82 per cent in 1987 to 84 per cent in 1997. Thus, decisions of these countries with regard to the control of export supply are likely to have a direct impact on world supply and prices. Therefore, it is useful to decompose the Latin American regional banana supply into the supplies of individual countries, as well as the supplies of sub-groups of countries, in order to arrive at some indication of the extent of monopoly power that countries command at both the individual and sub-group levels.

Figure 3.2   World banana exports, by region ('000 tons)

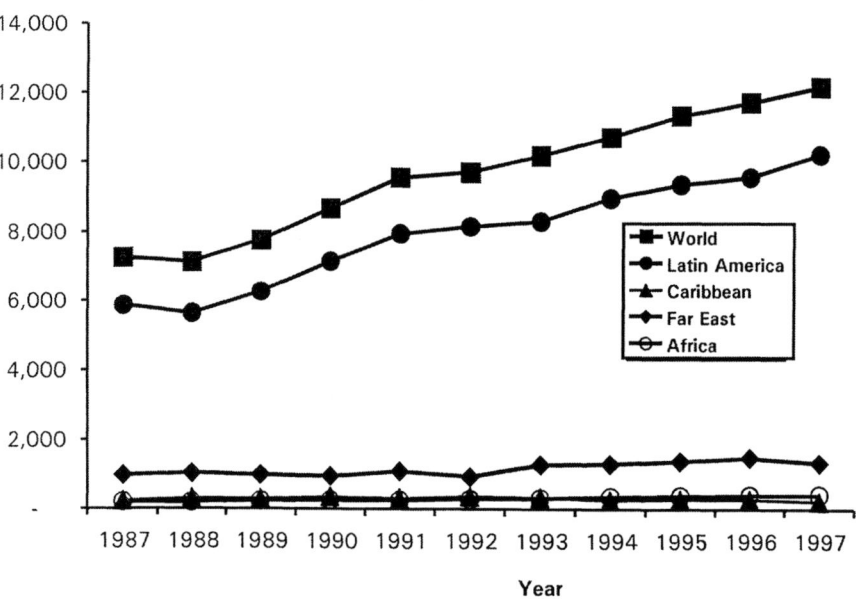

Source: Author's database.

3.2.1   Latin America's banana exports

Some 13 countries in Latin America account for all that region's banana exports, and export concentration is very high. On the average, particularly between 1995 and 1999, five of these countries accounted for 90 per cent of all that region's exports, while three of them accounted for more than 70 per cent (Figure 3.3).[2]

Ecuador alone accounted for 23.6 per cent of that region's banana exports in 1987, and by 1999 its share had increased to 44.3 per cent. Additionally, the joint export shares of Ecuador, Costa Rica and Colombia have increased steadily over time, with the first two accounting for 67.8 per cent, and all three accounting for 86.7 per cent of all Latin American banana exports in 1997. In order to better explain the preceding trends, let us analyse the export volumes of the top five countries in Latin America.

Figure 3.3 Banana export concentration among Latin American countries (as % of total regional banana exports)

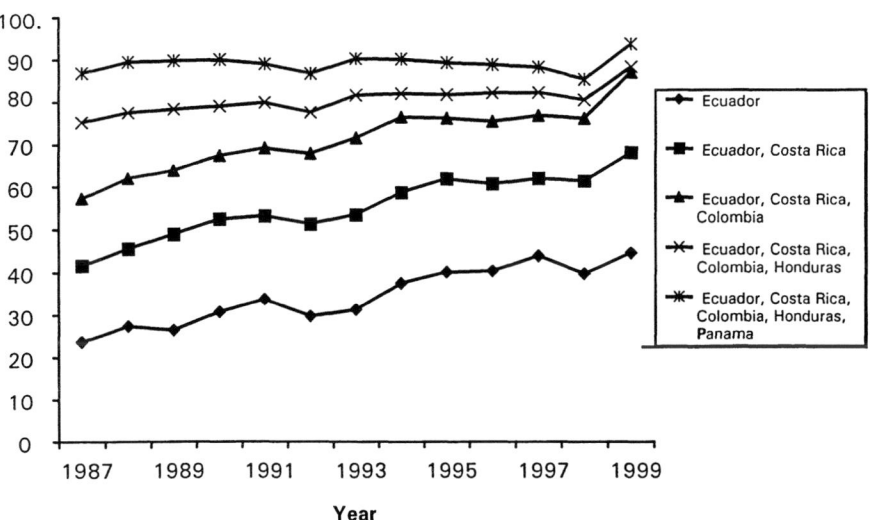

Source: Author's database.

Although Ecuador, Costa Rica and Colombia have consistently been the top three banana exporters from that region, in that order of relative importance, the tendency has been for the growth rate of Ecuador's exports to significantly outpace those of Costa Rica and Colombia, resulting in a widening gap in their export volumes (Figure 3.4). Therefore, at the level of individual countries, concentration in world banana export trade is extremely high, with Ecuador assuming the role of dominant actor.[3]

3.2.2   Banana exports to the EU

Detailed accurate data on banana exports to EU member-states are available only for the major importing countries. This is partly because exporting countries tend to report significant quantities of banana exports as exports to 'other countries' whenever those countries are not major importers.[4] Since only a few EU member-states (Germany, France and the United Kingdom) account for the bulk of all banana imports and most of subsequent analysis is based on these member-states, only exports to these countries are examined below.

Figure 3.4   Latin America banana exports, by country ('000 tons)

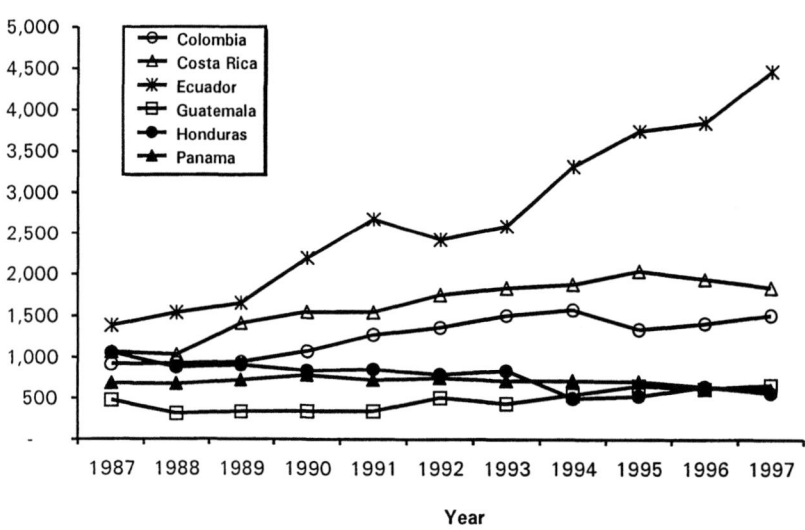

Source: Author's database

Banana exports to Germany originate exclusively from Latin America, with Ecuador, Costa Rica and Panama accounting for more than 75 per cent of supply and Colombia and Honduras accounting for residual shortfalls (Figure 3.5). From 1986 to 1990, Costa Rica was the major source of supply to Germany, with total exports peaking at 428,900 metric tons in 1990. However, since 1991, Ecuador has become the major supplier, with its exports peaking at 515,651 metric tons in 1997. A notable exception was in 1992, when Panama's exports to Germany were slightly larger than those of both Ecuador and Costa Rica.

Figure 3.5   World banana exports to Germany ('000 tons)

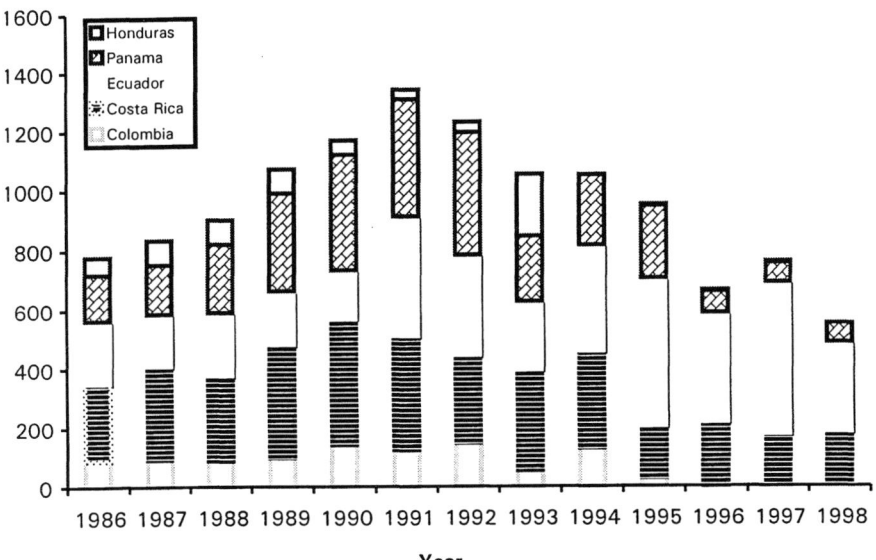

Legend:
- Honduras
- Panama
- Ecuador
- Costa Rica
- Colombia

Source: Author's database.

In contrast, banana exports to France originate almost exclusively from the DOMs and the ACP countries (Figure 3.6). During the pre-SEM period (1987-92) the DOMs accounted for 63 per cent, while the ACP countries accounted for 33 per cent of the French market, leaving 4 per cent for the dollar-zone on the average. The tendency since the SEM took effect has been for a decrease in the market share of the DOMs – 49 per cent, with a concomitant increase in the share of the ACP countries – 49 per cent, while the share of the dollar zone has declined to 2 per cent on the average.

Finally, the Caribbean ACP countries have dominated banana exports to the UK, particularly during the pre-SEM period (1986-92) when they accounted for over 70 per cent of that market on the average, while exports from Latin America accounted for shortfalls. Since the SEM took effect, however, there has been a slight decline in the Caribbean's market share, most of which was initially met by supplies from the dollar zone and, increasingly, from Africa.

The above evidence suggests the importance of different banana import policies in the major EU member-states in the pre-SEM period and the strategic actions that major suppliers in Germany and Britain are likely to have pursued prior to implementation of the SEM.

Figure 3.6   World banana exports to France (tons)

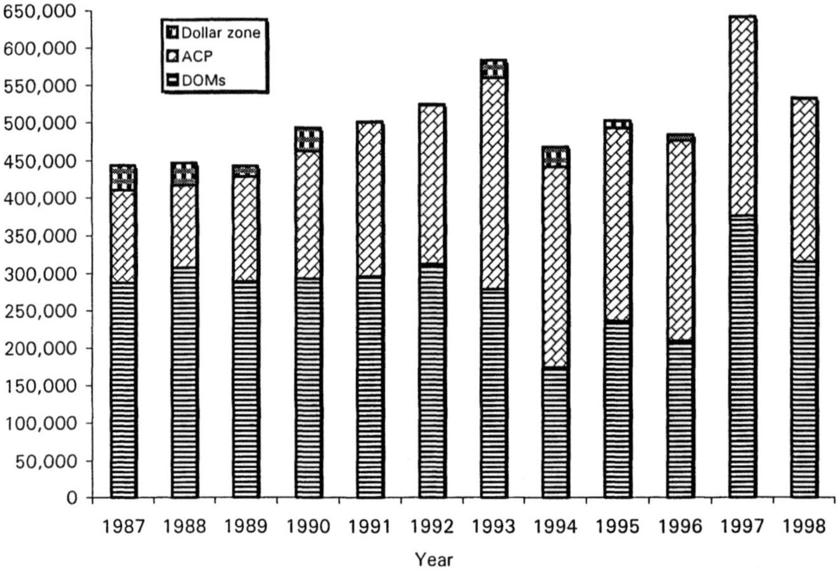

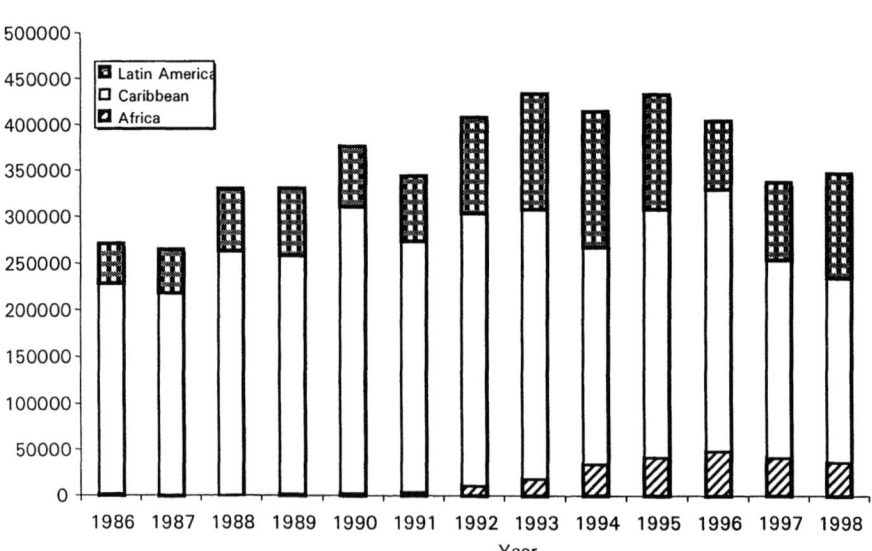

Source: Author's database.

Fig. 3.7   World banana exports to the UK (tons)

Source: Author's database.

In both the pre- and post-SEM periods the market in France is dominated by supplies from the DOMs and the ACP countries, while the market in Britain remains largely under ACP control. While banana volumes peaked in Germany in 1991, such volumes did not reflect increases in demand, but rather increases in supply from actors in the dollar zone in anticipation of increased market shares when the SEM took effect. Hence a secular decline in total exports since the SEM took effect. A similar explanation applies to Britain (Figure 3.7). Let us now examine the pattern of banana import demand.

3.3   Pattern of world and EU banana import demand

World banana imports show a rather similar trend to exports for the 1986-97 period, with imports increasing from 6.5 million metric tons in 1986 to 11.4 million metric tons in 1997, or an average growth rate of 6.9 per cent per annum (Figure 3.8).

Fig. 3.8   *World banana import demand, by region ('000 tons)*

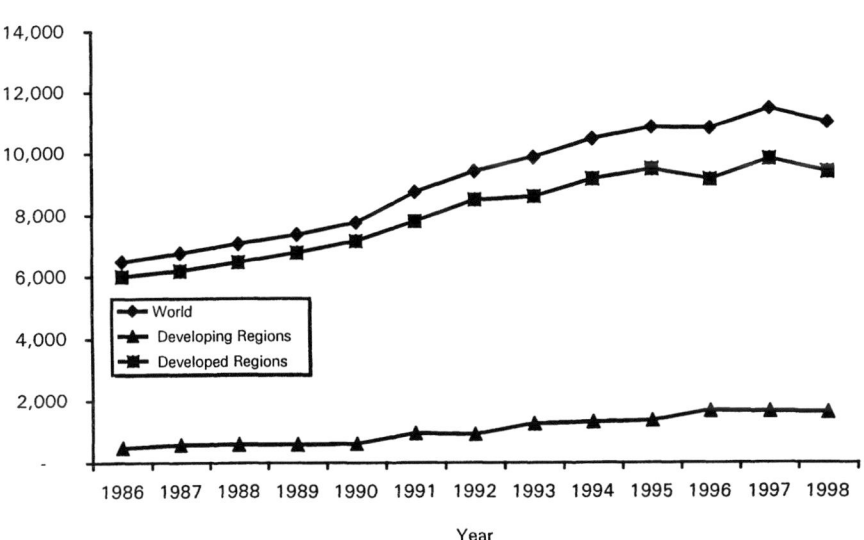

Source: Author's database.

Yet, the growth rate of banana import demand was not uniform through-out that period: import demand grew at 4.9 per cent per annum during the 1986-90 period, compared to a growth rate of 7.9 per cent per annum during the 1990-95 period. Although world banana imports in 1996 fell slightly below their 1995 level, the prospects for continued growth appear to be good.

World demand for banana imports is explained largely, but not invariably, by the import demand of the developed regions. In 1993, it was the growth of import demand within the developing regions that sustained the overall growth in world banana imports, since demand growth within the developed regions was sluggish. The demand for banana imports grew at an average of 20.3 per cent within the developing regions during the 1986-95 period, while the corresponding figure for the developed regions was only 6.4 per cent. Yet, given the import levels in both regions in 1986, it seems unlikely that developing regions' import demand will have any significant impact on world import demand in the near future, even if it is assumed that their demand for banana imports continues to grow at present rates.[5]

Since the demand for banana imports by the developing regions has little impact on world banana import demand, and this study is concerned with the EU banana trade, let us now examine the import trends among the developed regions in order to properly situate the EU within that category. This will be followed by an analysis of EU banana imports.

3.3.1   Developed regions' banana import demand

Among the developed regions, world banana import demand varies considerably, with two of those regions, North America and the EU, accounting for approximately 65 per cent of world imports.[6] While the North American region was a considerably more important market than the EU during the 1986-89 period, the gap has narrowed considerably since the mid-1990s (Figure 3.9).

Bananas are considered to be an important part of a healthy diet, and increasingly especially the diet of the elderly and the sick.[7] Yet they are produced in the tropics and the process of getting them to the tables of consumers in the temperate regions is complex and expensive (see Chapter 4). Consequently, the possibilities for their consumption in the temperate regions are highest in the relatively rich countries with large, well-developed markets, where the actors engaged in their distribution could enjoy some economies of scale. This explains why the North American and EU markets account for the greater part of world export consumption. The changing relative importance of these markets is explained by the dynamics of the EU since the late 1980s – increased consumption in Germany due to reunification, and enlargement of the EU to include Austria, Finland and Sweden in 1995.

Fig. 3.9   *Banana imports within the developed regions ('000 metric tons)*

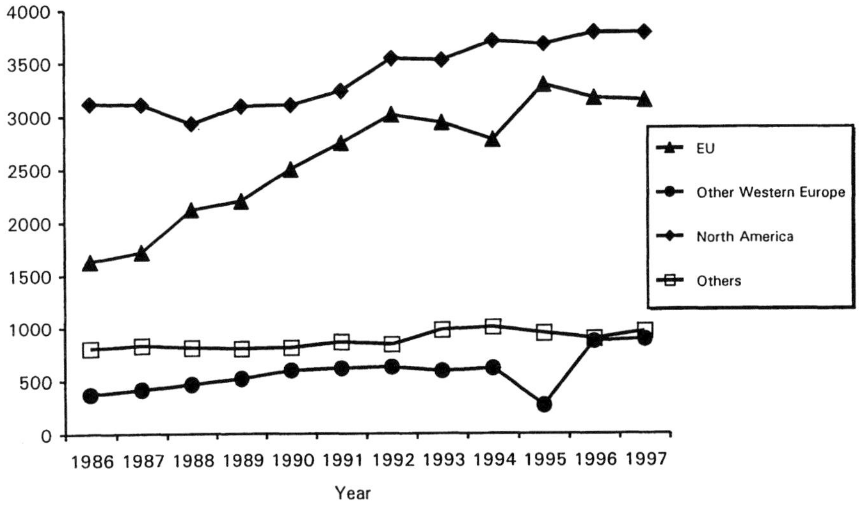

Source: Author's database.

There are three other features of the banana import trade among the developed regions that warrant discussion. Firstly, in Eastern Europe and the former USSR, imports grew from 86,000 metric tons in 1986 to 1.3 million metric tons in 1995, or an average growth rate of 157 per cent per annum. Most of this growth is explained by the collapse of communism and subsequent emergence of markets in these countries – imports grew at 149 per cent per annum on the average during the 1990-95 period, compared with a growth rate of only 19.8 per cent per annum on the average for the 1986-90 period. However, the recent economic crisis in the Russian Federation has resulted in reduced consumption (FAO, 1999: 42).

Secondly, the growth of banana imports into the other developed countries, primarily Japan, was rather sluggish during that period. In fact, in the 1986-92 period imports grew by slightly less than 1 per cent per annum on the average before recovering to an annual average of 4.3 per cent in the 1992-95 period.[8]

Thirdly, in the remainder of Western Europe, while imports grew at an average rate of 11.4 per cent per annum during the 1986-92 period, imports have been declining since 1994 at an average rate of 19.1 per cent per annum for the 1992-95 period. This precipitous decline in the import of bananas into the rest of Western Europe largely reflects the enlargement of the EU in 1995 to include Finland, Sweden and Austria, as opposed to changing demand for bananas in those countries *per se*.

3.3.2   EU banana import demand

Demand for banana imports into the EU grew steadily during the 1986-96 period, from 1.8 million metric tons to 3.3 million metric tons (Figure 3.10). We have seen earlier that banana exports to the EU originate primarily from three sources of supply – the dollar-zone countries, some banana-exporting ACP countries, and domestic production from some EU member-states, the DOMs (sub-section 3.2.2). Additionally, a small quantity of exports originate from a few countries which are not regular trading partners, labelled others.[9]

There are three salient features of the EU banana import trend. First, the import trend of bananas into the EU is explained largely by the import trend of dollar-zone bananas (Figure 3.10). This is not surprising because, as seen earlier, the trend in banana exports from Latin America explains the trend in world banana exports, and the EU is a principal consuming region.

Fig. 3.10   EU banana imports, by region ('000 metric tons)

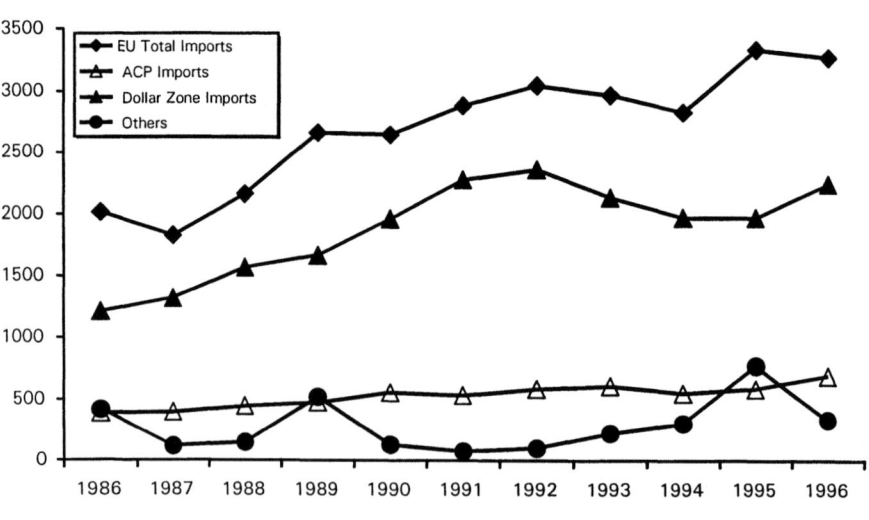

Source: Author's database.

Second, with the exception of the 1994-95 period, when there were moderate declines in the growth of banana imports from the ACP region, banana imports from that region grew at an average annual rate of 10.5 per cent, while in contrast growth in imports from the dollar-zone accelerated over the 1989-92 period (Figure 3.10). This further explains the strategic actions of operators from the dollar zone in the run-up to the SEM, in a bid to expand their market share when the SEM took effect. Subsequent deceleration in dollar-zone exports is a direct consequence of over-supply in the pre-SEM period.

Third, banana imports into the EU from other countries have increased steadily over the 1987-96 period, exceeding the levels of imports from the ACP region in 1988 and 1995. The import level in 1988 is largely explained by imports from the Philippines, which supplied 36,662 metric tons. More difficult to explain is the import level of that category for 1995 – 105,343 metric tons from unknown sources. Although these were not sustained for any considerable period they have been growing at an average annual rate of 21 per cent. Given the EU's strict tariff and quota policies on banana imports in both the pre- and post-SEM periods, the latter observation appears anomalous. We shall return to discussion of this anomaly in later chapters of the thesis.

Before proceeding to the arguments on market structure, it is useful to discuss whether or not, and the extent to which, the EU's banana policies have distorted demand, a hypothesis which is typically advanced by exponents of the neo-classical approach.[10] The EU's per capita banana import growth of 8.7 per cent per annum on the average during the 1986-95 period can be decomposed into two sub-periods: first, 1986-92, during which per capita banana imports grew at 13.0 per cent per annum on the average. Second, 1992-95, when they declined at 2.2 per cent per annum on average (Figure 3.11).

But we have seen earlier that the trend in total banana imports was rather similar. First, they grew at 13.4 per cent per annum on the average during the 1987-92 period; then they declined at 3.6 per cent per annum on the average during the 1992-94 period. The author has also argued that the decline in banana imports after the SEM took effect was a direct consequence of the over-supply situation created by dollar-zone sources. Therefore, once the strategic actions of dollar-zone operators are controlled for, it does appear that, contrary to neo-classical expectations, the EU member-states' policies on banana imports during the pre-SEM period were consistent with consumer demand.[11]

Fig 3.11   EU per capita banana imports (kg.)

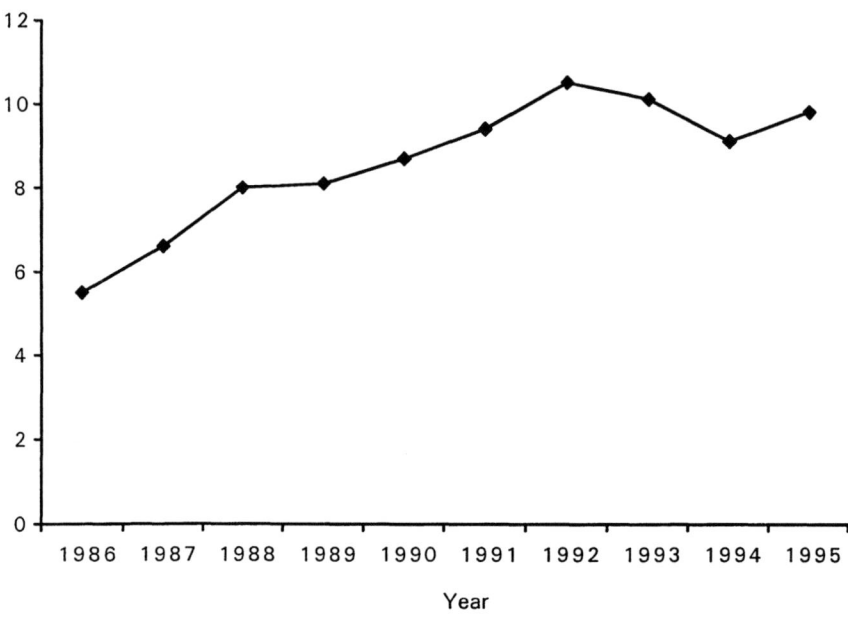

Year

Source: Author's database.

3.4   World and EU banana market structure

By market structure, we mean the nature of the typology facing buyers and
sellers in the banana trade. It will be recalled that the driving hypotheses
behind previous works on the EU banana market are that it is either
perfectly competitive and/or contestable. These hypotheses imply that: (i)
no firm can affect market price, or exercise any degree of market power;
and (ii) no barriers exist for entry into or exit from the EU banana market by
new firms. Yet, we have seen that at both the global and EU levels, the
banana trade tends to be characterized by high concentration levels in export
supply and import demand at the level of individual countries, suggesting
that the power of individual countries and/or firms might be more important
that previously thought. Let us, therefore, examine the banana market
structure at both the world and EU levels.

3.4.1   World banana market structure

The dominance of world banana export supply by a small number of countries in Latin America is by no means its only form of concentration in the commodity chain. In fact, as this study will argue, bananas are traded along a commodity chain with various stages and each stage of the chain adds value in the creation of the final product. In order to determine whether or not the hypotheses of perfect competition and/or contestability are reasonably satisfied, we need to identify the actors that control and/or own the value-adding activities at various stages along the commodity chain and the organizational nature of their activities. Vertical integration, for instance, is likely to confer superior advantages on actors directly involved in the banana trade than to those engaged in arm's length (conventional) trade.

At the global level, the banana trade takes place in an oligopolistic market, in which three TNCs: United Brands (Chiquita), Castle and Cooke (Dole) and Del Monte, command nearly 70 per cent of international trade in the commodity (Table 3.1). In 1966, 47.4 per cent of world banana trade took place under the direct control of these three TNCs, and by 1992 their joint market share had increased to 70 per cent.

Table 3.1   Market shares of transnational firms in world banana trade (%)

Firm	Year					
	1966	1972	1980	1992	1995	1997-98
Chiquita	34.0	30.5	28.7	35.0	25.0	24.5
Dole	12.3	18.0	21.2	20.0	22.5	25.5
Del Monte	1.1	5.5	15.4	15.0	15.5	16.0
CR3	47.4	54.0	65.3	70.0	63.0	66.0

Source: Author's database.

Yet, even these figures somewhat understate the authority of these firms in the banana trade, given the nature of its commodity chain. The marketing and distribution of bananas produced in most Latin American countries is done by these firms through contractual agreements with national banana associations in producing countries (FAO, 1986), and when these shares are added to their corporate shares, considerably more than 70 per cent of world banana trade falls under their control. In order to better explain the nature of the banana TNCs, why oligopolistic interdependence is high and the power which they command in international trade of the commodity, it is important to discuss their financial statements and corporate activity.

Chiquita Brands International Inc.

Chiquita Brands International Inc. (Chiquita) is an extremely powerful corporation by any standard: its total assets between 1995 and 1999 averaged well above $2.5 billion, total capitalization averaged slightly less than $2.0 billion over the same period and net sales were in line with total assets (Table 3.2).

Table 3.2   Financial condition and operations of Chiquita brands (US$000)

	Year				
	1995	1996	1997	1998	1999
Financial condition					
Working capital	366,893	379,977	300,348	308,805	414,445
Capital expenditures	64,640	74,641	76,248	118,250	152,080
Total assets	2,623,533	2,466,934	2,401,613	2,509,133	2,596,127
Capitalization:					
short-term debt	172,333	135,089	152,564	169,279	129,754
long-term debt	1,242,046	1,079,251	961,972	1,002,606	1,227,001
shareholders' equity	672,207	724,253	780,086	793,980	705,286
Operations					
Net sales	2,565,992	2,435,248	2,433,726	2,720,361	2,555,799
Operating income	175,770	84,336	2,433,726	78,609	42,038
Income / (loss) from continuing operations	27,969	(27,728)	343	(18,412)	(58,382)
Net income (loss)	9,212	(50,566)	343	(18,412)	(58,382)

Source: Author's database.

The fact that this firm has recorded net losses during the 1995-99 period is explained largely by its loss of market share since the implementation of the EU's NBR in July 1993 and its failure to diversify its banana supply sources to the producing countries that continue to enjoy preferential market access to the EU. Chiquita explains the decrease in net sales in 1999 over 1998 as a consequence of lower banana pricing, while the increase in net sales in 1998 over 1997 resulted from the expansion of its processed foods business, through acquisitions of vegetable canning operations in late 1997 and early 1998. With regards to its operating income, the firm attributes the decrease in 1999 to weak banana pricing, particularly in Europe, due to over-allocation of EU banana import licences earlier that year and weak demand in Eastern Europe and Russia. The firm's operating income in 1998 also reflects write-downs and other costs due to significant damage to its properties in Honduras and Guatemala by Hurricane Mitch.[12] In fact, Chiquita contends that if the Hurricane Mitch effect is excluded, its fresh produce operating income in 1998 improved, relative to 1997, due to increased farm productivity and reductions in transportation costs on higher world-wide banana volumes.[13] This supports the hypothesis that economies of scale, both on plantations as well as in the shipping of bananas, are extremely important.

A significant component of capital expenditures in 1999 was directed at rehabilitation of banana farms in Honduras and Guatemala following their extensive destruction and/or damage by Hurricane Mitch, and most of this capital expenditure was funded by proceeds from the firm's insurance as well as credit. Capital expenditures in the prior two years included expenditure on expansion of Chiquita's vegetable canning operations and the rehabilitation of farms in the firm's western Panama division following a two-month strike.[14]

Dole Food Company

Like Chiquita, Dole Food company (Dole) is an extremely powerful firm by any standard: its total assets averaged slightly less than \$3.0 billion between 1995 and 2000, total capitalization has averaged \$1.7 billion since 1998 and gross revenue has averaged more than \$4.0 billion since 1997 (Table 3.3). In fact, Dole's current financial performance is better than Chiquita's for two reasons: (i) whereas the long-term debt of both firms is of the same order of magnitude, Dole's short-term debt is several orders of magnitude smaller than Chiquita's; and (ii) whereas Chiquita has been essentially a loss-maker since 1996, Dole has consistently reported significant profits since 1995 (see Tables 3.2 and 3.3).

Table 3.3 Financial condition and operations of Dole Food Company ('000)

	Year					
	1995	1996	1997	1998	1999	2000
Financial condition						
Working capital	480,000	464,000	407,000	366,000	381,000	356,000
Capital expenditures	90,000	110,000	129,000	150,000	158,000	122,000
Total assets	2,442,000	2,487,000	2,464,000	2,915,000	3,034,000	2,845,000
Capitalization						
short-term debt	24,000	22,000	13,000	37,000	39,000	45,000
long-term debt	896,000	904,000	755,000	1,116,000	1,286,000	1,136,000
shareholders' equity	508,000	550,000	666,000	622,000	532,000	555,000
Operations						
Revenue	3,804,000	3,575,000	4,065,000	4,189,000	4,794,000	4,763,000
Operating income	193,000	164,000	244,000	85,000	140,000	184,000
Income (loss) from continuing operations	120,000	89,000	160,000	12,000	49,000	–
Net income (loss)	23,000	89,000	160,000	12,000	49,000	68,000

Source: Author's database.

The superiority of Dole's performance relative to Chiquita's in recent times could be explained by a combination of factors. First, Dole is a far more diversified firm than Chiquita: whereas Chiquita has depended largely on bananas for its operations and financial health, Dole produces and markets bananas and pineapples as its major line of operations, and in addition, it is a major marketer of a variety of other products including citrus fruits, table grapes and a wide range of fresh and processed vegetables.[15]

Second, Dole has been more proactive in adapting to the constraints of the EU's NBR, implemented in 1993, than Chiquita, which instead chose to fight the EU in the WTO and elsewhere (see Chapter 5). Since (and even prior to) the implementation of the EU's NBR in 1993, Dole has diversified its sources of banana supply to include countries in Africa and the Caribbean, which continue to enjoy preferential market access to the EU.[16] Additionally, beyond its ownership of banana ripening facilities throughout Europe, Dole: (i) is a partner in the largest French banana and pineapple producer and is also a minority partner in a banana exporting firm in Guadeloupe; (ii) holds minority partner shares in the Jamaican Producers Group of companies, which ripens and distributes bananas produced in Jamaica; and (iii) owns 60 per cent of Saba Trading AB in Sweden, Scandinavia's leading importer of fruits, vegetables and flowers.[17]

Dole asserts that the outcome of its operations and financial condition in 2000 represents an improvement over 1999, although it could have been even better were it not for the following factors: (i) a 13 per cent decline in the average exchange rate of the EUR to the USD; (ii) an increase of 40 per cent, on average, of end-user fuel rates in 2000 over 1999; and (iii) a continued situation of over-supply in the banana industry. Since Dole has significant European market sales denominated in EUR, and product and shipping costs associated with some of these sales are USD denominated, the depreciation of the EUR relative to the USD caused the firm's revenues and operating income to decline by $140 million and $40 million, respectively. Dole also estimates that the 40 per cent increase in end-user fuel rates resulted in a $20 million decline in the firm's operating income. Finally, the firm expects weak banana pricing to persist into the near future due to continued conditions of over-supply in the market as well as the collapse of previously emerging banana markets in eastern Europe.[18]

Fresh Del Monte Produce

Relative to Chiquita and Dole, Fresh Del Monte Produce (Del Monte)[19] is a smaller firm, with total assets averaging slightly less than $1 billion over

1996 to 2000, and total debt averaging less than \$0.5 billion over the same period (Table 3.4). Yet, this firm has managed to outperform Chiquita in terms of both operating and net incomes (see Tables 3.2 and 3.4), suggesting a much more efficient utilization of productive assets. Additionally, despite the fact that its average assets over 1995 to 2000 amounted to nearly one-third of Dole's, both its operating income and net income over the same period averaged nearly half those of Dole (see Tables 3.3 and 3.4).

Del Monte's performance can be explained by a number of factors. First, it is a far more diversified firm than Chiquita, although perhaps less so than Dole. In 1999, Del Monte was: (i) the third-largest marketer of bananas in the world, with an estimated market share of 19 per cent; (ii) the largest marketer of fresh pineapples in the world, with an estimated market share of 54 per cent; and (iii) the largest marketer of cantaloupes sold in the United States.[20]

Second, Del Monte functions as a fully vertically integrated firm, controlling, managing or supervising all aspects of the production, distribution and marketing of its fresh produce. This, the firm contends, enhances its ability to ensure high product quality, operate efficiently and generate high margins.[21]

Third, the firm distributes production and supply risks by sourcing its products from approximately 13 countries located in North America, South America, the Asia-Pacific region and Africa.[22] Additionally, Del Monte strategically divides its fresh produce between that cultivated on its own farms and that acquired through supply contracts with independent growers.[23]

Fourth, the firm has strategically divided its 43 globally managed refrigerated-vessel fleet between vessels owned by it and those that it charters. This enables the firm to function as a vertically integrated corporation with lower risks than those that might arise from deployment of capital in its vessel fleet.[24]

Notwithstanding its firm strategies, which have led to its impressive performance, Del Monte faces several risk factors which have adversely affected both its performance and financial condition in recent times. Del Monte points out that while bananas accounted for a significant share of its total net sales in 1999, it was pineapples that accounted for the significant share of its gross profit that year. It attributes this to the increasing power of wholesalers and distributors in the banana industry, which derives from increasing consolidation among leading grocery stores and other retail chains.[25]

Table 3.4   Financial condition and operations of Fresh Del Monte Produce ('000 $)

	Year					
	1995	1996	1997	1998	1999	2000
Financial condition						
Working capital	(2,300)	85,200	134,600	177,200	203,700	451,000
Total assets	274,300	920,800	1,009,300	1,034,000	1,216,200	1,221,600
Capitalization						
total debt	118,600	438,600	354,100	354,200	504,100	778,400
shareholders' equity	99,600	147,000	342,800	382,500	425,800	425,800
Operations						
Revenue	220,800	278,300	1,542,400	1,600,100	1,743,200	1,859,300
Operating income	3,100	17,500	110,800	104,200	84,500	82,600
Income (loss) from continuing operations	1,700	8,000	63,600	77,400	56,900	33,100
Net income (loss)	1,700	8,000	53,200	59,300	56,900	33,100

Source: Author's database.

Crop disease and adverse weather conditions routinely affect the financial condition of Del Monte. Recent such incidents include: a hurricane in Guatemala in 1998; flooding in Costa Rica in 1996; and a major outbreak of Black Sigatoka disease on banana farms in Costa Rica in 1993 and 1994.[26] Other factors that have adversely affected Del Monte's financial condition and performance in recent times include: legal action in relation to worker safety and the environment;[27] adverse regulation in export markets;[28] international exchange rate movements;[29] and the effective settlement of disputes with associates in export markets.[30] We shall now examine the structure of the EU banana market and demonstrate how the global organization of the banana market relates to it.

3.4.2   EU banana market structure

The oligopolistic market structure prevailing in the world banana trade persists at the level of the EU banana trade, despite the protectionist policies of the EU both prior to and since the implementation of the SEM. In the 1970s and 1980s, Chiquita, Dole, Del Monte and Noboa accounted for 54.1 per cent of the EU banana market on the average, and EU banana TNCs accounted for the remaining 45.9 per cent. However, in the 1990s the shares of the US banana TNCs along with Noboa increased considerably to 62.6 per cent on the average, leaving the remaining 37.4 per cent to EU banana firms (Table 3.5).

Table 3.5   Market shares of transnational firms in the EU banana trade (%)

Firms	Year						
	1976	1980	1984	1988	1992	1996	1998
Chiquita, Dole, Del Monte and Noboa	52.6	56.4	50.9	56.4	63.1	61.7	63.1
Fyffes, Geest, Pomona	47.4	43.6	49.1	43.6	36.9	38.1	36.9

Source: Author's database.

The fact that the US banana TNCs have managed to prosper in the EU banana market despite what is widely cited as a highly discriminatory banana import policy against them, gives some indication of: (i) their degree of market power relative to EU firms; and (ii) the difficulties that firms are likely to experience in contemplating entry into the market, that is, the market is not likely to be either perfectly competitive or contestable. We shall return to these arguments in Chapter 8 where the degree of market power in France and Germany is empirically measured. For the moment, let us examine the financial condition and performance of the EU's most significant banana firms.

Financial condition and performance of EU banana TNCs

Unlike the US banana TNCs, which command the lion's share of both world and EU banana trade, EU banana TNCs are rather modest, and most of them hardly qualify to be regarded as TNCs. In fact, the only thing that one could regard as being of a transnational nature about most of these firms is that they source bananas from one part of the world and distribute them to select locations, primarily in the UK, Ireland and France. Yet, even then, the activities of these firms that create value added at various stages of the commodity chain are not under their strict control, but are instead loosely coordinated through various contracts among actors. In fact, so limited is the scale and scope of operation of these firms that the vast majority of them are not publicly liable, with the exception of Fyffes, which has recently emerged to become a significant competitor to the US banana TNCs *within* the EU market.[31] Therefore, detailed data on the financial condition and performance of these firms are scant, and where available, are considered strictly confidential by firms. Moreover, since the onset of the banana controversy between the US and the EU in 1993, EU banana TNCs have tended to treat their internal data with even more secrecy;[32] perhaps this is out of fear that their weaknesses might be revealed to rival US TNCs, some of which have contended that the EU banana policy is designed primarily to provide monopolistic advantages to these firms, and not to the exporting ACP countries which enjoy preferential market access, as is commonly argued. Therefore, the following analysis is based on data for Fyffes.[33]

Fyffes is considered to be the fourth-largest fresh produce company in the world, employing in excess of 3000 people, nearly one-third of whom are based at the firm's headquarters in Ireland. Bananas, most of which are sourced from Belize, Surinam, Jamaica and the Eastern Caribbean, account for approximately one-third of the firm's sales and half its operating profit. Since the early 1990s the firm has undertaken the acquisition of a number of banana-related entities in Europe,[34] and has successfully diversified its sources of supply to include Honduras in Central America and the Dominican Republic.[35]

In the year 2000 Fyffes PLC had a market capitalization value of EUR 239 million, sales of EUR 1,859 million and total assets of EUR 224 million

(Table 3.6). Thus we see that Fyffes' total assets were only approximately one-tenth those of Dole and slightly less relative to Chiquita. Notwithstanding this, while Fyffes' pre-tax profit averaged slightly more than EUR 70 million during the 1996-99 period, Chiquita consistently recorded losses for that period. In fact, Fyffes' pre-tax profit was consistently higher than that of Dole, suggesting more efficient utilization of productive assets than by its rivals.[36] Additionally, the firm's debt position seems to be more resilient than those of both Dole and Chiquita.

Table 3.6 Financial condition and operations of Fyffes (€ 000,000)

	Year				
	1996	1997	1998	1999	2000
Financial condition					
Working capital	2.17	2.33	2.32	6.15	7.24
Fixed capital	134.00	148.00	165.00	156.00	161.00
Capital expenditures	0.95	13.70	18.60	44.90	55.60
Total assets	137.12	164.03	185.92	207.05	223.84
Capitalization:					
market capitalization	286.00	300.00	350.00	398.00	239.00
short-term debt	227.00	276.00	372.00	412.00	381.00
long-term debt	183.00	176.00	150.00	97.30	156.00
shareholders' equity	28.50	27.90	28.00	35.80	38.50
Operations					
Net sales	1,638	1,674	1,709	1,688	1,859
Pre-tax profit	61.50	68.60	78.90	83.90	7.53
Retained profit / (loss)	25.00	30.30	37.20	41.60	(26.40)

Source: Author's database.

3.5   Firm conduct in world and EU banana trade

It will be recalled that the underlying assumptions in previous work on the EU banana trade, which sought to promote liberalization as a means of increasing economic welfare, are that the banana market is perfectly competitive and/or contestable (Chapter 2). Yet, the empirical analysis presented so far in this chapter demonstrates that the market is in fact oligopolistic at both the world and EU levels, and that it is not likely to be contestable, given the large capital investment, risks, and organizational logistics that confront both incumbents and potential new entrants. Therefore, the question of whether or not liberalization of the EU banana trade is likely to result in increased welfare and efficiency should be answered in the context of an oligopolistic banana market, which is neither perfectly competitive nor contestable.

Since the presence of oligopoly and the absence of contestability in any market signals the possibility of perverse behaviour, we need to identify the nature of conduct of the banana TNCs as a precondition to simulating how they are likely to behave in a liberalized market. Specifically, we need to determine whether: (i) individual firms engage in conduct that seeks to uniquely identify their product to consumers; (ii) as a consequence of unique identification of the products of individual firms, they are capable of charging higher prices to consumers; (iii) any evidence exists on rivalry or co-operation between firms; and (iv) other forms of discrimination exist, based on the relative power of individual firms. Let us therefore go on to discuss these issues.

3.5.1   Monopoly power due to branding

A distinctive feature of the world and EU banana trade is that all major firms have sought to differentiate their bananas in some manner in order to obtain marketing and consumption advantages. The most obvious and widely known form of differentiation is branding, and the reader who eats a banana periodically will have come across at least one of the following brands: Chiquita, Dole, Del Monte, Fyffes, Bonita and Geest.[37] Branding is used by some firms to differentiate between classes of their own bananas, so that consumers are misled into thinking that they have a wider choice than they actually do, while firms command higher margins on the stronger brand names at the expense of possible losses on the weaker ones.

Table 3.7 shows the brands used by major firms in the international banana trade and their principal sources of supply. The fact that certain banana brands command a stronger presence in the market than others, and that the firms that control those brands are conscious that they do command a certain degree of monopoly pricing power in markets, is difficult to deny. In fact, practically all of the major banana firms go to considerable lengths to argue that their brand names give them distinct advantages in the market.

Table 3.7   Major banana brands in international trade, by firm and region of origin

Firm	Brands	Regions/countries of supply
Chiquita Brands International	Chiquita, Chiquita Jr., Consul, Amigo, Onkel Tuca, 1x1	Central America, Colombia, Ecuador, Philippines
Dole Food Company	Dole	Central America, Philippines, Cameroon, Côte d'Ivoire
Fresh Del Monte Produce	Del Monte	Central America, Cameroon, Philippines
Fyffes PLC	Fyffes	Jamaica, Central America, Colombia
Geest Bananas	5 Isles	Eastern Caribbean
Jamaica Producers	JPs, Turbana	Jamaica, Central America, Colombia
Noboa	Bonita	Ecuador
Uniban	Turbana	Colombia

Source: Author's database – Banana Brands!

The credibility of firms' claims with regard to their brands is derived largely from the length of time they have been exposed to consumers, the intensity of advertising used to stimulate consumer awareness, and their historical reputation for quality. Chiquita argues that "it derives competitive benefits in the marketing, distribution and sourcing of fresh produce" through a number of factors, the first of which it identifies as "recognized brand names and a reputation for quality".[38] A similar opinion is expressed by Del Monte. In explaining why it considers itself a global leader in the fresh produce industry, Del Monte asserts that its "products are marketed throughout the world under the Del Monte ® brand name which has been in existence since 1892 and is a widely recognized symbol of product quality and reliability".[39] Dole is perhaps even more explicit about how it views the importance of its brands. The firm contends that "recognition of the Dole-Registered Trademark- trademarks and related brands and the association of these brands with high-quality food products contribute significantly to

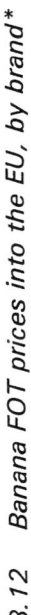

Fig. 3.12   Banana FOT prices into the EU, by brand*

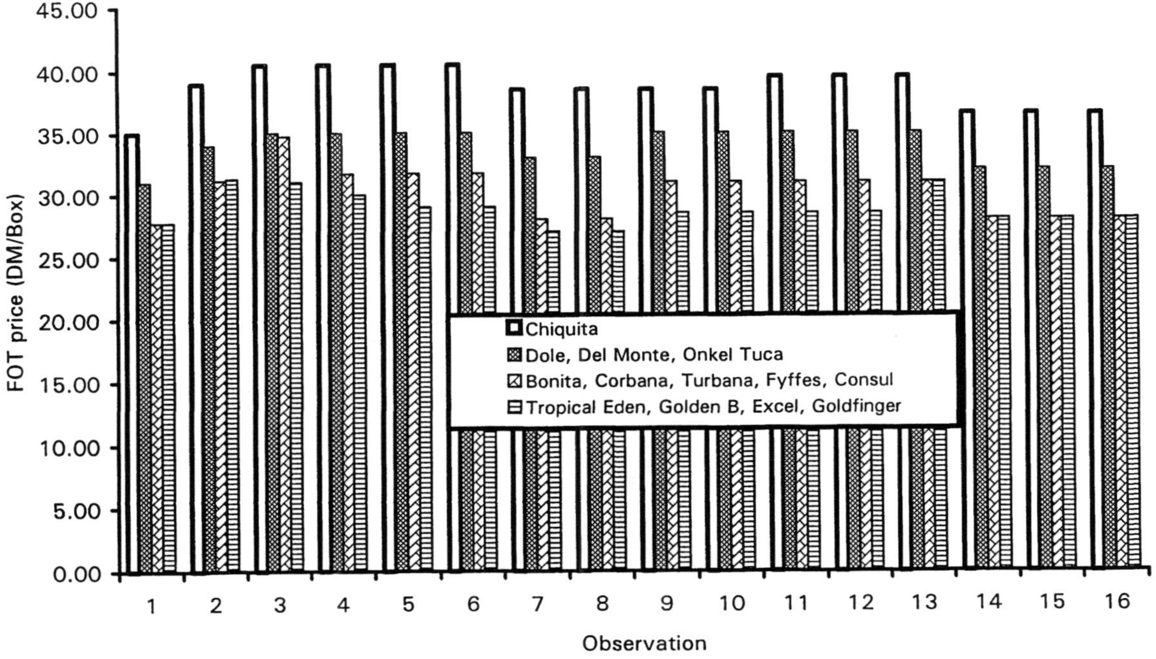

Note: FOT is the free on truck price of bananas when they have been imported into an EU member-state. In member-states where bananas are loaded onto trains, the equivalent price is the FOR, the free on rail price.

Source: Author's database.

Dole's ability to compete in the markets for fresh fruit and vegetables, packaged foods, dried fruit, nuts and pineapple juice and juice blends".[40]

Branding, therefore, does give individual firms some degree of monopolistic advantage; moreover, firms are capable of exercising their monopoly power by charging higher prices for strong brands than they do for weak or unbranded bananas (Figure 3.12).

Bananas are divided into four distinct price classes based on the strength of their brand names: (i) the "Chiquita" brand, generally referred to as the premium brand, is in the first price class; (ii) the "Dole", "Del Monte" and "Onkel Tuca" brands are in the second price class; (iii) the "Bonita", "Corbana", "Turbana", "Fyffes", and "Consul" brands are in the third price class; and (iv) the weakest brands – "Tropical Eden", "Golden B", "Excel", and "Goldfinger" – are in the fourth price class (Figure 3.12).

"Chiquita" bananas command a price up to 43.6 per cent higher than fourth-class bananas; 37.5 per cent higher than third-class bananas; and 16.7 per cent higher than second-class bananas. Although their margins are lower than that of the "Chiquita" brand, second price class bananas command a price up to 27.3 per cent higher than the lowest price class; and 17.9 per cent higher than third-class bananas. Therefore, although all the major banana TNCs command some degree of monopoly power, it is clear that Chiquita has managed to exploit such monopoly power to the greatest degree. Its biggest rivals, Dole and Del Monte, effectively compete against its "Onkel Tuca" brand, while the smaller EU and Latin American banana firms effectively compete against its "Consul" brand.

We shall demonstrate econometrically in Chapter 9 that there exists a causal relationship in price-setting among oligopolists based on banana brands, which is consistent with the concept of price leadership by a dominant firm.

3.5.2   Monopoly power due to advertising – changing the brand image

Despite the importance of branding as the major means of differentiating the bananas of one firm from those of its rivals, in practice firms use a number of additional strategies to promote the consumption of fresh produce. One strategy that is growing in popularity among firms for promotion of banana consumption is health and nutritional value. Chiquita has been aggressively utilizing this strategy since the autumn of 2000, when it launched its programme to combat fad diets and promote healthy eating. The firm first educates the US public on the importance of a well-balanced diet as opposed to fad diets, and emphasizes the importance of "regular exercise and a sensible diet that includes healthy food choices, such as Chiquita ® bananas".[41] It emphasizes the nutritional aspects of bananas as "an outstanding source of energy-sustaining complex carbohydrates", which "also provide essential vitamins (B6, C) and minerals the body needs, including all-important potassium".[42] By combining this health promotion programme with the seductive voice and looks of its "Miss Chiquita" – who supposedly epitomizes the beauty that every American woman should aspire to – Chiquita further entrenches its power in the banana market.[43] The other major banana TNCs also emphasize the nutritional value of the commodity and promote their brands as standard bearers of that quality, but in different ways. All of them feature the health and nutritional value of bananas in their annual reports, general advertising and websites.[44]

Given the oligopolistic structure of the banana industry, its non-contestability, and the importance of product differentiation, it is likely that some form of open rivalry or co-operative behaviour might persist at various stages. In fact, extensive evidence exists of other forms of anti-competitive conduct that characterizes the world banana industry from its early stages to the present time, all of which involve the Chiquita TNC in some way or the other. We shall briefly examine four of these: (i) the implementation of the Consent Decree in the United States; (ii) exclusive use of special assets; (iii) price discrimination against consumers; and (iv) control over firm equity after divestiture.

3.5.3   Consent Decree – Chiquita and the United States Department of Justice

The Consent Decree is an agreement entered into between the United Fruit Company (Chiquita)[45] and the United States Department of Justice in 1958, which forbade Chiquita from engaging in certain aspects of anti-competitive behaviour. In exchange for this, Chiquita was not required to admit any violation of United States antitrust laws (Litvak and Maule, 1977:540).

Prior to 1958, Chiquita and Castle and Cooke (Dole)[46] accounted for nearly 90 per cent of the United States banana market, with Chiquita alone accounting for 80 per cent in 1950 (ibid.:542). At the time, Chiquita functioned as a fully vertically integrated TNC, controlling every stage of the banana commodity chain from railways on its own plantations in Central America to shipping facilities and jobbing operations throughout the United States, thus commanding a considerable degree of market power. Under the Consent Decree, Chiquita was required to divest itself of significant assets and was prohibited from engaging in several activities related to the banana business after bananas enter the United States.[47]

3.5.4   Exclusive use of special assets

With regard to the exclusive use of special assets, the subject of diseases in the banana industry is extremely important. Bananas tend to be prone to certain diseases, the monitoring and eradication of which require continuous research and technological innovation for the creation of more resistant varieties, which calls for highly specialized scientific skills.[48] Although such skills are transferable across regions in principle, in practice they tend to be firm-specific, resulting in the dominance of world banana export production by a small number of firms (Casson, 1986:52).

More recently, there has been some rivalry between Dole and Del Monte over patents for marketing sweet pineapples. Del Monte brought a complaint before a Florida Court claiming that Dole's "extra-sweet Premium Select pineapple" was actually a "copy of Del Monte's own Del Monte Gold fruit". However, the Judge in the case ruled that Del Monte does not hold a patent on its Gold pineapple.[49]

Therefore, innovation in both product and process are important for maintaining monopoly power in the banana industry. This again adds to the non-contestability of the banana industry as a whole.

3.5.5   Price discrimination

In 1976 a Danish customer brought a complaint before the European Commission, alleging that Chiquita had charged it a higher price than it should have and had attempted to prevent that customer from selling green bananas in the market (Hallam, 1995:518).[50] The European Commission subsequently conducted an investigation of Chiquita's business practices to determine whether they were in contravention of Article 86 of the Treaty of Rome,[51] which prohibits any abuse of a dominant position in the common market that might affect trade between EU member-states.[52] Chiquita at the time did command a dominant position, since it accounted for 40 per cent of the EU market, and its biggest rivals, Dole and Del Monte, accounted for only 9 and 5 per cent of the market, respectively. The Commission found that Chiquita had indeed abused its dominant position in several ways, and as a consequence it fined Chiquita one million units of account and required the firm to cease all infringements of the Treaty of Rome.[53]

3.5.6   Control of equity after divestiture

In 1986 Chiquita divested itself of Fyffes, thus creating an autonomous firm, Fyffes PLC (Fyffes). However, as part of this divestiture Chiquita attempted to prevent Fyffes from using the "Fyffes" brand outside the UK and Ireland until 2006.

At the request of Fyffes in 1990, an inquiry by the European Commission found that Chiquita's action was in violation of Article 85(1) of the Treaty of Rome. As Deodhar and Sheldon (1995:339) put it, by attempting to restrict Fyffes' use of the "Fyffes" brand, Chiquita was trying to ensure that its equity in the "Chiquita" brand was not undermined by the "Fyffes" brand.[54]

Let us now examine the price formation process along the banana commodity chain.

3.6   Price formation along the banana commodity chain

In addition to the quantities of bananas that are traded globally and the strategic actions of TNCs, the prices that prevail at the various stages of the commodity chain are a key indicator of the performance of the world banana economy in general, and the EU banana market in particular. There are at least five distinct stages of value-adding activity along any banana commodity chain: (i) production; (ii) ocean transportation or shipping; (iii) importation; (iv) ripening; and (v) redistribution for retail sale.[55] Whether or not the welfare of producing countries is maximized depends on their relative efficiencies in production and the share of revenue and surplus that they retain from the commodity chain. Similarly, whether or not the welfare of consumers in the importing countries is maximized depends on the efficiencies of the various value-adding processes at each stage of the commodity chain and the share of revenue and surplus that they retain.

At any stage of the commodity chain, the extent to which price exceeds marginal cost serves as a proxy for the extent to which welfare and profits are maximized. If the tendency is for firms to enjoy monopoly profits, then policies that encourage freer trade are likely to decrease welfare, while the converse is expected if profit margins are relatively small. Therefore, in the remainder of this section we shall examine banana prices at various stages of the commodity chain and demonstrate, in aggregate terms, the extent of both absolute and relative margins between one stage and the next and their variations across different commodity chains.

Reliable time series data on world banana prices at *all stages* of the commodity chain are only available for a small number of importing countries: the United States, Germany, France, the UK, and Japan; and their principal banana exporting partners.[56] Consequently, the following analysis is based on prices in those countries only.

During the 1986-99 period, in median terms, world banana import prices were lowest and with the least variability in the United States, and highest and with considerable variability in France. Prices in Germany were comparable to those in France and showed the most variability (Figure 3.13).

Fig. 3.13   Dispersion of world banana import prices (1986-99)

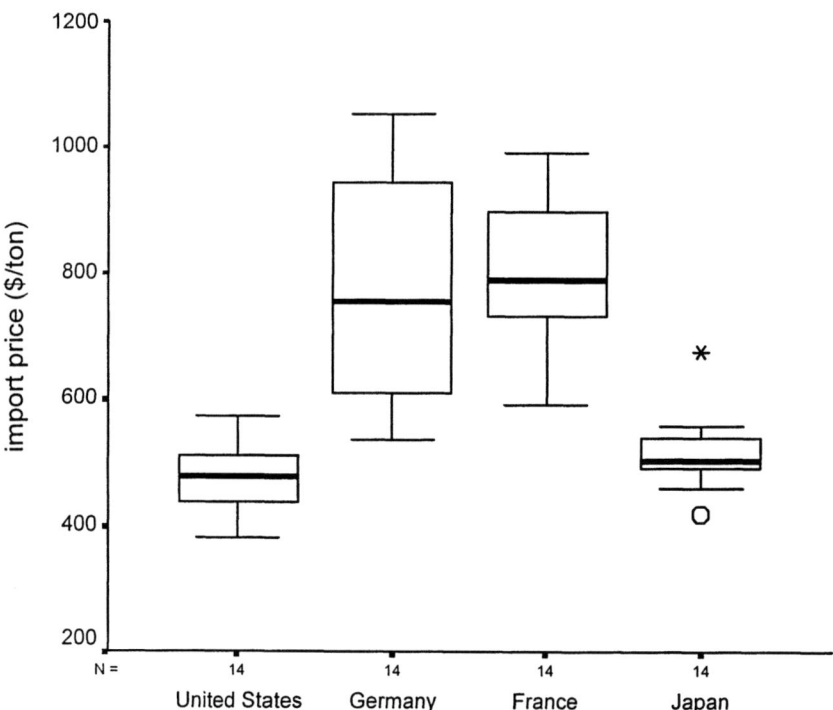

Source: Author's database.

The relatively low levels of United States banana import prices are explained by a combination of factors. First, the geographic proximity of the United States to its principal sources of supply, the dollar-zone countries, which are the most competitive in costs of production. Second, the vast size of the United States market makes it possible for TNCs to exploit econo-mies of scale in shipping by optimizing reefer sizes to meet market demand.

By contrast, banana import prices were highest in France because of significantly higher costs of production in the DOMs – France's principal source of supply – the greater geographic distance which bananas need to travel to reach the French ports and the relatively smaller size of the market, making it difficult to optimize scale economies in shipping to match market demand.

Where Germany is concerned, most of the variation in its banana import prices is explained by its implementation of the EU's NBR in 1993, under which it was required to introduce the EU's CET. In fact, when provision is made for Germany's implementation of the CET the degree of variability in import prices falls below that of France (Figure 3.14). The higher level of German banana import prices relative to those in the United States is explained by the greater geographic distance which reefers need to travel to access the market. However, their lower levels relative to those in France are a consequence of importation almost exclusively from the dollar zone.

Fig. 3.14   World banana import prices (US$ per metric ton)

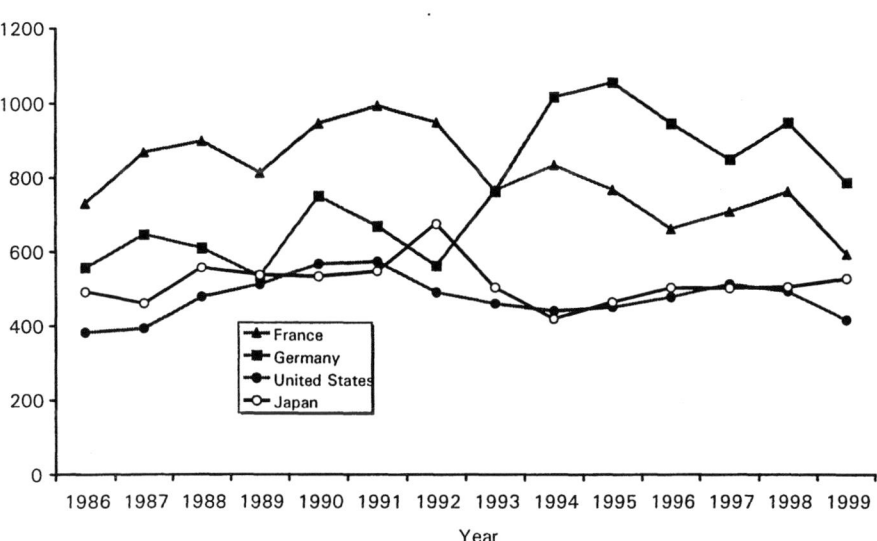

Source: Author's database.

Yet, while the CET is only the equivalent of a 20 per cent import duty, German banana import prices increased by more than 30 per cent in some years, relative to their 1992 levels (Figure 3.14). Therefore, it appears that banana TNCs operating in the German market might have seized the opportunity of the CET to increase their profit margins at the shipping stage. We shall further explore and discuss this proposition in Chapters 6, 7 and 8.

With the exception of a near outlier and an extreme outlier in the Japanese data for 1994 and 1992, respectively, banana import prices in Japan were remarkably stable throughout the same period. Relatively low Japanese banana import prices are explained by the geographic proximity of Japan's principal source of supply, the Philippines, where production costs are comparable to those in the dollar-zone.

3.6.1   Wholesale-import price margins along EU banana commodity chains

Absolute margins of banana wholesale prices over import prices (wholesale-import margins) generally increased for "Chiquita" bananas sold in Germany and all bananas sold in France during the 1986-98 period. However, the wholesale-import margins of "Other" brands of bananas sold in Germany over the same period did not increase (Figure 3.15).

Fig. 3.15   *Absolute banana wholesale-import margins in France and Germany (US$ per metric ton)*

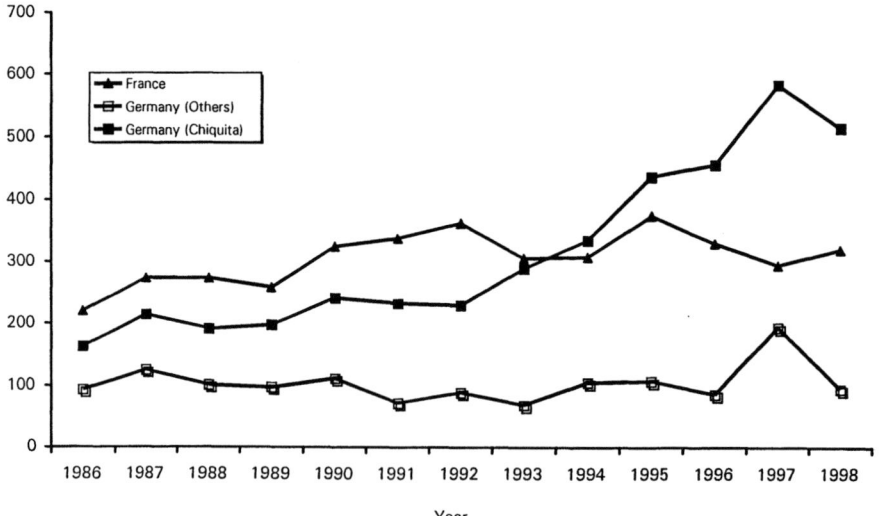

Source: Author's database.

Decomposing these trends reveals that during the 1986-92 sub-period, wholesale-import margins were highest for bananas sold in France; however, since 1993 they have been highest for "Chiquita" branded bananas sold in Germany (Figure 3.15).

This supports the hypothesis that since the implementation of the EU's NBR in 1993, firms that trade in "Chiquita" branded bananas at the wholesale stage of the commodity chain in the German market appear to be enjoying larger profits than before. Moreover, relative wholesale-import margins – the percentage increase of wholesale prices over import prices – reveal a similar trend to that of absolute wholesale-import margins. In fact, although firms at the wholesale stage of the banana commodity chain in France have enjoyed larger absolute margins than those in Germany on the average, in relative terms firms marketing "Chiquita" bananas have consistently enjoyed larger margins, while those marketing "other" brands have invariably enjoyed the least (Figure 3.16).

Fig. 3.16   Relative banana wholesale-import margins in France and Germany

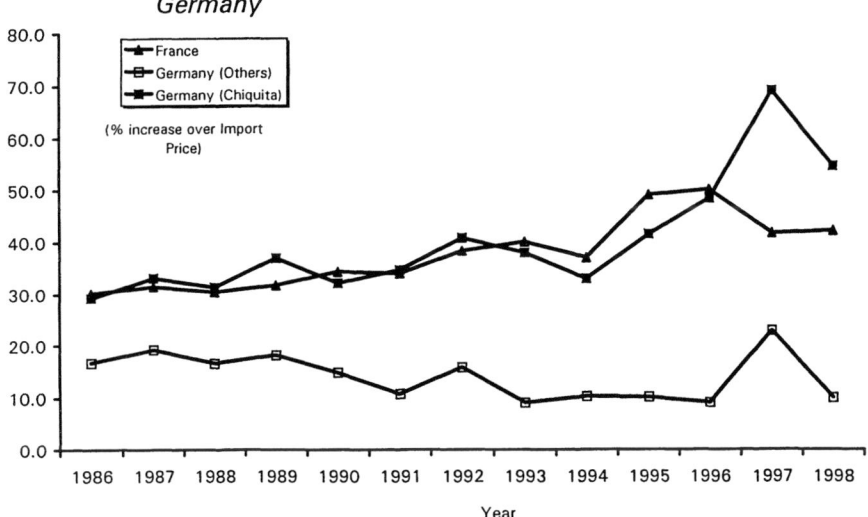

Source: Author's database.

The reader will recall that the underlying assumption in the arguments of earlier mainstream works on the EU banana trade is that, given that the German banana market was considered perfectly competitive and/or contestable, liberalization is likely to increase consumer welfare (Chapter

2). However, the empirical evidence discussed so far does not support such a hypothesis. Quite to the contrary, our finding so far presents two implications. First, the neo-classical hypothesis that consumer welfare is always maximized in a free market does not apply where firms enjoy some degree of market power derived from product differentiation. Second, relatively low import prices, which suggest low production costs, might reflect higher levels of efficiency in exploitation of sources of supply, so that firms appear to behave more competitively than they really are. In other words, the benefits of efficient exploitation of sources of supply are appropriated by firms as profits and not passed on to consumers as surplus.[57]

The latter implication of our finding is especially relevant in an environment of international production, where all stages of the banana commodity chain are under the control of a single TNC. Therefore, we shall return to it in Chapter 4 where we develop a theoretical framework which is used for the empirical analysis in the subsequent chapters of the thesis. Let us now examine banana retail-wholesale margins in order to determine whether retailers are engaged in conduct similar to that of wholesalers and how such conduct varies across the different commodity chains.

3.6.2   Retail-wholesale price margins along EU banana commodity chains

Trends in absolute margins of banana retail prices over wholesale prices (retail-wholesale margins) are rather similar to those observed at the wholesale-import stage of the commodity chain (Figure 3.17). Retail price data are not available for "Chiquita" bananas in Germany, but are available for "other" brands sold in Germany, as well as for bananas sold in the UK and France.

Decomposing these trends into the pre- and post-SEM periods results in the following. First, during the 1986-92 period there was little difference in the levels of margins, although those in the UK were slightly higher than elsewhere. Second, during the 1993-98 period margins in Germany rose considerably, while there was a secular decline in margins in the UK, and to a lesser extent in France.

Contrary to the expectations of exponents of the neo-classical approach that retail monopoly power was expected to be considerably higher in France and the UK given their protectionist import policies, we see that German retail margins were of comparable magnitude in the pre-SEM period and that they have increased the most since the SEM came into effect. Moreover, the trends in relative retail-wholesale banana margins are

Fig. 3.17   Absolute banana retail-wholesale margins in Germany, France and the UK (US$ per metric ton)

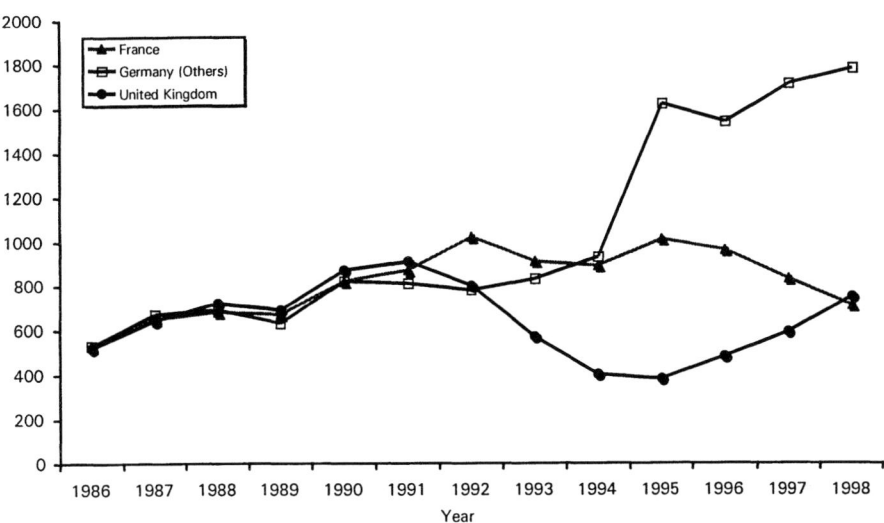

Source: Author's database.

even more revealing. While, in absolute terms, firms operating at the retail stage of the banana commodity chain in Britain enjoyed slightly larger margins than those elsewhere during the pre-SEM period, in relative terms it has been firms in the German market which have enjoyed considerably larger margins in the pre-SEM period, and those margins have increased significantly since the SEM took effect (Figure 3.18).[58]

The preceding analysis of retail-wholesale margins so far leads us to the following initial conclusions. First, whereas firms at the retail stage of the commodity chain in the UK obtained larger absolute margins in the pre-SEM period, in relative terms it was firms in Germany marketing "other" banana brands that were likely to have made the most profit. So although German consumers enjoyed the lowest absolute price for bananas in the pre-SEM period, in reality that price was considerably higher than it would have been if firms in that market had behaved more competitively.

Second, the fact that absolute banana retail prices in France and the UK were generally higher than those in Germany in the pre-SEM period is largely a reflection of higher production costs from their sources of supply, and not super-normal monopoly profits of marketing firms as exponents of the neo-classical approach predict. Thus, firms in the British and French markets are likely to be considerably less profitable than those in Germany. We shall further develop and discuss these arguments in Chapters 6 and 7.

*Fig. 3.18   Relative banana retail-wholesale margins in Germany,
France and the UK*

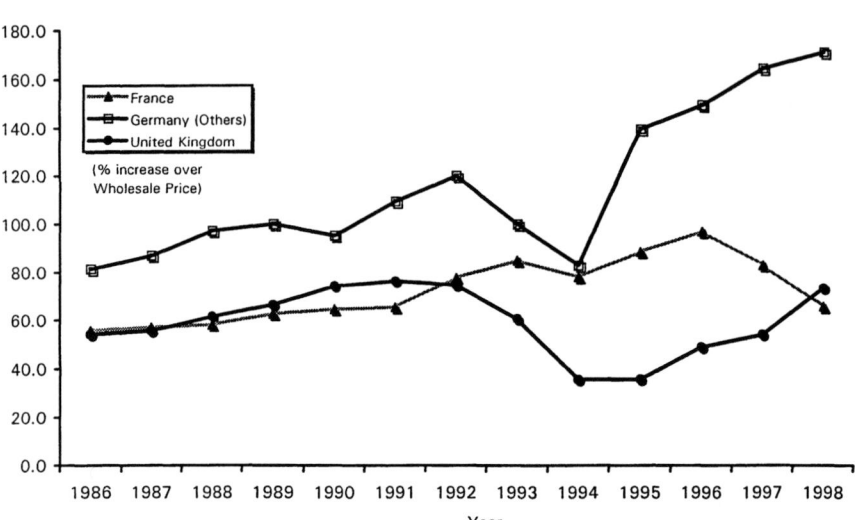

Source: Author's database.

3.6.3   Hypothetical implications of these findings

One hypothetical proposition that emerges from the preceding discussion is
that producers who supply the French and British banana markets are likely
to have received a larger share of revenue and surplus than their rivals who
supply the German market. A corollary to this hypothesis is that firms in the
German banana market appropriated a larger share of the commodity chain
as profits than did those in France and Britain.

   Although the hypothesis that firms in the German market are likely to be
most profitable might be challenged on the grounds that higher margins
might reflect higher costs of distribution of bananas, such a proposition
would seem unlikely. Since Germany accounts for more than one-third of
all EU banana imports, the likelihood that firms in that market enjoy
superior scale economies relative to those elsewhere in the EU is high. We
shall explore the preceding hypothesis in detail in Chapters 6 and 7, where
we shall decompose the banana commodity chains, that lead into those
countries to demonstrate how revenue and surplus are divided and distributed among the various countries.

3.7 EU banana trade policy: pre- and post-SEM

Having discussed the nature and structure of the EU banana trade, the conduct of dominant actors in the world banana industry and the price formation process, let us now shift the focus to EU banana import policy. Specifically, let us discuss the various banana import policies that existed in EU member-states during the pre-SEM period, the NBR which was implemented under the SEM, and briefly suggest why the NBR was challenged and defeated in the GATT and WTO.

3.7.1 Pre-SEM banana import policies in EU member-states

At the signing of the Treaty of Rome in 1957, EU member-states were granted a certain degree of latitude in setting their individual banana import policies under Article 115 of the Treaty, subject to two special conditions. First, bananas imported from overseas territories of EU member-states[59] and ACP countries[60] would be admitted duty free in all EU member-states, while those imported from other sources, primarily dollar-zone countries[61] would be subjected to the Community's common external tariff of 20 per cent (Hallam, 1995:526; Sutton, 1997:10-11). Second, given the size of the German market and the level of its banana consumption at the time, under a special protocol to the Treaty of Rome, Germany was granted the right to import bananas duty free regardless of their countries of origin (Sutton, 1997:10-11).

Consequently, there was considerable variation in banana import policies and patterns of trade across EU member-states, all of which fell within one of the following four categories. First, Germany operated a duty-free banana import market, and in practice more than 99 per cent of its bananas were imported from dollar-zone countries.[62]

Second, France, Spain, Portugal and Greece all imported bananas primarily from their colonies and/or overseas territories, but where demand exceeded supply they imported bananas first from the ACP countries, and if their supplies were exhausted then from dollar-zone countries. In the preceding EU member-states, in addition to tariffs, bananas from dollar-zone countries were subjected to a quota and, in some cases, a licence and a consumption tax.[63] Yet, this system of protection did not prevent bananas from dollar-zone countries from entering the markets, since they were able to command a small but significant presence in the French market prior to 1991[64] to such an extent that a significant part of the increase in demand in France in 1990 was furnished from dollar-zone countries.[65]

Third, the UK and Italy, both of which no longer owned banana-producing colonies, imported bananas primarily from ACP countries where they maintained considerable economic and political interests. UK banana imports were dominated by supplies from the Eastern Caribbean and Jamaica, all of which were admitted duty free, while supplies from the dollar zone were subjected to a licensing system and a quota in addition to the EU's 20 per cent tariff (Sutton, 1997:8).

Yet, dollar-zone supplies were extremely important to the UK market: although there was a slight decrease in imports in 1991 relative to 1990, the share of supplies from the dollar-zone nearly doubled, while imports from ACP countries actually decreased that year. Moreover, the increase in UK imports in 1992 was furnished largely from the dollar-zone, while imports from ACP countries stabilized at their original 1990 levels.[66]

In Italy, bananas imported from EU producer territories and ACP countries were not subjected to tax or quota restrictions from 1974, while those imported from dollar-zone countries were subjected to the EU's common external tariff of 20 per cent, a quota which ranged from 205,000 to 265,000 metric tons in 1974-77, and a consumption tax, which amounted to $270 per metric ton in 1982 (FAO, 1986:47). Italian Settlers in Somalia are known to have invested considerably in Somalia's banana industry since the 1930s, but the bananas produced were hardly competitive on world markets. The expansion of Somalia's banana industry since the 1930s is attributed to protection from Italy, which included the establishment of an Italian State monopoly, in 1935 (Houtkamp, 1996:96).

Finally, in The Netherlands, Belgium, Luxembourg, Ireland, Denmark, and Sweden, the EU's common external tariff was applied to all banana imports except those from EU territories or ACP countries. Yet, most of the bananas imported into these countries originated from the dollar zone; in The Netherlands for instance, dollar-zone bananas have dominated the market, consistently accounting for more than 95 per cent of imports, although imports from ACP countries have increased significantly since 1990.[67]

So, to summarize, the pattern of trade in the pre-SEM system was shaped largely by the import policies of EU member-states. Those that favoured *laissez-faire* trade policies had few political interests in the supplying countries, and consequently they imported bananas primarily from the relatively cheap dollar zone. Conversely, EU member-states that adopted relatively protectionist trade policies had considerably more strategic political interests in the supplying countries, and so they imported bananas primarily from their DOMs and the ACP countries even though they were relatively more expensive. We shall further develop this discussion in

Chapter 5, where we analyse the different interests in the EU banana trade in greater detail.

3.7.2   Common organization of the EU banana market – EEC Regulation 404/93

Although the SEM was intended to bring about the implementation of common trade policies in all commodities throughout the EU, in the case of bananas it was only implemented in July 1993; six months after its implementation for all other commodities. In its original form, the NBR implemented on 1 July 1993 comprised the following elements: (i) a general quota of duty-free entry for 854,000 metric tons of bananas from the EU's DOMs; (ii) another general quota of duty-free entry for 857,700 metric tons of bananas produced by ACP countries that were traditional[68] suppliers to the EU market; and (iii) a general tariff quota of 2 million metric tons for bananas produced in third countries (primarily dollar-zone) and/or non-traditional[69] quantities of ACP and EU bananas. In the latter case, bananas originating from an ACP country or EU territory could be admitted free of duty, provided that the quantity fell within that quota; otherwise they would be subjected to a tariff of ECU 750 per metric ton. Bananas originating from a third country were admitted at a duty rate of ECU 100 per metric ton, provided that the quantities fell within the established general quota of 2 million metric tons. Additionally, a much higher tariff of ECU 850 per metric ton applied in respect of any bananas in excess of the established general quota of 2 million metric tons originating from a third country (European Council, 1993).[70]

Even more complex was the operation of the tariff quota, since its implementation was subject to a licencing system, which in turn was based on a system of classification of operators according to three activity functions: purchase and transport, customs clearance, and ripening and selling to wholesale. Specifically, of the licences available, 66.5 per cent were for operators that marketed bananas originating in third-countries and/or non-traditional ACP bananas; 30 per cent were reserved for operators that marketed traditional ACP or EU bananas; and the remainder was for new operators (European Council, 1993:Article 19).[71]

Additionally, with reference to the activity functions,[72] 57 per cent of licences were issued to operators that were involved in primary import, 15 per cent were issued to operators that performed secondary import and 28 per cent to operators involved in the activities of ripening and selling wholesale to retailers. This system of licence allocation was used in order to ensure that large TNCs did not dominate the trade at the expense of other firms (European Commission, 1994:3-4).[73]

3.7.3   Why the NBR was challenged in the GATT and WTO

By now it should be evident that the EU's NBR, introduced under regulation 404/93, was naturally unstable and therefore vulnerable to attacks from several directions. In Chapter 5 we shall analyse and discuss in greater detail the various reasons why the EU's NBR was challenged first from within, by some of its member-states, then from outside in the GATT and WTO. Suffice it to say for now that the EU's NBR was challenged because of various conflicting interests of actors involved in the trade of the commodity and the difficulty of satisfying all these divergent interests simultaneously.

3.8   Conclusions

The objectives of this chapter have been threefold. First, to analyse and discuss the empirical evidence on market structure and firm conduct in the global and EU banana business. Second, to examine the various banana import policies that have existed in EU member-states and explain why a new policy was introduced under the SEM. Third, to prepare the reader with background detail orientation for the empirical work which will be done in the remainder of the thesis.

The chapter has demonstrated that world banana trade is characterized by very high concentration in both export supply, which is explained largely by the supply of a few countries in Latin America, and import demand which is explained largely by the demand for bananas in a few developed regions of the world, that is, the EU, North America, and Japan. These trends are largely maintained in the EU banana market, although, due to the EU's interventionist policy, a small fringe of suppliers – its own DOMs and the ACP countries – command significant market shares in France, Spain and the UK. But perhaps the most important argument developed in this chapter is the dominance and/or control of both world and EU banana trade by a few TNCs, accounting for nearly 70 per cent of the market in both cases. We also saw that, based on the financial condition and operations of these TNCs, the banana market cannot be considered to be perfectly competitive or contestable, neither at the world nor EU levels. Moreover, the conduct of firms in the banana business clearly demonstrates their willingness and ability to charge monopoly prices, with "Chiquita" branded bananas commanding the highest degree of monopoly power in the EU, and unbranded bananas the least. Essentially, we have attempted to quantify monopoly power in the world and EU banana trade in a useful manner by isolating the underlying factors that lead to natural monopoly in the first place – scale economies, innovation in product and process and barriers to entry.

Finally, we have seen that the considerable variation in banana import policies in EU member-states in the pre-SEM period, which largely reflected both the past and present economic interests of the EU member-states in the exporting countries, resulted in an NBR which sparked much discontent among actors, and was therefore challenged and defeated in the GATT and WTO. In Chapter 5 we shall return to the NBR, analysing and discussing the events that led to a WTO ruling against it, particularly from the perspective of the bargaining power of the Chiquita TNC, and the implications of the WTO ruling for future dispute settlement and the theory of international trade. However, in Chapter 4 let us first construct the theoretical framework that will be applied for analysis and discussion in the remainder of this work.

Notes

[1] Moreover, the minimum 15 per cent reduction of import price is on the assumption that price reductions at import are transmitted to retail – in practice, only a small percentage of import price reductions are transmitted to the final consumer.

[2] These countries are Belize, Brazil, Colombia, Costa Rica, Dominican Republic, Ecuador, Guatemala, Honduras, Mexico, Nicaragua, Panama, Suriname, and Venezuela.

[3] Ecuador's role of dominant actor is presently a subject of great controversy among the banana-exporting countries and the major banana TNCs, and it has drawn attention from both the press and social movements. Ecuador is known for paying the lowest wage on the planet to banana workers, with a large number of them earning the equivalent of $2 per day, while within the rest of Latin America wages of up to $10 per day are common (see US/LEAP, 1999; Frank, 2002). The perceived problem with Ecuador by its neighbours and the US TNCs is that of social dumping, in its bid for a race to the bottom (US/LEAP, 1999).

[4] Based on data compiled from several FAO sources.

[5] Growth of import demand for bananas among the developing countries has increased considerably since 1990. Whereas banana import demand grew at an

average of 6.5 per cent per annum during the 1986-90 period, the corresponding figure was 24.8 per cent during the 1990-95 period. This increase in the growth rate of import demand is explained largely by the increase in demand in Eastern Europe and the former Soviet Union following the end of the Cold War.

[6] Based on data from author's database, file: *World Banana Imports*.

[7] For a discussion of the importance of bananas in diets, see European Commission (1976) "Proceeding Under Article 86 of the EEC Treaty (IV/26999–Chiquita)", *Official Journal of the European Communities*, pp. 238-57. See also Section 3.5.

[8] The pattern of Japan's demand for bananas requires separate research. Whereas there exist at least *weak* causal links between growth in income and banana consumption in the developed countries in general, Japan is an exception.

[9] Among these "other" countries that recently exported bananas to the EU are Brazil, Argentina, Israel, Thailand and Taiwan (Author's database: Imports of EU12-15 1988+).

[10] Demand for bananas appears to be affected by both economic and non-economic factors. Among the economic factors, price and income (or per capita income) are expected to have some impact. We examine these in Chapter 8. Non-economic factors include quality, consumer preference and consumer lifestyles. These are discussed in more detail below.

[11] A recent study undertaken by the International Banana Association reports that EU banana per capita consumption remains at approximately 11Kg, while that of the US is approximately 14 Kg. The study also found that banana consumption is higher among senior citizens than young singles and couples with no children (*Banacol.com*, 2002).

[12] Damage by hurricanes and floods is a recurrent problem in the banana business. In November 2001 Honduras suffered rainfall and flooding on a scale unprecedented since that caused by Hurricane Mitch three years earlier.

[13] Chiquita Brands International, Inc. (2000) *1999 Annual Report and Form 10-K*, p. 3.

[14] Ibid., p. 4.

[15] To quote the firm, "Dole sources, distributes and markets fresh fruit products, including bananas, pineapples, table grapes, apples, pears, stone fruit, oranges, grapefruit, lemons, mangoes, kiwi, tangelos, melons, cherries, strawberries, raspberries and other tropical, deciduous and citrus fruits." In addition, the firm "grows, harvests, distributes and markets more than 40 kinds of fresh-cut flowers, including roses, spray roses, carnations, miniature carnations, pompons and standard chrysanthemums, among others" (Dole Annual Report, 2000:1-2).

[16] According to Dole, its European division sources bananas from Cameroon, Côte d'Ivoire, the Canary Islands, Martinique, Guadeloupe and Jamaica for the EU market (ibid., p. 4).

[17] An extended significance of Dole's holdings in Saba Trading AB is that the latter firm "has a wholly-owned subsidary in the Netherlands that is one of Europe's largest exotic fruit import and distribution companies" (ibid.).

[18] Ibid., p. 14.

[19] While we refer to Fresh Del Monte Produce as Del Monte in this thesis, the reader is cautioned not to confuse this firm with another fully independent and unrelated firm called Del Monte Foods Company. A major difference between these firms is that Fresh Del Monte Produce deals exclusively with the international production, trade and marketing of fresh produce: bananas, pineapples, deciduous fruit and melons; while Del Monte Foods Company deals primarily in the production and distribution of canned vegetables and canned fruit in the United States. Both firms share the "Del Monte" brand name largely for historical reasons of incorporation and subsequent divestment and acquisition activities, since 1892.

[20] Fresh Del Monte Produce (2000) *Annual Report for Fiscal Year Ended December 31, 1999*, p. 1.

[21] Ibid., p. 2.

[22] Ibid., p. 2.

[23] Del Monte indicates that, in 1999, 31 per cent of its fresh produce was grown on farms that it either owns or leases, directly or indirectly, while the remaining 69 per cent was obtained through supply contracts with independent growers (ibid., p. 2).

[24] Ibid., p. 2.

[25] Ibid., p. 3.

[26] Ibid., p. 3.

[27] Del Monte is presently engaged in several legal actions in both U.S. and international courts in relation to allegations by numerous Latin American and Philippine plaintiffs that they were injured during the 1970s and 1980s by their exposure to a nematocide containing the chemical Dibromochloropropane. Additionally, the United States Environmental Protection Agency is investigating Del Monte's alleged environmental damage in Hawaii, and Del Monte expects, should it lose the case, to be liable to pay compensation ranging from $4.2 to $28.1 million to the United States government (ibid., p. 4).

[28] Del Monte argues that the EU banana regime, implemented in July 1993, has restricted its access to the EU banana market and increased its cost of doing business there (ibid., p. 5).

[29] Appreciation of the U.S. dollar relative to major currencies in the EU adversely affects the financial condition of all banana transnationals. Del Monte's argues that, although approximately 41 per cent of its sales revenues was received in currencies other than the dollar in 1999, most of the its costs were incurred in dollars, and hence its operating income was adversely affected (ibid., p. 5).

[30] As a consequence of a dispute in 1997 between Del Monte and an EU firm with which it has a sales and purchase agreement for bananas, Del Monte informed the firm of its decision not to continue the agreement as of 31 December, 2002. Unless Del Monte is able to secure a new agreement with that firm or another equivalent one, it stands to lose considerable sales volume and revenue, since it needs the licences held by that firm for entry of its bananas into the EU (ibid., p. 6).

[31] Fyffes continues to grow as an important TNC in the banana business. Having changed its financial year to coincide with the calendar year in 2001, the company reported a stronger profit position in 2002 and is reported to have been considering taking over Chiquita in March 2002 (*Irish Sunday Independent*, 3 March, 2002).

[32] In the process of conducting research for this thesis, several of the major banana TNCs were contacted for information on trade in the commodity. Some, unfortunately did not respond at all, while others, at best provided information which should otherwise be available to public shareholders and directors.

[33] As recent as December 2001, the author made contact with an official at Fyffes in Ireland seeking a discussion of the EU's banana policy and how it had affected the company. Despite promises made by that official, no data has been provided to date.

[34] Fyffes has stock in several European banana companies, including: 50 per cent each in Eurobanane Canarias of Spain and Brdr Lembcke of Denmark in 1993; 50 per cent in Velleman and Tas of the Netherlands, 70 per cent in Kahl-Munich of Germany, 33 per cent in Sofiprim SA of France and 50 per cent in Tropic SA of France in 1994; and 50 per cent in Swithenbanks of the UK in 1995. It also totally owned Valley Gold of the UK in 1994 (Roche, 1998:144-5).

[35] In 1989 Fyffes expanded its wholesale activity by six units and secured an agreement with the Dominican Republic for exclusive rights to its bananas, which were grown primarily by independents. This can be viewed in part as the fulfilment of Fyffes' claim of "strengthening the production and commercial efficiency of the local grower in his own country, supporting the grower in achieving a more viable business and improving production and quality" (Roche, 1998:143).

[36] In fact, the year 2000 was the only one in recent history when the firm recorded after-tax losses. Fyffes' Chairman, Neil McCann, argued that the year 2000 was one of the toughest in the world-wide banana industry and that it adversely affected Fyffes' previous growth trends (Fyffes, 2001).

[37] While this study does not claim to present an exhaustive list of banana brands here, some other brands that are widely found in Europe are: Consul, Onkel Tuca,

Turbana, Five Isles, Corbana, Golden B, Tropical Eden, Goldfinger, Excel, Favorita, Pretty Liza, Pablitos, Ecuadorian Gold, Jamaican, Fruidor, and UTC.

[38] Chiquita Brands International, Inc. (2000) *1999 Annual Report and Form 10-K*, p. K-1.

[39] Fresh Del Monte Produce (2000) *Annual Report for Fiscal Year Ended December 31, 1999*, p. 1.

[40] Dole Food Company (2001) *Annual Report for Fiscal Year Ended December 30, 2000*, p. 1.

[41] Chiquita Brands International, Inc. (2000) "Chiquita launches program to combat fad diets and promote healthy eating", *Chiquita.com* (November 17).

[42] Ibid.

[43] Chiquita's current caption regarding its "Miss Chiquita" reads " Over fifty years and not a wrinkle. Must be the bananas!" See www.chiquita.com for more about "Miss Chiquita" – the "First Lady of Fruit".

[44] Del Monte features a full page on "healthy lifestyles and eating healthy" on its website, portraying a pretty, healthy-looking woman holding an apple, and a short write-up on the relationship between being healthy and what we eat. See www.freshdelmonte.com for more.

[45] From 1899 (its year of incorporation) to 1972, the firm's name was the United Fruit Company.

[46] The firm was named Castle and Cooke up to that time.

[47] Under the consent decree, Chiquita was required to: "...divest itself of any ownership of International Railways of Central America", "...liquidate its subsidiary, Banana Selling Corp., which had been engaged in jobbing operations in Mobile, Alabama" and "submit a plan by 30 June 1966 to turn over to a new company operating independently of any UFC control, land and purchasing arrangements, and integrated facilities for shipping to and distribution in the United States of nine million stems (16 million boxes) of bananas annually" (Litvak and Maule, 1977:539).

[48] In that regard, Black Sigatoka is one of the major diseases that has infested the plantations of banana producing countries in recent times. The disease has been recently spotted in Mexico where it has destroyed several thousand hectares of the commercial crop (Orozco-Santos et al., 2001).

[49] See "Del Monte loses bid to prevent Dole Foods marketing sweet pineapple", *Just-Food.com* (2002).

[50] Price discrimination means the practice of a firm charging different customers different prices for similar goods.

[51] Article 86 of the Treaty of Rome has since been renumbered as Article 82 of the Treaty of Amsterdam (Read, 2002).

[52] See *Journal of World Trade Law*, 1977, 11.1, pp. 84-9; and Nurse and Sandiford (1995:87).

[53] See European Commission (1978) "United Brands v Commission", *European Court Reports* 1987, p. 207; and *Journal of World Trade Law*, 1977, pp. 84-9.

[54] Chiquita appears to have also attempted to control Fyffes' sources of supply in Honduras. The Council on Hemispheric Affairs (COHA) has documented the conduct of Chiquita towards Fyffes in some detail, including intimidation of Fyffes' management and damage to or appropriation of millions of dollars' worth of Fyffes fruit, which eventually caused Fyffes to sell its Honduras operations. See Mangold et al. (1996).

[55] We shall return to these stages of the banana commodity chain in greater detail in Chapter 4, where we construct a theoretical framework which will be used in the remaining chapters of the thesis. This framework is based on the commodity chain concept, theories of international trade, production and industrial organization.

[56] Data at the retail stages are generally available for several other EU member-states, but not at the intermediate stages of import and wholesale.

[57] A recent example of exploitation of dollar-zone supply sources was reported by Ecuadorian Ambassador to the United Nations, who claimed that his country faced grim allegations and was being subjected to a smear campaign (*FreshInfo.com*, May 2002). The Campaign for Labor Rights (1998) has argued that Chiquita prefers to keep some of its Ecuadorian operations anonymous in order to facilitate relationships with unions, governments and suppliers. In so doing, it reduces costs, reduces exposure to strikes and increases its bargaining position.

[58] In 1998, relative retail-wholesale margins for "other" German brands stood at 171 per cent compared with 74 per cent and 66 per cent, for bananas sold in the UK and France, respectively.

[59] The overseas territories refer to colonies or departments of EU member-states. These include France's Département d'outré mer (DOMs): Martinique and Guadeloupe; Spain's Canary Islands; Portugal's Madeira and Greece's Crete.

[60] ACP refers to some countries in Africa, the Caribbean and the Pacific that are parties to the various Lomé Conventions, the first of which was created in 1974. The Lomé Conventions are programmes of aid and development co-operation between the EU and ACP countries. The Fourth Lomé Convention came to an end in February 2000, and the joint EU-ACP Council is in the process of renewing that agreement. For a detailed review and discussion of Lomé, particularly from an international legal perspective, see Arts (2000).

[61] The dollar-zone refers to a number of banana-exporting countries in Central and South America. Major suppliers to the EU market are Ecuador, Panama, Colombia,

Honduras and Costa Rica. Other dollar-zone exporters are the Dominican Republic, Nicaragua, Guatemala and Mexico.

[62] Based on data obtained from GATT (1994) "EEC – Import Regime for Bananas: Report of the Panel", DS38/R (18 January).

[63] In France, imports from the dollar-zone were subjected to a licence as well as the tariff, and the licence was only granted when import prices exceeded a certain level. In Spain and Portugal imports were supplied from the Canary Islands and Madeira, respectively, while Greece imposed a ban on all imports (Borrell and Yang, 1990:7-10).

[64] Based on data obtained from GATT (1994) "EEC – Import Regime for Bananas: Report of the Panel", DS38/R (18 January).

[65] Which also suggests that export supply from the DOMs and ACP countries is not very elastic, at least in the short run (1-2 years), and these countries are likely to be operating at output capacity limit. Therefore, the dollar-zone was *the* residual source of supply for any short-term increases in demand.

[66] Based on data obtained from GATT (1994) "EEC – Import Regime for Bananas: Report of the Panel", DS38/R (18 January).

[67] Based on data obtained from GATT (1994) "EEC – Import Regime for Bananas: Report of the Panel", DS38/R (18 January).

[68] Traditional banana imports means specific quantities of bananas, as set out in the Annex to Council Regulation 404/93, exported by each ACP State, that has traditionally exported bananas to the EU (European Council, 1993:Article 15).

[69] Non-traditional banana imports refer to bananas exported from ACP countries in excess of traditional levels, where 'traditional' is as defined in note above.

[70] Specifically, Article 12 declares the size of the production quota and its breakdown among EU territories; Article 15 sets out the size of the quota for imports from traditional ACP countries as well as the amount allocated to each country; and, Article 18 declares the size of the third-country tariff quota and the applicable tariffs with respect to different sources of supply (European Council, 1993).

[71] The new operators category refers to firms that started the banana import business in 1992 or later. In practice, these firms are considerably smaller than existing operators.

[72] These activity function rules were only applicable with respect to the first two categories of licences, in order words, they did not apply with respect to the newcomer category.

[73] In the Commission's wisdom, having experienced numerous trade disputes involving the large banana TNCs' exploitation of monopoly power in the market –

notably Chiquita's – it was felt necessary that some safeguards be put into place in order to pre-empt any such future attempts at market power abuse.

4 Theories of International Trade, Industrial Organization, Transnational Firms, Commodity Chains and the EU Banana Market

The coming age of multinational corporations will create grave social and political problems and will be very uneven in exploiting and distributing the benefits of modern science and technology.

— Hymer (1970:448)

4.1 Introduction

Chapter 2 showed that liberalization of the EU banana trade is likely to result in perverse welfare effects unless the assumptions of competition and contestability are reasonably satisfied. Chapter 3 argued further that firms repeatedly exercise such imperfectly competitive behaviour primarily through branding of bananas, the persistence of transnational oligopolistic interdependence, and the promotion of the health and nutritional value of the commodity. Moreover, we have seen that the behaviour of banana TNC oligopolists in the EU is precisely what it had been in the United States market prior to the implementation of the Consent Decree in 1958 (Chapter 3). Therefore, effectively the EU banana market is best conceptualized as an oligopoly in which dominant firms do exercise market power, and there is every indication that this will continue to be the case unless some intervention is undertaken along the lines of the Consent Decree.

Yet, reinforced by the waves of economic liberalism of the 1990s, WTO rules remain rooted within the view that liberalization of trade automatically increases economic efficiency and welfare.[1] In fact, as suggested in Chapter 2, most of the earlier studies conducted on the EU banana trade and/or import policy have largely sought to vindicate neo-liberal economic doctrine,[2] arguing that any losers created as a result of trade liberalization can be adequately compensated by the gainers.[3]

The fact that the EU banana market is neither competitive nor contestable, and TNC oligopolists do exercise some degree of market power, is likely to have significant implications for both efficiency and economic welfare under trade liberalization. Therefore, three questions arise. First, is there likely to be an overall increase (or decrease) in economic welfare and efficiency after trade is liberalized? Second, what are the magnitudes and directions of the welfare effects of trade liberalization under imperfect competition and how do they compare with those under workable competition? Third, how is revenue and surplus divided and distributed among the banana-exporting countries, the EU member-states and the TNCs involved in the various banana commodity chains?

In this chapter we shall create the theoretical framework that will be applied to address the preceding questions in the rest of the thesis. We shall begin with the theories of international trade (Section 4.2) and discuss the extent to which they are relevant for explaining the EU banana trade. The oligopolistic structure of the market and the nature of behaviour of banana TNCs necessitate theories of industrial organization, and the transnational firm (international production) as a special case of those theories, for analysing the EU banana trade. These are discussed in Sections 4.3 and 4.4, respectively. Finally, the concept of a commodity chain, which is discussed in Section 4.5, will be used to decompose the banana commodity chain and demonstrate how revenue and surplus are divided and distributed along it. We shall conclude the chapter by indicating how and where those theories will be applied in the rest of this study.

4.2   Theories of international trade and the EU's banana business

During its evolution, international trade theory has shifted from the classical doctrines of absolute advantage (Smith, 1776) and comparative advantage (Ricardo, 1817), to the neo-classical doctrine of factor endowments (Heckscher, 1919; Ohlin, 1933) and its extension to factor-price equalization (Samuelson, 1948). Subsequently, the need for explaining why differences in technology could serve as a basis for trade, as well as why new products entering into international trade went through various phases, led to the technology gap (Posner, 1961; Linder, 1961) and product cycle (Vernon, 1966) theories. All the preceding theories of international trade maintained common features; namely, they do not allow for imperfectly competitive markets, and for individual firms to enjoy scale economies. The New Trade Theories (NTTs) address these limitations by postulating that international trade could be caused by the existence of scale economies *within* firms, as opposed to the external economies that firms enjoy as a group within an industry (Krugman, 1994; Helpman and Krugman, 1985;

Helpman, 1981). Such scale economies arise due to the reduction in marginal and average costs of the firm's production. Additionally, in oligopolistic markets product differentiation gives rise to imperfect competition (Helpman, 1984,1981; Grubel and Lloyd, 1975), which then becomes another cause of international trade. Therefore, the NTTs allow for the possibility that under free trade different forms of market structure could result in different welfare effects (Helpman and Krugman, 1989; Dixit and Norman, 1980);[4] a hypothesis which was simply inconceivable in the traditions of both classical and neo-classical theories of international trade. We shall now briefly discuss the relevance of these theories of international trade for explaining the EU's banana trade.

4.2.1   Classical theory of international trade

Adam Smith (1776:401-3) advanced the theory that it was more advantageous for every nation to engage in the production and trade of the good in which it had an absolute advantage,[5] than to encourage exports while restricting imports, in the hope of generating a net inflow of gold, silver or bullion into the exporting country.[6] In so doing, he successfully challenged the dominant views of the Mercantilists, who at the time contended that to become rich and powerful a country should maintain a surplus in its trade balance. In the case of the banana-producing countries, their absolute advantage arises from their geographic locations, since bananas can be easily and cheaply cultivated only in some regions of the world, notably the tropics, and not in others.[7] Yet, Smith's theory of international trade cannot explain why considerable variability exists in both productivity and cost of production among the banana-producing countries, even where climatic conditions are generally similar.[8] Additionally, it cannot explain why, although only a few nations possess absolute advantages in producing all commodities, countries continue producing goods in which they do not necessarily have an absolute advantage. In fact, full specialization does not apply to banana-producing countries, which happen to also produce a range of other commodities including manufactures and services, the contribution of the latter to GDP being often larger than that of bananas.

The comparative advantage theory of David Ricardo (1817), which states that each country could mutually benefit from trade by specializing in the production and export of the good in which its absolute disadvantage is smaller, provides greater explanation of the EU's banana import business, because it allows for differences in both the productivity and cost of production in the producing countries, although it cannot explain why such differences exist. The relevance of the Ricardian theory of trade to the EU's banana import business becomes more evident when Ricardo's original labour theory of value is replaced by the opportunity cost theory of value put forward by Haberler (1936).[9] As we have seen earlier, although the production of bananas does require labour, capital and technology do play important, and in most cases, dominant roles as well (Chapter 3). Since the Ricardian theory of international trade does not explain what causes comparative advantage, the reasons for both the differences in labour productivity across nations as well as the impact of international trade on the earnings of the factors of production remain uncertain. Therefore, applied to the EU's banana import business, the Ricardian theory of international trade cannot explain why bananas are produced most efficiently in Latin America and least efficiently in the French DOMs in the Caribbean. More importantly, it cannot explain why, despite these differences in productivity, wages are lowest in the former and highest in the latter.

4.2.2   Heckscher-Ohlin (H-O) and Heckscher-Ohlin Samuelson (H-O-S) theory

The first explanation of the causes of comparative advantage is found in the works of Heckscher (1919) and Ohlin (1933), subsequently integrated by Samuelson (1948). The H-O theory comprises two distinct theorems: the theorem that explains and predicts the pattern of trade; and the factor-price equalization theorem, which explains the effect of international trade on factor prices, which now includes not only labour but also capital and technology. The first theorem isolates relative factor abundance among nations as the basic determinant of comparative advantage and international trade. Applying it to the EU's banana business could produce mixed results, depending on the assumptions that are made about factor proportions in banana production.[10] If it is the case that banana production is labour-intensive, then H-O theory correctly predicts the causes of differences in productivity between Latin America and the Caribbean. However, as we have seen in Chapter 3, banana production is also capital- and technology-intensive and so such a proposition would need further investigation. This is particularly so when one considers the predictions of H-O-S theory, which is the second theorem: when each nation partially specializes in producing the commodity in which it has a comparative advantage, international trade tends to bring about equalization in the relative and absolute returns to homogeneous factors across nations, since in the labour-abundant nation the wage rate rises while the return to capital falls and in the capital-abundant nation the wage rate falls while the return to capital rises (Samuelson, 1948:169-70). In the case of the EU's banana trade, however, the latter theorem contradicts the former. If it is the case that labour is abundant in Latin America relative to other producing countries, then the wage rate should have increased considerably over time relative to the labour-scarce producing countries. However, wages in Latin American banana-producing countries have remained substantially lower than in other banana-producing countries, particularly those in the Caribbean (see Chapter 3).

Therefore, to summarize, the classical and neo-classical theories of international trade provide only a partial explanation of the working of the EU's banana business. They do explain essentially why bananas are produced in some regions of the world and not others, and, to some extent, why differences in productivity exist across regions. However, they cannot explain the existence of persistently low wages in labour-abundant countries and considerably higher wages among the labour-scarce countries. Additionally, since they assume a technology of constant returns, they do not allow for the possibility that increases in productivity might arise from increases in efficiency due to economies of scale. But, given the importance of technology in banana production and marketing (Chapter 3), further explanations are needed, which necessitate going beyond the H-O theory.

4.2.3   New trade theories (NTTs)

NTTs explain why imperfect competition arising from economies of scale is a cause of comparative advantage, and thus of trade.[11] They predict that in the presence of increasing returns (scale economies), mutually beneficial trade is possible even when two nations are identical in every respect (Krugman, 1994:18-21).[12] Additionally, they predict that where scale economies persist over a sufficiently long range of outputs, imperfect competition results and the entire market for a commodity becomes a monopoly or an oligopoly. Here, the argument is that since trade is caused by increasing returns in individual differentiated products, then each is produced in only one country "for the same reasons that each good is produced by only one firm" (Krugman, 1994:25-6).[13] Applying the NTTs to the EU's banana business provides a deeper understanding of how it works. We have seen that one distinct feature of the EU's banana business is its highly concentrated oligopolistic market structure, in which more than 60 per cent of all banana trade takes place under the direct control of three TNCs (Chapter 3).[14] Additionally, these TNCs own plantations for banana export production in Latin America, on which they enjoy economies of scale.[15] Therefore, the oligopolistic market structure for banana imports in the EU is likely to have arisen, at least in part, from the scale economies enjoyed by these firms in production and their differentiated products (see Chapter 3).[16] Krugman (1994)'s notion could then apply if, instead of differentiated products being associated with individual countries, they are associated with individual TNCs.

Notwithstanding the strengths of the NTTs in providing a deeper and more general explanation of the causes of international trade, their explanation of the EU's banana business presents limitations. First, the NTTs do not address the question that capital employed on plantations in producing countries might be of foreign ownership; in that case, the returns to capital (profits) might be of greater concern to investors than returns to labour (wages). Second, and more importantly, the NTTs do not address the question that banana retail prices in destination markets are likely to be a function of not only production costs but also ocean transportation (shipping), ripening, and redistribution to retail. Nested within each of these intermediate stages in the banana commodity chain are important scale economies, which confer considerable monopolistic advantages to beneficiary firms. As such, banana retail prices, P_{eu}^r, are likely to be determined by a function of the following form:

$$P_{eu}^r = P\left(C_a^p, C_a^s, C_a^r, C_a^d, Z\right) \tag{4.1}$$

which, in reduced form might be expressed as:

$$P_{eu}^r = \alpha_0 + \alpha_1 C_a^p + \alpha_2 C_a^s + \alpha_3 C_a^r + \alpha_4 C_a^d + \alpha_5 Z + \varepsilon \tag{4.2}$$

where α_0 is a constant reflecting fixed minimum margins for firms to engage in the banana business; C_a^i is the cost of operation at stage i in the commodity chain for bananas from a producing country a (so that, C_a^p, C_a^s, C_a^r and C_a^d represent production, shipping, ripening and distribution costs, respectively); α_j $\left(j \neq 0\right)$ represents the level of significance of the cost factor at successive stages; Z is a vector of exogenous factors that also affect retail price; and ε is a random error term, such that $\varepsilon \sim N\left(\mu, \sigma^2\right)$.

The importance of scale economies at *all* stages of the commodity chain implies that market structure is likely to have a significant influence on price. And since the entire commodity chain is not nationally but transnationally controlled, then determining the nature and distribution of gains from trade is complex. Hence we need to introduce theories of industrial organization and international production.

4.3   Industrial organization and the EU's banana business

Industrial organization or industrial economics is the broad field within microeconomics that focuses on business behaviour and its implications both for market structures and processes, and for public policies towards them (Schmalensee and Willig, 1989). Theories of industrial organization are concerned with how markets are structured, how firms behave in markets and what the implications such behaviour might have for both producers and consumers of goods in markets. While much of textbook economics tends to view markets as being perfectly competitive (in which case production decisions of firms and consumption decisions of buyers have no impact on market price) industrial organization theory allows for other possibilities. Industrial organization theory begins with the premise that markets are imperfectly competitive and, therefore, the concern is to develop models of imperfect markets. In such models the typically recurrent themes include the measurement of structural variables; measurement of performance variables; assessment of various forms of market conduct; and attempting to establish relationships between them. Such measurements are typically carried out in the form of inter-industry studies, or as the study of a single industry.

In order to explore the relevant themes of industrial organization the remainder of this section begins with an overview of the various forms of market structure. This is followed by the structure, conduct, performance (SCP) approach to industrial organization analysis, and the section concludes with an overview of the new empirical industrial organization (NEIO) methods.

4.3.1   Market structure defined

Market structure refers to the organizational characteristics of a market. It includes buyer-buyer relations; seller-seller relations; seller-buyer relations and seller-new entrant relations. Generally, markets tend to fall within one of four extremes: perfectly competitive, in which many buyers and sellers exist; monopoly, in which a single seller and many buyers exist; oligopoly, in which a few sellers and a number of buyers exist; and oligopsony, in which many sellers and only a few buyers exist. Since both the cases of monopoly and perfect competition are rare, and neither features significantly in the EU's banana business, this section will focus on oligopoly.[17] At least four distinct theories of oligopoly can be identified: static oligopoly theory, repeated oligopoly games, two-stage competition, and dynamic rivalry.[18] Rather than attempting to examine any of these in detail, attention will be given to the Cournot and Bertrand models of oligopoly, since they constitute the basis of the most advanced developments in the field (Shapiro, 1989:330). Nevertheless, for completeness let us begin with a review of the SCP approach to industrial economics.

4.3.1.1 *Structure, conduct, performance (SCP)*

The SCP approach, originally introduced by Bain (1968), assumes that the overall performance of an industry is a function of market structure and the conduct of firms within markets. Additionally, it argues that firm conduct within an industry could result in changes in market structure over time, which, in turn, affects industrial performance. The SCP approach has its basis in several case-studies of US enterprises in the period from the Civil War up to 1963, and its major findings relate to the relationship between the size of an enterprise and the degree of concentration within an industry; the reasons for some industries being highly concentrated and others not; the various forms of barriers to entry into an industry; and the conduct and performance of firms within industries.[19]

It appears that highly concentrated markets and industries arise as a consequence of several firm-specific considerations, namely the firm's pursuit of technical efficiency, its profit maximizing objectives, and the determination of dominant firms to keep out potential entrants (Bain, 1968:255). Where a firm pursues higher levels of technical efficiency, it might consider establishing a plant of minimum scale that minimizes its average costs. However, in doing so, the firm might seek to supply a minimum quantity of industry output and create a barrier to entry for potential entrants.[20] Where a firm's objective is to maximize profits, it might differentiate its product significantly through branding or design, such that it is perceived to be noticeably different from that of rivals.[21]

The SCP approach has been used extensively for industry analysis since its introduction. Prior to Bain's work, many economists used concentration and firm size as the primary description of industry structure;[22] however, the literature during and since the 1970s has sought alternative analytical tools. Some authors have openly criticized earlier methods in support of Bain's approach (Boyle and Sorensen, 1970), while others have gone further to argue that the choice of concentration index that is used does matter (Kwoka, 1981). Subsequently, it has been argued that profits-concentration correlations "cannot be given a causal interpretation of the conventional kind running from structure to performance" (Geroski, 1982), a direct challenge to Bain. Yet, the SCP approach has withstood criticism and has been used very recently for empirical work in the European food sector (Viaene and Gellynck, 1995). The authors relate differences between EU member-states to the structure of the FDT industry and compare perform-ance criteria of individual countries with the regional EU industry as a whole.[23] Despite the usefulness of the various SCP methods for industry analysis, the major weakness is that these methods are not tractable.[24] Hence, while we make use of it in this study we shall also apply the conjectural variations approach along with some basic concepts from game theory for empirical analysis.

4.3.1.2 New empirical industrial organization (NEIO)

Having been formulated in the late 1980s, the NEIO is essentially a relatively new structural approach for conducting empirical analysis in industrial economics. As already noted, earlier empirical methods relied on the SCP approach, and were characterized by cross-section regression analysis of industries, in which it was assumed that market power existed. These constituted the inter-industry studies of industrial organization (Bresnahan and Schmalensee, 1987:372-3).[25] However, the NEIO is characterized by empirical investigation for the presence of market power within an industry and relies on the use of structural econometric methods for such analysis (Bresnahan and Schmalensee, 1987:373-4).[26] Underlying these methods are the concepts of various Nash equilibria, from Cournot to Bertrand, and their applicability.[27] These are dealt with below in some detail.[28] As hinted earlier on, their relevance for our analysis will be in the construction of a structural econometric model for measuring market power and making predictions about firm conduct and economic welfare (Chapters 8 and 9).

Cournot model

Consider two firms competing to supply a homogeneous good, and the demand for the good is given by $p(X)$, where p is the price, and $X = x_1 + x_2$, is the total output of the industry.[29] Firm 1 produces according to the cost function $C_1(x_1)$ and firm 2 produces according to the cost function $C_2(x_2)$. The marginal costs of production for the firms are $C_1'(x_1)$ and $C_2'(x_2)$ respectively.[30] The profit for each firm is given by:

$$\pi_1 = p(X)x_1 - C_1(x_1), \text{ and } \pi_2 = p(X)x_2 - C_2(x_2), \text{ respectively.}$$

In the Cournot model, each firm makes a single decision on output that captures how vigorously it attempts to sell, and both firms make their decisions simultaneously, resulting in Nash equilibrium in quantities. With a given set of outputs $\{x_1, x_2\}$, price adjusts to clear the market, so that $p = p(X)$. The Cournot equilibrium output vector, $\{x_1, x_2\}$, is determined by the two equations, $\dfrac{\partial \pi_1}{\partial x_1} = 0$ and $\dfrac{\partial \pi_2}{\partial x_2} = 0$, which are the reaction curves[31] of firm 1 and firm 2 respectively. The profit-maximizing condition for each firm is derived from its reaction curve as follows:

$$\frac{\partial \pi_1}{\partial x_1} = p(X) + x_1 p'(X) - C_1'(x_1) = 0, \text{ from which}$$

$$p(X) - C_1'(x_1) = -x_1 p'(X),$$

and

$$\frac{\partial \pi_2}{\partial x_2} = p(X) + x_2 p'(X) - C_2'(x_2) = 0, \text{ from which}$$

$$p(X) - C_2'(x_2) = -x_2 p'(X).$$

Dividing both sides of these equations by $p(X)$ gives the Cournot oligopoly pricing formula:

$$\frac{[p(X) - C_1'(x_1)]}{p(X)} = \frac{-x_1 p'(X)}{p(X)} = \frac{s_1}{\varepsilon} \text{ with respect to firm 1, and}$$

$$\frac{[p(X) - C_2'(x_2)]}{p(X)} = \frac{-x_2 p'(X)}{p(X)} = \frac{s_2}{\varepsilon} \text{ with respect to firm 2,}$$

where $s_1 = \dfrac{x_1}{X}$ and $s_2 = \dfrac{x_2}{X}$ are the market shares of firms 1 and 2 respectively; and $\varepsilon = \dfrac{-p(X)}{Xp'(X)}$ is the market elasticity of demand at output X, with $\varepsilon > 0$. Where more than two firms are involved in the oligopoly to produce total output X, the Cournot equilibrium output vector, $\{x_1, x_2, ..., x_n\}$, is determined by the sum of the reaction curves for n firms, $\dfrac{\partial \pi_1}{\partial x_1} = 0$, $\dfrac{\partial \pi_2}{\partial x_2} = 0, ...,$ $\dfrac{\partial \pi_n}{\partial x_n} = 0$. Following from the above, when n firms compete to produce output in a Cournot equilibrium, the oligopoly solution formula generalizes to:

$$\frac{[p(X) - C_n'(x_n)]}{p(X)} = \frac{-x_n p'(X)}{p(X)} = \frac{s_n}{\varepsilon} \text{ for the } n^{th} \text{ firm.}$$

The Cournot oligopoly solution formula captures several features of the behaviour of oligopolists. Suppose that all firms are symmetric, so that they have identical cost functions, the formula reduces to $\dfrac{[p - c]}{p} = \dfrac{1}{n\varepsilon}$. It tells us that: each firm knows that it possesses market power; the Cournot equilibrium lies between the competitive and the monopoly solutions; if market elasticity of demand is high, firm mark-ups are small; firm mark-ups are proportional to their market shares;[32] firm market shares are related to their efficiencies, but less-efficient firms are able to survive with smaller market shares.

Yet, there are two limitations to the basic Cournot model. First, since it is a static model, it imposes the need for firms to make their output decisions simultaneously, only once, with no provision for dynamic adjustment. In practice, firms may adjust their initial supplies subject to market conditions. Secondly, in many industries price is the strategic variable through which firms compete as opposed to quantities of output.

One model that attempts to capture the reaction decision of a firm in response to the output decision of a rival firm is the Stackelberg model. This model is essentially the Cournot model adjusted by the assumption that a particular firm decides upon the quantity to supply and supplies the market first, then the other firm makes its output decision. It predicts that the firm that starts supplying the market has a first mover advantage, since it chooses an output such that its marginal revenue equals marginal cost, taking into account the knowledge of its rival's reaction curve. On the other hand, the reacting firm treats the output of the first mover as fixed then decides upon the amount for it to supply. In such a situation although the first mover firm makes significantly more profit than the reacting firm, the reacting firm is likely to accept such an outcome, since, if it were to produce a large output both firms would simply lose money. Hence the reacting firm prefers to earn some profit, rather than have both firms losing money through lower prices.

Bertrand model

In this model, the strategic variable that firms manipulate in order to compete is price. In the case of symmetric firms, if the goods are perfectly homogeneous, then consumers will only purchase the lower-priced good. Hence the Bertrand model predicts that, for perfectly homogeneous goods, the firm that sets the lower price captures the entire market, and, the resulting Nash equilibrium will equal the competitive equilibrium, since firms will set price to equal marginal cost and earn zero profits.[33]

This model of oligopoly has been criticized on several fronts with respect to perfectly homogeneous goods. Generally, when goods are perfectly homogeneous firms tend to compete by setting quantities as opposed to prices. Moreover, even if firms were to compete through prices and each firm were to set a price to equal marginal cost, the model cannot predict how the sales will be divided among the firms. Additionally, the Bertrand model implies that individual firms are likely to possess unlimited capacity; a suggestion which does not conform with general observation. Finally, it is quite normal for firms in an oligopoly to earn positive economic profit; hence, the proposition that firms would undercut each others' prices until price equals marginal cost does not hold well with observed empirical evidence.[34] Therefore, the Bertrand model is inappropriate for perfectly homogeneous goods, but it is useful for heterogeneous or differentiated goods.

Consider two firms competing to supply two differentiated goods x_1 and x_2, at price p_1 and p_2 respectively. The demand system for these goods is given as follows:

$x_1 = D_1(p_1, p_2)$ and $x_2 = D_2(p_1, p_2)$, respectively.

Let $p = (p_1, p_2)$, be the Bertrand equilibrium price.
Profits for firm 1 and firm 2 are given by:

$$\pi_1 = p_1 D_1(p) - C_1(D_1(p)), \text{ and } \pi_2 = p_2 D_2(p) - C_2(D_2(p)),$$

respectively.

The reaction functions for the Bertrand equilibrium for firms 1 and 2 are the first-order profit-maximizing conditions $\dfrac{\partial \pi_1}{\partial p_1} = 0$ and $\dfrac{\partial \pi_2}{\partial p_2} = 0$, respectively.

So, for firm 1:

$$\frac{\partial \pi_1}{\partial p_1} = D_1(p) + p_1 \frac{\partial[D_1(p)]}{\partial p_1} - C_1 \frac{\partial[D_1(p)]}{\partial p_1} = 0$$

$$\Rightarrow \frac{\partial \pi_1}{\partial p_1} = D_1(p) + (p_1 - c_1) \frac{\partial D_1}{\partial p_1} = 0, \text{ where } c_1 = \frac{\partial[D_1(p)]}{\partial p_1}$$

$$\therefore \ p_1 = \frac{D_1(p)}{[\partial D_1 / \partial p_1]} - c_1$$

And, for firm 2:

$$\frac{\partial \pi_2}{\partial p_2} = D_2(p) + p_2 \frac{\partial[D_2(p)]}{\partial p_2} - C_2 \frac{\partial[D_2(p)]}{\partial p_2} = 0$$

$$\Rightarrow \frac{\partial \pi_2}{\partial p_2} = D_2(p) + (p_2 - c_2) \frac{\partial D_2}{\partial p_2} = 0, \text{ where } c_2 = \frac{\partial[D_2(p)]}{\partial p_2}$$

$$\therefore \ p_2 = \frac{D_2(p)}{[\partial D_2 / \partial p_2]} - c_2$$

These results imply that the optimal price for the goods of each firm is an increasing function of its rival's price, that is, the firm is able to sell more as its rival increases price.

4.3.2   Empirical studies in industrial organization

The Cournot and Bertrand models of oligopoly serve as the foundation for recent empirical work in the area of measuring market power. Some of this work is reviewed in this section, with particular attention being paid to their applications in the food and agriculture sectors. Lopez (1984) uses a linear specification of a structural econometric model[35] to test for competitive behaviour and measure the degree of market power in the Canadian food processing industry. He rejects the hypothesis that firms in that industry are price-takers, and moreover, he finds that the average degree of market power has increased over the 1965-79 period (Lopez, 1984:229). In response to a doubling of the four-firm concentration ratio in the United States' beef-packing industry, Schroeter (1988) employed a similar technique to estimate the degree of market power. He found that although there were small and statistically significant price distortions in both the slaughter cattle and wholesale markets, there was no indication that firms had become less competitive (Schroeter, 1988:158). Since most rice-exporting countries use a central agency for controlling export supply, Karp and Perloff (1989) use a dynamic oligopoly model to estimate the degree of competitiveness in the rice market.[36] They find that although their model confirms an oligopolistic market structure for rice, the behaviour of firms is closer to being competitive than collusive (Karp and Perloff, 1989:469). These studies suggest that where markets are concentrated it is likely that firms do not behave competitively; however, the outcome for any particular market needs to be determined on a case by case basis.

4.3.3   Industrial organization and the EU's banana import business

The importance of industrial organization theory to this work is explained by the nature of EU banana import business. We have seen that the EU's banana market is oligopolistic, with approximately 60 per cent of all bananas traded falling under the control of three TNCs (Chapter 3). Additionally, even bananas not subject to the control of these firms fall under the influence of other small groups of firms operating elsewhere within the EU. For instance, three firms supply more than 90 per cent of the market in Germany, the Benelux and Scandinavian countries; another three firms supply more than 80 per cent of the market in the UK; and four firms supply more than 75 per cent of the French market.[37] All of this suggests that within member-countries of the EU, as well as the EU in general, firms in the banana market are likely to enjoy some degree of market power. This implies that whether or not, and how much, consumers benefit from trade liberalization depends on the extent to which firms are capable of exercising market power. Therefore, the basic propositions of SCP – that market structure and the conduct of firms within markets are important in determining overall performance – have direct relevance in explaining whether or not liberalization of the EU banana trade is desirable. We shall develop and test the preceding propositions in subsequent chapters.

Applications of elements of the Cournot and Bertrand models of oligopoly to simulate 'games' of reaction behaviour are likely to result in estimates of the degree of market power in markets within EU member-states and for the EU as a whole. These estimates of market power can be used to determine the potential welfare effects of implementing free trade.[38] In Germany, for instance, the market is structured in such a way that Chiquita supplies 44 per cent, while Dole and Bonita account for 20-22 per cent each. Therefore, if the presence of strong oligopolistic interdependence among firms is confirmed, then the Stackelberg model could be used to predict one possible market outcome. Chiquita takes the lead and supplies its market share (44 per cent), leaving Dole and Bonita to following their reaction functions and supply the remainder of the market. Alternatively, again with the assumption of strong oligopolistic interdependence, firms might compete on the basis of differentiated products, so that some brands of bananas command a higher price than others, while firms take quantity decisions as fixed.[39] Thus, by using the relevant data for *representative* EU member-states and for the EU banana market as a whole, the degree of market power and the related welfare and efficiency effects of trade liberalization will be estimated in Chapters 8 and 9, respectively.

4.4 Theories of the transnational firm and the EU's banana import business

Although the different forms of industrial organization and methods of analysis discussed in the preceding section will be applied directly in some chapters of this work, the fact that the key players in the EU banana trade are transnationals necessitates a deeper discussion of the relevant theory. We shall now undertake this task.

4.4.1   Theories of the transnational firm

Transnational firms are companies that own or control value-added activities in two or more countries, usually through foreign direct investment (FDI) although they may choose to exercise ownership in foreign production through co-operative alliances with foreign firms (Cantwell, 2000; Dunning, 1996; Teece, 1982). FDI involves the transfer of a package of resources across national boundaries in such a manner that the ownership and control of those resources remains in the hands of the transferring firms or is at least shared with the transferring firms. This package of resources could include technology, management skills, organizational capacity and entrepreneurship (Dunning, 1996:38). Conceptually, two interrelated issues are important here: first, why firms engage in transnational production and, second, what specific factors determine foreign-owned production.[40] Below, we shall briefly discuss the two major paradigms that are used for analysing transnational production. In the context of the EU's banana trade, these paradigms will help explain both the transnational nature of the trade as well as why firms choose to invest in banana production in some countries and not in others.

Although two approaches dominate the theory of transnational production – namely the internalization paradigm (see Casson, 1987; Caves, 1982; Rugman, 1979; and Teece, 1982; among others)[41] and Dunning's eclectic paradigm (Dunning, 1996),[42] other attempts at explaining FDI exist.[43] Yet, the basis for explaining FDI remains Hymer's seminal work,[44] which presents "multinational corporations as a substitute for the market as a method of organizing international exchange" (Hymer, 1970:441). In other words, Hymer saw FDI as a form of corporate behaviour associated with imperfections in home country markets, particularly high entry barriers.[45] For Dunning and Rugman (1985:3) Hymer's major argument was that "...the MNE has the ability to use its international operations to separate markets and remove competition, or to exploit an advantage". Therefore, it requires control over the use of its assets abroad in order to minimize risks and to achieve monopolistic power. Firms operating in those markets usually possessed a combination of intangible assets, such as proprietary technology, a differentiated product and management experience. Hymer (1970:443) found that the concept of the TNC allowed business firms to transfer capital, technology and organizational skill from one country to another, while at the same time, TNCs served to restrain competition between firms of different nations. He further argued that the logic of economists who are proponents of free trade and factor mobility is based on allocative efficiency, a concept which "does not apply to foreign investment because of the anticompetitive effect inherently associated with it" (Hymer, 1970: 443). Since a major objective of TNCs "is to gain control over marketing facilities in order to facilitate the spread of their products" (Hymer, 1970:445), and invariably such products are available only in oligopolistic markets, then "bigness is thus paid for, in part, by fewness, and a decline in competition since the size of the market is limited by the size of the firm" (Hymer, 1970:443). Dunning and Rugman (1985:4) have suggested that a major weakness of Hymer's work is that he based all his analysis on structural market imperfections, following the tradition of Bain (1956), and paid no attention to transactions cost market imperfections. They contend it is largely for this reason that Hymer appears to have placed too much emphasis on the TNC as an entity seeking to exploit monopoly power.[46] Yet, as Yamin (1991:74) has pointed out, even in Hymer's doctoral dissertation he did not totally ignore transaction costs, an opinion shared by the author, and that in a paper that he wrote in 1968 he explicitly utilized Coase (1937)'s framework.[47]

Internalization emphasizes the efficiency with which transactions between units of productive activity are organized (Cantwell, 2000:17). It develops the concept of TNCs by explaining why transnational hierarchies, as opposed to market forces, are important in organizing the cross-border transactions of intermediate products (Teece, 1982, 1993). It is premised on the hypothesis that a firm is likely to engage in FDI if it perceives that net benefits achievable through joint ownership of domestic and foreign activities are likely to be greater than those achievable through external trading relationships (Teece, 1982:3-4; Cantwell, 2000:17).[48] Therefore, it predicts that, for a given distribution of factor endowments a positive relationship is expected between transnational activity and the costs of organizing cross-border markets in intermediate products; and, that the specificity of physical and human assets serve as incentives for vertical integration of TNCs (Teece, 1982:22).[49] However, Dunning (1993:75-6) points out that this approach does not adequately explain the level and structure of production of a country's own firms outside its boundaries, nor the production of foreign-owned firms within that country. Furthermore, internalization fails to identify location-specific variables as a requirement for explaining FDI. Let us briefly discuss Dunning's approach.

By establishing a relationship between the H-O-S theory of international trade and the microeconomic theory of the firm, Dunning (1996:27-8) demonstrates that whether or not international economic activity takes place depends on variables like market structure, transaction costs and firm-level management strategies. More specifically, the variables introduced by Dunning are: (a) ownership-specific, or 'O' advantages, that is, special assets that are assumed to be unique to a particular firm. These assets, apart from tangible ones like natural resources, capital and labour, include technology and information; managerial, marketing and entrepreneurial skills; organizational systems; and access to goods markets; (b) location-specific, or 'L' advantages, available to all firms in a given environment. In addition to ordinary H-O-S-type factor endowments, advantages include a nexus of cultural, legal, political and institutional environments in the country concerned, as well as market structure and government investment and other related policies; and (c) internalization, or 'I' advantages, as presented earlier (Dunning, 1993:79-81). Dunning's eclectic paradigm predicts that at any point in time, the more 'O' advantages the firms in one country have relative to firms in another country, the greater the incentive for such firms to internalize rather than externalize the use of such advantages. Additionally, the more firms find it convenient to exploit their 'O' advantages from a foreign location, the more likely they are to engage in international production (Dunning, 1993:80).[50] Therefore, it is such combinations of 'O', 'L' and 'I' advantages, along with other factors, that dictate the causes of transnationality.

However, Teece (1982:41) contends that there are three limitations to Dunning's eclectic paradigm of FDI. First, it cannot predict which firm-specific assets are likely to be traded within the TNC and the circumstances under which the TNC might choose so to do. Second, it cannot distinguish individual cost components (production and transaction) nor can it demonstrate the relationship between these costs. Third, it does not take into consideration the incentives for vertical integration. Yet, in the broader scheme of things both the internalization and eclectic paradigms share a common limitation – they focus on factors internal to the firm in analysing why TNCs make the decisions they do and fail to take strategic management behaviour into account (Graham, 2000:162).[51]

4.4.2   Empirical evidence on transnational firms

Since one objective of this research is to explain the nature of the contributions of TNCs to the EU's banana business, below we shall examine some empirical evidence on the involvement of TNCs elsewhere, and discuss the extent to which such evidence supports or refutes existing theories. Particular attention will be given to: (i) the evidence on the involvement of TNCs in international trade, (ii) their effect on market structure, and (iii) their contribution to economic development and production.

The nature of involvement of TNCs in host countries can determine whether or not those countries might benefit from international trade. Since TNCs tend to replace markets with organizational relationships between hosts and affiliates, internalization theory generally predicts an increase in trade volume, which is expected to arise from the increased economies of vertical and horizontal integration (Gray, 1996:251).[52] While empirical evidence tends to support this, it also shows that export-oriented host countries, or better TNC-affiliates, tend to benefit more from the growth of trade than others do (Gray, 1996:254),[53] and in addition, TNCs contribution to growth of exports is greatest when specialized marketing arrangements are required. According to Lall (1996:59) it appears that TNCs' contribution to export promotion is greatest when "...the marketing of exports requires an established network of vertically integrated facilities across countries, or powerful brand names, or when production involves easily transferred proprietary inputs or knowledge." Yet, where TNCs are involved in manipulative transfer pricing, host countries are not likely to enjoy full potential benefits from trade (Gray, 1996:251; Lall, 1973:190-191) and the process results in complex problems for both TNCs and host governments (Plasschaert, 1996:394).[54] Nevertheless, Gray (1996:257) contends that unless the costs of manipulative transfer pricing are far higher than presently known, the benefits that host countries enjoy from intra-firm trade are likely to involve spillovers of indeterminable size to trading countries; an opinion which is supported by Lall (1996:62-3).[55]

Our second area of interest regarding TNCs is their effect on, or relationship with, different forms of market structure. The fact that TNCs have greater access to special assets (technological, managerial, marketing, and other resources) confers two advantages on them. First, these special assets become a source of market power, and second, they render TNCs more attractive to host countries (Frischtak and Newfarmer, 1996:296-7). Although Vernon's product cycle theory predicts that, as a product matures, its market gradually transits from monopoly to oligopoly and, finally, to workable competition (Vernon, 1977:91), a study conducted by Connor and Mueller (1977) in Brazil and Mexico found that, after controlling for other factors, there was a strong positive relationship between market concentration and two other measures of market imperfection (product differentiation and relative market share) and the level of foreign ownership in industry.[56] Additionally, a cross-sectional econometric study of Brazil's manufacturing sector in 1994 found a positive correlation between foreign ownership of an industry and industrial concentration (Frischtak and Newfarmer, 1996:301).[57]

Another theoretical proposition advanced by Vernon (1994) is that the market share of the leading established foreign and domestic firms should decline as a function of new, foreign-based, entry. However, other studies have shown that average market share does not necessarily decline, but instead might increase slightly, both at entry and post entry (Frischtak and Newfarmer, 1996:303).[58] In addition, it appears that whatever the potentially pro-competitive effects of TNCs might be in reducing concentration at entry, these tend to be mitigated by their subsequent growth strategies (Frischtak and Newfarmer, 1996:304).[59] But, perhaps, the explanation of these 'anomalies' might come from Vernon himself. By his own admission, as the product matures, the need for flexibility declines and the commitment to certain product standards opens up the possibilities for achieving economies of scale, as initial concerns about product characteristics are replaced by those related to production cost (Vernon, 1966:196).[60] Therefore, the innovating firm might then consider the possibility of investing abroad, provided that it is likely to enjoy savings in its overall costs.[61] But we have seen that the NTTs, notably Krugman (1994), argue that scale economies (increasing returns) that are inherent in innovation lead to imperfect competition and that it might not be possible to predict the outcome for consumer welfare.[62] Therefore, the implications of Fischtak and Newfarmer's findings are that Vernon's above propositions are not correct, since TNCs, while pursuing scale economies, as Vernon rightly predicts, nevertheless, engage in anti-competitive behaviour in accordance with the predictions of the NTTs.

The third aspect of TNCs that is of interest to us is their contribution to economic development and production. TNCs can and do provide positive contributions to the economic development of developing countries through foreign investment and the associated products and services created. In particular, they could make a positive contribution through (i) the balance of payments, (ii) provision of access to modern technology and (iii) employment. Let us examine each of these in turn.

Balance of payments

FDI directly affects a country's balance of payments in a number of ways, the first of which is the direct effect of capital outflows and inflows which are used for financing outward and inward FDI, respectively, except in situations where FDI is financed through other means.[63] The second direct effect concerns the outflow and inflow of profits and dividends from earlier inward and outward FDI, which could be significant for countries that are heavily engaged in FDI (Ietto-Gillies, 1992:168-9). Whether or not developing countries gain from FDI depends on whether the profits and dividends to foreign investors are smaller or larger than the inflow of new FDI.[64] Additionally, the balance of payments could be indirectly affected if TNCs engage in transfer price manipulations, a practice which they might engage in to take advantage of exchange rate movements and/or the desire to transfer profits otherwise subjected to legal restrictions (ibid., pp.169-70).

Technological diffusion

Since most technological innovation takes place in TNCs, which invariably originate in developed countries, these entities have become extremely important in the transfer of technology (Cantwell, 2000; Hennart 2000) to the developing countries. Yet, there are both costs and difficulties associated with technological transfer, which Cantwell (2000:47) links to the research and production experience accumulated within the TNC, while Yamin (2000:62) sees these costs as arising "from the difficulties involved in conveying and obtaining knowledge across organisational boundaries". The issue of appropriateness of the technology being transferred is extremely important, given that TNCs tend to invent technologies that are capital-intensive, while those that might be most appropriate for developing countries might be the labour-intensive variety, given the relative abundance of labour to capital in the developing countries. In this context Ietto-Gillies (1992:170) contends that the use of inappropriate technology in the developing countries might lead to greater income inequalities. Yet, she continues, if introduced carefully, developing countries might imitate both the technology and management and marketing techniques of TNCs.

Employment and organized labour

International production unquestionably affects employment and organized labour in both the home and host countries in various ways. TNCs are thought to have directly employed in excess of 65 million people and indirectly approximately 130 million people world-wide, in the 1980s (Ietto-Gillies, 1992:174). Yet, exactly how job creation by TNCs impacts on developing countries depends on the nature of FDI undertaken. If FDI activity is largely the acquisition of an existing firm it might not necessarily create new jobs and might even reduce jobs once operations are rational-ized. Also, if FDI results in the crowding out of domestic investment, then again no new jobs might be created; and TNCs might employ fewer employees than an equivalent domestic firm if they use capital-intensive technologies (Ietto-Gillies, 1992:174-5). So, in fact, it is not automatic that a home country would lose jobs due to FDI, and whether or not the host country gains remains equally inconclusive. Moreover, if TNCs pursue a 'divide and rule' strategy, that is, the division of labour into country-specific groups so that employers improve their bargaining positions, then they might gain at the expense of labour by producing in the country where wages are lowest (Peoples and Sugden, 2000:178). Nonetheless, because the transnationalization of production is likely to create wider investment opportunities world-wide, direct employment opportunities are likely to increase. Additionally, a number of indirect employment opportunities are likely to arise due to the effects of FDI on trade, competition and the spread of technology (Ietto-Gillies, 1992:175).

Although labour productivity tends to be higher in TNCs than in domestic firms in many countries, there is considerable debate over their labour relations practices. TNCs appear to be keen on transferring their labour relations practices from their headquarters to the host country, a practice which they normally engaged in as part of their negotiations for entry into a new host country (Ietto-Gillies, 1992:177). Another practice of TNCs that is associated with their centralized system of management and foreignness is their treatment of managerial jobs in host countries, most of which tend to be awarded to nationals from their home country (Ietto-Gillies, 1992:177-8). Therefore, "the geographical fragmentation of labour across many nations resulting from companies' internalization over many countries, rather than one, definitely weakens labour" (Ietto-Gillies, 1992:179).

Other contributions

Finally, other aspects of TNC behaviour impact on the potential gains of host countries from TNC investment, and Frischtak and Newfarmer (1996:306-7) have identified three of these. First, TNCs tend to bring different marketing abilities and a higher propensity to advertise than do domestic firms in the same industry, and, it is evident that the share of TNCs in a market is a principal determinant of the level of its product differentiation. Second, it appears that product differentiation tends to heighten industrial concentration in consumer industries primarily serving local markets. Third, foreign firms have a greater tendency to acquire domestic firms than the other way round for two reasons: they have greater access to large pools of investment resources, and the absence of an insulated domestic capital market usually prevents domestic management from assuming control of foreign corporations in transition.

4.4.3   Theories of the TNC and the EU's banana business

Let us now apply the above theories of the TNC to explain different aspects of the EU's banana business. Starting with Dunning (1993, 1996)'s approach, we argue that 'O','L' and 'I' advantages are important for explaining the EU banana business. Bananas are most suitable for cultivation on vast expanses of flat land in tropical regions of the world. Since they are fragile and perishable commodities, the *harvesting* process is very delicate and is best done manually, making it rather labour intensive.[65] The choice of region for production of bananas for export is explained by the 'L' advantages of host countries. In fact, so important are these 'L' advantages that an observed prime barrier to entry into the industry has arisen from the historical access to the best plantation sites of the world by the US TNCs. These firms acquired most of their plantations in Latin America through concessions, in return for which they agreed to provide improvements to existing infrastructure (Read, 1986:320). The 'L' advantages of Latin American countries in banana export production derive from their vast expanses of arable land and extremely low wages. Efficient inputs into production coupled with extremely low wages result in high productivity, which explains Latin America's competitiveness.

Dunning (1993, 1996)'s 'O' type advantages in the banana business arise from the importance of a combination of capital of high specificity, and research and development. Banana production is capital-intensive, demanding considerable amounts of fixed investment in plantations as well as appropriate technology for irrigation and harvesting. Additionally, since bananas are fragile and disease prone, research needs to be conducted on a continuous basis to develop more resistant varieties (see Chapter 3).[66] The relative ease of access to finance by US and EU TNCs, coupled with their advanced technologies in research and development, confer natural 'O' advantages on them. Read (1986:340) has brought out the importance of capital and technological know-how in the banana business in his analysis of how the US TNCs were able to penetrate the Japanese market. He argues that the "possession of cultivation scale economies, technological know-how, risk-diversifying supply contracts and a high degree of internalisation through branding, shipping and marketing, has enabled them to obtain an increasing market share", and that "the dominance of the banana MNEs in Japan was achieved at the expense of high-cost fruit from Taiwan and low quality Ecuadorian imports".

Yet, Dunning (1993, 1996)'s 'I' type advantages are also relevant for explaining the EU's banana business. Since bananas are highly fragile and easily damaged through inappropriate handling, co-ordination of the activities at different stages of the commodity chain is crucial in order to minimize risks that may arise due to spoilage and to maximize returns. By internalizing the various stages of the commodity chain in the manner suggested by Teece (1982, 1993) TNCs are able to realize greater benefits than if they were engaged in arm's-length trading relationships. In fact, Teece (1982:28) has suggested that the processes of international banana production appear to be broadly consistent with internalization theory,[67] although internalization does not explain the persistence of transnational oligopolistic interdependence in the banana industry. Hymer (1970)'s original market power approach for explaining TNC behaviour better explains the persistence of transnational oligopoly in the EU banana industry. By functioning as vertically integrated entities, TNCs in the EU banana business have effectively removed competition, and their product differentiation strategies have enabled them to exploit monopoly power. Moreover, technological innovation required to develop more disease-resistant banana varieties, coupled with the high specificity of capital – factors which are conducive to the creation of natural monopoly – explains the non-contestability of the EU banana market. It is for such reasons that in the absence of intervention along the lines of the Consent Decree (see Chapter 3) the EU banana industry will continue to be characterized by transnational oligopolistic interdependence, as opposed to transition from oligopoly to workable competition in the manner suggested by Vernon (1977).

Nevertheless, the theories of the TNC do not explain how value added is divided among various actors (or affiliates) in the banana commodity chain despite the importance of its intermediate stages. After they are produced on plantations in the tropics, bananas need to be transported, marketed, ripened and distributed in the country of destination. Each of these intermediate stages in the commodity chain is capital intensive and the banana is subjected to value-adding activities throughout. Thus, a deeper explanation of the value-adding processes that bananas are subjected to requires going beyond the conventional theoretical frameworks of international trade and production and introduction of the concept of a 'commodity chain' to provide deeper insights into the production and marketing of bananas.

4.5   Commodity chains

As should be evident from the preceding analysis, bananas are produced and marketed in a complex international network of firms and countries, the relationships between which cannot be fully explained and/or understood through theories of international trade, industrial organization and transnational firms, alone. This implies that bananas are subjected to continuous value transformation along the commodity chain, that is, from initial production to final consumption. The terms 'commodity chain', 'production chain' and 'value-added chain' are all used interchangeably in the literature. For instance, Gereffi (1994) prefers the term commodity chain, while Dicken (1998) prefers the term 'production chain'. This study will use the term 'commodity chain' to avoid confusing the reader, who may otherwise think we are dealing only with the banana *production* process; or are only concerned with value-addition. In fact, our central concern is not on the individual processes *per se*, but rather on the interconnections between processes. Therefore, in this sub-section we begin with a definition of a commodity chain, followed by an overview of its application for analysing the international production and processes of a commodity. The sub-section will then attempt to show how both international trade and production theories are absorbed into the commodity chain approach. Finally, the sub-section will discuss how this concept will be applied for an analysis of the EU's banana business.

4.5.1   Commodity chain defined

A commodity chain is a transactionally linked sequence of functions in which each stage adds value to the process of production of goods or services (Dicken, 1998:7). The basic stages of any commodity chain are as follows: materials, procurement, transformation, marketing and sales, distribution and service (Figure 4.1). Each basic stage is subjected to technology, research and/or development, as well as transport and communications processes. The entire system is subject to a financial system, as well as systems of regulation, co-ordination and control (Gereffi, 1994:96; Dicken 1998:6). A commodity chain can be either buyer- or producer-driven, depending upon the governance structure that characterizes the processes of ownership, control and management along the chain.

In a producer-driven commodity chain, TNCs or other large integrated enterprises usually play the central role in controlling the entire production system, including its forward and backward linkages (Gereffi, 1994:97; Dicken, 1998:9).[68] In contrast, a buyer-driven commodity chain refers to an industry in which large retailers, brand-name merchandisers, and trading companies play a central role in organizing decentralized production networks in several exporting countries (Gereffi, 1994:97). The networks of exporting countries include many of the developing countries. In a buyer-

Fig. 4.1   *The commodity chain*

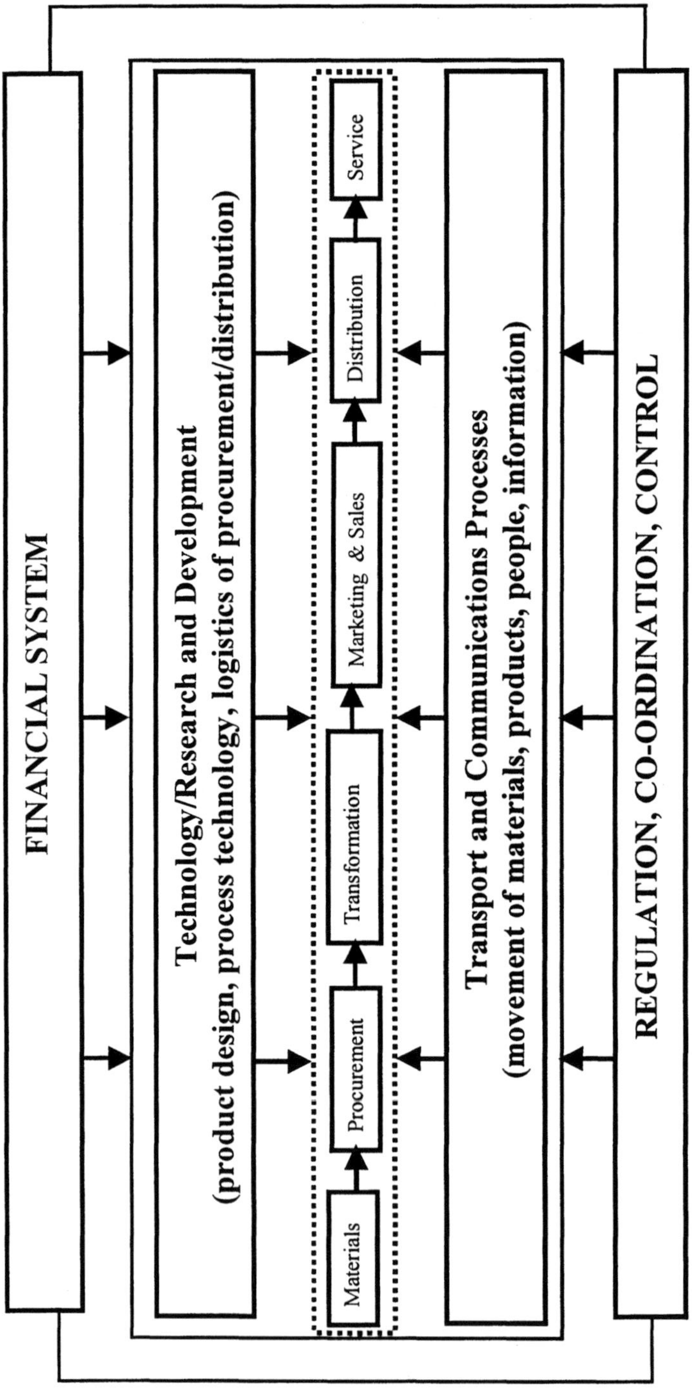

FINANCIAL SYSTEM

Technology/Research and Development
(product design, process technology, logistics of procurement/distribution)

| Materials | Procurement | Transformation | Marketing & Sales | Distribution | Service |

Transport and Communications Processes
(movement of materials, products, people, information)

REGULATION, CO-ORDINATION, CONTROL

Source: Dicken (1998).

driven commodity chain independent factories in developing countries, which produce finished goods under original equipment manufacturer arrangements, generally carry out production. This type of commodity chain is closely linked to export-oriented industrialization among the labour-intensive consumer-goods industries, that is, garments, footwear, toys and consumer electronics (Gereffi, 1994:97).

.Regardless of the governance structure that characterizes a commodity chain, the concept is useful for explaining and understanding the linkages between firms, industries, and countries (Gereffi, 1995:101). Specifically, there are two major strengths of the commodity chain concept. Firstly, it allows analysis to be undertaken at the level of specific products and industries, as opposed to broad zones of economic development which tends to characterize other methods. Secondly, its greater emphasis on contemporary patterns of international competition makes it useful for both cross-sectional and time series data analysis (Gereffi, 1996:65).

4.5.2   International production and commodity chains

We begin this sub-section with a brief examination of how global commodity chains tend to be distributed and continue with a review of the relevance of the concept in some specific industries.

The existence of both producer- and buyer-driven commodity chains in the global economy is in itself a manifestation of the presence of asymmetric market power. Gereffi argues, that both producer- and buyer-driven commodity chains arise from the barriers to entry that allow core industrial and commercial firms, to control the backward and forward linkages in the production processes, respectively. Since producer-driven chains tend to be capital- and technology-intensive, their source of profits lies in their ability to enjoy scale economies through optimal production volumes and their pace in technological advances (Gereffi, 1995:117). On the other hand, since buyer-driven commodity chains are labour-intensive in production, they tend to be *relatively* competitive and so profits arise from the ability of firms to assemble unique combinations of high-value research, design, sales, marketing, and financial services. Thus, in the latter case retailers and branded marketers are capable of acting as strategic brokers, linking overseas factories and traders with evolving product niches in their main consumer markets (Gereffi, 1995:116). Therefore, assuming that Gereffi's propositions are correct, one would expect the greater value of all global production to be located in the capital-, knowledge- and technology-rich countries. A number of empirical studies have applied the concept of commodity chains to decompose and analyse the distribution of production in the world economy.[69] Korzeniewicz and Martin (1994) conducted a study to determine whether the global distribution and integration of production processes is related to the existence of world economic zones.[70] The results of that study confirm the existence of a tri-modal economic zone structure of production in the world economy, which is fairly stable over the long run (Korzeniewicz and Martin, 1994:71).[71] Additionally, their analysis of the share of involvement of each economic zone in major industries of global production confirms that most of the technology-, knowledge- and capital-intensive industries tend to be located in the industrialized countries, while most of the labour-intensive industries tend to be located in the developing countries (Korzeniewicz and Martin, 1994:76-9).[72]

Raynolds (1994) uses the commodity chains concept to analyse the configuration of firms in the non-traditional agricultural export sector of the Dominican Republic during the 1980s.[73] She finds that, in general, fresh fruit and vegetable export firms rely primarily on internal plantation production (66 per cent), for their supply of exportable produce, followed by contract production (22 per cent), while open-market production accounts for the remaining 12 per cent of all production. Internal production is most important for pineapples since they demand heavy capital investment and require over one year to mature. Hence, Raynolds (1994:151) argues that their production tends to be dominated by transnationals for the following reasons: (i) they have easier access to capital than do domestic firms; and (ii) the transnationals appear to prefer plantation production because it guarantees higher quality of supply, greater efficiency and lower administrative cost. Contract production was found to be most important in oriental vegetables and melons. In the case of melons, production requires moderate levels of capital not readily available to farmers, while the US market for melons, their only seasonal principal market, requires the fruit to be of a high quality. Thus, by entering into short-term contracts with farmers, melon firms distribute production risk while ensuring that they are capable of retaining their markets with high-quality fruit (Raynolds, 1994:151-2). Finally, since winter vegetables are short-cycle crops which are readily available, there is a significant level of reliance on open-market purchases of these commodities for export. Here, firms can avoid direct production costs while maximizing their product flexibility (Raynolds, 1994:152).

The preparation of fresh produce for export, the type of marketing channel that is used, and whether or not barriers to trade exist in the destination market, are all crucial factors that determine the overall efficiency and viability of an exporting firm. Before they are admitted into the United States, fresh produce must satisfy strict health and safety guidelines, which have been designed to protect the US population from unsanitary food and prevent the spread of plant diseases. But given the highly perishable nature of fresh fruit, the most efficient way to ensure that such standards are complied with, without imposing substantial costs on firms, is to use a system of advance monitoring.[74] However, this is extremely expensive and can only be afforded by large transnationals; thus, it constitutes a barrier to entry for smaller firms (Raynolds, 1994:152).[75] Smaller firms also suffer losses in the ocean transportation of fresh fruit since they, unlike the large transnationals, do not own dedicated vessels for this purpose. Consequently, their fruit is shipped via indirect routes involving several transit points, and the delays encountered result in deterioration of the quality even before arrival in the destination market.

There is also considerable variation in the organization of relationships between entities in the producing and importing countries. In general, the capital-intensive pineapple chain is far more vertically integrated than others, and, so exports are essentially direct transfers from a subsidiary firm in the Dominican Republic to its parent in the US.[76] At the other extreme, oriental vegetable firms market their produce on consignment to independent brokers and wholesalers in the US.[77] These firms enjoy the least favourable conditions of exportation since they are required to absorb the costs of transportation as well as losses from damage in transit.

Distribution, the final major stage in the commodity chain, varies from commodity to commodity, since they enter separate marketing networks. Oriental vegetables enter growing specialty food networks and are sold primarily to ethnic restaurants or specialty stores.[78] Melons and winter vegetables enter the off-season produce circuits and are sold to supermarkets, greengrocers and institutional food services (Raynolds, 1994:154). Finally, pineapples enter the global sourcing networks governed by Dole Foods and Chiquita Brands, two of the largest distributors of fresh produce in the world.[79] Chiquita and Dole have increased pineapple consumption through extensive *advertising* as well as through *product differentiation*. Their retail divisions effectively shape their markets and provide projections through company networks, which are used in planning pineapple planting and harvesting (Raynolds, 1994:155).[80]

4.5.3   Commodity chains and the EU's banana business

We shall now examine the extent to which the commodity chain concept, in which transnationals play important roles elsewhere according to the literature so far, might be relevant for explaining and understanding the EU's banana import business. All of the issues discussed above could be applied in some way to explain and understand the nature and structure of the EU's banana import business, since all banana trade flows into the EU are either subject to direct control by, or influence of, transnational firms to varying degrees.

The basic stages in a banana commodity chain are presented in Figure 4.2. Bananas are first cultivated on plantations or small farms, where the *natural* gestation period is nine months. After harvest, bananas are subjected to strict quality controls and firms label and brand the fruits on the basis of their overall quality before they are packaged into 18kg boxes. The bananas are then *rapidly* transported by rail or bus to shipping ports where they are loaded onto specialized refrigerated ships, known as reefers, which *rapidly* transport them across the Atlantic to various European ports. At their port of entry into Europe they are again subjected to quality controls before being *rapidly* transported in refrigerated containers to various ripening centres. Ripeners have some control over the pace at which the fruit ripens, with the process taking from three to seven days.[81] Once the bananas are ripe (that is, they become yellow), they are sold to retail outlets where they have a shelf life of 2-3 days.

Fig. 4.2   The stages in a banana commodity chain

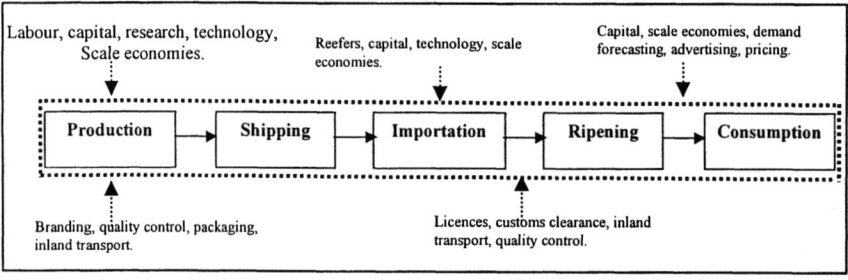

In all cases, the advantages of transnationals involved in the EU's banana import business are of the 'O' type. To appreciate this point, and why some transnationals command a significantly larger share of the EU's banana market than others, it is important to understand the nature and structure of the banana commodity chains that new firms face. Banana commodity chains have two distinct forms: some are completely vertically integrated, while others are only partially so (Chapter 3). Therefore, some firms own considerably more assets and capital than others do. Since the banana is an extremely fragile and highly perishable commodity, efficient dissemination of information along its commodity chain is of paramount importance in order to minimize losses and risks, maximize returns and preserve superior quality. Vertically integrated firms provide such advantages, which arise from economies of not only scale and scope, but importantly, common governance. Therefore, these differences in production chains confer certain efficiency advantages on some firms (large-scale vertically integrated TNCs), while they constitute efficiency disadvantages for others (small-scale producers with contractual agreements).

The extent to which a banana chain is vertically integrated is likely to give rise to different forms of market structure. Conceptually, completely vertically integrated chains tend towards monopolistic or oligopolistic market structures, while those characterized by contractual agreements tend towards more competitive market structures. In the case of the EU banana import business, an example of the two extremes are bananas produced on large plantations in Costa Rica by Chiquita, which are subsequently marketed through completely vertically integrated chains in Germany, and bananas produced on small-holder farms in St. Lucia, which are marketed in a rather loosely vertically integrated chain in the United Kingdom.[82] In the latter case, the production stage is characterized by strong oligopsony, where thousands of farmers sell all their bananas to one of two wholesale marketing firms,[83] which in turn work with a single international marketing firm, WIBDECO/Fyffes, which has the responsibility for packaging and preparing bananas for ocean transportation to the United Kingdom. This last stage is vertically integrated backwards to wholesale buying. Upon their arrival at ports in the UK, WIBDECO/Fyffes bananas are sold to three ripening centres, the transactions between two of which are partially internalized while the other constitutes a market transaction. From their point of entry into ripening facilities, all subsequent value added activities except the final point of retail sale to consumers, constitute internalized transactions. At the retail level, the market structure becomes oligopolistic.[84]

In the case of Costa Rican bananas, which are exported to and consumed in Germany, we consider the chain for which all of the stages are vertically integrated, although alternative commodity chains exist. Costa Rican banana production for export takes place on a combination of plantations owned by transnational firms and a number of independent firms that are associates of these transnationals. In 1984, 45 per cent of all banana production acreage was owned directly by Chiquita, Dole and Del Monte, with the remaining 55 per cent under the ownership of associate firms.[85] Despite the fact that a larger share of banana production acreage is owned by associate firms, subsequent stages of the chain are controlled by the three TNCs. Therefore, while only 2 per cent of all bananas exported from Costa Rica were marketed directly by independent growers in 1984; Chiquita, Dole and Del Monte accounted for the marketing of 25 per cent, 35 per cent and 38 per cent of all banana exports, respectively (FAO, 1986:79). Moreover, based on several unstructured interviews between the author and industry experts, while there has been slight changes in the shares of individual TNCs, the overall picture remains the same.

The commodity chain that moves Chiquita bananas from Costa Rica to Germany is a representative chain for bananas produced in Latin America that are exported to and consumed in Europe under the control of the US TNCs. First, since all the bananas produced for export originate either directly from Chiquita's own plantations or from those owned by one of its associate producer firms, for all intents and purposes this stage of the production chain is vertically integrated. Secondly, two firms, Chiquita and Atlanta, handle all the ocean transportation of bananas up to their point of entry into Germany, and since Chiquita is a major shareholder in Atlanta, for practical reasons that stage of the commodity chain is also vertically integrated. Atlanta handles the ripening of 85 to 90 per cent of all imported fruit, with the remainder being ripened by other independent companies. Finally, bananas are distributed primarily to retail chain outlets and other outlets for sale to consumers.

4.6   Conclusions

This chapter has discussed some of the theories of international trade, industrial organization, transnational corporations and commodity chains and applied them to illuminate the nature and structure of the EU banana trade. We have seen that while classical and neo-classical trade theories explain why tropical countries produce bananas for export, it is the NTTs that help explain why production in certain countries is more efficient than others, and why some brands of bananas command a higher price than others. Yet, the common assumption of the NTTs that firms are engaged in monopolistic competition and profits are driven to zero imposes some limitations on their analytical power. Invariably, 'monopolistic competition' models of international trade are likely to incorrectly predict that global welfare will increase under trade liberalization in any commodity. In the case of Europe's banana import business, firms are better conceptualized as being engaged in oligopolistic reaction behaviour, with the implication that whether or not welfare improves from trade liberalization depends on the nature of competition among firms in the market. Moreover, even if global welfare might increase under trade liberalization, neither the NTTs nor the classical and neo-classical trade theories predict the nature and structure of distribution of gains from trade. This is where the commodity chain concept provides deeper explanation of how value added is distributed, from the point of initial production to final consumption. Such commodity chains need to be explained in terms of the intra-firm transfers, or internalized transactions as opposed to arm's-length trade, since the dominant firms in the EU's banana business are transnational in nature. When the need to exploit economies of scale at various stages of the commodity chain is combined with the need for co-ordination of the activities of different stages, economies of common governance as suggested by Gereffi (1999) and Dicken (1998), become extremely important. It is these economies, coupled with the exploitation of market power by TNCs through control of the commodity chain, in the manner suggested by Hymer (1970, 1976) that explains the persistence of transnational oligopolistic interdependence. The commodity chain concept therefore allows us to go beyond the conventional meaning of a commodity, to capture the various stages of 'service value-addition' to which the physical commodity is subjected. These successive stages of 'service value-addition' transform and/or become embodied within the physical commodity, thus becoming a construction of the transnational.[86]

So, to conclude, in this study we conceptualize the EU's banana import business as comprising a number of commodity chains, some of which are characterized by successive stages of arm's-length transactions, and others that compose wholly internalized transactions. In all cases, the markets in both the banana-exporting countries and EU member-states are dominated by a small number of transnationals, which possess and exercise considerable market power. Therefore, the central proposition in this work is that the extent to which firms are capable of exploiting market power at successive stages of the commodity chain, and at the final point of retail sale determines the welfare outcomes for producers and consumers under trade liberalization.

In Chapter 5 we shall use a simple approach to lobbying and apply our concept of a commodity as comprising a physical good embodied within a 'vector' of services to explain and interpret the behaviour of the Chiquita TNC in instigating US action that led to the WTO ruling. Then we shall use the commodity chain concept along with the theories of international trade and transnational firms to decompose and analyse the revenue and surplus along the banana commodity chain in Chapters 6 and 7. Chapter 8 will draw upon the NEIO theory to construct a model and empirically measure the degree of market power in the EU banana business. Finally, we shall construct a three-period sequential oligopoly 'game' in Chapter 9 to estimate the welfare effects of trade liberalization under imperfect competition, using the empirical evidence on oligopolistic interdependence and strategic price-setting behaviour due to branding.

Notes

[1] The WTO Director-General was quoted as saying in a recent address to the *National Press Club* in the United States, "The WTO is an intergovernmental organization. Governments meet in Geneva to discuss trade issues, to negotiate rules for further liberalization of trade, to settle disputes. Governments deal directly with each other, face to face" (Moore, 2000:1).

[2] In particular, the works of Borrell and Yang (1990, 1992), Borrell and Cuthbertson (1991), Borrell (1994, 1996) and Kersten (1995) have all used the case of the EU banana trade to promote economic liberalism. See Chapter 2 for a summary of these.

[3] Compensation is defined here in terms of the Kaldor-Hicks-Scitovsky criterion. See Nath (1969) for a detailed discussion of the subject, but particularly pp. 95-6.

[4] As Dixit and Norman (1980:265) put it, "Because of imperfect competition, the gains from trade may not materialize; conceivably there could even be a loss from trade due to an increase in certain distortions".

[5] In fact, Smith argues that "If a foreign country can supply us with a commodity cheaper than we ourselves can make it, better buy it of them with some part of the produce of our own industry employed in a way in which we have some advantage" (Smith, 1776:401). He continues, "As long as the one country has those advantages, and the other wants them, it will always be more advantageous for the latter rather to buy of the former than to make" (Smith, 1776:403).

[6] As Smith puts it, the Mercantilists had sought to establish two fundamental points. First, "that wealth consisted of gold and silver"; and second, "that those metals could be brought into a country which had no mines only by the balance of trade, or by exporting to a greater value than it imported" (Smith, 1776:395-6).

[7] This is largely because the cultivation of bananas requires soils of a certain mineral composition as well as weather and climatic conditions that are only readily available in the tropics.

[8] In the Eastern Caribbean for instance, while average yields per hectare ranged from 9.9 to 12.3 metric tons in the 1980s, in the neighboring French DOMs yields of between 30 and 40 metric tons were common on certain farms (FAO, 1986:27-9).

[9] See G. Haberler (1936) *The Theory of International Trade.* London, UK: W. Hodge and Co., particularly chapters 9-10.

[10] Factor proportions in banana production are expected to depend on the production technology utilized. In the traditional system of production, labour is the dominant factor while increasing levels of capital and technology tend to characterize the semi-modern and modern systems, respectively. See Fonsah, E. and A. Chidebelu (1996) *Economics of Banana Production and Marketing in the Tropics: A Case Study of Cameroon.* Montreux, London and Washington: Minerva Press.

[11] Major contributions to the NTTs are found in the works of Krugman (1979), Dixit and Norman (1980), Lancaster (1980), Helpman (1981) Ethier (1982), Brander and Spencer (1985) and Grossman and Helpman (1991). All of these works use models of monopolistic competition for modelling trade under imperfect competition.

[12] With his monopolistically competitive Chamberlinian model of trade, Krugman (1994:19) argues that "economies of scale can be shown to give rise to trade and to gains from trade even when there is no international differences in tastes, technology, or factor endowments", although he acknowledges that the model cannot predict which country will export which good; but is able to determine the volume of trade.

[13] This model of trade is developed in some detail in P. R. Krugman (1994) *Rethinking International Trade.* Cambridge, MA: The MIT Press. For further discussion of trade under imperfect competition, see E. Helpman, and P. R. Krugman (1989) *Trade Policy and Market Structure.* Cambridge, MA: The MIT Press.

[14] We have also seen that an even higher degree of concentration exists at the level of the world banana trade, where three transnationals account for approximately 70 per cent of the market, with a similar feature characterizing both the American and Japanese banana markets.

[15] See, for instance, J. Roche (1998) *The International Banana Trade.* Cambridge, UK: Woodhead Publishing Limited; particularly, pp. 114-5 on these TNC advantages.

[16] In fact, the importance of concentration in the banana industry is a phenomenon that is common to the major banana importing regions of the world. Concentration in the US banana industry is also extremely high, where three TNCs "...United Brands, Castle and Cooke, and Del Monte – account for approximately 90 per cent of market sales" (Litvak and Maule, 1977:537).

[17] Oligopoly is most useful in analysing the EU's banana import business, although evidence also suggests the presence of oligopsony. However, given the rather similar approaches to explaining both oligopoly and oligopsony, a detailed treatment of one could lead sufficiently to inferences about the other.

[18] For a detailed treatment of each of these, see Shapiro (1989:330-414).

[19] Details of the findings and conclusions in the cases can be found in Bain (1968:Chapters 4-8).

[20] According to Bain (1968:251) barriers to entry essentially measure the extent of disadvantages that new sellers face should they try to compete in an industry. These barriers could be one of four types: (i) Blockaded entry – maximum entry forestalling price is so high as to be above the full joint monopoly price at which the established firms would maximize total industry profits. (ii) Effectively impeded entry – the maximum entry forestalling price is below that which would maximize total industry profits and above minimal average costs, and the established firms expect that it will yield them greater long-run profits than a higher price that would attract entry. (iii) Ineffectively impeded entry – the limit is below that which would maximize total profits and above minimal average costs, but low enough so that the established firms expect to make greater long-run profits by charging a higher price and inducing entry. (iv) Easy entry, or no barriers to entry (Bain, 1968:274).

[21] Bain (1968:233) argues that product differentiation in an industry exerts influence on prices, market shares, and the scope of market conduct open to sellers. Additionally, it could result from: differences in quality of design; ignorance of buyers regarding characteristics of goods being bought; persuasive sales promotion through advertising; gift or prestige goods; or differences in locations of sellers (Bain, 1968:226-8).

[22] See, for instance, Norman Collins and Lee Preston (1961) "The Size Structure of the Largest Industrial Firms, 1909-1958", *The American Economic Review*, 51:986-1003.

[23] See, for instance, Jacques Viaene and Xavier Gellynck (1995) "Structure, conduct and performance of the European food sector", *European Review of Agricultural Economics*, 22(3):282-95.

[24] The tractability problem has two dimensions: first, indicators of comparison tend to be of a strict qualitative nature, in which definitions could be rather arbitrary; and second, it is difficult to attach a measure of statistical significance to the results. Examples of both these problems are evident in the findings and conclusions section in the recent work of Viaene and Gellynck (1995:291-4).

[25] As observed by Bresnahan and Schmalensee (1987:372), while "some econometric industry studies were done in the 1970s, the early part of that decade saw the publication of many more cross-section studies of industry-level, government-supplied data." However, that approach was criticized extensively on the grounds "that industry-level cross-section data could not be used to identify and estimate structural relationships of interest" (Bresnahan and Schmalensee, 1987:373).

[26] The NEIO method stresses systematic statistical analysis and focuses on single industries or groups of closely related industries, and there is a tendency to focus on individual firms as the unit of observation (Bresnahan and Schmalensee, 1987:373-4).

[27] A Nash equilibrium is one in which each agent is doing the best that he can given what other agents are doing. As McMillan (2001:9) puts it, in a Nash equilibrium "No agent can do better than play his Nash strategy given that all the other agents are playing their Nash strategies." This concept was first formalized by the mathematician John Nash in 1951. For an introduction to Nash's seminal work, see: John Nash (1951) "Non-Cooperative Games", *Annals of Mathematics*; and John Nash (1950) "The Bargaining Problem", *Econometrica*.

[28] The models of Cournot and Bertrand oligopoly discussed here draw heavily upon the work of Carl Shapiro in his contribution "Theories of Oligopoly Behaviour" to the *Handbook of Industrial Organization*. Volume 1, 1989.

[29] Where x_1 corresponds to output produced by firm 1 and x_2 corresponds to output produced by firm 2.

[30] Here $C_i'(x_i)$ refers to the first derivative of the cost function for the ith firm and

$$i = 1 \text{ or } 2. \text{ So that } C_1'(x_1) = \frac{\partial C(x_1)}{\partial x_1} \text{ and } C_2'(x_2) = \frac{\partial C(x_2)}{\partial x_2}.$$

[31] The reaction curve for a firm shows how much it will produce as a function of how much it believes the other firm will produce, and so the reaction curve of firm 1 is a decreasing schedule of how much it believes firm 2 will produce and *vice versa*.

[32] Of course if we assume firms to be symmetric then all firms have equal market shares.

[33] The Bertrand model of oligopoly suggests that "with prices as strategic variables, each of two rival firms would have a strong incentive to undercut the other's price in order to capture the entire market" (Shapiro, 1989:344).

[34] Moreover, Shapiro has argued that Bertrand equilibria cannot exist in pure strategies unless it is assumed that firms exhibit constant returns. Where firms enjoy increasing returns to scale, "<u>destructive competition</u> drives prices down to marginal cost, but this cannot be an equilibrium as prices then fail to cover average costs" (Shapiro, 1989:344; emphasis in original).

[35] The basis of this model is the profit-maximization problem that faces an oligopolist, and is simulated using conjectural variations.

[36] The study uses rice export data for the 1961-85 period for Thailand, Pakistan and China (Karp and Perloff, 1989:465-6).

[37] Based on data in FAO (1986) and several other sources in the author's database.

[38] It is worthwhile to note that Deodhar and Sheldon (1995) have conducted a study to estimate the degree of market power in the German banana market for the pre-SEM period *only*. That study found the German market to be imperfectly competi-

tive and that firms were marking up price above marginal cost (Deodhar and Sheldon, 1995:345-6).

[39] In fact, we have demonstrated in Chapter 3 that firms do, indeed, command some degree of market power through branding of bananas, with Chiquita receiving the highest price and unbranded or fourth class bananas receiving the lowest.

[40] As Dunning puts it, while the theory of the transnational corporation (TNC) seeks to explain the existence and growth of TNCs, the theory of the activities of TNCs aims to identify and evaluate the determinants of foreign-owned production of such firms. Thus, while the former is concerned with the reasons for transnationality of firms at the micro level the latter is concerned with explaining the factors influencing the ability and willingness of groups of firms or countries to engage in foreign value-added activities (Dunning, 1996:27).

[41] As Cantwell (2000:12) put it, in this approach authors adopt a Coasian or institutionalist view of the firm as a device for raising efficiency by replacing markets. Teece (1982:1), for instance, attempts to "dimentionalize the transactions cost properties of the multinational enterprise in such a fashion that the theory predicts when and where the internalization of economic activity within the firm is likely to be the more efficient mode for organizing economic activity". Emphasis is placed on the transactions cost properties of multinationals, which, for Teece, explain why plants in different countries are likely to fall under common ownership and control as opposed to trading with each other through contracts (Teece, 1982:12).

[42] While Dunning (1996) represents one of the author's most recent works, the eclectic theory of FDI has been developed since the early 1970s. See, for instance, Dunning (1973) 'The Determinants of International Production', *Oxford Economic Papers*, 25:289-336; Dunning (1979) 'Explaining Changing Patterns of International Production: In Defence of Eclectic Theory', *Oxford Bulletin of Economics and Statistics*, 41:269-95; and Dunning (1980) 'Towards an Eclectic Theory of International Production: Some Empirical Test', *Journal of International Business Studies*, II:9-31.

[43] Among other noted theoretical explanations of FDI are the capital arbitrage and appropriability theories. Capital arbitrage theory views the TNC as a firm which essentially transfers equity capital from countries where returns are low to those where they are high, earning economic rents in the process. This theory predicts that TNCs would be based mainly in countries that are generously endowed with capital (with low domestic marginal productivity of capital) and that they would arbitrage capital towards countries less so endowed, where the marginal productivity of capital is higher (Teece, 1982:35). The appropriability theory promotes the view that the most important consideration facing innovating transnationals is the possible loss of their technology to rivals and copiers. Therefore, it is more efficient and desirable to transfer high technology to other countries from inside the firm than through the market, since there would be less likelihood of the technology

being copied and stolen by outsiders if under control of a single firm (Teece, 1982:39).

[44] Developed in his Ph.D. thesis in 1960, Hymer's seminal work entitled *The International Operations of National Firms: A Study of Direct Foreign Investment*, was published by The MIT Press in 1976. Hymer (1976:23-5) identified two motives for foreign direct investment, both of which are linked to *control* of the foreign enterprise. In the first type of foreign investment, control is sought "to ensure safety of his investment", while in the second type of foreign investment, control is sought "in order to remove competition between that foreign enterprise and enterprises in other countries" or "to appropriate fully the returns on certain skills and abilities".

[45] According to Cantwell (2000:12) Hymer's original framework for analysing transnational production views the TNC as an agent for market power and collusion, and has been subsequently developed using both Marxist [Baran and Sweezy, 1966] and non-Marxist [Cowling and Sugden, 1987] modes of analysis.

[46] Dunning and Rugman (1985:4) contend that internalization is not necessarily a bad thing leading to the exploitation of monopoly power. In fact, they insist that if "an exogenous market imperfection leads the MNE to organize an internal market as a substitute for either a missing regular (external) market...then the process of internalization improves efficiency". Hence, if the MNE is exercising transaction-cost power no rents are expected to accrue to it.

[47] While the transaction cost approach (briefly discussed) to the TNC is important for explaining the EU banana trade, the author holds the view that it is a combination of control and the ability of TNCs to exploit monopoly surplus through imperfect competition that is central in explaining the EU banana trade.

[48] As Cantwell (2000:17) put it, where "the transaction costs of an administered exchange are lower than those of a market exchange, then the market is internalized and the collective efficiency of the group is thereby increased".

[49] Teece supports his argument with empirical evidence on the investment of American enterprises abroad. Drawing upon the work of Pugel (1978), he argues that US manufacturing industries with greater involvement in natural resources tend to invest larger proportions of their assets abroad. Additionally, drawing upon the seminal work of Stuckey (1981) he argues that in the aluminium industry, switching cost tends to be high for the ore refiner because alumina refining facilities need to be located physically close to bauxite mines in order to minimize transport costs. Moreover, they are designed to handle the properties of specific ores (Teece, 1982:27).

[50] As observed by Teece (1982:41), the eclectic theory also implies that changes in the outward or inward investment position of a particular country can be explained in terms of changes in the ownership and internalization advantages of its enterprises, relative to those of other nationalities, and/or changes in the location

specific endowments relative to those of other countries, as perceived by its own and foreign enterprises.

[51] Graham (2000) applies some concepts from non-cooperative game theory for understanding rivalry of TNC activity. He develops a model comprising two monopolists, initially in their national markets, who face insurmountable barriers to trade, then derives the conditions under which they would consider entering each others market.

[52] In fact, it has been argued that the modern corporation is a response to the need for firms to co-ordinate and control the high volume of throughput that is required to realize scale economies that arise from the ability of a firm to integrate and co-ordinate the flow of materials through its plant, rather than through greater specialization and subdivision of labour (Teece, 1982:3).

[53] In addition Lall (1996:51) argues that "Investment in highly protected import-substituting environments generated much lower benefits than those that were undertaken under export-oriented regimes, or those that were exposed to significant foreign competition".

[54] Manipulative transfer pricing is the process whereby TNCs strategically vary prices at which intra-firm trade takes place away from an appropriate or full-cost price. This is done in order to reduce the total taxes paid, as well as to bypass host-country controls over the repatriation of profits to hard currency areas (Gray, 1996:251). When a parent company sells to an affiliate abroad there might be several motivations for it to consider transfer-pricing manipulations, including: corporate profits tax, repatriation of profits or capital, responding to anti-monopoly charges and enlarging market share, among others. In all of these cases the TNC has an incentive to under-price its goods or service, except when its motive is to repatriate profits or capital, in which case it overprices the goods or services (Plasschaert, 1996:395).

[55] Lall (1996:62-3) argues that although TNCs might engage in undesirable practices including transfer pricing, predatory behaviour, or failure to allow linkage capabilities of local counterparts to develop, "Given the incentive and capability structures of the host economy, and considering only marginal changes in FDI...it would appear that TNCs *generally offer net benefits* to host developing countries"(emphasis in original).

[56] See J. M. Connor and W. F. Mueller (1977) 'The shaping of market structures by multinationals: Brazil, Mexico, and the United States', Staff Paper Series No. 120, Department of Agricultural and Applied Economics, University of Wisconsin-Madison.

[57] See M. Blomstrom (1994) 'Multinationals and market structure in Mexico', in C. R. Frischtak and R. S. Newfarmer (eds) *Transnational Corporations: Market Structure and Industrial Performance*. Volume 15, UNLTNC. London: Routledge, pp. 83-95.

[58] The methodology used in these studies is considered superior to that used by Vernon since it entails a more direct measure of competitive market effects by looking at the average market share of subsidiaries of TNCs from the United States in Brazil and Mexico.

[59] TNCs tend to grow through take-overs of domestic firms and/or raising barriers to entry linked to advertising and to economies of scale. All of these explanations of TNC growth are, of course, anti-competitive in nature.

[60] For Vernon (1966:198), the main production cost differences between a US producing facility and that from another developed country arise from scale economies and labour costs. Therefore, if scale economies are fully exploited, the principal differences are likely to be due to labour costs. It is with this guiding hypothesis in mind he further argues, that "...if labor cost differences are large enough to offset transport costs, then exports back to the United States may become a possibility as well" (Vernon, 1966:198-200).

[61] Vernon (1966:197) argues that since there are risks and uncertainties in investment abroad, "as long as the marginal production cost plus the transport cost of the goods exported from the United States is lower than the average cost of prospective production in the market of import, United States producers will presumably prefer to avoid an investment".

[62] It appears that in the presence of scale economies, protection might result in desirable outcomes for consumers. Krugman (1994) argues that, while in traditional trade models a tariff or import quota is always bad since both tend to depress welfare, with new trade theory protection could lead to inefficient scale production at one extreme, or increased scale of production to reap benefits to consumers at the other.

[63] These other means include borrowing on international markets, loans from the host country, or profits from other affiliates abroad.

[64] An example of the adverse effect of FDI on development is the net outflow of funds of $11.3 billion from Latin America in response to an inflow of $3.8 billion (Magdoff, 1966:198, cited in Ietto-Gillies, 1992:169).

[65] However, this does not mean that the banana chain as a whole is labour intensive. It is only the harvesting process, which requires careful handling to avoid spoilage, that is labour intensive.

[66] The problem of disease, and the need for ongoing research to contain it, is a recurrent concern in the banana business. According to Read (1986:321-2), "In the 1930s Sigatoka disease presented a major threat to the continued operations of UFCo and Standard Fruit (the major US banana TNCs)" and "after Sigatoka, research was switched to the problem of Panamá Disease. Panamá Disease attacks and destroys banana plants and then lies dormant in the soil after infection". See also Chapter 3 for further discussion.

[67] Like Read (1986), Teece (1982:28) advances the view that in the case of bananas, it is the co-ordination and scheduling of production and distribution that appears to give distinct advantages to the TNCs such as United Fruit Company (Chiquita).

[68] This is most characteristic of capital- and technology-intensive industries, such as automobiles, computers, aircraft, and electrical machinery. Control is exercised by the administrative headquarters of the TNCs (Dicken, 1998:9).

[69] Although not exhaustive, a list of these studies runs as follows: Peter Dicken (1998) *Global Shift: Transforming the World Economy* – contains case-studies on 'textiles and clothing', 'the automobile industry', 'the electronics industries' and the 'internationalization of services'; Gary Gereffi (1996) 'The Elusive Last Lap in the Quest for Developed-Country Status', in J. H. Mittelman (ed.) *Globalization: Critical Reflections* – contains case-studies on changing patterns in global manufacturing with reference to triangle manufacturing among Asia's newly industrialized countries; Korzeniewicz and Martin (1994) 'The Global Distribution of Commodity Chains', – looks at evidence on the global distribution and integration of production processes in relation to the existence of world economic zones; Laura Raynolds (1994) 'Institutionalizing Flexibility: A Comparative Analysis of Fordist and Post-Fordist Models of Third World Agro-Export Production', – looks at the configuration of firms in the non-traditional export sector of the Dominican Republic; and Goldfrank (1994) 'Fresh Demand: The Consumption of Chilean Produce in the United States', uses the concept to look at how changing patterns in the diets of US consumers affect the commodity chain for non-traditional fresh fruit imports from Chile.

[70] Their methodology entailed an analysis of the distribution of global GNP, which was done by plotting national population (as a percentage of total population) against the log of GNP per capita in current dollars over the 1938-91 period (Korzeniewicz and Martin, 1994:71).

[71] The stability of this relationship was established by plotting the modes of Log GNP per capita over time for the three economic zones of production identified in the global economy (core, periphery, and semi-periphery), and determining whether there was convergence or not.

[72] The authors used six commodities for this analysis: motor vehicles, tires, crude steel, cotton fiber, cotton yarn and wheat. Although wheat is a labour-intensive primary commodity, the share of industrialized countries in wheat production was larger than that of the lowest income countries.

[73] Raynolds defines the traditional agricultural export sector as comprising the commodities that historically prevailed and integrated Latin America and the Caribbean into the colonial-based international division of labour. For the Dominican Republic, these products include sugar, coffee, cocoa, and tobacco. In contrast, the non-traditional export sector is dominated by an array of specialty horticultural crops and off-season fruits and vegetables. It includes pineapples, melons, and oriental and winter vegetables.

[74] Advance monitoring is the process whereby an US Department of Agriculture representative inspects the fruit in the country of origin before it is sealed into containers for export, so that upon arrival in the US the fruit is allowed to pass through customs unhampered.

[75] Raynolds (1994:152) points out that the delays which small firms incur at the port of entry have in the past resulted in the loss of numerous shipments of produce due to discovery of pests and pesticide residues among the produce by US customs agents.

[76] In this case, the main advantages of vertical integration are the following: (i) it ensures the rapid and controlled movement of fresh produce, and (ii) it facilitates efficient feedback on any problems encountered during shipping (Raynolds, 1994:153).

[77] Under this arrangement, importers take 13-15 per cent commission on the selling price, with the balance going to the exporter (World Bank, 1985:92, cited in Raynolds, 1994:153).

[78] Since enterprises involved in this sector are relatively modest, they cannot afford the expensive advertising necessary to introduce these 'exotic' foods to the mass US consumer market. Therefore, only a few oriental vegetables, such as snow peas and Chinese eggplants, make it into large supermarkets (Raynolds, 1994:154).

[79] Of course, these firms are the same ones that were presented in Chapter 3 and Raynolds's argument simply reinforces the one we have made earlier on.

[80] Again, the exercise of dominant firm behaviour and market power by these transnationals.

[81] Based on own interviews with ripeners in the banana trade in Europe. As one ripener put it, vessels typically arrive in European ports on a Monday or Tuesday each week, by Wednesday the bananas are with ripeners and by Friday in the supermarkets.

[82] The case of St. Lucia is highly representative of all the remaining Eastern Caribbean islands. The only difference is at the production-wholesale buyer stage, which is characterized by a single firm in the other Eastern Caribbean islands, as opposed to two in St. Lucia.

[83] Until March 1998 only one firm, the Sate owned St. Lucia Banana Growers Association, bought bananas from all farmers, but in April 1998 it was privatized and became the St. Lucia Banana Corporation (SLBC). At about the same time, a rival firm – Tropical Quality Fruit (TQF) – was also created, which initially served the interest of primarily larger farmers. In principle, the farmers have the choice of selling their bananas to either of the firms. However, in practice farmers are required to be members of only one firm and essentially enter into some sort of contractual agreement with it. The firm provides farmers with production inputs, and general technical assistance, and is responsible to the farmer, for handling all

subsequent stages of the marketing process (author's interviews with firms and other industry sources).

[84] Based on numerous discussions (unstructured interviews) between the author and industry experts.

[85] Associate firms produce bananas under contract with the transnationals.

[86] We shall return to, and further develop this concept of a commodity in Chapter 5, which will argue in part that the effect of the WTO ruling in the case of the EU banana regime has been to call for a new concept of a commodity, along the lines of what has been proposed in the present chapter.

5 Lobbies, Market Power, and the Creation of World Trade Policy – the WTO Banana Dispute

Little of the orthodox literature of the theory of international trade addresses the question of the political sources of trade policies.

– Helleiner (1977:102)

5.1 Introduction

In Chapter 3 we discussed the structure of the world banana market and the conduct of TNCs in it. Particular attention was paid to the structure of the EU banana market and the conduct of firms there, with reference to the US banana market, from where several of the main TNCs originate and operate. The chapter argued that the international banana trade is characterized by an oligopolistic market structure in which dominant TNCs have repeatedly exercised anti-competitive behaviour. It further suggested that the WTO ruling against the EU's NBR was the culmination of actions of discontent exercised by several actors, all of which pursued different interests in the trade of the commodity.

However, the question of what motivated WTO action in the case of the EU's NBR remains. Was WTO action against the EU's NBR the outcome of discontent of individual nation states as envisaged by conventional trade theory, or are there other possibly more significant factors that explain the WTO action? Related to this, can we adequately interpret the WTO ruling in the context of conventional trade theory, or has that ruling necessitated the need to go beyond the theory? These questions are addressed in the present chapter, the remainder of which is organized as follows. Section 5.2 examines the interests of different actors in the EU banana trade and the extent to which such interests influenced the decision for establishment of a Panel. In section 5.3 we then isolate the US as the most influential nation-state in the process of establishment of the WTO Panel and demonstrate that the US action could be explained by the political contributions of one of its TNCs, Chiquita, to both the Democratic and Republican parties. The individual elements of the WTO Panel and Appellate Body rulings are then discussed in section 5.4, where the specific articles of world trade policy that the EU violated are identified. We then discuss the WTO Panel and Appellate Body rulings in the context of conventional international trade theory in section 5.5. Finally, the conclusions arising from this chapter are presented in section 5.6.

5.2   Different interests in the EU banana trade

When we discussed the structure of the EU banana trade and the different systems of organization that dominated various market segments in the pre-SEM period in Chapter 3, it became apparent that any common banana policy would have to reconcile divergent interests of various actors. Thus, while the banana does not feature prominently in international trade, where trade policy is concerned, it is the only commodity that has been subjected to every possible trade litigation procedure, both within the EU and in the WTO. Exactly why this is so is linked to the structure of the banana commodity chain and the relative power and interests of various actors involved in the production, shipping, marketing and distribution of the commodity. The major actors in the EU's banana commodity chain are: (i) producer organizations in supplier countries and their governments, (ii) consumer organizations in importing EU member-states and their governments, (iii) the European Commission, and (iv) TNCs that are linked variously at all stages of the commodity chain. Although it is largely the latter aspect – that is, the presence and role of TNCs in the banana commodity chain – that makes it so controversial, we examine the interests of each of these actors below.

5.2.1   Producer organizations and the exporting countries

The interest of all exporting countries is to maximize export revenue (sales), if not profits, from bananas. However, within the context of the NBR, the possibilities for doing so depend on whether or not the policy favours or discourages exports from certain countries, and so the interests of some countries are diametrically opposed to those of others.

Dollar-zone countries are by far the most efficient, with yields per hectare ranging from 36.4 to 45.5 metric tons and cost of production ranging from $162 to $200 per metric ton. This contrasts with production within EU territories, where yields range from 10 to 12 metric tons per hectare, and, in 1984 the f.o.b. cost for one metric ton of bananas was $334.10.[1] Although ACP countries are slightly more efficient than EU territories, they have considerably higher costs and lower yields per hectare than their dollar-zone trade rivals. These differences in productivity and cost of production of the exporting regions manifest themselves as differences in import prices in major destination markets in the EU (see Chapter 3).[2] We have also seen that c.i.f. prices in France for bananas produced in EU territories were consistently higher than those for dollar-zone bananas in Germany during the 1983-94 period, with the gap widening to 33 per cent in 1989. Additionally, there was far more convergence between ACP countries' and EU territories' c.i.f. prices, with a tendency for ACP countries' c.i.f. prices to be slightly lower in the 1980s while those of EU territories tend to be slightly lower at the beginning of the 1990s (Chapter 3).

Therefore, it was in the interest of dollar-zone producers that the EU implement as *laissez-faire* a banana import policy as possible, since such a policy would have resulted in an increase in their market share and export revenue.[3] On the other hand, it was in the interest of the EU territories and ACP countries that the EU implement as strict an import policy as possible so that they could retain a presence in the market.[4] Moreover, the EU found itself confronted by an even bigger dilemma concerning its choice of banana import policy where the supplier countries were concerned: its own territories and the ACP countries were more dependent on bananas for their survival than dollar-zone exporters, and so their economies were considerably more vulnerable to sudden changes in the pattern of trade (Chapter 3).[5]

5.2.2   Consumer organizations and the importing EU member-states

Considering the prevailing EU member-states' trade policies and the resulting patterns of trade during the pre-SEM period (Chapter 3), the considerable degree of heterogeneity that existed derived, at least in part, from their specific interests. For countries like France, Spain, Portugal and Greece the primary interest was the preservation of banana production in their respective overseas territories. Given a structural allocation of land for agriculture in their overseas territories in which bananas feature very prominently, any sudden reduction in exports would result in major economic and social unrest, at least in the short run.[6] But it seems that the concern in France might be more about the social and political consequences than the economic ones.[7] Although the Commission has intervened in various ways, providing subsidies, aid, and other financial schemes to encourage farmers to cease export production, such measures have not been particularly successful so far. Even had they been, they would most likely have resulted in increased structural unemployment.

Where countries like the UK and Italy are concerned, the primary interest has been to protect their investments in the banana business since World War II, while a secondary interest has been the preservation of political stability and economic viability of the very vulnerable ACP countries. Since the early 1950s, the UK has given loans and/or grants in excess of £100 million to Geest Industries, one of the largest EU banana TNCs *up to* the mid-1990s. Most of this investment went into the acquisition of a banana reefer fleet and the creation of ripening and distribution facilities in the UK. Additionally, at various times, particularly in the 1960s and 1970s, Geest either actually owned or had considerable interests in banana plantations in some Caribbean countries (Nurse and Sandiford, 1995). In 1995, in the face of increased competition since implementation of the SEM, Geest was acquired by a joint venture between Fyffes (Ireland) and WIBDECO (St. Lucia);[8] the assets for capitalization in the case of the latter firm comprised loans from a major Irish bank at market interest rates (Sandiford, 2000:51).[9] Although Italy had made similar investments in Somalia prior to World War II, those were not as successful, and, since the overthrow of Somalia's military regime in 1991, banana production there has plummeted (Chapter 2).

As for the remaining EU member-states, since they have no direct investment in the banana production business their sole interest was to consume the best-quality bananas at the lowest possible price. Questions of sustainable production and the *fairness* of trade have only recently been gaining in importance.[10] None of these countries have significant related economic investments in their producing trade partners, neither are they of significant strategic political importance. All the high-value-adding activities of dollar-zone bananas in Europe, that is, ocean transportation, ripening, marketing and distribution, take place largely under the control of US-based TNCs. These firms may form alliances with EU firms, particularly in the ripening and retail business, although their preferred form of corporate organization is vertical integration (see Chapter 3). Since the US TNCs account for more than 60 per cent of all EU banana trade, the banana business has become quite lucrative in these countries. Therefore, the interests of these EU member-states are linked closer with profits from the activities of the US TNCs, with whom a number of their firms have formed alliances (see Chapter 3), than with safeguarding the preferential access of ACP countries.

5.2.3   TNCs operating along EU banana commodity chains

Three categories of TNCs are involved in the EU banana importing business: (i) three US-based firms, Chiquita, Dole and Del Monte, which jointly account for approximately 70 and 60 per cent of world and EU banana trade, respectively; (ii) a few firms based in the UK and France, primarily Geest, Fyffes, and Pomona, which jointly account for approximately 10 and 15 per cent of world and EU banana trade, respectively; and (iii) a few smaller firms based in Latin America, primarily NOBOA and UNIBAN, which jointly account for less than 10 per cent of EU and world trade, respectively (Chapter 3). The distinguishing features of these categories of TNCs are their levels of capital stock and the geographic reach of their operations. Firms in the first category have a global scope of operations and command the highest levels of capital, while those in the third category are the most modest, both in terms of levels of capital investment and scope of operations. Firms in the second category tend to concentrate their activities *within* the EU market, but operate at slightly higher levels of capitalization than those in the third category (Chapter 3).

At the very least, all of these firms have the common interest of maximizing sales, if not profits, which translates to market share and power. However, in practical terms, there exists some variation in strategic interests across categories, in particular within those from the US. The pattern of involvement of the US-based TNCs has tended to favour vertically integrated systems, from ownership of plantation production to ocean transportation, ripening and retail sale in Europe. Since the banana commodity chain is highly capital intensive and demand for bananas is highly income- and price-inelastic, these firms have pursued strategies of anti-competitive behaviour by creating huge barriers to entry.[11] At the same time, the higher levels of efficiency that they enjoy due to economies of scale and co-ordination of all stages of the commodity chain results in extremely low per unit costs and high product quality. These firms obtain all their bananas for export to the EU either from their own plantations or through contractual agreements with grower associations in the dollar-zone (Chapter 3). As such, it was in their interest that the EU implement a *laissez-faire* banana import policy, since it would strengthen their market positions, both in terms of shares and profits.

Conversely, the pattern of involvement of the EU-based TNCs has not tended to vertical integration throughout their respective commodity chains. Their role has been restricted to the higher-value-adding stages of the commodity chain: ocean transportation, ripening, marketing and distribution (Nurse and Sandiford, 1995:34-8). In fact, EU-based TNCs do not typically own plantations in producing countries; instead, production is owned by local farmers and takes place on small-holdings, typically of 5 hectares or less (Chapter 3). The principal sources of supply of their bananas have been EU territories and ACP countries. Since these firms are generally much smaller than their US rivals and have higher production costs in supplier countries, their per unit costs have been higher, making them less competitive. Consequently, it was in their interest that the EU implement as protectionist a banana import policy as possible so that they could retain their market positions.

The final category comprises the Latin American TNCs, in which the Ecuadorian TNC, NOBOA, plays a dominant role. For reasons similar to those of the TNCs of US origin, it was in their interest that the EU implement as *laissez-faire* a banana import policy as possible. Lower banana prices in the EU would present opportunities for them to increase market shares and profits, provided that such price decreases resulted in significantly increased consumption.

5.2.4   Difficulties confronting the European Commission and Parliament

As the technical arm of the EU, the European Commission was confronted by challenges that were far more diverse than those facing any other actor in the EU banana trade. In pursuance of its objective of the SEM, the European Commission was required to implement a banana import policy that would result in increased consumption, efficiency and economic welfare, but without increasing tensions between EU member-states or jeopardizing relations between the EU and its trading partners. At the same time, it needed to implement a banana import policy consistent with the EU's obligations to WTO members, particularly under the completed Uruguay Round of the GATT [1994] and the GATS.

Yet, when we consider the preceding discussion of the interests of the various actors involved in the EU banana trade, it is clear that reconciling their differences could not have been straightforward. If the Commission had chosen a *laissez-faire* trade policy, it would have improved trade relations with dollar-zone countries, increased tensions between EU member-states and jeopardized relations with the ACP countries.[12] Conversely, had the Commission chosen a very protectionist trade policy, it would have increased tensions between EU member-states, jeopardized relations with dollar zone countries and preserved relations with ACP countries.[13] But the relations with ACP countries could not have been systematically bypassed, since these relations represent a long history of trade and development co-operation, which is legally binding through the Lomé Convention. Additionally, the strategic economic and political interests of various EU member-states (see above) in the pre-SEM period had to be taken into consideration. Consequently, the Commission adopted the position that the prevailing pattern of trade in the pre-SEM period should be preserved, at least in the short run, even if it appeared that such a decision might be inconsistent with its commitments to the WTO.

5.3   Challenges to the EU's NBR by different actors

Against a background of various actors with contrasting interests and the radically different banana import policies of EU member-states, it is not surprising that the NBR made necessary by the implementation of the SEM could not simultaneously satisfy all the actors. Even at its conceptual formulation stage, the proposed EU banana regime caused considerable disagreement between the actors. Below we examine the nature of the disagreement and the extent to which the different actors contributed to the demise of the EU's NBR.

5.3.1   Challenges to the NBR by EU member-states

Since the proposed NBR was opposed by Germany, Denmark and the Benelux countries on the grounds that it would not fulfil the objectives of the single market and was likely to impact adversely upon the welfare of consumers, several modifications were introduced before its adoption for implementation in July 1993.[14] The modifications included monthly adjustments of the quota in line with demand; licensing arrangements that would not disadvantage traditional importers from Latin America; and the treatment of any significant rise in price as an indication of shortage, which would require a review of the NBR (Sutton, 1997:14).

In a last attempt to prevent its implementation, German consumers, importers and the government lodged an injunction with the European Court of Justice against the proposed NBR.[15] On 29 June 1993 the European Court of Justice disallowed the injunction and hence paved the way for the implementation of the NBR as from 1 July 1993 (European Court of Justice, 1993:para. 55). That ruling has led legal scholars and practitioners to pose the question of who should be the final judge of constitutionality in Europe (Kumm, 1998; Everling, 1996; Kuilwijk, 1996a; Kuilwijk, 1996b), causing the contentious banana regime to contribute to the setting of another precedent.[16]

5.3.2   Challenges to the NBR by dollar-zone exporting countries under the GATT

Several countries in Latin America responded with hostility towards the EU's NBR through joint action, following consultations between themselves at a special meeting called by Ecuador in February 1993.[17] Specifically, these countries appealed to the GATT for its intervention and issued a joint declaration, which charged that the EU's banana import policy was protectionist, discriminatory and restrictive (Sutton, 1997:18). However, since these actions yielded no satisfactory results the complaining countries formally referred the matter to the GATT. They called upon the GATT to establish two panels: the first was to examine the pre-SEM banana import policies of EU member-states, and the second to examine the NBR implemented in July 1993. The first Panel found that the quantitative restrictions in force in France, Italy, Spain, Portugal and the UK were inconsistent with both the relevant articles of the GATT and the existing legislation under which member-states of the EU had become contracting parties to the GATT. Specifically, the Panel found that the preferential tariff on bananas originating from ACP countries was inconsistent with Article 1 of the GATT and that the EU's obligations under the Lomé Convention were not a sufficient legal basis for granting such a preference (GATT, 1993:67-83). Although these findings had no practical implications for the EU since a new import policy was due to come into force shortly,[18] EU and ACP countries jointly opposed adoption of the panel report when the GATT Council met in June 1993.[19]

The second Panel presented its report on 18 January 1994. It deplored the legal shortcomings of the NBR, finding that both the NBR and the procedure through which the EU extended its Lomé preferences to ACP countries were in contravention to the rules of the GATT (GATT, 1994:para. 169-70). Additionally, while it recognized that the EU had a legal obligation to discharge to ACP countries, the panel was of the view that the proper way of doing so was by seeking a waiver from the GATT on an annual basis (GATT, 1994:para. 168). In response to the Panel report, the EU adopted a two-prong strategy to defuse the problem:[20] seeking the support of ACP countries to prevent the GATT Council's adoption of the report and creating a Framework Agreement for banana imports with some Latin American countries.[21] In addition to guaranteeing market shares for these countries, the EU agreed to expand the tariff quota annually and reduce the in-quota tariff to ECU 75 per metric ton (European Council, 1998:Article 18).

Although at that stage the US had not initiated any direct action against the EU banana regime, in negotiating the Framework Agreement the EU had attempted to pursue a pre-emptive strategy. It had ensured that the Framework Agreement was agreed to by the US as part of the completion of negotiations under the Uruguay Round.[22] Meanwhile, the GATT Council agreed to grant the EU a waiver of Article I.1, thus allowing the EU to give preferential treatment to the goods originating from the ACP countries (European Commission, 1995:16). Therefore, as discussed below, it appears that subsequent action by the US against the EU's banana regime could only be explained by Chiquita's vigorous lobbying of both the Democratic and Republican parties. In so doing, Chiquita took advantage of both its authoritative market power position in the world banana trade and its political connections with major players in the US to dictate EU banana trade policy.

5.3.3   Challenges to the EU's NBR by the US and the Chiquita factor

The US' official challenges to the EU's NBR commenced in the autumn of 1994, when Chiquita Brands International filed an application with the office of the US Trade Representative (USTR)[23] for an inquiry into the EU banana regime under Section 301 of the US Trade Act.[24] Chiquita alleged that the implementation of the EU's NBR had resulted in considerable damage to its business interests and so it sought the intervention of the US government in the matter (USTR, 1995).[25] The initial reaction of the US was cautious because no GATT precedent existed allowing a country that was not an exporter of the commodity in question to seek suspension of concessions against a producer, and the US was not an exporter of bananas.[26] Moreover, it was common knowledge at the highest level in the US that some Caribbean countries, while highly dependent on bananas, were also among the most inefficient producers, which made them extremely vulnerable to any sudden change in the pattern of trade.[27] For these reasons the US had always supported the Caribbean's EU banana preferences as both internal memoranda of the USTR and communiqués between the US and Caribbean governments show (Barlett and Steele, 2000:4).[28] However, Chiquita now made two moves that brought about a shift in US' position on EU banana trade policy. First, it convinced the

Hawaii Banana Industry Association to submit a joint application requesting
action under Section 301 (Sutton, 1997:25).[29] Second, it initiated vigorous
and expensive lobbying of both the Republican and Democratic parties of
the US.

It is estimated that Chiquita and affiliated firms and individuals made
financial contributions in excess of $5 million dollars to the Democratic and
Republican parties between 1990 and 1999 (Figure 5.1).[30]

Fig. 5.1   *Chiquita's financial contributions to the Democratic and*
             Republican parties in the US (1991-99)

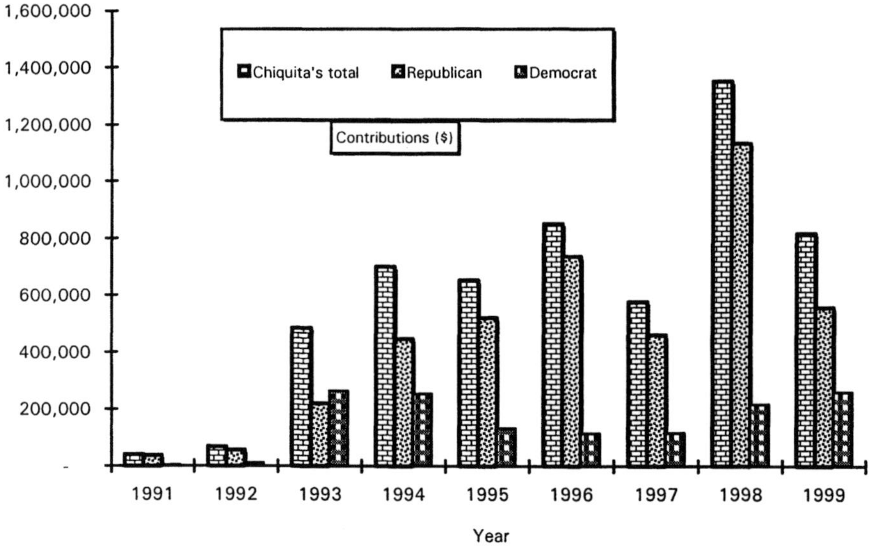

Source: Barlett and Steele (2000)

Although the Republican Party's share of Chiquita's contributions most
of the time exceeded that of the Democratic Party, when the Democrats
assumed the presidency in 1992 there was a shift in Chiquita's financial
contributions towards the Democratic Party (Figure 5.1). Moreover, in
December 1994 alone, Carl Lindner, Chairman and Chief Executive of
Chiquita Brands International, contributed $250,000 to the Democratic
National Committee (Barlett and Steele, 2000:2-3).[31] By thus increasing the
level of its financial contributions to the Democratic Party, Chiquita ensured
that both the Congress and the Executive would be prepared to act on its
behalf.

In fact, there appears to be a strong relationship between the financial
contributions of Chiquita to the various political parties and the severity of

political action that the US government subsequently undertook against the EU's banana regime (Figure 5.2).[32]

Fig. 5.2   *Relationship between the financial contributions of Chiquita to US political parties and political action against the EU's NBR*

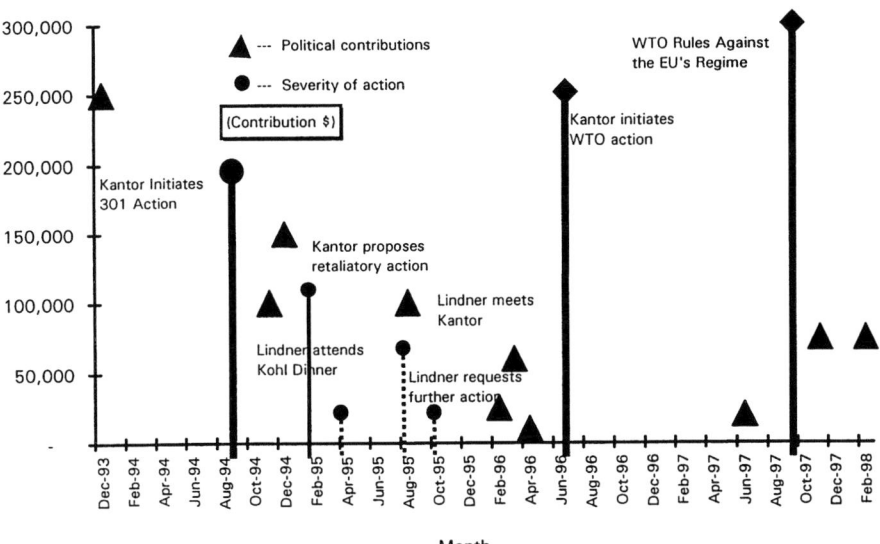

Source: Author's construction based on data from Barlett and Steele (2000).

Chiquita's lobbying appears to have paid off rather swiftly: as early as January 1995, the USTR indicated that the results of its preliminary investigation into the EU's NBR confirmed that it adversely affected the US' economic interest.[33] In December of that year, the USTR confirmed that it would file a complaint with the WTO because the system of allocation of licences and the assignment of quotas discriminated against US firms. Subsequently, in June 1996, the USTR requested the WTO to establish a panel. The relationship between Chiquita's financial contributions and political actions taken by the US government is quite revealing (Figure 5.2).

Whereas prior to October 1994, Chiquita's task was to get the US' government to engage in the dispute with the EU, which it achieved by making a very large contribution, once the USTR had initiated a Section 301 action, Chiquita's strategy shifted to making slightly smaller but more frequent contributions at critical moments until WTO action commenced. Interestingly, while the matter was under consideration in the WTO, both the level and frequency of financial contributions diminished considerably, since it had then become a *national* issue.[34] But Chiquita was not alone in the campaign to dismantle the EU's NBR. The disunity among Latin American exporters over the Framework Agreement provided a source of leverage for the US, since it convinced the countries that had not accepted the Agreement to join with it in requesting a Panel against the banana regime.[35] The fact that most of the Complaining Parties were banana-exporting countries made it extremely difficult, if not impossible, for the WTO to dismiss the case.

5.4   WTO dispute and rulings of the Panel and Appellate Body

The WTO dispute process began on 5 February 1996, with joint and individual requests for consultations with the European Communities by Ecuador, Guatemala, Honduras, Mexico and the US. Consultations were requested on the regime for importation, sale and distribution of bananas established under Regulation (EEC) 404/93,[36] as well as subsequent legislation, regulations and administrative processes related to it.[37] However, since the consultations were unsuccessful, the Complaining Parties requested the establishment of a Panel on 11 April 1996. Their request covered a rather broad scope to include violations under the GATT, the Agreement on Import Licensing Procedures, the Agreement on Agriculture, the GATS, and the Agreement on Trade Related Investment Measures.[38] The Dispute Settlement Body (DSB) established the Panel on 8 May 1996 and provided specific terms of reference for its work (WTO, 1997a:1).[39]

In its defence, the EU deplored the manner in which the panel had been established, questioning the adequacy of consultations[40] as well as the clarity of the issue[41] under dispute. However, the Complaining Parties countered that their action was consistent with Article 4.7 of the DSU, which provides for establishment of a Panel 60 days after the start of consultations (WTO, 1997a:3-7). Additionally, the EU questioned the legitimacy of the US' interests in the claim that was being pursued, since there was no banana trade between those countries. The US argued in turn that it had a significant commercial interest since two of its firms, Chiquita and Dole, had played a major role in developing the EU's banana market in the past. Moreover, the US argued that under Article XXIII of the GATT, dispute settlement action could be initiated by any Member if, in its view, one Member's action was inconsistent with another's interests (WTO,

1997a:8-9). What seems to be clear from the arguments leading up to the establishment of the Panel is that while the EU had sought to create a regime based on good faith, the Complaining Parties essentially ignored that motive and placed emphasis on the letter of the law.

In its ruling against the EU's banana regime, the Panel concluded that certain aspects of the regime were inconsistent with its obligations under Articles I:1, III:4, X:3 and XIII:1 of the GATT,[42] Article 1.2 of the Licensing Agreement and Articles II and XVII of the GATS.[43] Additionally, it recommended that the Dispute Settlement Body request the EU to modify its banana regime, to make it conform with its obligations under the GATT, the Licensing Agreement and the GATS (WTO, 1997a: para. 9.1- 9.2).

The EU was not prepared to concede defeat and immediately announced its intention to appeal certain issues of law as well as some of the legal interpretations developed by the Panel on 11 June 1997 (WTO, 1997b: para. 2). In its appeal, the EU again took issue with the right of the US to advance claims under the GATT and the manner in which the Panel had been established (WTO, 1997b: paras. 15-18). Where the legal interpretations of the Panel were concerned, the EU brought many issues into question, taking them in turn under the categories of measures affecting trade in goods and services. Regarding measures affecting trade in goods, the EU challenged the Panel's interpretation of: the Agreement on Agriculture; Articles I:1, III:4 and XIII of the GATT; the Lomé Convention as well as the scope of the Lomé Waiver; and the Licensing Agreement.[44] Additionally, it brought into question the difficulty of simultaneously fulfilling obligations under Articles I:1 and X:3(a) of the GATT and Article 1.3 of the Licensing Agreement (WTO, 1997b: paras. 19-39).

Where the measures affecting trade in services were concerned, the EU argued that the broad scope of interpretation of the GATS by the Panel had resulted in "a 'total overlap' between the GATT 1994 and the other Annex 1A agreements of the *WTO Agreement*, on the one hand, and the GATS on the other hand." (WTO, 1997b: para. 40).[45] Moreover, the EU argued that the Panel erred in assuming that the drafters of the GATS desired to widen its scope by substituting the term "delivery of a service" with "supply of a service". This is because it would still need to be shown that the measures concerned had been taken in respect of the production, marketing, sale and delivery of a service, as the term is defined under Article XXVIII(b) of the GATS (WTO, 1997b: para. 42).[46]

The Appellate Body largely upheld the findings of the Panel. In particular, it upheld the Panel's conclusion that the US had a right to bring a claim in the dispute and that the establishment of the Panel was consistent with requirements under Article 6.2 of the DSU (WTO, 1997b: para. 255ab). Additionally, it upheld the conclusion of the Panel that the Agreement on Agriculture did not permit the EU to act in a manner inconsistent with its obligations under Article XIII of the GATT 1994; and that the allocation of shares of the tariff quota was not consistent with Article XIII:1 of the GATT 1994 (WTO, 1997b: para. 255d-e).

5.5   WTO rulings and the conventional theories of international trade

Until the advent of the WTO ruling in the case of the EU's NBR, there existed clear lines of demarcation between what constituted a violation under the GATS as opposed to that under the GATT. Essentially, GATS violations were originally intended to cover trade in services and the services sector in general, while GATT violations were intended to apply to the trade in physical goods. In the case of the EU's NBR, however, both the Panel and Appellate Body have adopted a broad interpretation of the scope of coverage of the GATS. Consequently, the distinction between violations under the GATT and the GATS is rather blurred and it poses a major challenge to the conventional theories of international trade, where the definition of the concept of a commodity is concerned.

During its evolution from the classical traditions based on absolute advantage (Smith, 1776) to comparative advantage (Ricardo, 1817) and factor endowments (Heckscher, 1919; Ohlin, 1933; Samuelson, 1948) international trade theory had always focused on physical goods and assumed perfectly competitive markets. The contributions of the 1960s sought to explain why new products were developed at different times in different regions of the world due to differences in technology (Posner, 1961) or development cycle (Vernon, 1966). However, these approaches retained the perfect competition assumptions of earlier theory. It was only with the advent of the 'new trade theories' that a decisive attempt was made to relax the assumptions of perfect competition in modelling international trade. In fact, the major contribution of the 'new trade theories' is that the existence of economies of scale within a firm producing a commodity results in imperfect competition and a certain degree of monopoly power in markets (Krugman, 1994; Helpman and Krugman, 1985; Helpman, 1981). The 'new trade theories' predict that under free trade different forms of market structure could lead to different welfare effects (Helpman and Krugman, 1989).[47] Yet, even the 'new trade theories' restrict their analysis to the point where the commodity's crossing the border into the foreign country constitutes a final transaction. Moreover, not even the extensive literature on theories of the TNC (Chapter 4) has focused on the value-adding stages of a commodity chain as a basis for explaining welfare effects of trade policy reform. It follows that, whether or not commodities are subjected to further transformation or value-adding processes after clearance at a border has hardly been taken into consideration in conventional trade theory for explaining the potential welfare effects of trade policy reforms.[48]

The analysis undertaken in this chapter therefore suggests that there are two potential problems with the WTO ruling from the point of view of conventional international trade theories. First, conventional trade theories advocate *laissez-faire* as *the* optimal trade policy, on the assumption that individual firms in international trade cannot exercise market power and so the lobbying by TNCs, for instance, cannot influence trade policy. Yet, we have argued that not only do certain firms in the EU banana trade possess market power, but also that the Chiquita TNC has demonstrated its ability and willingness to exercise such power by lobbying political parties in the US to affect EU banana trade policy. Unfortunately, since the WTO envisions its members as commanding equal 'market power', the question of violations of the covered agreements and their implications for trade policy reform only arises within the context of one member not fulfilling its obligations to other members, whereas the driving force behind trade policy reforms might be the power of TNCs, instead.

The second effect of the WTO ruling against the EU's NBR is to extend the reach of international trade to include all processes that a physical commodity might be subjected to, even after it has entered into a foreign country. The implications are that the concept of a commodity in international trade has to be redefined to include the services that the physical commodity might be subjected to at any stage from its original point of production to its final point of consumption. Therefore, conceptually, a commodity should comprise a physical good embodied within a 'vector' of services, the importance of which changes over space and time.

5.6 Conclusions

The preceding analysis leads to three conclusions. First, a combination of the historical trade policies and patterns of trade of individual EU member-states, as well as the divergent and conflicting interests of the various actors, explains the instability of the EU's NBR. Reconciling these differences is further complicated by the fact that individual EU member-states continue to maintain strong bilateral ties with specific countries, whose interests in some cases are given precedence over the collective interest of the Union (Peers, 1999).[49]

Second, the processes that led to the establishment of a WTO Panel to investigate the EU's NBR demonstrate the power that one TNC can command in influencing international trade policy, contradicting the prevailing assumption of international trade theory that since individual firms do not possess market power they cannot shape world trade policy. This supports the independent conclusions of Helleiner (1977:115) that US trade policy is primarily the product of political pressures from its TNCs. Coupled with the strong oligopolistic market structure (Chapter 3), it casts doubt on whether or not, and the extent to which consumers in the EU are likely to gain economic welfare in a fully liberalized banana market.[50] Yet, at the same time, the loss of rents from market access of high-cost Caribbean producers is not likely to be transferred to the lower-cost Latin American producers, but to the US TNCs that operate there.[51] We shall further develop this argument in Chapters 6 and 7 where we analyse the division of wealth.

Third, the ruling might have profound implications both for the future of the working of the dispute settlement process in the WTO and for conventional theory of international trade. The US' claim that any member can bring a complaint against any other has the effect of pushing international trade law to its limit and, in the process, a precedent has been established: that trade in physical goods could become subject to very broad rules that were primarily intended to cover trade in services. An immediate consequence of this precedent is that it has made it possible for unpredictable and undesirable action by members when retaliating[52] and calls for a definition of a commodity as a physical good embodied within a "vector" of services, the importance of which changes over space and time. Additionally, the numerous preferential agreements (regarding trade in goods) that exist between many countries could now all be subject to measures under the GATS, in addition to those under GATT 1994.[53]

In demonstration of its resolve to create a system that works not only in the interest of US TNCs but for all the actors involved in the trade of the commodity, the EU has endured the suspension of its trade concessions by the US for over one year.[54] After a protracted period of indecision and further challenges to the EU's proposals to revise its NBR, in April 2001 the US and EU arrived at an understanding in the banana dispute.[55] Consequently, the dollar-zone countries have finally agreed to a request by the EU for a conditional waiver from WTO rules in order to fulfil its obligations to the ACP countries under the Cotonou Agreement, and in turn, the EU has promised to replace all its banana quotas with tariffs by 1

January 2006.[56] However, while accepting the inevitability of their loss of EU preferences, Caribbean governments have argued that the Commission's proposal for re-allocation of licenses will result in decreasing market share.[57]

Notes

[1] All prices in current dollars.

[2] However, it should be noted that differences in cost of production only explain part of the differences in import price. Equally, if not more important, are the superior economies of scale in shipping dollar-zone bananas than ACP and EU bananas to various ports in Europe as was argued in Chapter 3. We shall return to this argument in Chapters 6 and 7.

[3] Panama's position on the protection of the EU banana market was made clear in a letter under the signature of its Minister of Foreign Affairs, H. A. Cerjack, to the Minister of Foreign Affairs of Trinidad and Tobago in 2000. Cerjack (2000:2) argued that "as long as the European Union maintains a banana trade regime based on simple discrimination between production of two groups of developing countries, the final result will be the economic detriment of one group for the benefit of the other, thus an endless continuation of the dispute." It was for these reasons that Panama had certain reservations with regard to endorsing a WTO waiver which would give the EU *carte blanche* authority to implement the Cotonou Agreement with the ACP countries.

[4] The vulnerability of the economies of ACP countries, especially Caribbean ones, to sudden changes in the EU banana regime (that is, liberalization) is captured in a statement by St. Lucia's Minister of Foreign Affairs, George Odlum, to the Second Annual Meeting of Caribbean Foreign Ministers and the United States Secretary of State. Odlum (2000:2) argued that "It is our view that the most effective means of securing access for ACP bananas would be through a separate allocation or set of country quotas for ACP suppliers. This would require a WTO waiver from GATT under Article XIII."

[5] It is estimated that in Martinique bananas are grown on approximately 9,000 hectares of the best agricultural land, some 23 per cent of all the agricultural land area. Moreover, bananas account for approximately 50 per cent of total exports and employs 15,000 people.

[6] France's sensitivity to the banana trade of its overseas territories was brought out in 1999, when Prime Minister Lionel Jospin undertook a four-day mission to these territories to personally unveil an emergency plan to help banana producers in Guadeloupe and Martinique, where bananas occupy the first and second positions in their trade, respectively. Banana prices had fallen by 25 per cent at the start of the

year threatening farmers with bankruptcy ("France to Support West Indies Banana Growers", Reuters, 25 October, 1999).

[7] Social unrest in the French overseas territories is a swift and prominent form of action. When banana prices fell by more than 25 per cent at the beginning of 1999, 100 farm unionists from the regional and young farmers' unions protested in Fort de France by occupying the naval headquarters (ibid.).

[8] WIBDECO, the Windward Islands Banana Development and Export Company, is a regional firm representing the collective production, research and marketing interests of national banana associations in the Eastern Caribbean. It succeeds WINBAN, the Windward Islands Banana Organisation.

[9] As Sandiford (2000:51) has recorded it, "the equity contribution of Fyffes and WIBDECO to the joint venture was £20.0m each". While Fyffes financed its equity contribution using a combination of "existing bank facilities" and "external bank indebtedness provided by Allied Irish Bank PLC", "WIBDECO borrowed its equity contribution to the joint venture from the same bank with the loan secured by the assets of the joint venture and guaranteed by the governments of the Windward Islands". That loan was at an interest rate of 7 per cent and payable within six years with a three year grace period.

[10] Since the last decade of the twentieth century, there has been increasing awareness of the need to promote economically and environmentally sustainable production of bananas. Such initiatives have been led by organizations like the Fair Trade Labelling Organisation (FLO) and the European Banana Action Network (EUROBAN). Both these organizations have a membership that spans the breadth of the EU and they appear to have been capable of influencing the direction of the Commission on future banana policy. See FLO and EUROBAN (2000) for their recent joint position on bananas.

[11] Barriers to entry into the banana business are of two principal types. First, the tremendous levels of capital that are required to finance and efficiently govern the various stages of the commodity chain, which has resulted in a highly vertically-integrated industry. Second, the conduct of firms in ensuring that they continue to enjoy some degree of monopoly power. See Chapter 3 for a detailed discussion of these.

[12] Objection to *laissez-faire* was forcefully articulated by the European Parliament in September 1997, when a majority of its members called upon the EU to indicate to the WTO that its banana regime was an instrument for *development* and so should be preserved. The European Parliament adopted a joint resolution by the Union for Europe, United Left, Greens, European Radical Alliance and Europe of Nations group stating that the WTO's ruling against the NBR affected both the Common Agricultural Policy and the EU's development policy and it mandated the Commission and Council to find "an appropriate response guaranteeing the preservation of Community banana production and the retention of privileged flows from ACP countries" ("EP/Bananas: Majority of Parliament call on EU to Point out

to WTO that its Banana Regime is an Instrument for Development to be Preserved, and Recommend a Review of Geneva Procedures", Agence Europe, 18, September 1997).

[13] In fact, because the EU opted for protectionism it resulted in deterioration of relations with the dollar-zone countries. Six months after the NBR had been finally condemned by an Arbitration Body, Ecuador threatened to seek authority from the WTO to impose $450 million of sanctions on European Union exports unless there was a change in the NBR. Among other things, Ecuador indicated that the European Union had failed "to remove country specific quotas", an action which it could have taken immediately ("Ecuador Threatens Sanctions on EU over Bananas", *Reuters*, 28 October, 1999).

[14] Germany's objection to the NBR also stemmed from the fact that it would lose its national derogation under the Special Protocol to the Treaty of Rome. Among the numerous actions instigated against the European Union were the following. In European Court of Justice, Case C-257/93 R, Léon Van Parijs NV (Belgium), Bananic International (Belgium), International Fruchtimport Gesellschaft Weichert and Co. (Belgium), Velleman and Tas (Netherlands), Banana Marketing Belgium (Belgium), and Jan Van Den Brink (Netherlands) took both the European Communities and the Commission of the European Communities to court. Specifically, they made an application "for interim measures seeking, inter alia, suspension of operation of certain provisions of Council Regulation (EEC) No 404/93 of 13 February 1993 on the common organization of the market in bananas". On 6 July 1993 the president of the European Court of Justice ruled that the "application for interim measures is dismissed as inadmissible."

[15] See, for instance, European Court of Justice (1993) "Federal Republic of Germany v Council of the European Communities", Case C-280/93, *European Court Reports*.

[16] Kumm (1998) examines and discusses the dominating conceptions and doctrines that are used by the German Federal Constitutional Court for determining the constitutionality of Regulation 404/93, under which the SEM was introduced. An interesting perspective developed by the author is that the question of who is the final arbiter of constitutionality in Europe is not answered because "within a pluralist framework, it does not make sense to speak of a final arbiter of constitutionality in Europe." Kuilwijk (1996) advances the thesis that the EU's protectionist banana trade policy is detrimental to the interests of importers in the EU as well as the public interest of the Community; while GATT law serves both to protect these individual interests as well as the overall 'public good'. Everling (1996), a former Judge of the Court of Justice, applies a historical legal perspective to the EU's NBR and poses the central question of whether or not the EU will slip on bananas. The author begins with the quarrels over bananas which existed in the EU since the establishment of the EEC in 1956, which were only settled after intervention of Heads of Governments, then shows how essentially the same problem had re-emerged under the SEM.

[17] The countries that actively participated in this joint action were Ecuador, Colombia, Costa Rica, Guatemala, Nicaragua and Panama, while Mexico and Venezuela were in attendance as observers.

[18] The first panel submitted its report on 3 June 1993, while the NBR was due to be implemented in July 1993. Since under GATT rules contracting parties had a reasonable period of time (not less than 60 days) to remedy any trade-distorting measure, the report posed no direct threat to the EU. However, it might have been part of a strategy of the complaining parties to show over the long run that the EU's banana import policies had always violated world trade rules.

[19] Under GATT 1947 rules, the findings of a panel could only be implemented against a contracting party if a two-thirds majority of contracting parties agree to an adoption of the report at a meeting of the GATT Council.

[20] By then, the EU had realized that unless it adequately addressed the concerns of the Latin American complaining parties, this would become a recurrent problem. Moreover, in anticipation of the creation of the WTO under the Uruguay Round, the EU was aware that any further attacks on the banana regime would most likely result in its defeat.

[21] Under the proposed Framework Agreement, the complaining parties would be allocated certain shares of the import quota based on past performance, and the quota would be increased annually by an autonomous amount. But the Latin American countries were divided on the matter, both in terms of the size of the quota and their individual shares, rendering the agreement unstable. Notably, Ecuador, Guatemala, Honduras and Panama objected to the agreement, while Costa Rica, Colombia, Nicaragua and Venezuela accepted it (European Commission, 1994:11-12).

[22] As the EU explains, although the Framework Agreement was subjected to "criticism both inside and outside the Community", it nevertheless formed "an integral part of the Uruguay Round as signed in April in Marakesh." European Commission (1994:12). The US was one of the signatories.

[23] Actually, Chiquita and the Hawaii Banana Industry Association jointly filed a Section 301 action before the USTR on 2 September 1994, seeking unilateral action against the countries that were parties to the Framework Agreement.

[24] Section 301 of the United States Trade Act of 1974 is essentially a set of policy instruments available to the US government and its citizens for conducting and safeguarding their interests in international trade. Its coverage includes any type of foreign direct investment with implications for trade in goods or services in general; and the right to initiate action might arise from any act, policy or practice of a foreign government that denies market opportunities to a US firm or citizen. Up to 1994, over 100 actions had been initiated under Section 301, of which 10 per cent had been taken to the stage of international consultations or dispute settlement procedures, and 30 per cent had been solved through mutual understandings. For a

competent discussion of Section 301 and how the EU's Trade Barrier Regulations (TBR) measure up to it, see Mavroidis and Zdouc (1998:424-31).

[25] In deciding to initiate Section 301 action against the EU's NBR, Michael Kantor, the USTR, said that the United States had "repeatedly sought changes in the European banana regime to address the discrimination against U.S. companies, but unfortunately the EU has been inflexible." (USTR, 1995). See also the 25 April edition of the *Federal Register* (1996) in which the United States Trade Representative served public notice of intent to establish a dispute settlement panel.

[26] Barlett and Steele (2000:4) note that, in an October 1994 memorandum to the USTR, Michael Kantor, two of his staff members commented that if the investigation were initiated they would be setting a new precedent. It would be the first time ever that the US would be using Section 301 in connection with a product not exported from the US, but from a third country.

[27] The vulnerability of several Caribbean countries to sudden changes in the EU banana trade is well known by the US. In fact, in May 1997, at a special meeting of Heads of State and Government of the Caribbean Community and President Clinton of the US, held in Bridgetown, Barbados, the parties entered into a special understanding on the EU banana trade. Specifically, an agreement, subsequently called the Bridgetown Accord, enjoined these countries to "work with all concerned parties to achieve mutually satisfactory marketing arrangements for Caribbean bananas, recognizing the critical importance to Caribbean countries of the continued access of Caribbean bananas to the traditional markets of the European Union." (Heads of State and Government of the Caribbean Community, 1999).

[28] This point emerges forcefully in a letter from Sir John Compton, Prime Minister of St. Lucia, to President Clinton in 1995, where he argued in connection with the initiation of Section 301 action by the USTR that "I am particularly concerned since this is taking place in spite of your [President Clinton's] and Ambassador Kantor's repeated assurances that it is not the intention of the United States to harm the banana industry in the Caribbean." He further argued that "no United States vital economic interests are at stake and that United States based companies and, in particular Chiquita Brands International Inc., which has turned a massive loss in 1992 into a substantial profit, have improved their profitability in the European Market." (Compton, 1995:2).

[29] Hawaii is an outlying Pacific state of the US. Bananas are grown there, but only on a very small scale and primarily for domestic consumption. There is no history of banana trade between Hawaii and any of its neighbouring islands, nor the EU. Nevertheless, as Hallam and Peston (1997:17) have argued, the fact that bananas are grown there provided the opportunity for a complaint by the US that the EU's NBR affected its *potential* trade interest.

[30] It appears that Chiquita and affiliated firms were traditionally stronger supporters of the Republican Party, since most of the $5 million contributed from 1990 has been directed at it. However, Chiquita did make strategic adjustments to its pattern

of financial contributions after the implementation of the EU's banana regime, with increasing shares of its contributions going to the Democratic Party (Bartlett and Steele, 2000:2).

[31] This could only be meaningful as part of a strategic move. At that stage, Chiquita was anxious to engage official US action in the matter, so it redirected some of its financial contributions. In addition to the one-off payment of $250,000 in December 1994, Chiquita is alleged to have contributed considerably more money to earn its CEO a night at the White House (Barlett and Steele, 2000:2).

[32] Mangold et al. (1996) also supports this viewpoint, claiming on the basis of a wealth of primary sources that, Chiquita had spent considerable sums "of money in Washington buying influence, and when the time came to use it, it was at Lindner's disposal."

[33] In the 4 October issue of the *Federal Register*, the USTR lays down the history of the dispute, citing the chronology of the events, which starts with the joint petition filed by Chiquita and the Hawaii Banana Industry Association (*Federal Register*, 1995:52026-7).

[34] In that regard, the notice issued by the USTR on 10 November 1998 is supportive. According to the USTR, "Section 306(b) of the Trade Act requires the USTR to determine what further action it shall take under section 301(a) if the USTR considers that a foreign country has failed to implement a recommendation made pursuant to dispute settlement proceedings under the WTO." (*Federal Register*, 1998:63099).

[35] Two requests for consultations on the banana regime were made in the WTO. The US, Guatemala, Honduras and Mexico made the first, in September 1995, while the subsequent one in February 1996, which superseded the first, included Ecuador (WTO, 1997a).

[36] Consultations were actually held between the Parties on 14 and 15 March 1996, but did not result in a solution that was mutually acceptable (WTO, 1997a: paragraph 1.2).

[37] Included among these regulations and administrative measures was the Framework Agreement on Bananas, which had been agreed to by the US in December 1994 and negotiated between the EU and several Latin American exporters.

[38] The Complaining Parties requested specific consultations and or action pursuant to the following: Article 4 of the Understanding on Rules and Procedures governing the Settlement of Disputes; Article XXIII of the GATT 1994; Article 6 of the Agreement on Import Licensing Procedures, to the extent that it relates to Article XXIII of GATT 1994; Article XXIII of the GATS; Article 19 of the Agreement on Agriculture, to the extent that it relates to Article XXIII of GATT 1994; and Article 8 of the Agreement on Trade-Related Investment Measures, to the extent that it relates to Article XXIII of GATT 1994 (WTO, 1997a:1).

[39] "To examine, in the light of the relevant provisions of the covered agreements cited by Ecuador, Guatemala, Honduras, Mexico and the United States in document WT/DS27/6, the matter referred to the DSB by Ecuador, Guatemala, Honduras, Mexico and the United States in that document and to make such findings as will assist the DSB in making recommendations or in giving the rulings provided for in those agreements" (WTO, 1997a:1).

[40] The EU argued that only the barest outline of complaints had been presented during consultations, and that Complaining Parties had not exhausted the possibility of reaching a mutually satisfactory solution as foreseen under Article 4.3 of the DSU (WTO, 1997a: paras. II.2, II.5).

[41] Specifically, the EU argued that at the consultations stage of dispute settlement the responding party should be given as clear a picture as possible of the case against it. It said it had prepared several questions for consideration of the Complaining Parties and had been in the process of preparing relevant responses to questions submitted by them when they announced a decision to establish a panel. Moreover, the request for establishment of a panel did not identify the specific measure at issue, but merely cited "the regime" (WTO, 1997a: paras. II.3, II.9).

[42] These articles deal with the most favoured nation (MFN) treatment requirement of trade in goods. Specifically, Article I:1 deals with non-discriminatory tariff treatment; and Article XIII:1 deals with quota restrictions on sources of supply.

[43] These are the GATS non-discrimination clauses, which require that WTO members accord all "services" and "service suppliers" similar treatment, regardless of the mode of supply of such services.

[44] Specifically, as far as the EU was concerned, "the Panel erred in interpreting Article 4.1 of the *Agreement on Agriculture*" in two specific ways. The first was that "the transition from a highly restrictive system, largely based on non-tariff barriers, to more open market access for agricultural products had to be progressive."; and the second was that "the process of reform initiated by the *Agreement on Agriculture* was aimed at achieving binding commitments in three areas: market access, domestic support and export competition." (WTO, 1997b: para. 19).

[45] Thus, the EU argued that any measure could simultaneously fall under the Annex 1A Agreements and the GATS, and that there was no indication whether the panel examined a different aspect or part of the EC licence allocation rules under the GATS, from that examined under GATT 1994 or the *Licensing Agreement* (WTO, 1997b: para. 40).

[46] The argument developed by the EU was that the interpretation of the panel was not supported by the relevant provisions of the GATS, the preamble of which gives "no indication that the GATS is concerned with the indirect effects on trade in services of measures relating to trade in goods." (WTO, 1997b: para. 42).

[47] As Krugman (1994) puts it, in "traditional trade models a tariff or import quota is always bad since it depresses welfare. In new trade theory protection could lead to inefficient scale production at one extreme, or increased scale of production to reap benefits to consumers at the other."

[48] An important exception to this is the advent of intra-industry trade, which explicitly recognizes the movement of semi-processed commodities between nations (Grubel and Lloyd, 1975). However, the focus of intra-industry trade has been on the actual flows of commodities and not on the transformation processes that these semi-processed commodities are further subjected to.

[49] Peers (1999:195) suggests that, a likely consequence of the WTO ruling for the EU will be a decline in its preferences to the numerous third countries with which it has preferential trade agreements. He postulates that "the predominance of preferential agreements in the Community's legal order may be starting to diminish."

[50] That EU consumers are likely to enjoy significant welfare gains from freer trade in bananas has been the driving force behind liberalization of trade in the commodity.

[51] Upon reflection, given the inelastic price and income demand for bananas, it is likely that the outcome of any further liberalization would be a transfer of rents from the less-efficient EU-based TNCs to the more-efficient ones of the US.

[52] In fact, Ecuador requested the WTO to establish a panel to determine whether the revised EU banana regime under Council Regulation (EC) No 1637/98 was sufficiently modified so that its trade benefits were no longer being nullified or impaired (WTO, 1999:1). The panel concluded "that there is nullification or impairment of the benefits accruing to Ecuador under the GATT 1994 and the GATS within the meaning of Article 3.8 of the DSU." (WTO, 1999:99). In March 2000, the panel that had been asked to make an arbitration decision on the level of retaliation which Ecuador could apply against the EU authorized Ecuador to suspend concessions in trade with the EU to the amount of US$201.6 million per year. The Panel also authorized Ecuador to exercise cross-retaliation, that is, to retaliate under the TRIPS agreement although the EU's violations were under the GATT and the GATS. Specifically, Ecuador had requested authorization to retaliate with respect to the protection of industrial designs, geographical indications and the protection of performers, producers of sound recordings and broadcasting organizations (Zdouc et al., 2000:1).

[53] Examples include the Multifibre Arrangement (see Navaretti et al., 1995) and the Agreement on ASEAN preferential trading arrangements (see ASEAN 1977).

[54] In April 1999, the USTR decided to suspend trade concessions to the EU by applying 100% *ad valorem* duties on a range of products from the EU, including bath preparations, handbags, lead-acid storage batteries, and bed linen, among others (*Federal Register*, 19 April, 1999). Subsequently, in one of its reports to the WTO on its progress in implementation of the Panel and Appellate Body reports,

the EU noted that "...there continue to be divergent views expressed by the main parties concerned, and even where there is apparent agreement, differences emerge regarding the details. As a result, no agreed conclusions have been reached yet" (WTO, 2000).

[55] Consequently, the USTR decided to terminate its application of 100 per cent *ad valorem* duties against EU products, but reserved the right to initiate further action under Section 301 should the EU fail to comply with that understanding (*Federal Register*, 6 July 2001).

[56] This decision was taken at the WTO Ministerial Conference in Doha on 14 November 2001. As part of the conditions for granting the EU this waiver, Latin American countries reserve the right to challenge any future EU banana tariffs if they in any way adversely affect market access. ACP countries had earlier threatened to join the EU in blocking any new negotiations for further trade liberalization in this new trade round unless the request for the EU waiver was granted. See WTO (2001) "Conference ends with agreement on new programme", *Doha WTO Ministerial 2001: Summary of 14 November*.

[57] In a letter to the President of the European Commission, Romano Prodi, the Prime Minister of St. Vincent, Ralph Gonsalves, has said that while the Caribbean understands the need for the EU to facilitate newcomers, it would prefer a 6 per cent share of licenses to be allocated to non-traditional operators instead of the 11 per cent presently proposed by the Commission, in order not to undermine the predictability of marketing their bananas (*Sopisconews.com*, 2002).

6 Division and Distribution of Revenue Along the EU Banana Commodity Chains

6.1 Introduction

Thus far, our emphasis has been on the likely magnitude of the gains that might be realized from liberalization of trade in bananas in the EU. In particular, in Chapter 2 we reviewed and criticized earlier studies of these potential gains. The fact that the EU banana market is neither perfectly competitive nor contestable (Chapter 3) implies that the welfare effects of trade liberalization are likely to be considerably different from those predicted by previous studies that utilized the foregoing assumptions about the EU banana market. In Chapter 8, we shall first estimate the degree of market power in the banana business for two *representative* EU member-states, then we use the knowledge of market power so derived to estimate the welfare effects of liberalization, taking into consideration the oligopolistic market structure, which will be detailed in Chapter 9. Yet, a mere knowledge of the magnitude of the welfare effects, whether under competition or Cournot-Nash conditions, cannot give any indication of their *division and distribution* along various banana chains, which in itself is a prerequisite for explaining how the various actors might be affected by trade liberalization. Therefore, we need to determine how the total wealth (revenue and surplus) that is created along the various banana commodity chains into EU member-states is divided and distributed among nations. Specifically, we need to undertake a comparative analysis of how that wealth is divided between the exporting countries and EU member-states. We shall divide this task into two related analytical inquiries, distinguishing first how revenue, and then surplus, have been divided and distributed between EU member-states and exporting countries. The extent to which firms enjoy rents due to Commission intervention is quantified in Chapter 9.

The present chapter is concerned with answering the first of these questions – the division and distribution of revenue along the various EU banana commodity chains. We shall compare the division and distribution of revenue along banana commodity chains into France, Germany and the UK. The specific questions that we seek to answer are: how is revenue divided and distributed along various EU banana chains? Is there any evidence that a particular mode of organization of EU banana commodity chains results in a more progressive division and distribution of revenue than others? How has the implementation of the SEM affected the division of revenue between EU member-states and exporting countries? Is liberalization of trade in the commodity likely to affect all banana chains in a similar way, or, is it likely to result in the displacement of some in favour of others? The remainder of the chapter is organized as follows. Section 6.2 presents the methodology, which draws upon the concept of commodity chains discussed in Chapter 4, followed by the data that are used in this chapter. This is followed by an analysis of the division and distribution of revenue along banana commodity chains into Germany, France and the UK in Section 6.3. Section 6.4 discusses the implications of the findings in the three cases analysed, and Section 6.5 concludes the chapter.

6.2   Methodology and sources of data

Conceptually, the division and distribution of revenue and surplus along the banana chain will be done using the commodity chain concept that was introduced in some detail in Chapter 4. We shall estimate the value of each of these variables at the export, import, wholesale and retail stages of the banana commodity chain.

Few of the studies that have used the commodity chain concept attempt a systematic, quantitative breakdown and distribution of revenue at the various stages of a chain. Gary Gereffi has used the concept extensively to depict changing patterns in international production in the apparel (Gereffi, 1999) and more generally, the manufactures (Gereffi, 1996) sectors. In both these studies, emphasis is placed on the changing gross value of trade in the commodities by country and region of origin.[1] Raynolds (1994) used the commodity chain concept to analyse the organization of production, marketing and distribution of non-traditional agricultural products in the Dominican Republic. She identifies the factors, commodities and conditions under which certain firms have enjoyed exceptional performance in that market.[2] However, her study does not quantify the division and distribution of revenue between the various actors along the respective commodity chains. The analysis of the demand for fresh Chilean produce in the US conducted by Goldfrank (1994) places emphasis on changing consumption patterns by income and age categories, but only glosses over the various stages of individual commodity chains.[3] One notable exception is found in the work of Talbot, who has undertaken such an analysis for the coffee commodity chain. Talbot (1997:65-7) uses the retail price per pound of coffee in US cents as a proxy for the total income generated from coffee and estimates the shares paid to growers in producing countries and transport costs between production and retail. The author concludes that the distribution of coffee surplus between producing and consuming countries has changed between the 1960s and the 1980s. Up to the mid-1980s, the surplus from coffee was distributed equally between producing and consuming countries; however, after the mid-1980s there was a massive shift in surplus from coffee-producing countries to developed country TNCs (Talbot, 1997:86).[4]

Although our analysis of the EU banana commodity chains draws upon Talbot's approach, there are a few differences. First, although it is not explicit in his study, it appears that Talbot's analysis is based on nominal coffee prices only, and that the quantities of coffee traded have not been taken into consideration. Since the banana commodity chain traverses several countries, real prices cannot be applied, so this study takes the quantities of bananas traded into consideration to derive estimates of revenue generated. As Chapter 8 argues, if firms exercise market power, price is not the only variable of interest. Instead, it is the change in quantity of bananas supplied by one firm at a given price in response to a unit change in quantity supplied by another that captures the exercise of market power. Secondly, the prices used in Talbot's analysis are weighted average retail prices of member-countries of the International Coffee Organization (ICO), and not the prices obtained by a particular producing country in its trade with a developed importing country. Thus, while Talbot's analysis gives some indication of what happened in the coffee chain at the global level, it does not answer the question of whether a particular mode of organization of the coffee chain results in a superior division and distribution of income. By analysing three different banana commodity chains between the producing countries and a consuming EU member-state, this chapter will demonstrate that certain forms of organization of the banana chain result in superior divisions and distributions of revenue. Thirdly, since Talbot's analysis treats coffee-producing and consuming countries in aggregate form, it is unable to explain whether a particular country, or group of countries, is likely to survive in a liberalized coffee market, and what the resulting division and distribution of income would be. Since this study analyses three different banana commodity chains, it will be able to reach some conclusions with regard to gainers and losers from liberalization. Finally, this chapter will apply the concept of exploratory data analysis, using box plots to quantify and map out the dynamics of revenue division and distribution in the EU banana trade. The data used in this chapter (see the

Author's database) were collected and compiled during the author's field-work in 2000.

The distribution of revenue along the banana commodity chain is presented for the case of trade between three EU member-states: Germany, France and the UK, and their trading partners. At any stage i in the banana chain, the Revenue R_i, is the product of price P_i and Quantity, Q_i, i.e.

$$R_i = P_i Q_i \tag{6.1}$$

The share of revenue retained at the ith stage in the banana commodity chain, σ_i, is the ratio of revenue at that stage, R_i, to the sum of revenue retained at all stages, $\sum_{i=1}^{3} R_i$, i.e.

$$\sigma_i = \frac{R_i}{\sum_{i=1}^{3} R_i} \tag{6.2}$$

6.3 Division and distribution of revenue along EU banana commodity chains

The trends in the division and distribution of banana revenue between Germany, France and the UK and their banana-exporting partners are analysed in the sections below. In light of the fact that in the pre-SEM period these EU member-states applied different banana trade policies, which typify those that were in force in all other member-states (Chapter 3), and given that their aggregate share of EU banana consumption exceeds 70 per cent (Chapter 3), explanations of the distribution of banana revenue along their commodity chains in the pre-SEM period could be generalized to other EU member-states. Moreover, given that the marketing and distribution of bananas throughout the EU is undertaken by the same TNCs that operate in the above three member-states, the division and distribution of banana revenue along the commodity chains of these countries and the banana-exporting countries in the post-SEM period is likely to be highly representative of other EU member-states and their banana-exporting partners as well. Let us begin with the German commodity chain.

6.3.1   Division and distribution of banana revenue along the German commodity chain

Although bananas represent a very small segment of the German economy, they are extremely important in the fresh fruit and vegetable trade: between the late 1970s and the late 1990s, total revenue generated from bananas at the retail level ranged from DEM 879 million (USD 437 million) in 1978 to DEM 3.5 billion (USD 2 billion) in 1991, or approximately a five-fold increase in value over a period of two decades (Figure 6.1).

Fig. 6.1   *Banana revenue in Germany (current prices)*

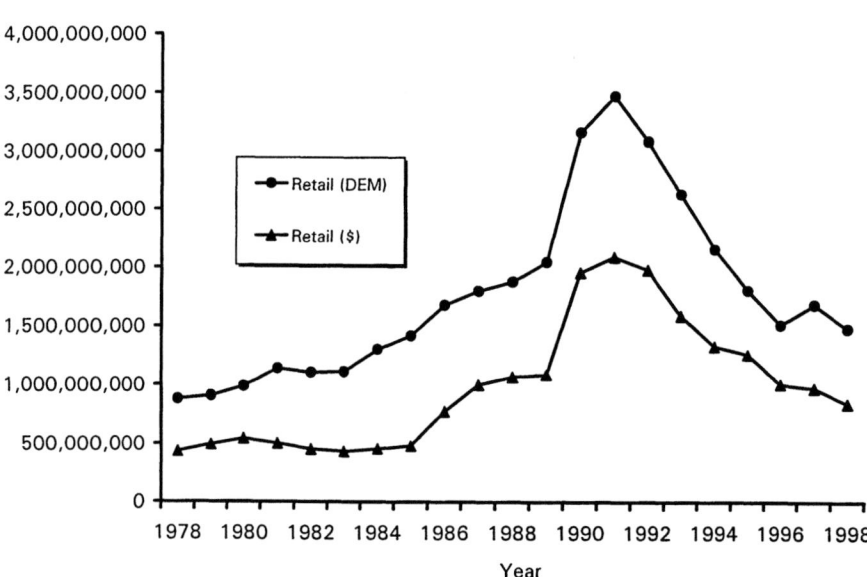

Source: Author's database.

German banana revenue increased steadily from the 1970s to the late 1980s and then accelerated in the 1990-92 period. While part of that acceleration reflected increased demand due to German reunification, reunification alone cannot explain a two-fold increase in banana consumption, since the population of Germany did not double as a consequence. Instead, most of this acceleration is explained by the strategic actions of US TNCs operating in the German market, which, in anticipation of the EU's implementation of a quota-based banana import policy under the SEM, conjectured that the EU's allocation of licences for accessing the quota would be based on the most recent supplies of operators. Acceleration of German banana revenue, which is linked to over-supply in the run-up to the SEM, is further explained in Table 6.1, which shows that although there was no significant change in the retail price of bananas between 1987 and 1993, the quantity sold effectively doubled. Since the sale of such quantities in the German market were unsustainable – they did not reflect increased per capita consumption – there has been a drastic decrease in revenue since 1992.

Table 6.1   Retail price and quantity of bananas in Germany (1987-93)

Year	Quantity (metric tons)	Retail price (DEM/metric ton)
1987	695,416	2,582.50
1988	762,103	2,460.83
1989	864,938	2,363.33
1990	1,165,548	2,711.67
1991	1,346,616	2,576.67
1992	1,374,693	2,243.33
1993	1,035,575	2,537.50

Source: Author's database.

However, while the trend in total banana revenue is important for explaining the trade in the commodity in Germany, even more important in the context of this study is how that revenue has been divided and distributed between the exporting countries and various actors in Germany (Figure 6.2), and how the implementation of the SEM has impacted upon it.

Figure 6.2 shows that the perceived value of the German banana trade is different for the various actors along the commodity chain. Whereas German banana retailers realized revenues of DEM 3.5 billion (USD 2 billion) in 1991, wholesalers obtained only DEM 2.0 billion (USD 1.2 billion), importers DEM 1.5 billion (USD 898 million), and exporters a meagre DEM 657 million (USD 395 million) (Figure 6.2). In fact, throughout the period under study German banana importers, wholesalers and retailers appropriated slightly more than 84 per cent of all revenue generated by the banana commodity chain, while slightly less than 16 per cent was retained in the producing countries, on average (Figure 6.3). Therefore, the division of revenue between the actors in Germany and the banana-exporting countries is highly skewed in the favour of the former.

Even when we use the median as opposed to the mean, as the measure of centre for the shares of revenue retained by actors in Germany, we come to

Fig. 6.2   Distribution of banana revenue in the German commodity
              chain (current DEM)

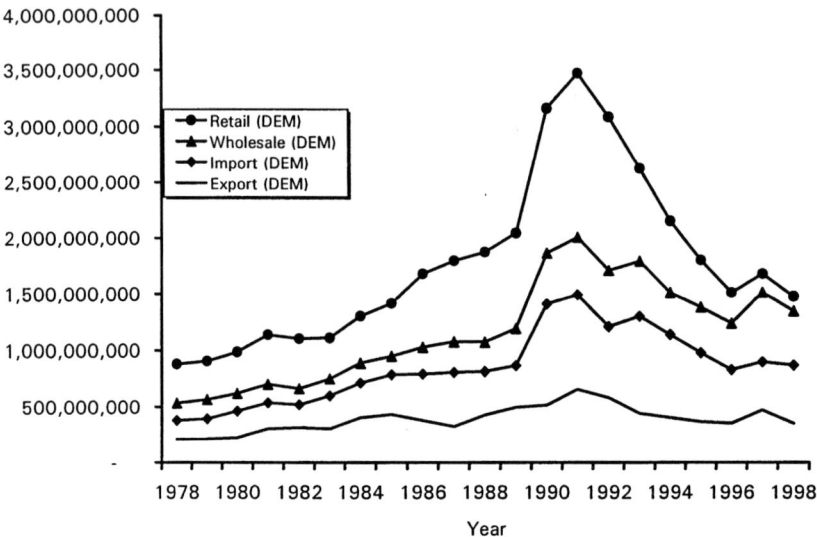

Source: Author's database.

Fig. 6.3   Division of banana revenue between Germany and the
              Exporting countries along the commodity chain (%)

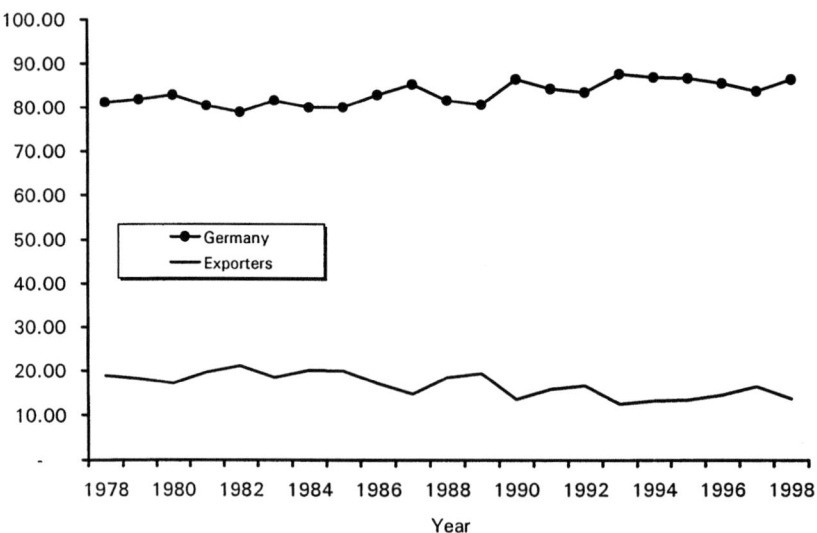

Source: Author's database.

the same conclusions as above. Moreover, not only is the median share of revenue retained in Germany 82.9 per cent, but, as Figure 6.4 shows, that share has increased since the SEM came into effect. In fact, whereas the pre-SEM (1978-92) median share of revenue retained in Germany was 81.6 per cent, with all observations within 4.6 per cent of the upper and lower quartiles,[5] for the post-SEM period (1993-98) it moved to 86.5 per cent with all observations within 2.9 per cent of the upper and lower quartiles[6] (Figure 6.4). Thus, the SEM has made the division of revenue between actors in Germany and the exporting countries more regressive. Up to 1989, retailers were responsible for most of the revenue appropriation; however, the increased revenue appropriation from 1990 was achieved through increased shares of wholesalers and importers, as well (Figure 6.2).

Fig. 6.4   *Box plots of banana revenue in Germany (%)*

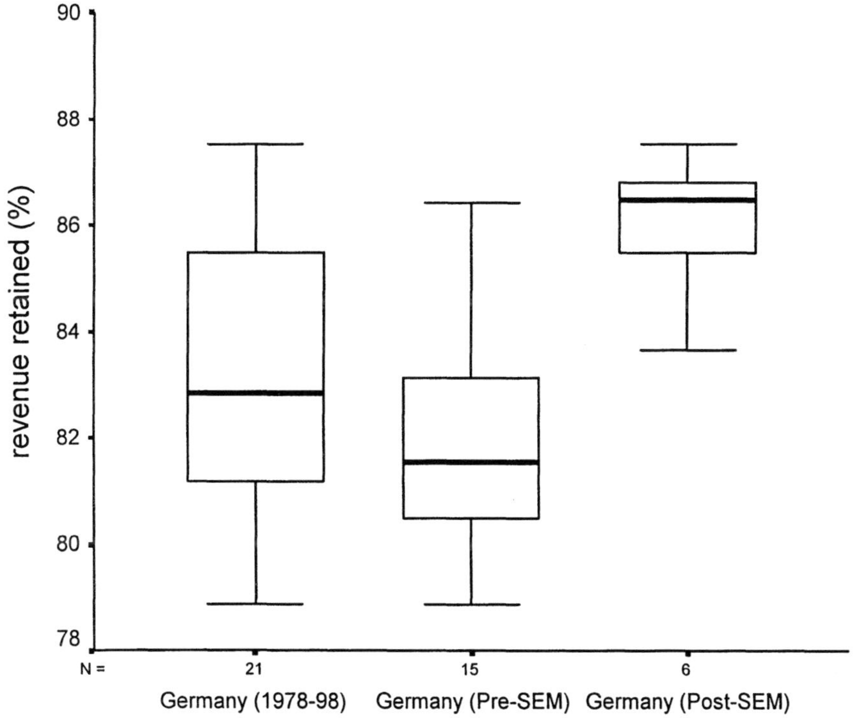

Source: Author's database.

Examination of the performance of the exporting countries for the entire period under study (Figure 6.5) reveals that they managed to retain different revenue shares of the banana commodity chain. Costa Rica obtained the highest median revenue share (20.8 per cent),[7] while Nicaragua was the worst performer with a median revenue share of only 11.9 per cent.[8] Moreover, with the exception of Honduras, which captured approximately 19 per cent of the revenue of its commodity chain, the remaining countries were only able to retain approximately 14 per cent (see Figure 6.5) of the revenue of their respective commodity chains, on average.[9] Therefore, while the tendency in the German commodity chain is to squeeze all sources of supply, Costa Rica, Honduras, and to a lesser extent Panama, have outperformed their competitors due to two factors. First, productivity on plantations in these countries is significantly higher on average than in the others. Second, because labour is more professionally organized in these countries, local trade unions command stronger bargaining power when negotiating conditions of work with the US TNCs that operate there. Thus, the larger revenue shares of the chain retained in these countries is a reflection of relatively higher wages.[10]

Fig. 6.5   *Box plots of banana revenue of the exporting countries in the German commodity chain (1978-98)*

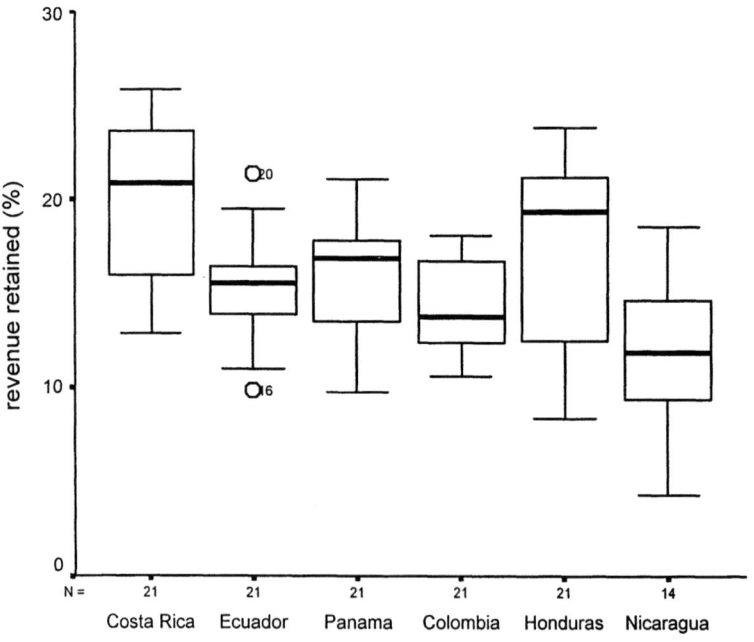

Source: Author's database.

Notwithstanding the foregoing argument that actors in Germany appear to have been appropriating larger revenue shares of the banana commodity chain since the SEM took effect, it is of interest to this study to determine whether or not the SEM has had an even impact on all the banana-exporting countries. Expectations of economists following the neo-classical approach, like Borrell and Yang (1990, 1992), are that all supplier countries would be adversely affected by the EU's tariff quota. If these expectations are correct, all exporting countries should retain significantly larger revenue shares in the pre-SEM relative to the post-SEM period. Box plots constructed for these periods (Figures 6.6 and 6.7) typically confirm these expectations, that is, the median revenue shares retained in most exporting countries were larger in the pre-SEM period.

Fig. 6.6   *Box plots of banana revenue of the exporting countries in the German commodity chain (pre-SEM)*

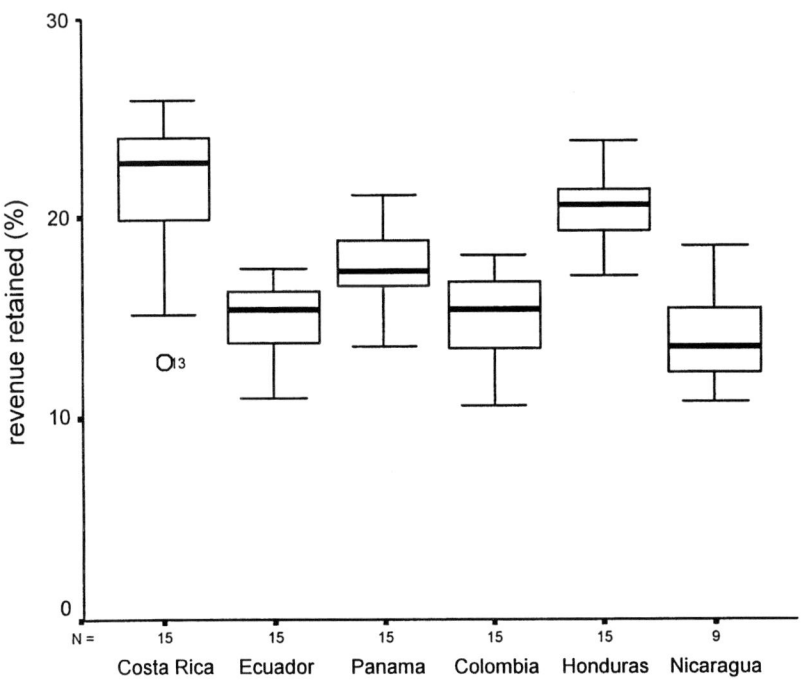

Source: Author's database.

Costa Rica, the best performer in both periods, witnessed a decline in its median share from 22.8 per cent in the pre-SEM period to 17.0 per cent in the post-SEM period, while Honduras, which retained the second-largest median revenue share in the pre-SEM period (20.6 per cent), plummeted to last place with a median share of 8.6 per cent. However, contrary to the neo-classical expectation, Ecuador managed to marginally *increase* its median revenue share, from 15.4 per cent to 16.0 per cent (see Figures 6.6 and 6.7). Exactly why this is so requires further investigation of the commodity chains leading into France and the UK, but at this stage we conclude that while the tariff-quota explains most of the decline in revenue of the banana-exporting countries, some other factor explains why Ecuador's median share increased. We hypothesize that in addition to the tariff-quota, the structure of production, marketing and distribution of bananas is likely to explain the changes in the median revenue shares of the exporting countries. Whereas the US TNCs control the production, marketing and distribution of bananas in the other exporting countries, Ecuador controls these activities along its commodity chain. So let us now examine the division and distribution of banana revenue along the French commodity chain.

Fig. 6.7   Box plots of banana revenue of the exporting countries in the German commodity chain (post-SEM)

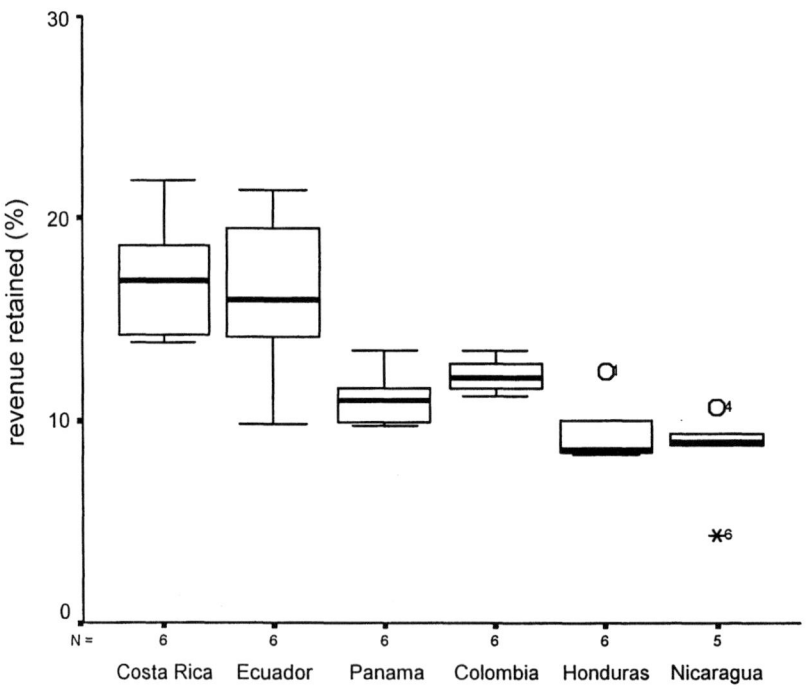

Source: Author's database.

6.3.2 Division and distribution of banana revenue along the French commodity chain

As in Germany, bananas are extremely important in France's fresh fruit and vegetable trade, where total revenue generated from them at the retail level ranged from FFR 2.2 billion (USD 500 million) in 1978 to a maximum of FFR 6.5 billion (USD 1.2 billion) in 1993, followed by a steep decline since (Figure 6.8).[11] Banana revenue in France grew steadily over the 1978-89 period, averaging 7.6 per cent per annum, before growth rates accelerated to 12 per cent per annum in the 1989-91 period. Unlike in Germany, where we attributed the acceleration in revenue to a combination of reunification and the strategic behaviour of TNCs operating in that market, in France revenue acceleration is better explained by higher retail prices, coupled with relative exchange rate stability during the 1990-93 period (Table 6.2). It will be recalled that in the pre-SEM period France applied a tariff-quota on bananas from the dollar zone (Chapter 3), so the option to over-supply the French market in the run-up to the SEM was not available to US TNCs. The subsequent decline in French banana revenue in 1994 is explained by a major decline in demand in the market, coupled with over-supply from dollar-zone sources; while in 1996, it was due to a combination of exchange rate appreciation and a considerable decrease in the retail price (Table 6.2).

Fig. 6.8   Banana revenue in France (current prices)

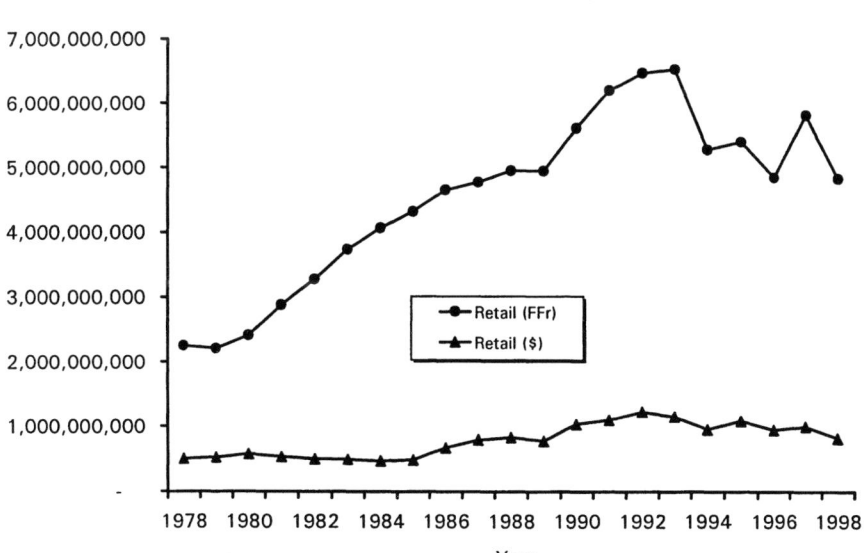

Source: Author's database.

*Table 6.2   Retail price and quantity of bananas, and exchange rate in
             France (1989-96)*

Year	Quantity (metric tons)	Retail Price (FFR/metric ton)	Exchange Rate (FFR/USD)
1989	447,096	11,072.50	6.38
1990	494,563	11,360.83	5.44
1991	500,491	12,382.50	5.65
1992	523,509	12,358.33	5.29
1993	582,682	11,201.67	5.67
1994	467,614	11,300.00	5.54
1995	503,119	10,740.00	4.99
1996	485,748	9,979.17	5.11

Source: Author's database.

Let us now discuss how banana revenue has been divided and distributed among the major actors along the French commodity chain since the late 1970s and determine whether or not it has been affected by the implementation of the NBR in July 1993. As in the case of Germany, the perceived value of the banana trade in France is different for the various actors in the commodity chain at different points in time and these values appear to have been more correlated in the pre-SEM than in the post-SEM period (Figure 6.9). French banana revenue peaked for retailers in 1993, with the commodity chain generating FFR 6.5 billion (USD 1.2 billion), while the corresponding maxima for French banana wholesalers and importers – FFR 3.8 billion (USD 666 million) and FFR 2.8 billion (USD 496 million) respectively – were realized in 1991 and exporters realized their maximum revenue of FFR 1.9 billion (USD 337 million) in 1997 (Figure 6.9). Unlike the typical German commodity chain, which is highly vertically integrated from production to retail and tends to be controlled exclusively by one TNC, the typical French commodity chain tends to be characterized by a number of supply contracts among various actors, making its overall co-ordination less efficient (Chapter 4). Thus, there is a lag in adjustment to price-quantity decisions of retailers (which are based on market demand) by other actors in the commodity chain, which explains why banana revenue peaked in different years for different actors.

Co-ordination between French banana wholesalers and importers tends to be highest due to the relatively higher degree of risk that these actors are subjected to. Once bananas are imported into an EU member-state they need to be *rapidly* transported to wholesalers for ripening in order to minimize spoilage and ensure high quality (Chapter 4). However, wholesalers have

Fig. 6.9 Distribution of banana revenue in the French commodity chain (current FFR)

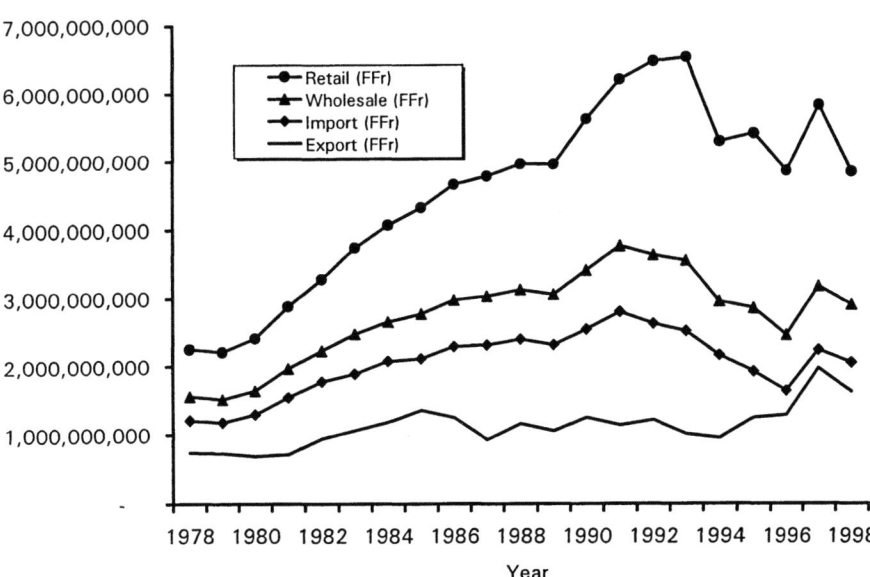

Source: Author's database.

some degree of control over the pace of the ripening process, and hence, for the purposes of minimizing spoilage and quality control, the degree of co-ordination between the wholesale and retail stages is not as mission critical as it is between the import and wholesale stages. Let us now examine how French banana revenue is divided between actors in France and the exporting countries (Figure 6.10).

It is evident that throughout the 1978-98 period, French banana importers, wholesalers and retailers appropriated 81 per cent of the commodity chain, leaving 19 per cent on average for the exporting countries. Comparison of these figures with those for Germany leads to the conclusion that banana exporters to the French market have enjoyed a significantly larger share of the commodity chain relative to those that exported bananas to the German market. If the neo-classical hypothesis that free markets always result in superior allocation of the benefits of trade relative to protected markets is correct, then we would expect the pre-SEM division of banana revenue along the German commodity chain to be superior to that along the French commodity chain. Yet, even in the pre-SEM period a marginally smaller median revenue share was retained by importers, wholesalers and retailers in France (Figure 6.11) than those in

Fig. 6.10   *Division of banana revenue between France and the*
             exporting countries (%)

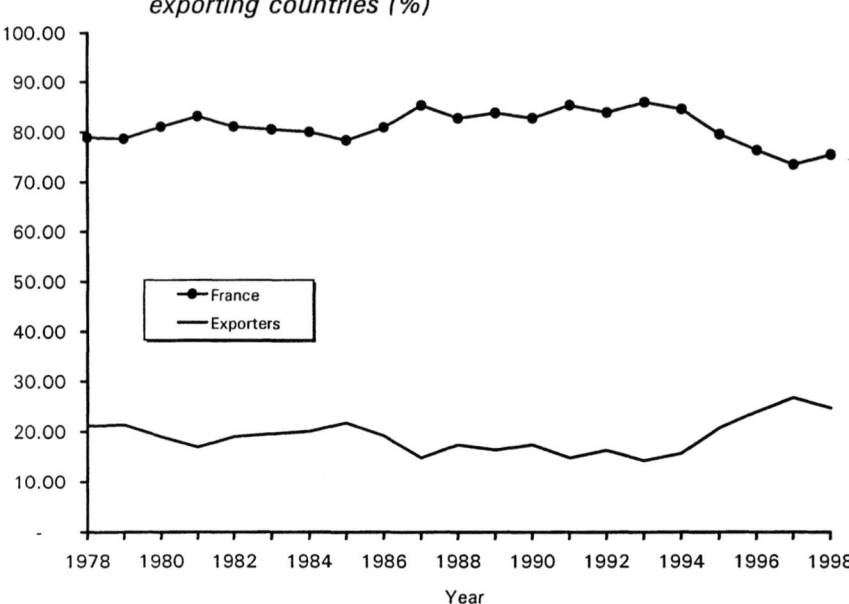

Source: Author's database.

Germany (Figure 6.4),[12] contradicting the above neo-classical hypothesis.
Moreover, unlike in Germany where the median share of revenue retained
by importers, wholesalers and retailers increased after the SEM came into
effect (Figure 6.4), that in France actually decreased, significantly (Figure
6.11).[13]

During the post-SEM period, most of the decline in the median revenue
share of the commodity chain retained by actors in France took place
between 1993-96, a period characterized by shrinking gaps between the
shares of revenue retained by retailers and wholesalers on the one hand, and
importers and exporters on the other (Figure 6.9). Thus, we have established
that countries exporting bananas to France retained significantly larger
median revenue shares of the commodity chain than those exporting to
Germany. What remains to be explained is whether or not some of these
countries benefited more than others.

Examination of the revenue shares of the banana commodity chain
retained by the various exporting countries to France (Figure 6.12), reveals
that some of these countries benefited significantly more than others. The
best performers were Martinique (21.4 per cent) and Guadeloupe (19.8 per
cent), followed by the former French African colonies of Ivory Coast (16.1
per cent), Madagascar (15.3 per cent) and Cameroon (14.9 per cent).[14] The

Fig. 6.11   Box plots of banana revenue in France (%)

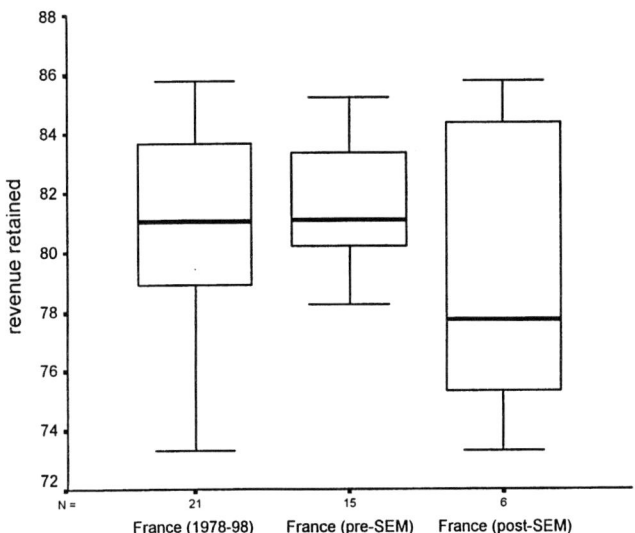

Source: Author's database.

Fig. 6.12   Box plots of banana revenue of the exporting countries in
the French commodity chain (1978-98)

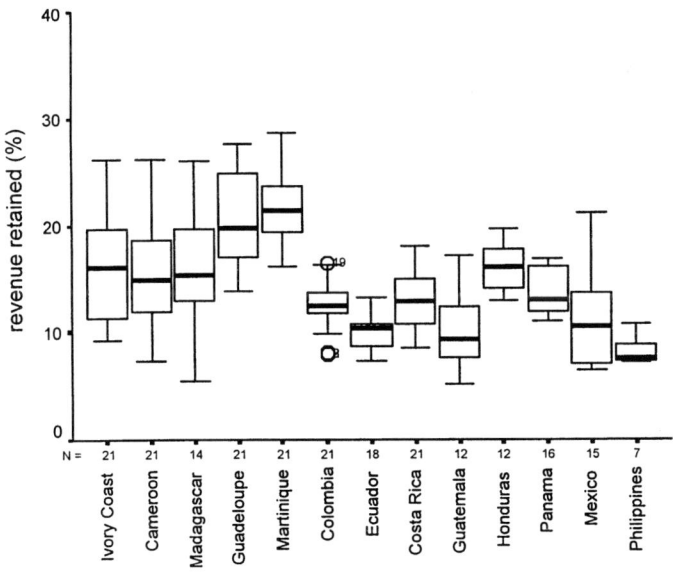

Source: Author's database.

superior performance of the French DOMs and former African colonies above is explained by their higher costs of production and preferential access to the market in France.

At the other extreme, dollar-zone banana-exporting countries retained comparatively lower median revenue shares of the commodity chain – Honduras retained the largest median revenue share in this group (16.1 per cent) followed by Panama (13.0 per cent) and Costa Rica (12.8 per cent). Excluding the Philippines from this analysis,[15] the worst performers among the dollar-zone countries in terms of median shares of revenue retained were Ecuador (10.3 per cent) and Guatemala (9.3 per cent).

The above clearly suggests that the protectionist banana import policy in France during the pre-SEM period is likely to have adversely affected dollar-zone suppliers. Yet, the median revenue shares of the dollar-zone countries in the French commodity chain, on the average are of the same order of magnitude as those that they received in the German commodity chain. So, let us analyse the median revenue shares of the countries that exported bananas to France in the pre-SEM period (Figure 6.13), in order to isolate the extent to which the dollar-zone countries are likely to have been discriminated against.

Fig. 6.13   *Box plots of banana revenue of the exporting countries in the French commodity chain (pre-SEM)*

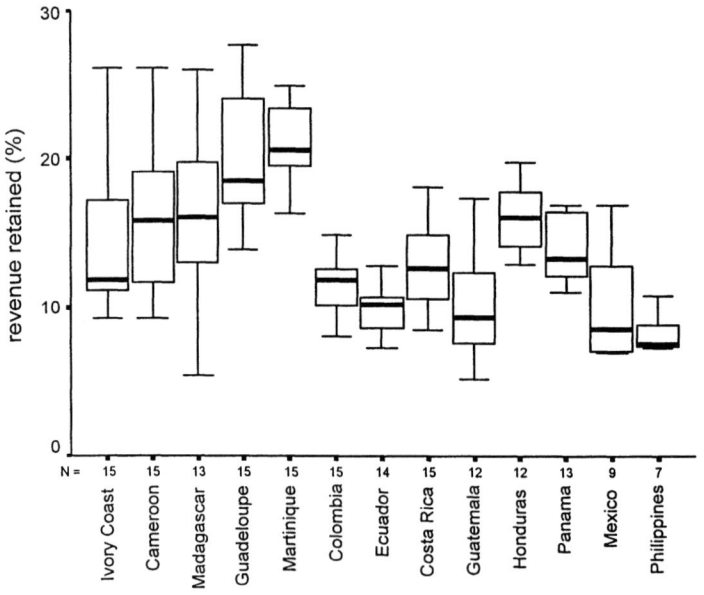

Source: Author's database.

Not surprisingly, the French DOMs retained the largest median revenue shares, and these shares were slightly larger than those which they retained during the entire period under study.[16] Equally not surprising is the performance of most of the former French African colonies, which retained larger median revenue shares.[17] An important exception was the Ivory Coast, which experienced a complete reversal of fortune – its median share of revenue retained in the pre-SEM period was only 11.8 per cent, almost 5 per cent less than that for the entire period under study.

The revenue distributions of most of the dollar-zone countries in the pre-SEM period and the entire period under study were rather similar, and there was little change in their relative positions. Mexico, the only exception, retained the least median revenue share of its commodity chain in the pre-SEM period: 8.5 per cent. The reader will recall that as far as France was concerned, the SEM effectively maintained its pre-SEM banana import policy, whereby a tariff was applied with respect to bananas from the dollar-zone (Chapter 3). Therefore, the SEM would not be expected to have any major impact on the foregoing revenue distributions of the dollar-zone countries. Figure 6.14 typically confirms that expectation – the revenue distribution of the dollar-zone countries has either remained unchanged, or improved in the case of Mexico and Ecuador.[18] This explains why there was

Fig. 6.14   *Box plots of banana revenue of the exporting countries in the French commodity chain (post-SEM)*

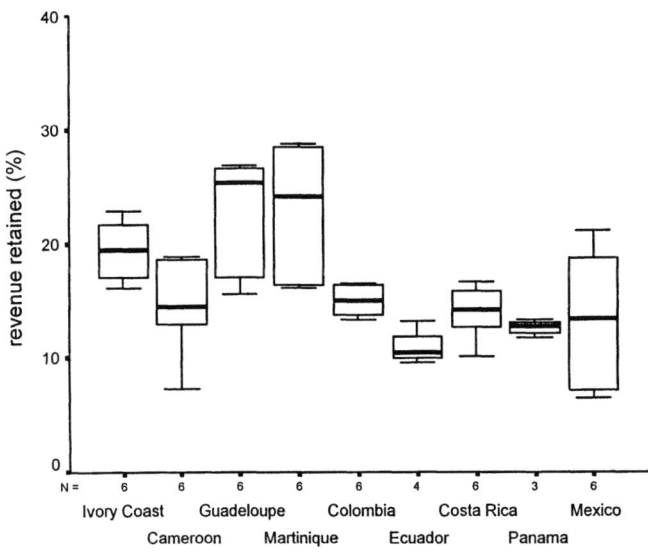

Source: Author's database.

little change in the distribution of revenue for these countries between the
pre-SEM and post-SEM periods. The SEM also had a positive impact on the
median revenue shares of the DOMs, with Guadeloupe and Martinique
recording increases of 25.3 and 24.1 per cent, respectively. Finally, among
the former French African colonies, the Ivory Coast managed to increase its
median revenue share of the French banana commodity chain to 19.4 per
cent with somewhat reduced variability, while for Cameroon it was a slight
reversal of fortune – its median revenue share reduced to 14.4 per cent in
the post-SEM period. Let us now examine the division of banana revenue
along the British commodity chain.

6.3.3   Division and distribution of banana revenue along the British commodity chain

While French and German revenue from bananas peaked in the early 1990s,
in the UK banana revenue at the retail level peaked at about GBP 510
million (USD 844 million) in 1998 (Figure 6.15), representing an
almost four-fold increase in value over the entire period under study.

Fig. 6.15   *Banana revenue in the British commodity chain (current prices)*

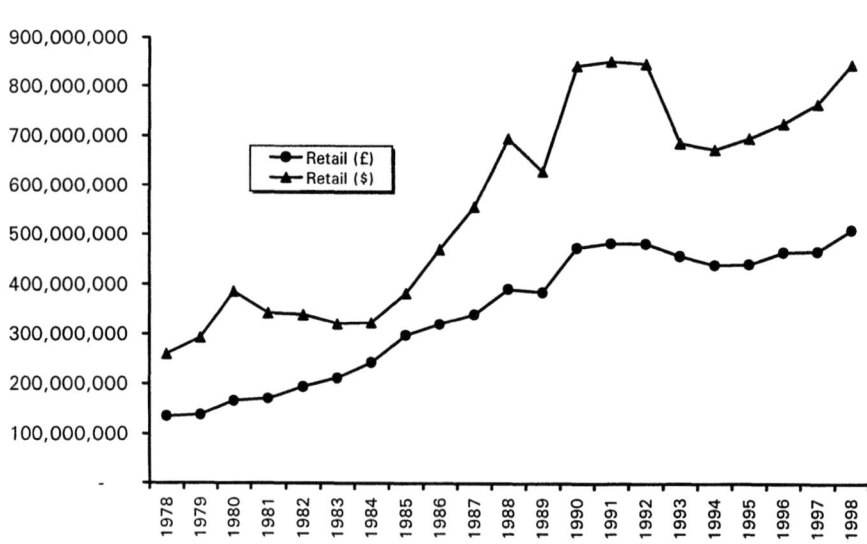

Source: Author's database.

In GBP sterling terms, banana retail revenue in the UK grew steadily over 1978-88, averaging 11.4 per cent per annum, then accelerated to 23 per cent in 1989-90. Whereas the growth trend in retail revenue over the 1978-88 period reflected increased demand and consumption, the acceleration of retail revenue in 1989-90 is explained by the strategic actions of US TNCs operating in the UK market in a similar way as in Germany. Despite the preferential access which the UK extended to the ACP countries in the pre-SEM period, dollar-zone supplies have always accounted for approximately 30 per cent of its market, due in part to the capacity limit constraints of the ACP countries.

Declines in the UK banana retail revenue are explained by a general decline in UK banana retail prices over the 1987-97 period, reaching a ten-year low of GBP 914.53 per metric ton in 1995 (Table 6.3).

Table 6.3   Retail price and quantity of bananas, and exchange rate in the UK (1987-97)

Year	Quantity (metric tons)	Retail Price (GBP/metric ton)	Exchange Rate (GBP/USD)
1987	319,679	1,065.50	0.611
1988	368,144	1,062.92	0.563
1989	364,516	1,056.17	0.613
1990	415,156	1,141.17	0.563
1991	407,446	1,185.58	0.568
1992	455,700	1,058.00	0.570
1993	454,722	1,006.25	0.666
1994	441,754	995.33	0.653
1995	482,280	914.53	0.634
1996	500,212	929.57	0.641
1997	457,180	1,021.30	0.611

Source: Author's database.

During that period, particularly the 1993-96 sub-period, the exchange rate of the GBP sterling to the USD remained relatively stable and the growth in quantities of bananas consumed was in line with previous years. Let us now discuss how banana revenue has been divided among the various actors in the British commodity chain (Figure 6.16) and determine how such revenue division has been affected by the EU's NBR.

Similarly to France and Germany, the perceived value of the banana trade in Britain is different for the various actors in the commodity chain at different points in time, and there have been three distinct trends. First, the

1978-85 period, during which the revenue shares of each component of the chain generally grew together. This is explained by the relatively high degree of predictability of demand at the time, which largely reflected increased consumption. Second, the 1986-91 period, characterized by a widening gap between the shares of wholesalers and retailers, and to a lesser extent importers and exporters. The explanation for this trend is linked to the strategic actions of US TNCs in the run-up to the SEM: the quantity of bananas sold in the market accelerated from 319,679 metric tons in 1987 to 455,700 metric tons in 1992. Although the middlemen (importers and wholesalers) in the chain were able to squeeze exporters somewhat, resulting in some divergence in their shares, retailers were able to exercise greater power over the middlemen, hence more divergence between these.

Fig. 6.16   Distribution of banana revenue in the British commodity chain (current GBP)

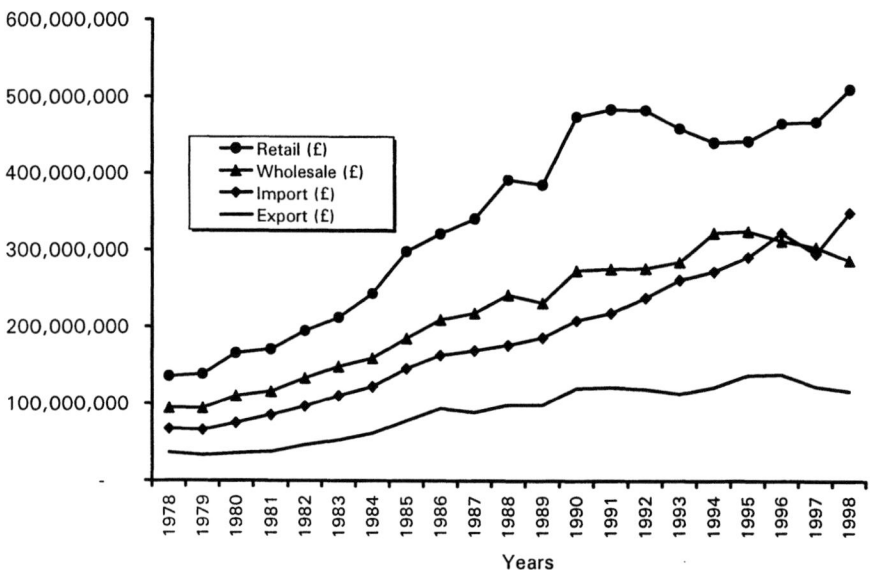

Source: Author's database.

Third, the 1992-98 period, which is characterized by convergence between shares of retailers and wholesalers and divergence between shares of importers and exporters. Here, once the NBR came into force the quantities of bananas returned to their *natural* levels, i.e., those levels which reflected demand. However now, since the middlemen owned a certain quantity of the licences, they were able to maintain their shares of the chain at the expense of retailers, which explains their convergence. Exporters on the other hand, given the general situation of over-supply which arose from the strategic actions of US TNCs in the pre-SEM period, were forced to accept a lower share of the chain, hence their divergence. This tendency for widening gaps between the revenue shares retained by wholesalers and exporters (Figure 6.17) effectively resulted in British banana importers, wholesalers and retailers appropriating slightly more than 82 per cent of the value of the commodity chain throughout the period under study, leaving on average just under 18 per cent for the exporting countries.

Fig. 6.17   *Division of banana revenue between Britain and the exporting countries along the commodity chain (%)*

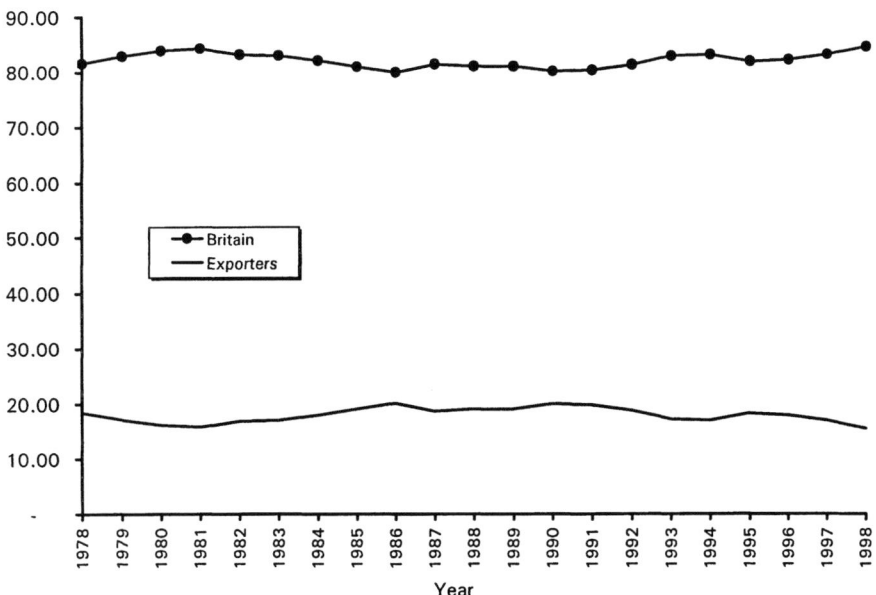

Source: Author's database.

It is evident, however, that for the pre-SEM period the median share of revenue retained by actors in Britain was somewhat lower at 81.4 per cent, compared with the post-SEM period when it increased slightly to 82.9 per cent (Figure 6.18). Once again, if the neo-classical hypothesis that free markets always result in superior division of the benefits of trade relative to protected markets is correct, then we would expect the pre-SEM division of banana revenue along the German commodity chain to be superior to that along the British commodity chain.

Fig. 6.18   Box plots of banana revenue in Britain (%)

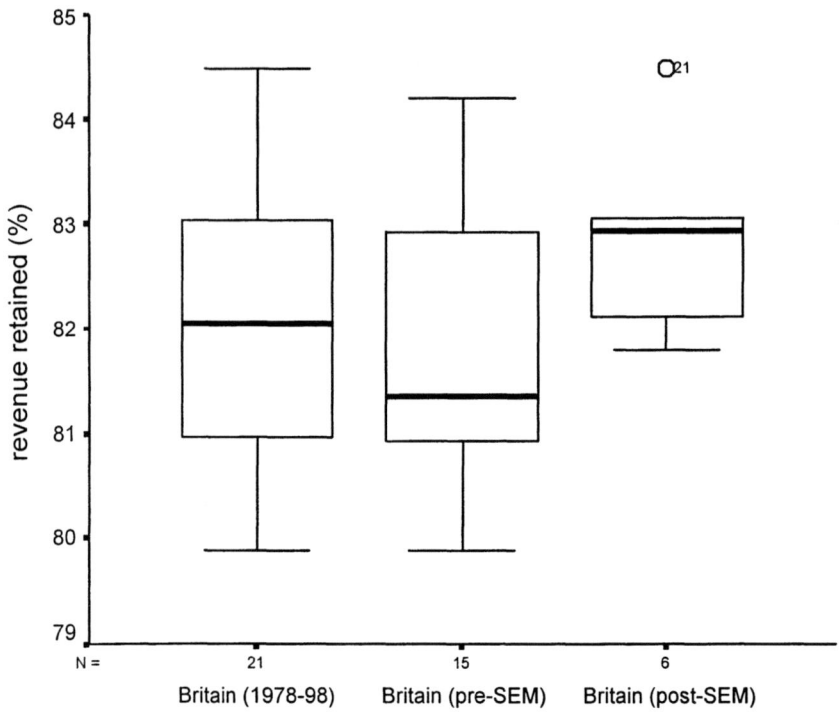

Source: Author's database.

Yet, in contradiction to the above neo-classical hypothesis, even in the pre-SEM period a marginally smaller median revenue share was retained by importers, wholesalers and retailers in the British commodity chain (Figure 6.18) compared with the German commodity chain (Figure 6.4).[19] Thus, up to this point we have established that the countries that exported bananas to the UK enjoyed significantly larger median revenue shares of the commodity chain than those that exported to Germany. What we shall now determine is whether or not some of these countries benefited more than others.

Examination of the revenue shares of the commodity chain retained by the various countries that exported bananas to the UK shows that some of them benefited significantly more than others. In order to avoid cluttering up the box plots (given the large number of countries that exported bananas to Britain) we shall focus on the shares of the commodity chain retained by the dollar-zone countries (Figure 6.19) and the ACP countries (Figure 6.20) separately.

Fig. 6.19   *Box plots of banana revenue of the dollar-zone countries in the British commodity chain (1978-98)*

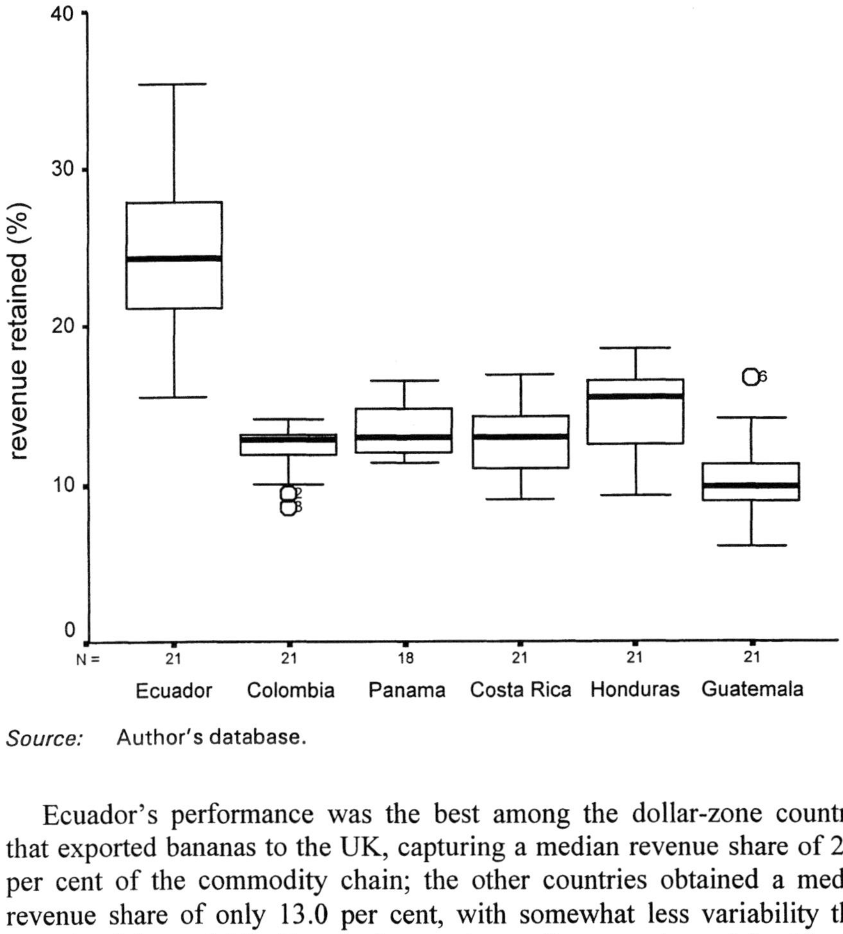

Source: Author's database.

Ecuador's performance was the best among the dollar-zone countries that exported bananas to the UK, capturing a median revenue share of 24.3 per cent of the commodity chain; the other countries obtained a median revenue share of only 13.0 per cent, with somewhat less variability than Ecuador (Figure 6.19). Ecuador's superior performance is explained by the direct involvement of its TNC, NOBOA, at all of the stages of the British commodity chain – production, marketing and distribution, an advantage which the other dollar-zone countries do not enjoy. Since ownership of all stages of the commodity chain is under Ecuador's control, it is in the interest of its TNC that production's share of the chain is significant relative to those retained in the UK. However, where the US TNCs are concerned, it is in their best interest to maximize their share of the commodity chain; therefore, significantly smaller shares of its value are transferred to the exporting countries. Additionally, the lower degree of variability of the median revenue shares retained by the other exporting countries is explained

by the relatively greater degree of efficiency of co-ordination of the
activities along these chains derived from the advantages that US TNCs
enjoy as fully vertically integrated entities – economies of scale and
common governance. Where the banana-exporting ACP countries were
concerned, those from the Caribbean have retained the largest median
revenue shares of the British commodity chain, with the least variability; the
African countries have retained the least revenue shares of the British
commodity chain, with the most variability; and the performance of
Suriname and Belize is somewhere between these two (Figure 6.20).

*Fig. 6.20   Box plots of banana revenue of the ACP countries in the
British commodity chain (1978-98)*

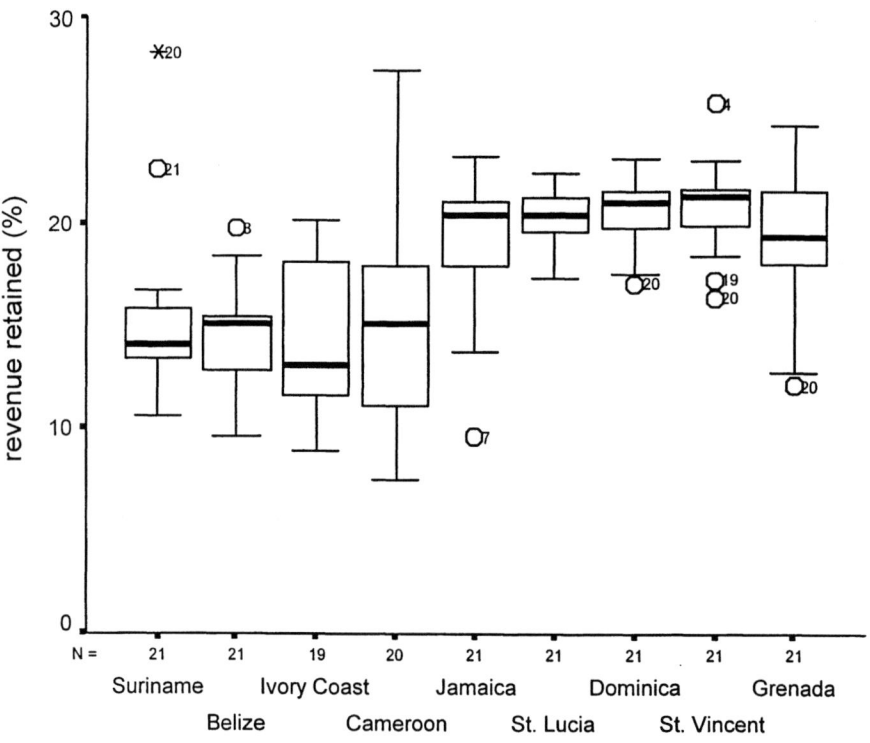

Source: Author's database.

The median revenue share of the commodity chain retained among the
Caribbean countries was 20.4 per cent,[20] and within that sub-category the
largest median revenue was retained by St. Vincent (21.3 per cent), while
the least was retained by Grenada (19.3 per cent). Among the remaining

ACP countries, Belize retained the largest median revenue share of the commodity chain (15.0 per cent), with relatively little variability, while the Ivory Coast retained the least share (13.0 per cent), with considerable variability. The explanation for the relatively larger median revenue shares of the Caribbean countries is their higher costs of production and their more organized collective bargaining approach towards actors in the UK. Joint shipping, marketing and distribution of bananas from the Eastern Caribbean countries makes it possible for them to exploit some economies of scale. Caribbean countries have attempted to integrate their production, shipping, marketing and distribution activities to a greater extent than their African counterparts. The relatively lower median revenue shares of the African ACP countries are explained by a combination of relatively lower costs of production and the fact that the UK is a residual market, and not a major market for these countries (see Chapters 2 and 3).

Fig. 6.21   Box plots of banana revenue of the dollar-zone countries in the British commodity chain (pre-SEM)

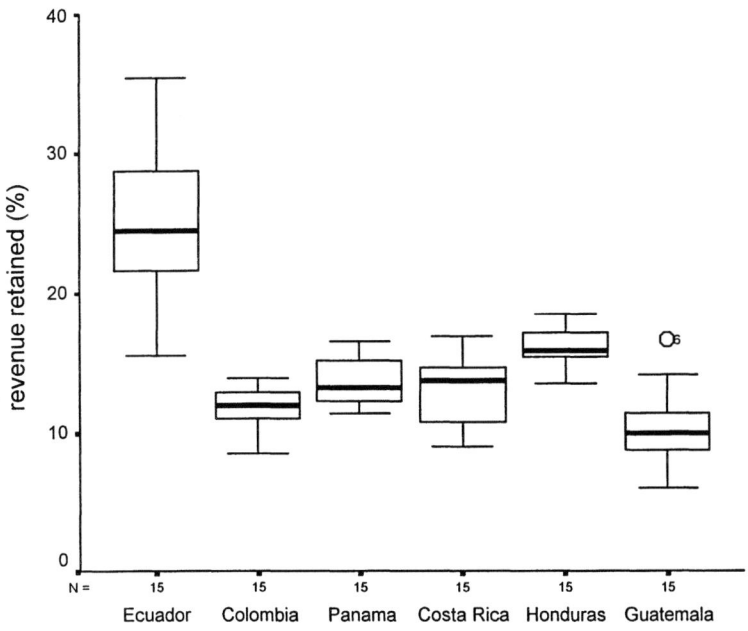

Source: Author's database.

The above discussion suggests typically, but not invariably, that preferential access to the British market by ACP countries, particularly those from the

Caribbean, explains in part why they retained relatively larger median revenue shares of the commodity chain than the dollar-zone countries. Yet, we have seen that it was Ecuador which appeared to have benefited the most. Let us therefore examine the distributions of revenue shares of all countries in the pre-SEM period and determine how the SEM has impacted upon them.

Conceptually, as for France, the SEM would not be expected to have any major impact on the distribution of revenue along the British commodity chain since it largely retained the UK's pre-SEM policy (Chapter 3). Figure 6.21 suggests that dollar-zone countries were marginally better off in the pre-SEM period, compared with the entire period under study, with Ecuador retaining the largest median revenue share of the commodity chain at 24.4 per cent, and Guatemala the least, at 10.0 per cent. Additionally, on the whole the ACP countries also appear to have been better off in the pre-SEM period, when all the Caribbean countries retained larger median revenue shares of the commodity chain with considerably less variability (Figure 6.22).

Fig. 6.22   Box plots of banana revenue of the ACP countries in the British commodity chain (pre-SEM)

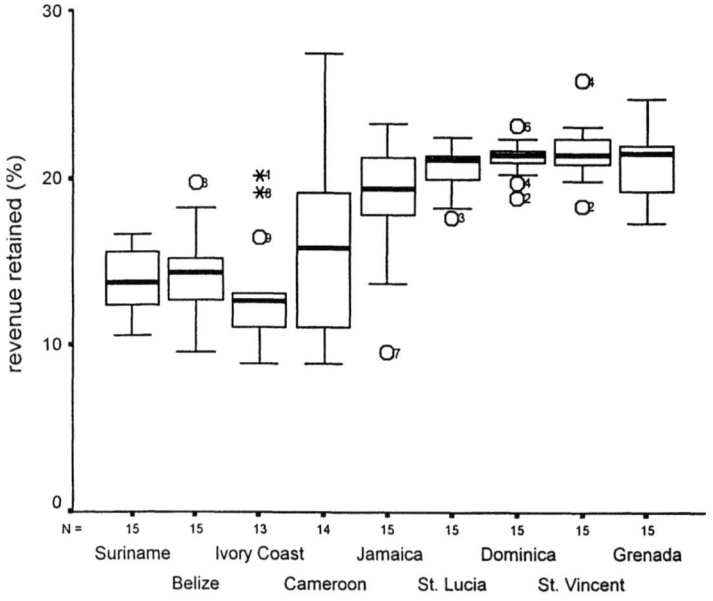

Source: Author's database.

Dominica, which retained a median revenue share of 21.4 per cent, had the best performance among this sub-group of countries,[21] while Jamaica appears to have been relatively worse off in the pre-SEM period.

Figure 6.23 suggests that in general, the SEM has not had any major negative effect on exporters from Latin America, leaving their median shares of revenue relatively unchanged, in conformity with expectations. Exceptions were Ecuador and Honduras. Ecuador's median revenue in the post-SEM period is 22.5 per cent, almost 2 per cent less than it had been in the pre-SEM period, while Honduras' revenue share fell to 10.0 per cent. In the case of Ecuador, this is explained in terms of increased cost of operation (due to acquisition of licences) for its TNCs in the British market and reduced volumes due to the tariff-quota. By contrast, any increased costs incurred by US TNCs were redistributed along the commodity chain through transfer-pricing.

Fig. 6.23　　*Box plots of banana revenue of the dollar-zone countries in the British commodity chain (post-SEM)*

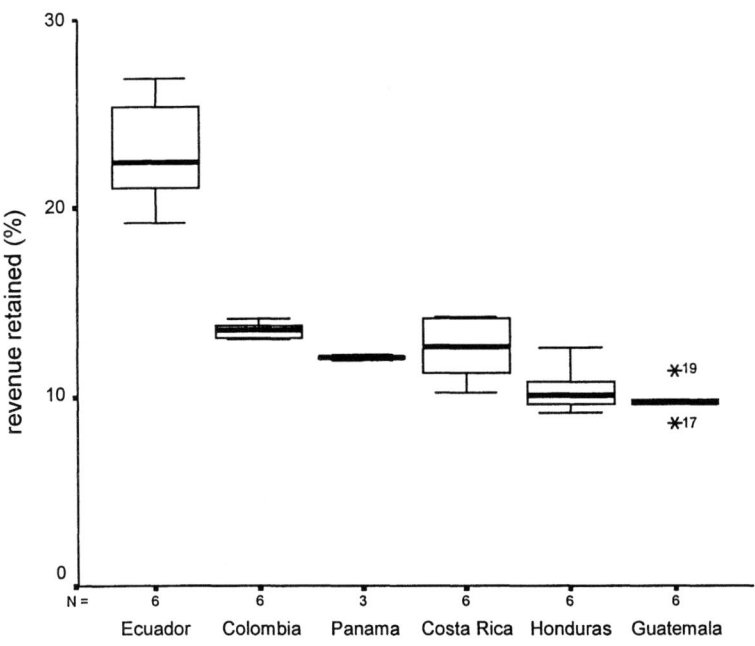

Source:　　Author's database.

Finally, regarding the Caribbean countries, it does appear that the implementation of the SEM has slightly adversely affected their median

revenue shares, which declined from approximately 20.9 per cent in the pre-
SEM period to approximately 19.4 per cent in the post-SEM period (Figure
6.24). The explanation for the decline in the Caribbean median share is
linked to uncertainty and rationalization of costs along the British
commodity chain. We have seen that the EU's NBR has been highly
criticized for extending preferential market access to particularly the
Caribbean ACP countries, which was the basis of the WTO action by the
US TNCs against the EU's NBR (Chapter 5). The threat of such preferential
access being removed by the WTO ruling has resulted in declining export
production and cost rationalization by Fyffes and WIBDECO. In particular,
Fyffes is increasingly sourcing bananas from some countries in Central
America, while WIBDECO is implementing a certification programme as
the basis on which farmers in the Eastern Caribbean receive larger revenue
shares. The Ivory Coast is the only country among the other ACP countries
whose median revenue share increased to 18.0 per cent from 12.6 per cent,
while those of the remaining countries were relatively unchanged.

Fig. 6.24   *Box plots of banana revenue of the ACP countries in the*
              British commodity chain (post-SEM)

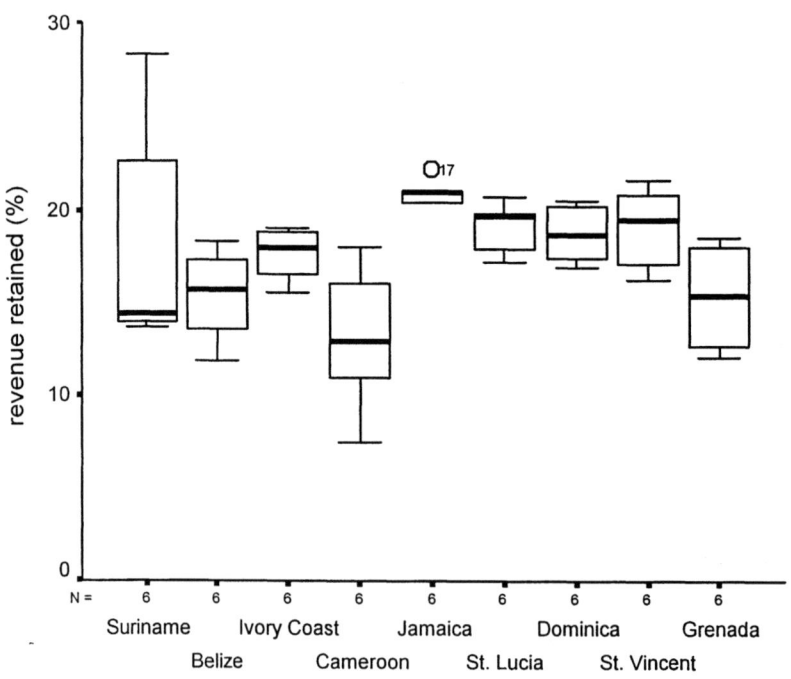

Source: Author's database.

6.4 Discussion and implications of the division and distribution of revenue

There are three findings in this chapter which require further discussion. First, the division of revenue between the various banana-exporting countries and the importing EU member-states is highly skewed in the favour of EU member-states, which were able to capture median revenues ranging from 81 to 86 per cent of the total commodity chain. This result is consistent with findings of previous research on the division of revenue between exporting and importing countries in the agricultural trade sector, e.g., Maizels (1992) and Talbot (1997), and suggests that the international division of trade revenue in the agricultural sector is likely to have remained largely unchanged since the 1980s.

Second, since the implementation of the SEM the shares of the banana commodity chain retained by actors in Germany and the UK have increased, while that retained in France has decreased. This supports the hypothesis that TNCs in the German market (and to a lesser extent those in the UK) have taken advantage of the tariff to increase their margins through higher retail prices. Additionally, because the German banana market is dominated by US TNCs this also suggests increased vertical integration of the commodity chain.

Third, the shares of revenue retained by the exporting countries differed considerably according to the EU member countries supplied, particularly to those with some form of protectionism. In France, the French DOMs enjoyed the largest median shares of their commodity chains while the dollar-zone exporters retained the least. In Britain, although on average the Caribbean countries retained the largest revenue share of their commodity chains, it is Ecuador that has enjoyed the best performance in that market. Yet, the Ecuadorian performance does not typify the dollar-zone countries, since on average, their median share of revenue retained was 7 per cent less than that of the Caribbean countries. Therefore, the type of trade policy in the destination market can and has influenced the division of revenue along the commodity chain. More importantly though, the exporting country is likely to retain a larger share of the commodity chain if its own TNC controls not only production of the commodity, but also its marketing and distribution.

The fact that the share of revenue retained in Germany was the largest of all the commodity chains analysed weakens the neo-classical arguments in favour of banana trade liberalization in the EU (see Chapter 2), all of which were premised on the assumption that consumers in the German market were likely to have enjoyed the best economic welfare in the pre-SEM system. That EU banana retail prices were lowest in Germany in the pre-SEM period was considered a natural outcome of its *laissez-faire* trade policies and so consumers there were assumed to be best off. However, now it appears that although German banana consumers enjoyed the lowest relative retail prices in the EU during the pre-SEM period, it was at the expense of the Latin American countries who retained the least revenue share of the commodity chain.

At the other extreme, protection of the French market in the pre-SEM period appeared not to harm those producing countries which had access to France, since they retained considerably larger shares of revenue along their commodity chains. This is particularly true of the DOMs and France's former African colonies. Even in the British market, where a mix of protectionism and *laissez-faire* existed in the pre-SEM period, supplying countries retained larger shares of their commodity chains than those in the German market. Furthermore, the fact that among all countries supplying Britain, Ecuador retained the largest share of its commodity chain, despite having its bananas subjected to a tariff, implies that there is no causal relationship between the protection afforded to an individual country and the share of revenue that it retains. Other factors matter too! Ecuador's superior performance is explained by the direct involvement of its banana TNC, NOBOA, in all aspects of the commodity chain. In so doing, NOBOA is able to exploit economies of scale and common governance in a manner rather similar to its major rival TNCs from the US and hence the appropriation of a greater share of the revenue of the commodity chain by Ecuador than comparable exporting countries.

Protectionism, therefore, appears to have had the obliging effect of transferring a larger share of revenue to the producing countries and possibly increased surplus along their respective commodity chains. This result is consistent with Talbot (1997)'s finding on the effect of the International Coffee Agreements on producing countries, where export quotas were utilized.[22] Moreover, it could be the case that the relatively free market in Germany in the pre-SEM period served to create more surplus throughout the banana commodity chains; however, more of that surplus was retained in Germany in the form of profits, at the expense of lesser revenue to its supplying countries. This hypothesis will be further investigated in Chapter 7.

6.5   Conclusion

Prior to the implementation of a common policy for the importation of bananas, three distinct types of trade policy existed in the European Union:

laissez-faire in Germany; protectionism in France; and a mix of the two in Britain (Chapter 3). Advocates of EU-wide trade liberalization have maintained that such liberalization would improve consumer and producer welfare, relative to the pre-SEM system.

This chapter has demonstrated that the pre-SEM system of organization of banana markets in the EU had some impact on the relative shares of revenue retained in the exporting countries and EU member-states. Contrary to the expectations of neo-classical theory (Borrell and Yang, 1990; 1992), countries exporting bananas to the free market in Germany retained the least revenue, while those exporting to France retained the most, with the outcome for those exporting to the British market somewhere in between. Therefore, the type of trade policy that was implemented in the destination market can, and has affected the division and distribution of revenue between the supplying and consuming countries. While in the pre-SEM period the relatively lower retail prices of bananas in Germany might have been good for consumers, this benefit was achieved at the expense of considerably lower revenue shares to the exporting countries. Additionally, since the SEM took effect the median shares of revenue retained by countries exporting to Germany have declined while those of countries exporting to France have increased.

So if liberalized EU banana trade seems to be an instrument for encouraging lowest cost producers to supply the market, they are also bound to retain the least shares of revenue generated at the various stages of the commodity chain. Consequently, if the objective is to widen the gap between the shares of revenue retained in the consuming and producing countries, then liberalization is the correct policy. If, instead, the objective is to promote a more equitable division and distribution of revenue, then the protected markets of the pre-SEM period seem to be more suitable. This result, which is not consistent with theoretical expectations, suggests that TNC oligopolists operating in the relatively free market appropriated some of the benefits which should have been passed onto consumers as super normal profits – a hypothesis which we shall explore in subsequent chapters.

Notes

[1] For instance, Gereffi (1999:50) argues that between the early 1980s and the mid-1990s there have been changes in global sourcing of apparel for the United States market. Whereas in 1983 Northeast Asia accounted for 68 per cent of all US apparel imports, with Southeast Asia, South Asia and Central America and the Caribbean accounting for 8 per cent, 4 per cent and 4 per cent, respectively; in 1997

Northeast Asia accounted for only 33 per cent, while Southeast Asia, South Asia and Central America and the Caribbean accounted for 13 per cent, 10 per cent and 16 per cent, respectively.

[2] The process appears to be rather complex and depends upon, among other things, the retail channels in the US through which products are marketed, the level of capital required to produce commodities and whether or not demand might vary according to season. The pineapple sector is dominated by TNCs because of its high capital requirements (Raynolds, 1994:151), while production in the melon and oriental vegetables sector takes place largely under contract, due to lower capital requirements and high seasonality of demand (Raynolds, 1994:152).

[3] Although Goldfrank (1994:272-5) identifies the major actors involved at the various stages of commodity chains, from shipping to retail, no attempt is made to quantify the distribution of revenue from these commodities between Chile and the United States.

[4] According to Talbot (1997:86), TNCs managed to cause a shift in coffee surplus from the exporting countries to the core, by exercising their market power in keeping the price of green coffee low while the price of processed coffee was increased artificially.

[5] The inter-quartile range (IQR) for these observations was 3.1, with lower and upper quartile values of 80.4 and 83.4, respectively. As such, both the maximum (86.4) and minimum (78.9) observed values, were well within the largest and smallest calculated values outside of the box, respectively.

[6] Here the IQR was 2.0, with lower and upper quartile values of 85.0 and 87.0, respectively. Thus both the maximum (87.5) and minimum (83.7) observed values were well within the largest and smallest calculated values outside of the box, respectively.

[7] All of Costa Rica's observations were within 11.8 per cent of the upper and lower quartiles. Costa Rica's IQR was 7.8, with lower and upper quartile values of 15.9 and 23.7, respectively. Both the maximum (25.9) and minimum (12.8) observed values were well within the largest and smallest calculated values outside of the box, respectively.

[8] All of Nicaragua's observations were within 8.3 per cent of the upper and lower quartiles. In this case the IQR was 5.6 and the lower and upper quartile values were 9.3 and 14.8, respectively. Both the maximum (18.5) and the minimum (4.3) observed values were well within the largest and smallest calculated values outside of the box, respectively.

[9] Ecuador was the only one of these countries to record outliers at either extremes of its box plot. Its IQR was 3.0, with lower and upper quartile values of 13.8 and 16.8, respectively. However, its minimum (9.8) and maximum (21.3) observed values were both slightly outside the smallest and largest calculated values outside of the box, respectively.

[10] Roche (1998) provides some evidence in support of better organization of labour in Costa Rica. He argues that the "longest strike in the banana industry, 72 days in 1984, did so much damage to the plantation of UFC in Palmar, Costa Rica, that the company found it uneconomic to rehabilitate the area" (p.120).

Regarding Honduras, Roche (1998:119) continues with the emergence of the modern labor movement there in May 1954 "when approximately 12000 workers of the Tela Railroad company in Honduras, a UFC subsidiary, went on strike for 67 days".

[11] Persistent fluctuations in the exchange rate between the French franc and the United States dollar imply that revenue growth was only 2.5 times in dollar terms. Moreover, while revenue peaked in 1992 in dollar terms, the corresponding maximum is in 1993, in French francs.

[12] In the pre-SEM period, importers, wholesalers and retailers in France retained a median revenue share of 81.1 per cent, compared with those in Germany, who retained a median revenue share of 81.6 per cent.

[13] France's median share of the commodity chain actually decreased from 81.1 per cent in the pre-SEM period to 77.7 per cent in the post-SEM period, although with increased variability.

[14] As is evident from Figure 6.12, the median share of revenue retained in Honduras is slightly more than that retained in Cameroon and Madagascar, and shows considerably less variability. However, equally evident is the smaller number of observations in the case of Honduras, 12, compared with those of Cameroon and Madagascar; 21 and 14, respectively.

[15] The basis for exclusion of the Philippines is two-fold: first, it is only a residual supplier of bananas to the EU market, and second, for the period under review it only supplied bananas to France in seven out of 21 years. Therefore, its revenue distribution cannot be taken as being representative of a typical dollar-zone supplier.

[16] As part of France, Martinique and Guadeloupe have guaranteed market access at higher prices than all other exporting countries, which explains why their median revenue shares of the banana commodity chain are considerably larger than those of all other countries.

[17] Madagascar and Cameroon were able to retain 16.0 per cent and 15.9 per cent of their commodity chains in the pre-SEM period, respectively, although with slightly increased variability than for the entire period under study.

[18] Mexico has managed to increase its median share of revenue in the banana commodity chain to 13.3 per cent, although with somewhat more variability than in the pre-SEM period. Additionally, it does appear that the SEM has been *relatively* favourable to Ecuador, whose median share of revenue retained along the French commodity chain increased to 10.4 per cent with considerably less variability.

[19] In the pre-SEM period, importers, wholesalers and retailers in the UK retained a median revenue share of 81.4 per cent, compared with those in Germany, who retained a median revenue share of 81.6 per cent.

[20] Based on St. Lucia's performance. Although St. Lucia's median is somewhat lower than that of St. Vincent and Dominica, the latter two tend to be characterized by outliers and extreme values and somewhat greater variability than the St. Lucia data.

[21] Although there are three outliers in Dominica's data (Figure 6.22) it is clear that the overall variability is much less, compared with the data for the entire 1978-98 period (Figure 6.20).

[22] As Talbot (1997:86) put it, the "main reason producing countries fared so well for so long seems to have been the International Coffee Agreements, which were instituted in response to collective action by producing states attempting to increase their incomes from coffee exporting".

7 Division and Distribution of Margins Along the EU Banana Commodity Chains

7.1 Introduction

Chapter 6 demonstrated how revenue is distributed along EU banana commodity chains and it advanced two specific arguments. First, in the pre-SEM period, countries exporting to the 'free market' in Germany retained the least revenue from trade in the commodity, while those exporting to the protected market in France retained the most. Second, since the implementation of the SEM, the shares of revenue retained by actors in Germany and the UK have increased, while that of France has declined. Yet, countries exporting to the previously 'free market' of Germany continue to retain the least share of revenue, while those exporting to France continue to retain the most.

As for the EU consumers, in the pre-SEM period, those in Germany enjoyed superior economic welfare relative to those in France, since they paid a lower price for bananas. Therefore, two important questions remain to be answered: (i) What are the relative magnitudes of the margins generated along the various banana commodity chains? (ii) How are they divided and distributed between the various actors: exporting countries, shipping and importing countries, at each stage of the banana commodity chain? These are the questions that are addressed in this chapter, the remainder of which is organized as follows. Section 7.2 presents the methodology, followed by a brief note on the data that are used. Section 7.3 demonstrates and discusses the division and distribution of the margins along the various banana commodity chains, while Section 7.4 demonstrates that these margins could be used as proxies for isolating the surplus. Section 7.5 discusses the implications of these findings and Section 7.6 presents the conclusions.

7.2 Methodology and sources of data

The methodology that is used for analysing the division and distribution of the margins is similar to that used in Chapter 6 for analysing the division and distribution of revenue, in the sense that both use the global commodity chain perspective presented in detail in Chapter 4. However, what differs here is the objective variables that are used in each case and how their values are arrived at. It will be recalled that in Chapter 6, the methodology for revenue generated at any stage in the banana commodity chain, R_i, is the product of the price, P_i, and the quantity of bananas transacted at that stage, Q_i.

$$R_i = P_i Q_i \tag{7.1}$$

Since the objective here is to demonstrate the division and distribution of the margins, the following methodology will be used. First, the difference in revenue at two successive stages of the chain, i and j, $(j = i+1)$, is derived. This is the aggregate margin realized at the jth stage of the chain, ∂_{ji}.

$$\partial_{ji} = R_j - R_i \tag{7.2}$$

Then, aggregate margins, ∂_{ji}, are decomposed into costs, c_{ji}, taxes, t_{ji}, wages, w_{ji} and profits, π_{ji}, as follows.

$$\partial_{ji} = c_{ji} + t_{ji} + w_{ji} + \pi_{ji} \tag{7.3}$$

Repeated application of this methodology at each stage of the banana commodity chain for imports into Germany, France and the UK gives the division and distribution of the margins in each case, from which the surplus is isolated.[1] The data used in this chapter are from the same sources as those used in Chapter 6.

7.3   Division and distribution of margins along EU banana commodity chains

The trends in division of *relative* banana margins between France, Germany and the UK and their banana-exporting partners are analysed below. In each case, trends in export margins will be used as a proxy to capture the extent to which exporters of bananas benefit from the trade in the commodity;

trends in import-export margins as a proxy to capture the extent of profitability of the shipping stage; and trends in wholesale-import, and retail-wholesale margins (aggregated as retail-import margins) as a proxy to capture both the extent of profitability of bananas for actors in the importing country as a whole, as well as the specific stages in the chain that are more or less profitable. We shall then see how decomposing these aggregate margins results in the actual surplus generated and retained at each stage.

7.3.1   Division and distribution of relative banana margins along the French commodity chain

The division of the total banana margin (from retail to export) between France and its trading partners is shown in Figure 7.1. It is evident that, over time, a disproportionately larger, and generally increasing share of the total banana margin is retained by actors in France, relative to that which is retained in its exporting partners.

Fig. 7.1   *Division of relative banana margins in the French commodity chain (%)*

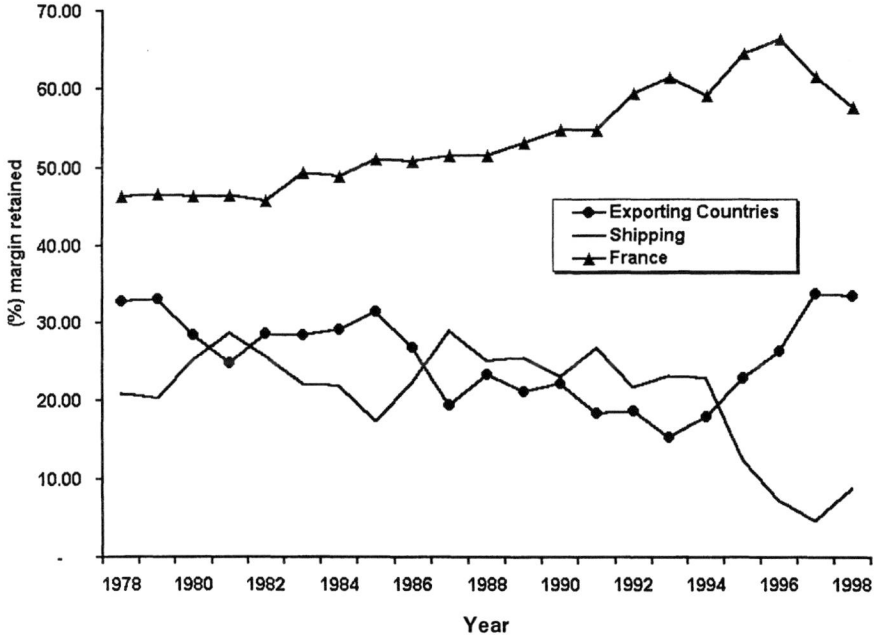

Source: Author's database.

During the pre-SEM period, the exporting countries retained their largest share of the banana margin between 1978 and 1979, when it averaged 33.0 per cent. Subsequently, during the 1980-92 period there was a cyclic but secular decline in the share of margins retained among the exporting countries, reaching an all-time low of 15.4 per cent in 1993. Part of the explanation for the decline in the margins retained in the exporting countries comes from the increased margin retained at the shipping stage during the 1980-81 period,[2] while the rest of that explanation comes from the exploitation of the market power of French banana firms during the pre-SEM period.[3] The apparent cost savings at the shipping stage during that period were largely appropriated by importers, wholesalers and retailers in France. By 1992, France's share of the banana margin had increased to just under 60 per cent, with shippers accounting for a further 22 per cent, leaving 18 per cent for the exporting countries.

Fig. 7.2   *Box plots of banana margins in the French commodity chain (%)*

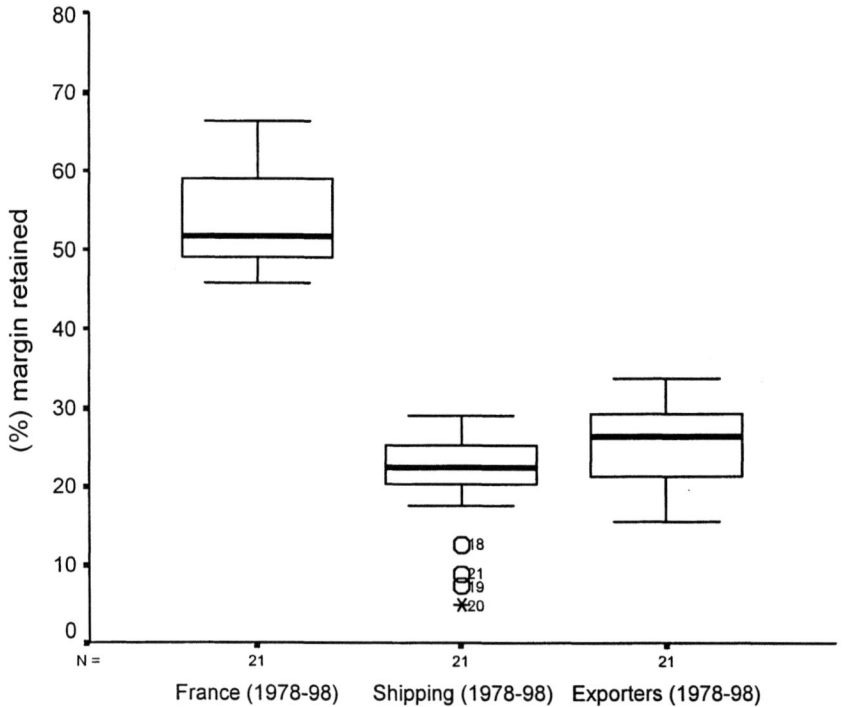

Source: Author's database.

However, the implementation of the SEM seems to have had a positive impact on the exporting countries, which retained a record high 33.8 per cent of the margin in 1997, as well as France, which retained a record 66.3 per cent of the margin in 1996. Shippers appear to have been made worse off, with their shares falling below 10 per cent (Figure 7.2). A possible explanation for these shifts in the shares of the margin retained comes from changing conditions in production and marketing of bananas along the French commodity chain. Prior to implementation of the SEM, Dole, and to a lesser extent Del Monte, had strategically invested in banana commodity chains in the French DOMs and the Ivory Coast (Chapter 3), resulting in increased productivity. Increased retention of the margin by France, therefore, reflects the increasing power of the US TNCs in the commodity chain. The questions that remain are: What were the relative positions of the various exporting countries with regard to the distribution of these margins? Did they all receive similar shares of the chain, or did some countries benefit more relative to others? How has the SEM impacted on individual exporting countries?

Fig. 7.3　　*Box plots of banana margins of the exporting countries in the French commodity chain (1978-98)*

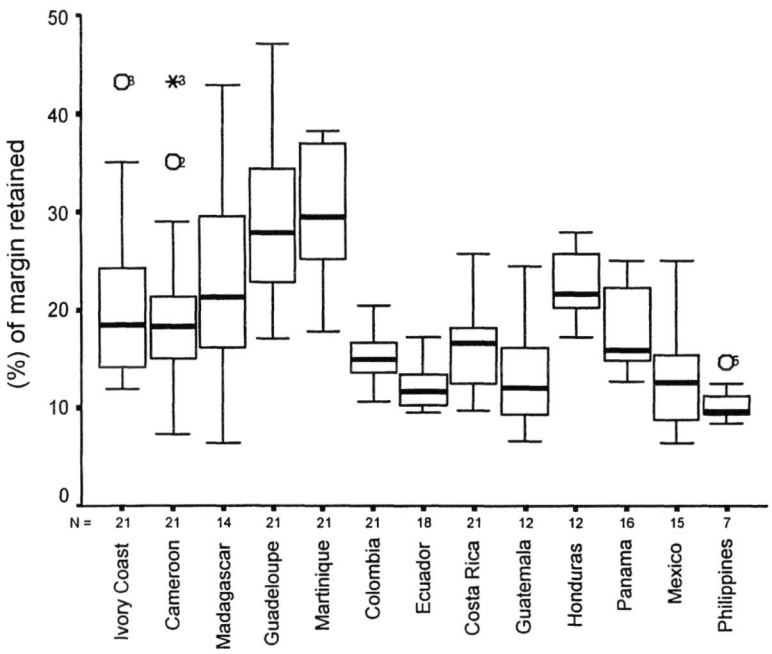

Source:　Author's database.

Figure 7.3 suggests that different exporting countries benefited differently from the banana trade with France during the 1978-98 period. In general, the French DOMs received the largest share of the banana margin,[4] while the dollar-zone exporters received the least[5] and the performance of former French colonies was somewhere in between.[6]

The most important exception to this generalization is Honduras, whose performance, with a median margin of 21.6 per cent, was third among all exporting countries to France.[7] These results are consistent with expectations from the banana import policy that was in force in France during the pre-SEM period (Chapter 3), and the fact that the SEM had not changed market access for the various countries in any significant way. Preferential access to the French market by the DOMs and former French colonies in Africa resulted in competitive advantages relative to their dollar-zone rivals, and co-operatives were placed in a strong position to exercise some degree of market power. This is confirmed when we compare the structures of the distribution of banana margins in the pre-SEM period (Figure 7.4) with the entire period (Figure 7.3).

Fig. 7.4   *Box plots of banana margins of the exporting countries in the French commodity chain (pre-SEM)*

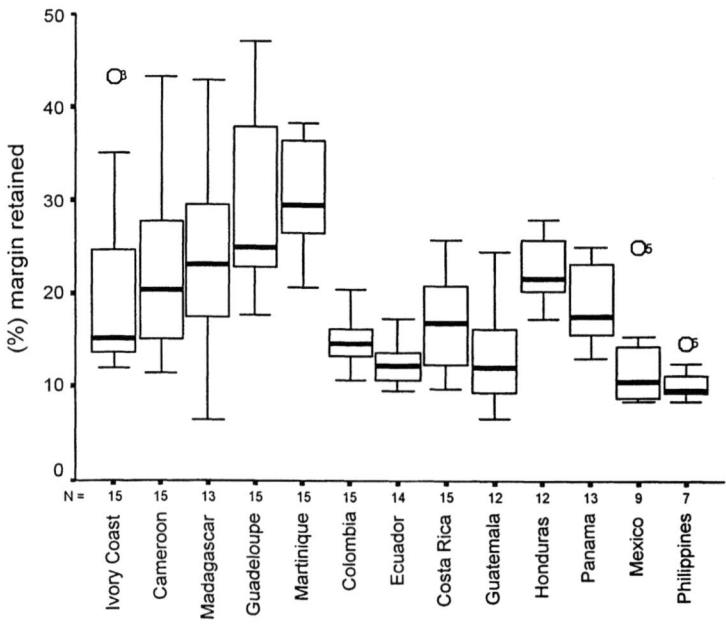

Source: Author's database.

As Figure 7.4 shows, the French DOMs retained a larger median share of banana margins in the pre-SEM period, while the dollar-zone exporters retained a smaller share. Martinique retained the largest median share of 29.5 per cent, while Guadeloupe retained the next-largest share of 25.0 per cent. Madagascar and Cameroon retained larger median shares in the pre-SEM period, of 23.0 per cent and 20.3 per cent, respectively; the Ivory Coast's share was lower, at 15.2 per cent. Among the dollar-zone exporting countries, the best performance came from Panama, which retained a median share of 17.6 per cent, followed by Costa Rica, which retained a median share of 16.8 per cent. However, for the remaining dollar-zone countries, the median share of the margin retained was considerably less, averaging just over 10 per cent. When the post-SEM period is considered (Figure 7.5) we see that the relative positions of the various supplying countries remain largely unchanged.

Fig. 7.5   *Box plots of banana margins of the exporting countries in the French commodity chain (post-SEM)*

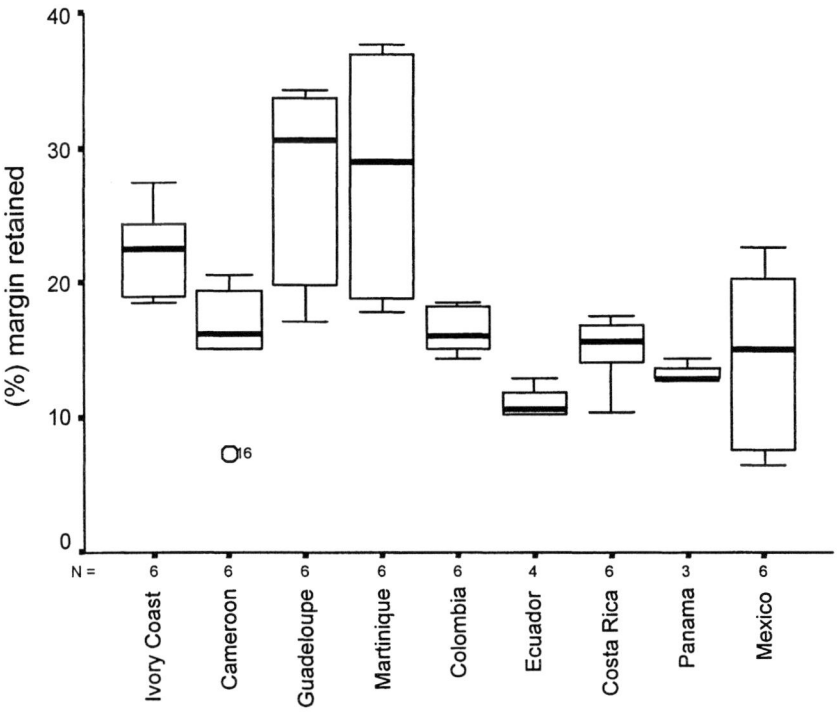

Source: Author's database.

Guadeloupe and Martinique outperformed all countries, retaining median shares of the chain of 30.5 per cent and 29.0 per cent, respectively.[8] Among the former French colonies, the Ivory Coast's median share of the banana margin improved relative to the pre-SEM period (from 15.2 per cent to 22.5 per cent), while Cameroon's median share worsened (from 20.3 per cent to 16.1 per cent). Where the dollar-zone countries were concerned, Costa Rica's median share of the margin retained decreased slightly (from 16.8 per cent to 15.6 per cent) while Colombia's improved marginally (from 14.6 per cent to 16.0 per cent). Mexico appears to have benefited the most from the SEM, with its median share of the margin retained actually increasing from 10.5 per cent in the pre-SEM period to 15.0 per cent in the post-SEM period.[9]

To summarize, the exporting countries retained relatively larger shares of the margin compared to revenue, although the DOMs and former French colonies retained disproportionately larger shares than the dollar-zone countries. Additionally, since the SEM took effect, actors both in France and the exporting countries have retained even larger shares of the margin than the shippers, suggesting increased control over retail by TNCs. Let us now examine how the margins are divided along the British commodity chain.

7.3.2   Division and distribution of relative banana margins along the British commodity chain

The division of the total banana margin (from retail to export) between the UK and its trading partners (Figure 7.6) is typified by two distinct trends: the 1978-90 period, when relatively stable but periodically fluctuating shares of margins were retained among actors; and the 1991-98 period, when there were major shifts in these shares.

During the 1978-90 period, growth in the shares of the margin retained by the exporting countries and the UK was at the expense of that retained at the shipping stage. The initial decline in the shares of the margins of the exporting countries is explained by increases in the share retained by importers, wholesalers and retailers in the UK.[10] However, the increases in the share of the margin retained at the shipping stage during the 1981-83 sub-period resulted in a simultaneous decrease in the shares retained in the UK and slight improvements in the shares retained among the exporting countries.[11] Subsequent decreases in the share of the margin retained at the shipping stage were initially evenly distributed between the UK and the exporting countries; however, since 1987 decreases in the margin retained at the shipping stage have resulted in increases in the margin retained in the UK and little change in that retained by the exporting countries.[12] This suggests that the actors who controlled the shipping stage of the British commodity chain largely influenced the division of surplus between the exporting countries and the UK, and so the exploitation of scale economies in shipping is important in order to keep the division of surplus stable.

Fig. 7.6   *Division of relative banana margins in the British*
              commodity chain (%)

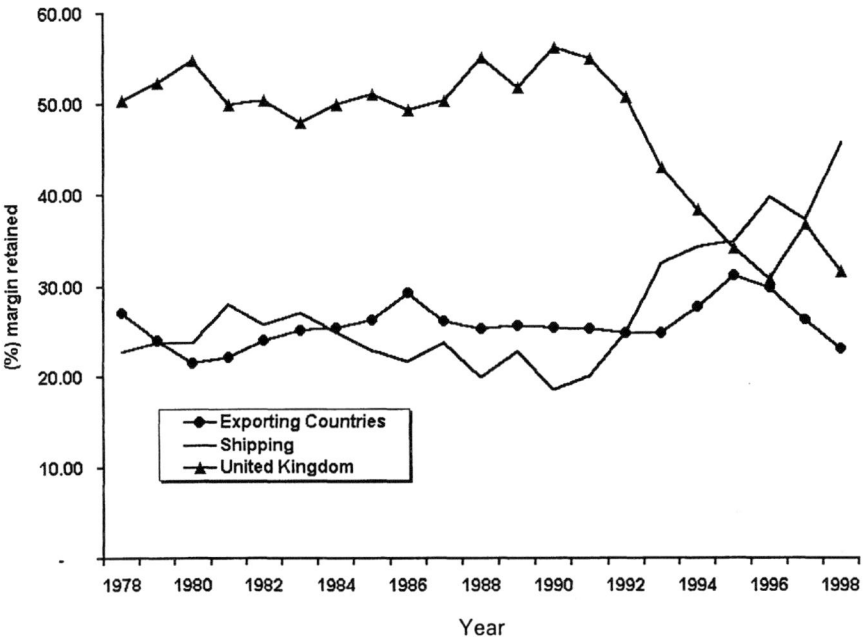

Source: Author's database.

Since 1991, there has been an increasing trend in the share of the banana margin retained at the shipping stage, peaking at 45.5 per cent in 1998. This has resulted in considerable declines in the share of the margin retained in the UK, falling to a record low of 30.7 per cent in 1996. Interestingly, the shares of the exporting countries actually increased initially, peaking at 31.1 per cent in 1995; however, their shares, like those of the UK, show a declining trend since 1996. This again emphasizes the importance of scale economies in shipping along the banana commodity chain, if both the exporting countries and the UK are to retain larger shares of the surplus.

Examining the variations in the shares of the banana margin retained by all the actors in the commodity chain (Figure 7.7) further brings out the crucial importance of shipping. The shares of the banana margin retained in the UK and at the shipping stage both show considerable variation, with standard deviations of 8.0 and 7.2, respectively. However, the shares of the banana margin retained among the exporting countries show considerable stability, with a median of 25.3 per cent and standard deviation of 2.4.[13] The stability in the median share of the margin retained by the exporting countries could be attributed to the relative price inelasticity of demand for bananas and the constraints on the costs of production that the major supplying countries to the UK face (Chapter 3). Therefore, shocks to the British commodity chain (for example, increases in shipping costs) are more easily coped with by importers, wholesalers and retailers, who control the price formation process, than by exporters. But the question of the relative positions of the exporting countries to the UK remains: Did all exporting countries receive similar shares of the banana margins along their commodity chains? And how has the SEM impacted on the performance of individual countries?

Fig. 7.7   *Box plots of banana margins in the British commodity chain (%)*

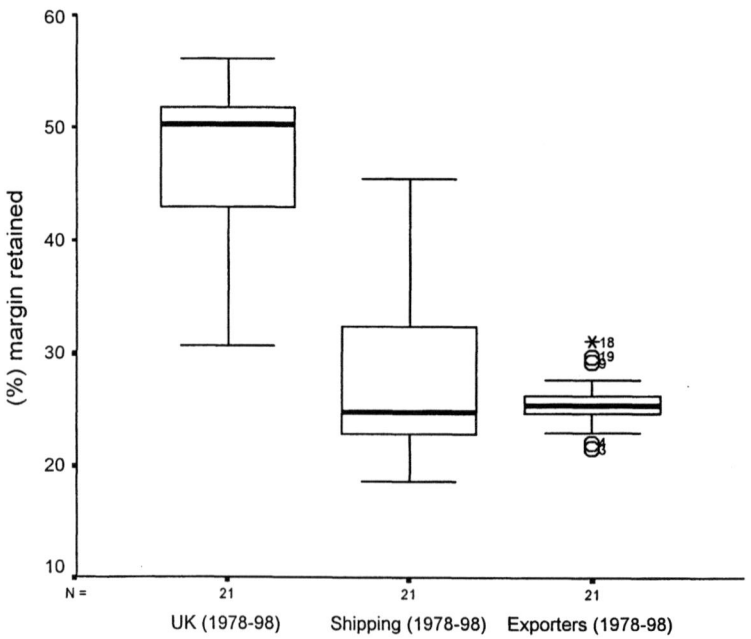

Source: Author's database.

Although the median share of the margin retained by the dollar-zone countries is less than 20 per cent, there is considerable variation in their individual performance and there are important exceptions (Figure 7.8). First, Ecuador has managed to retain a median margin of 39.2 per cent over the 1978-98 period, the largest median share retained by dollar-zone exporters to the British market. Despite the considerable variability in Ecuador's performance,[14] the minimum share retained over the entire period (20.4 per cent) was slightly larger than that of the second-best exporting country, Honduras; and Ecuador's maximum share of the UK commodity chain ever retained was 61.0 per cent.[15] Second, both Honduras and Costa Rica enjoyed relatively large shares of their British banana margins, with medians of 20.3 per cent,[16] and 18.8 per cent,[17] respectively.

Fig. 7.8   *Box plots of banana margins of dollar-zone countries in the British commodity chain (1978-98)*

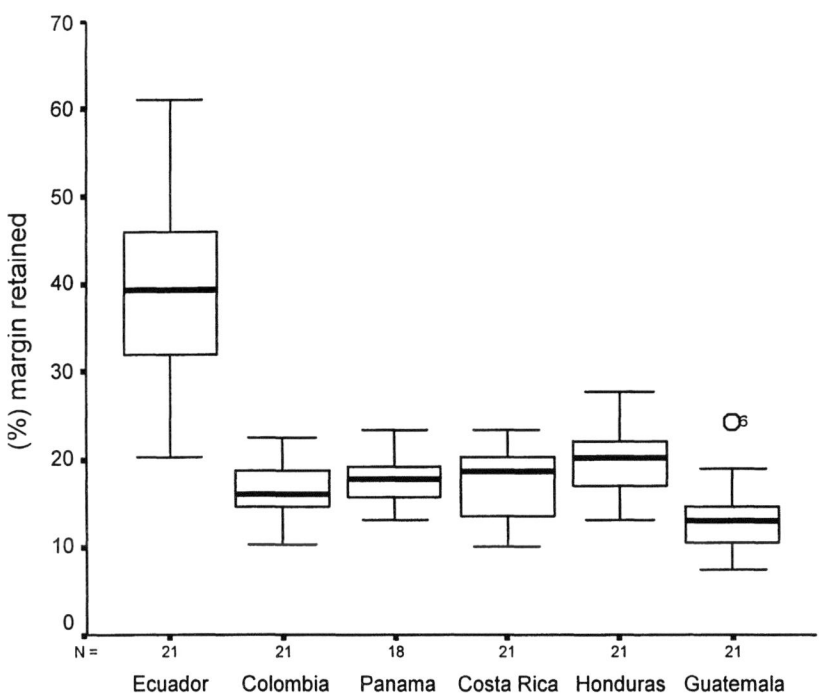

Source: Author's database.

Finally, despite somewhat lower median margins than Honduras, both Panama and Colombia performed reasonably well in the British banana market.[18] Therefore, as further discussed below, despite the imposition of tariffs against dollar-zone bananas, these countries were capable of commanding some presence in the market and retaining margins comparable to those of countries that enjoyed preferential access. Examining the variations in the margins of the ACP countries (Figure 7.9) further elucidates this point.

Fig. 7.9   Box plots of banana margins for ACP countries in the British commodity chain (1978-98)

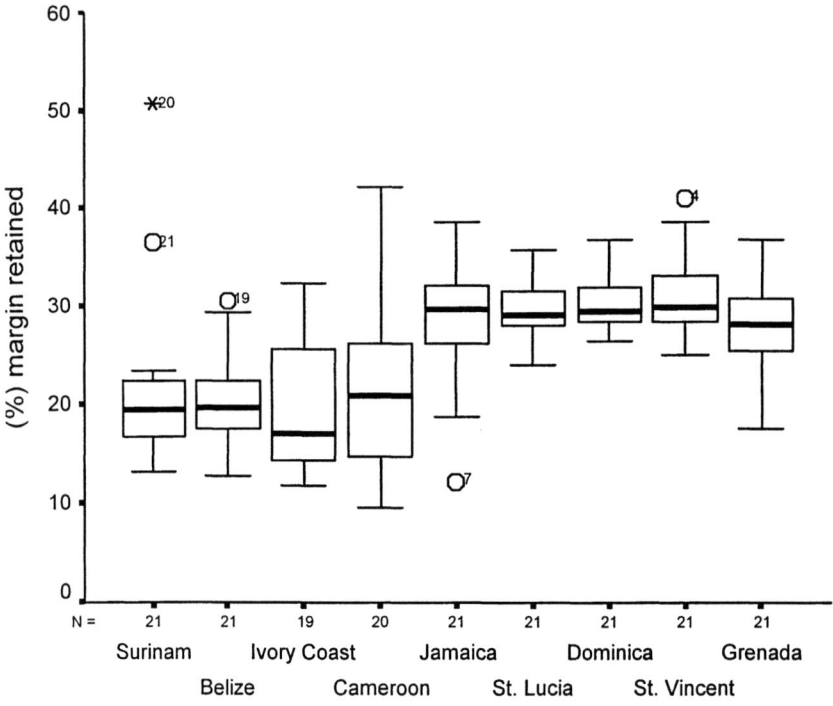

Source: Author's database.

Figure 7.9 shows that the Caribbean ACP countries appear to have performed the best in the group with larger median shares, and have generally less variability and extreme values or outliers, than the other ACP countries.[19] The magnitude of the shares retained by the Caribbean is explained by the preferential access which these countries enjoy in the British market, while the relative stability of these shares is explained by their joint shipping and marketing strategies, which allow them to enjoy some economies of scale (in shipping) and governance (in marketing and distribution). Figure 7.9 also shows that unlike the dollar-zone countries, where Ecuador captured a significantly larger share of the margin than all other countries, among the ACP countries the variations across groups is much less. This is explained by two factors. First, all ACP countries enjoy similar preferential market access to the EU, thus giving them similar competitive advantages. Second, all of these countries face similar constraints in production and marketing of bananas. Ecuador's decisive lead over the other dollar-zone countries is explained by the marketing and distribution of its bananas by its own TNC, NOBOA.

Over the 1978-98 period, St. Vincent demonstrated the best median margin performance among Caribbean ACP countries, retaining 29.9 per cent,[20] followed by Jamaica with 29.5 per cent,[21] Dominica with 29.5 per cent,[22] St. Lucia with 28.9 per cent,[23] and Grenada with 27.9 per cent.[24] Regarding the other ACP countries, the best performance in terms of median margins came from Cameroon, which retained 20.8 per cent,[25] followed by Belize with 19.7 per cent,[26] Surinam with 19.4 per cent,[27] and the Ivory Coast with 17.0 per cent.[28]

Fig. 7.10   Box plots of banana margins for dollar-zone countries in the British commodity chain (pre-SEM)

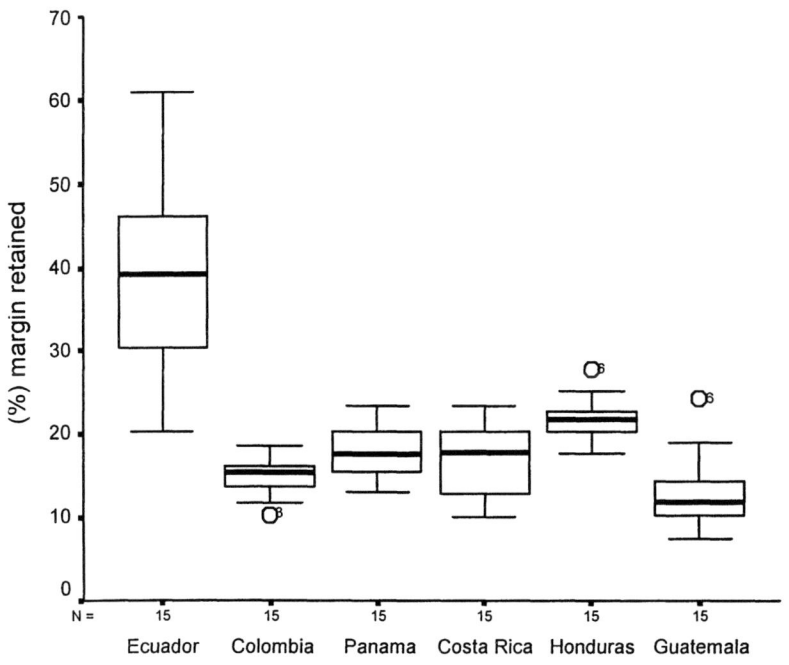

Source: Author's database.

Since implementation of the SEM largely preserved the UK's banana import policy, the SEM would not be expected to have any major impact on the distribution of these margins. Box plots constructed for the dollar-zone countries in the pre-SEM period (Figure 7.10) seem to support this in the case of Ecuador, whose median margin in the pre-SEM period, 39.2 per cent, is identical to that for the entire period under study (1978-98), although there was somewhat more variation in the pre-SEM data.[29]

Regarding the other dollar-zone exporters however, it appears that the majority were slightly worse off in the pre-SEM period (Figure 7.10) possibly because there was more arbitrariness in allocation of licences and quotas compared with that under the SEM. Yet they were certainly not as worse off as one might have expected, considering there was only a slight percentage change in the medians in most cases. Colombia's median margin was 15.5 per cent in the pre-SEM period, compared with 16.2 per cent for the entire period; Costa Rica's median margin was 17.8 per cent in the pre-SEM period, compared with 18.8 per cent for the entire period; and Guatemala's median margin was 11.9 per cent in the pre-SEM period, compared with 13.0 per cent for the entire period.[30]

Fig. 7.11   Box plots of banana margins for ACP countries in the British commodity chain (pre-SEM)

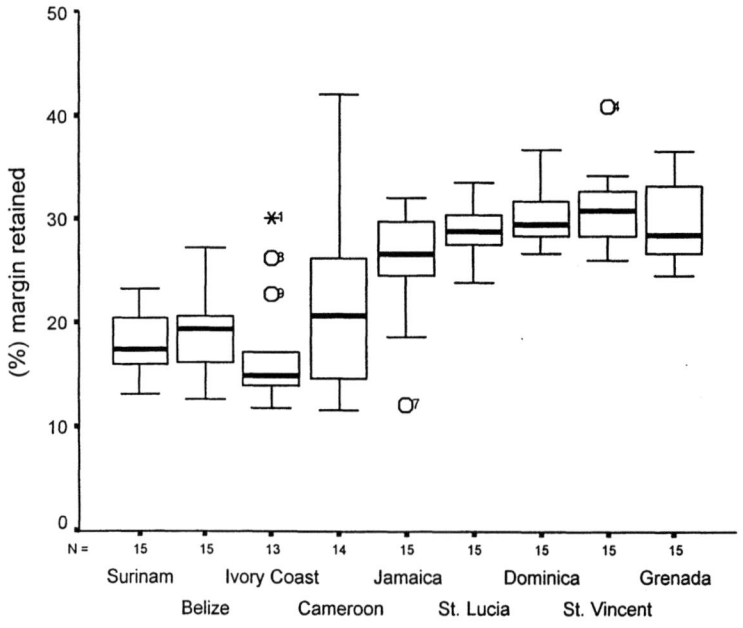

Source: Author's database.

If preferential access of ACP countries to the British banana market in the pre-SEM period was expected to result in super-normal monopoly profits as suggested by Borrell and Yang (1990, 1992), one would expect their median margins retained in the pre-SEM period to be larger relative to the entire period under study (1978-98). Yet, box plots for the ACP countries in the pre-SEM period (Figure 7.11) do not confirm this.

On the contrary, Figure 7.11 shows that while there were some differences in both the absolute and relative positions of ACP exporting countries in the pre-SEM period, such differences were not in the expected direction. In general, ACP countries either retained slightly lower median margins in the pre-SEM period, or their margins remained unchanged relative to the entire period under study. This is explained by the general trends in the margin shares retained by the exporting countries, shipping and in the UK, as presented earlier (see Figure 7.6). During the pre-SEM period, actors in the UK retained a disproportionately larger share of the margin than in the exporting countries, and the tendency was for an increase in the UK's share whenever shipping costs fell.

St. Vincent and Grenada were the only exceptions, with slightly larger median margins of 30.8 per cent and 28.4 per cent, respectively, in the pre-SEM period. These exceptions are explained by the ability of these countries to secure higher lower-bounds in the pre-SEM period, compared with the entire period under study (Figure 7.12). St. Vincent's lower-bound started within the 24-26 per cent interval in the pre-SEM period, compared with the 22-24 per cent interval for the entire 1978-98 period; Grenada's lower-bound started within the 22-24 per cent interval in the pre-SEM period, compared with the 16-18 per cent interval for the entire 1978-98 period.

So although Caribbean ACP countries were not badly off on the whole in both the entire 1978-98 period and the pre-SEM period, it is evident that the protection provided to these countries did not necessarily result in superior monopoly advantages in the British market, when they are compared with other major suppliers like Ecuador. Ecuador's exceptional performance in the face of tariff quotas clearly underscores the importance of *control* of the commodity chain and *internalization* of its various stages as a means of retaining surplus. By over-emphasizing the potentially pernicious effects of tariffs and quotas while ignoring the strategic advantages that TNCs enjoy through internalization of the banana commodity chain, Borrell and Yang (1990, 1992) and other exponents of the neo-classical approach are likely to have grossly over-estimated the potential welfare and efficiency effects of trade liberalization.

Fig. 7.12   *Comparative distribution of margins in Grenada and St.*
               Vincent

St. Vincent, 1978-98

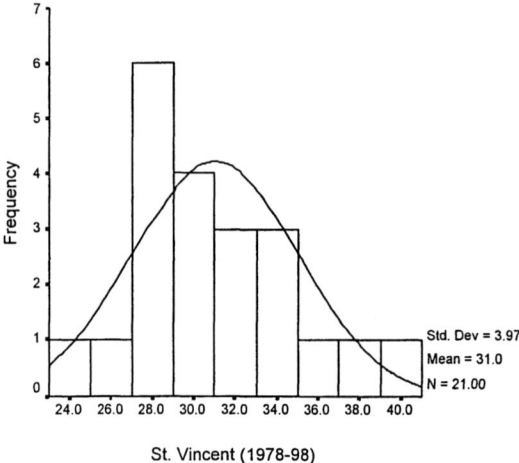

St. Vincent (1978-98)

Source: Author's database.

Grenada, 1978-98

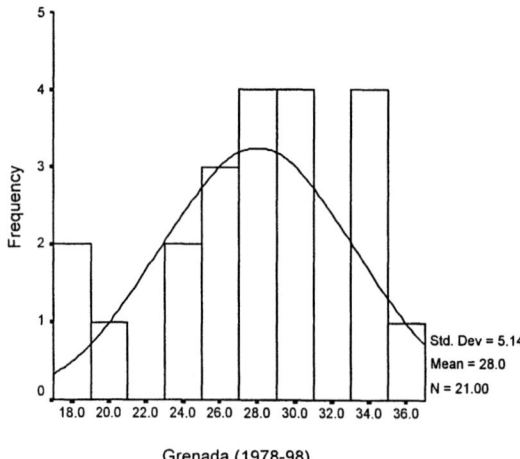

Grenada (1978-98)

Source: Author's database.

Fig. 7.12 Continued...

St. Vincent, pre-SEM

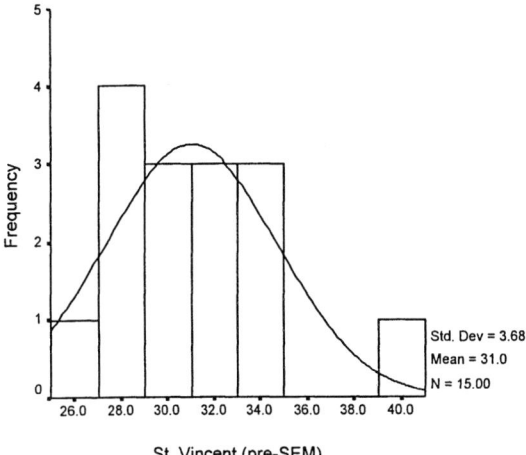

St. Vincent (pre-SEM)

Source: Author's database.

Grenada, pre-SEM

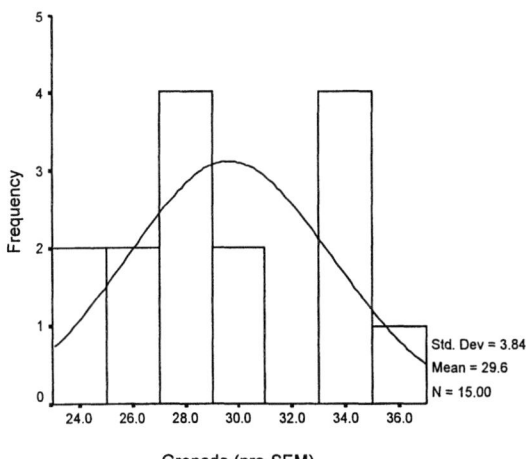

Grenada (pre-SEM)

Source: Author's database.

Regarding the other ACP countries, there was little change in the median margin retained by Belize, while Cameroon's remained unchanged. However, both the Ivory Coast and Surinam appear to have been disadvantaged in the pre-SEM period, with median margins of 14.9 per cent and 17.4 per cent, respectively. Again, this supports the argument that there is not likely to be any causal relationship between monopoly surplus appropriation by the exporting countries and preferential market access. The disadvantages suffered by the Ivory Coast and Surinam are explained by a relative lack of internalization of their commodity chains.

Let us now examine how the SEM has impacted on the distribution of banana margins along the commodity chains of the exporting countries in the dollar-zone (Figure 7.13).

Fig. 7.13   *Box plots of banana margins for dollar-zone countries in the British commodity chain (post-SEM)*

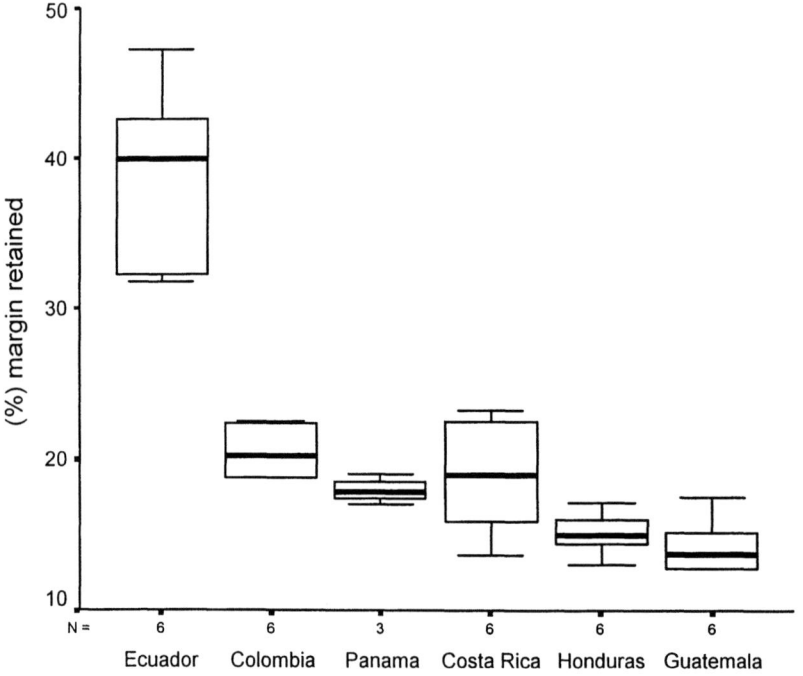

Source: Author's database.

The SEM appears to have benefited most of the Latin American banana-exporting countries in the British commodity chain, since they have generally managed to retain larger median margins. Ecuador, Panama, Costa Rica and Guatemala have all enjoyed a marginal increase in their median margins, ranging from 1 to 2 per cent, while Colombia has enjoyed the largest increase in the share of the margin retained, growing from 15.5 per cent in the pre-SEM period to 20.2 per cent since the SEM took effect (Figure 7.13).[31] This is an expected outcome since all of these countries now face similar rules regarding access to the EU market. However, Honduras' median margin has deteriorated since the SEM took effect, falling from 21.7 per cent to 15.0 per cent. This is explained by supply-side factors in the mid-1990s, including a number of hurricanes, labour unrest and crop disease.[32]

Additionally, the SEM appears to have reduced the degree of variability in median margins retained by the dollar-zone countries (Figure 7.13). Since access to the EU tariff quota requires licences and TNCs operating in these countries have advance knowledge of this, it is likely that plantation output in these countries is being matched to licence quantities in order to obtain cultivation scale economies. Additionally, since TNCs control the shipping of bananas, again they are likely to match the quantities of bananas shipped to optimal reefer sizes so as to exploit scale economies in shipping. When these two sources of scale economies are brought together, TNCs can predict the shares of the margin that will be retained at all stages of the commodity chain and hence the stability in the returns to these banana-exporting countries.

Regarding the ACP countries, if the logic of exponents of the neo-classical approach like Borrell and Yang (1990, 1992) is correct, the SEM would not be expected to affect them adversely to a significant extent provided their preferential market access was maintained. However, the empirical evidence (Figure 7.14) does not suggest any causal relation between their median margins retained in the post-SEM period and preferential market access. Most of the Caribbean ACP countries witnessed some decline in the median share of the margins that they retained, relative to the pre-SEM period. For Dominica, St. Vincent and Grenada, the median shares of the margin retained all decreased,[33] while for St. Lucia and Jamaica they increased by 2.5 and 8 per cent, respectively (Figure 7.14). We saw earlier (Figure 7.6) that since 1992 there has been an upswing in the share of the margin retained at the shipping stage of the commodity chain (a trend which persists up to 1998), most of which is explained by increasing shipping costs. Therefore, the relatively smaller[34] Caribbean ACP countries have fallen victim to these increased costs, while the relatively larger ones have survived.[35] So, for the ACP countries, economic *size* does matter.

Fig. 7.14   Box plots of banana margins for ACP countries in the British commodity chain (post-SEM)

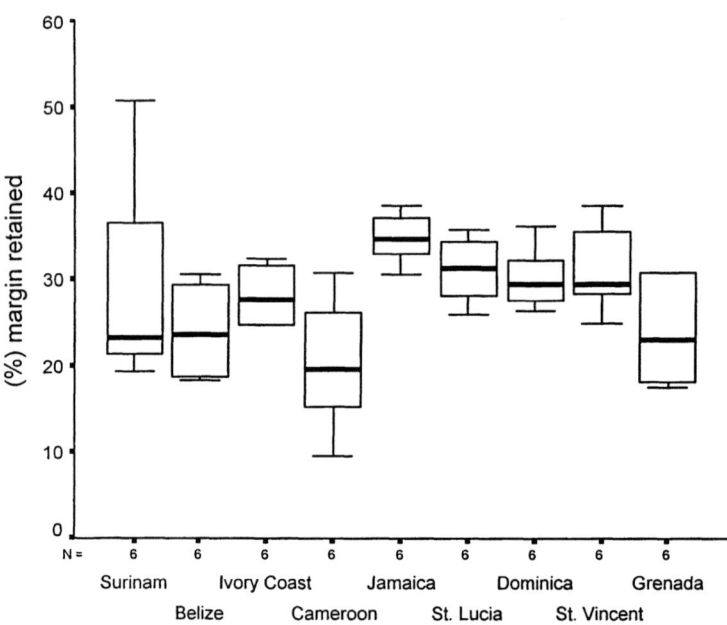

Source: Author's database.

Examination of the rest of the ACP countries (Figure 7.14) shows that, with the exception of Cameroon, whose median share of margin retained decreased from 20.8 per cent to 19.6 per cent between the pre-SEM and post-SEM periods, they were all made better off by the SEM. The Ivory Coast experienced a slightly more than 14 per cent increase in its median margin, Belize slightly more than 4 per cent, and Surinam just under 6 per cent. Explanation of these trends seems linked to the increased economies of scale and common governance of the respective commodity chains which took place within the last decade of the twentieth century with increased involvement of US TNCs in the production and marketing of bananas from these countries.

7.3.3   Division and distribution of relative banana margins along the German commodity chain

The division of the total banana margin (from retail to export) between Germany and its trading partners for the 1978-98 period (Figure 7.15) is typified by three distinct trends. First, the 1978-85 period is characterized by a general decline in the shares of the banana margin retained in Germany and a general increase in that retained by the exporting countries. Second, the 1986-92 period is characterized by a general increase in the shares of the banana margin retained in Germany and a decrease in that retained by the exporting countries. Third, the 1992-98 period is characterized by a general decline in the shares of the banana margin retained in Germany and a moderate increase in that retained by the exporting countries.

Fig. 7.15   Division of relative banana margins in the German commodity chain (%)

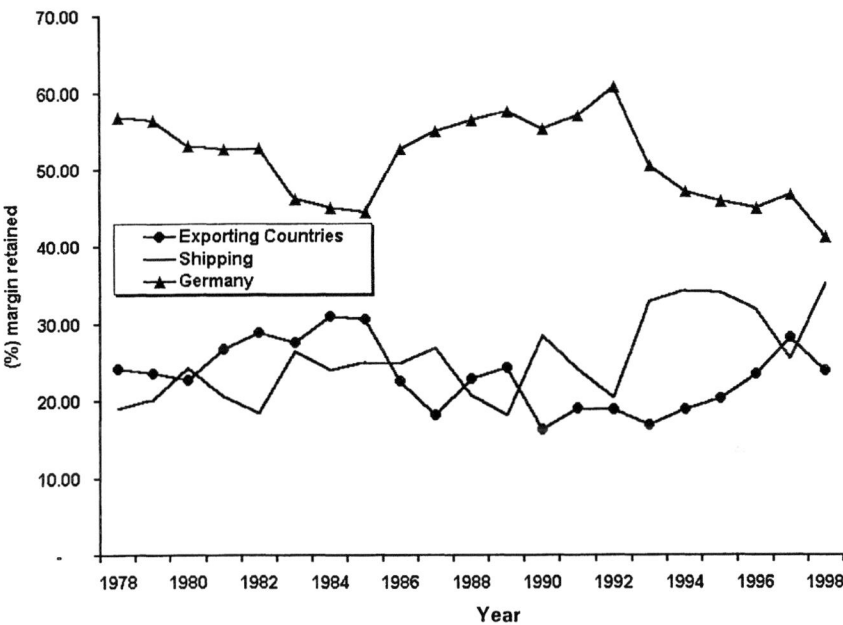

Source: Author's database.

During the 1978-85 period, the share of the banana margin retained by actors in Germany fell from 57.0 per cent to 44.6 per cent while that retained among the exporting countries increased from 24.0 per cent to 30.5 per cent. Consequently, more than 50 per cent of the decrease in the share of the banana margin originally retained in Germany was accompanied by an equivalent higher margin share for the exporting countries, with the remainder being retained at the shipping stage of the chain.[36] The increase in the share of the banana margin retained in the exporting countries is explained by increased demands for higher wages and improved conditions of work on dollar-zone plantations; the increase in the share of the banana margin retained at the shipping stage is attributed largely to technological progress made at that time.[37] Therefore, the 1978-85 period was one of progressive redistribution of the banana margin from Germany to its exporting partners. In the subsequent period, 1986-92, once the shipping technology had matured and its cost stabilized, German importers, wholesalers and retailers resumed appropriating increasing shares of the commodity chain at the expense of the exporting countries. During that period, the share of the banana margin retained in Germany increased from 52.7 per cent to 60.7 per cent, while that retained in the exporting countries decreased from 22.5 per cent to 18.8 per cent. Direct control of the various stages of the banana commodity chain by US TNCs served as a mechanism for redistribution of margins along the chain, resulting in increased monopoly profits for TNCs in Germany. Therefore, all of the loss of the margin originally retained in the exporting countries was appropriated in Germany, and, in addition, Germany appropriated some of the margin originally retained at the shipping stage.[38] Finally, during the 1993-98 period, there was a general decline in the share of the banana margin retained in Germany, which is explained largely by increasing shipping costs[39] and marginal improvements in the shares of the margin retained by the exporting countries. Germany's median share of the banana margin retained fell from 50.4 per cent in 1993 to a record low 41.2 per cent in 1998, while that retained by the exporting countries increased from 16.8 per cent to 23.8 per cent for the same period. Therefore, since the implementation of the SEM the tendency has been for a more progressive redistribution of the total banana margin among all actors in the German chain.[40] As will be argued later (in Chapter 8) these changes can be interpreted in the context of decreasing market power in the EU banana industry after the SEM took effect. Since the effect of the EU's tariff is to increase the perceived marginal cost of bananas for importers and wholesalers, their market power would be expected to decline.

Analysis of the variations in the shares of the banana margin retained among the actors along the German commodity chain (Figure 7.16) further supports the preceding discussion. In comparison with the French and British commodity chains, there is a remarkable amount of stability in the variation of the share of the banana margin retained among all actors in the German commodity chain.[41] German banana operators retained the largest share of the commodity chain (52.8 per cent), followed by operators at the shipping stage (24.8 per cent) and exporters (23.3 per cent). More importantly, there was somewhat less variation in the shares of the commodity chain retained by exporters compared with all other actors. This is explained by two factors: first, the relative price inelasticity of demand for bananas; and second the relatively weaker bargaining power of the exporting countries *vis-à-vis* other actors (TNCs) in the banana commodity chain.

Fig, 7.16   *Box plots of banana margins in the German commodity chain (%)*

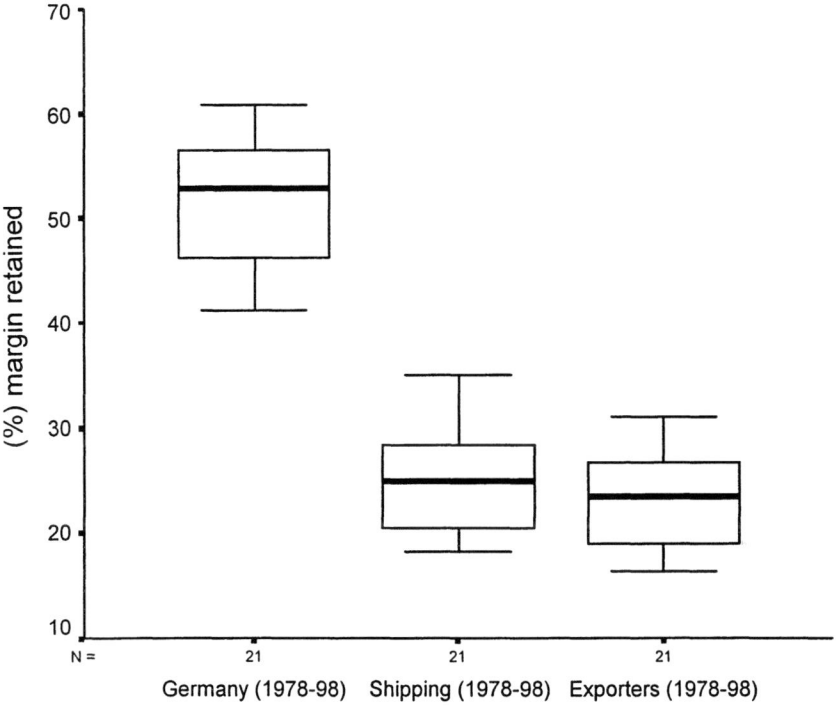

Let us now analyse the distributions of banana margins among the exporting countries (Figure 7.17) and discuss how the SEM has impacted upon such distributions. The exporting countries have enjoyed different levels of success in their exports to the German market, with Costa Rica enjoying the greatest success and Nicaragua the least. Costa Rica's median margin of the commodity chain retained was 31.1 per cent, but showed considerable variability with a standard deviation of 7.4.[42] Honduras had the next-largest median share of the commodity chain, at 25.4 per cent, but with slightly more variability than Costa Rica with a standard deviation of 7.5.[43] Ecuador and Panama were next, with practically coincident medians; however, there was considerably more variability in Ecuador's data, in terms of both the standard deviation and the presence of outliers.[44] Colombia's data, with a standard deviation of 3.1, showed the least variability of all countries exporting to Germany, and its median margin, at 19.4 per cent, was slightly less than that of Panama.[45] Finally, with a median margin of 16.1 per cent and standard deviation of 4.4, Nicaragua benefited the least. Not only was its margin the smallest, but its stability suggests that the prospects for improvement are minimal.[46]

Fig. 7.17   Box plots of banana margins of the exporting countries in the German commodity chain (1978-98)

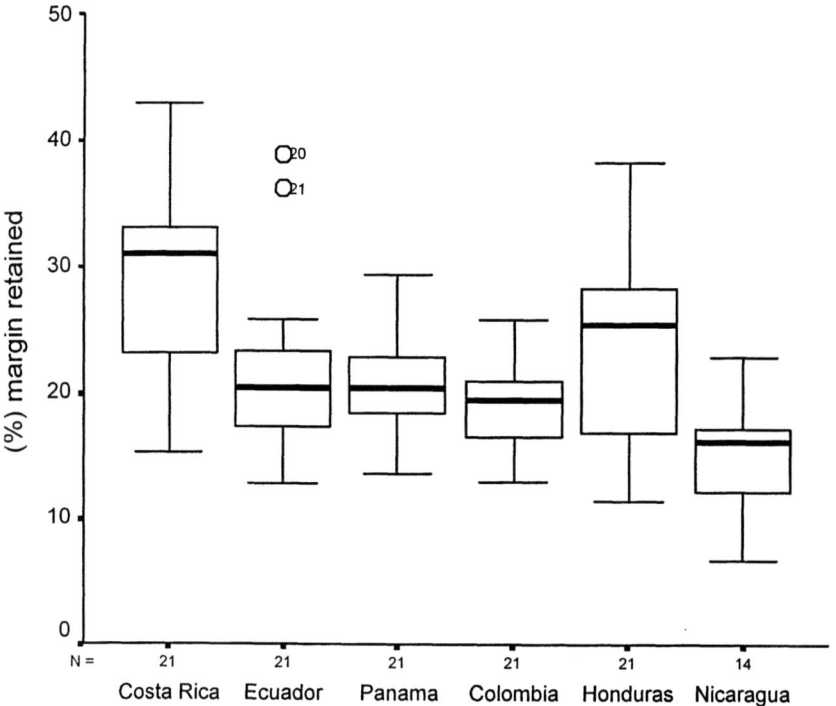

Source: Author's database.

Comparison of the median shares of the commodity chain retained by the dollar-zone countries exporting to Germany (Figure 7.17), France (Figure 7.3) and the UK (Figure 7.8) reveals that, on average, these countries were worst off in France and best off in Germany. This suggests that the SEM is likely to have had an adverse impact on the distribution of their margins in Germany. In fact, the pre-SEM distribution of these margins (Figure 7.18) suggests that most of these countries were somewhat better off in the pre-SEM period, relative to the entire period under study, and that the SEM has affected their relative positions as well. Costa Rica remains the leader, with a slightly larger median margin of 31.2 per cent, and Honduras remains in second place with an increased margin of 26.8 per cent.[47] However the relative positions of most other countries were affected: Panama was in third place with a median margin of 21.9 per cent, Colombia in fourth place with a median margin of 19.6 per cent and Ecuador in fifth place with a median margin of 19.5 per cent.[48] Finally, although Nicaragua remained in last place, when the pre-SEM period is considered its performance improved marginally, with its median margin increasing to 17.2 per cent and variability improving slightly.

Fig. 7.18   *Box plots of banana margins of the exporting countries   in the German commodity chain (pre-SEM)*

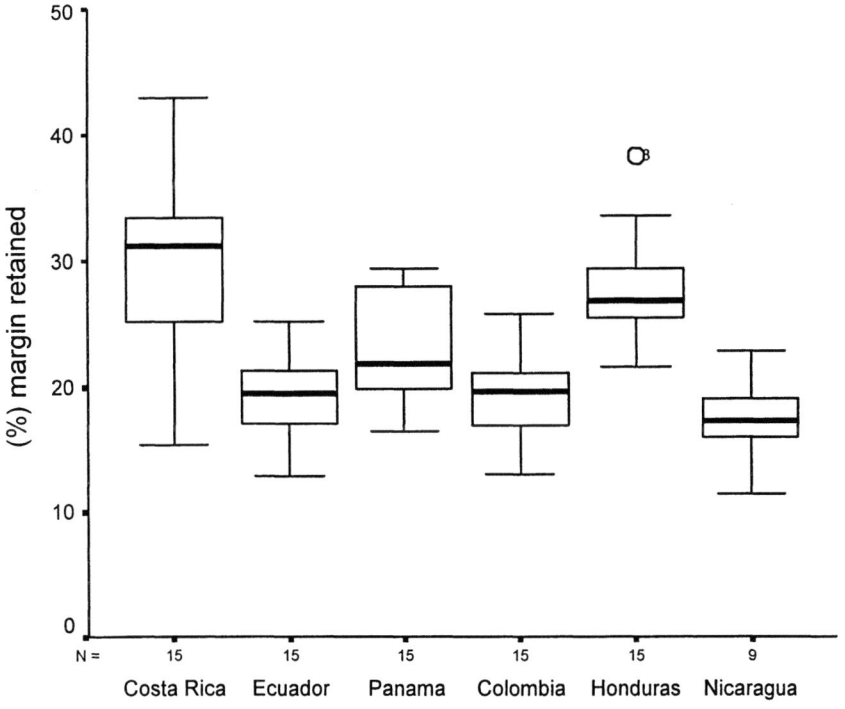

Source: Author's database.

When the distributions of banana margins among the exporting countries in the German commodity chain for the post-SEM period (Figure 7.19) are examined, at first it seems evident that the SEM has typically had a perverse effect. Costa Rica remains the top performer, with a median margin of 27.4 per cent, followed by Ecuador with a median margin of 25.5 per cent.[49] Colombia, the third-best performer, suffered a slight decrease of under 1 per cent in its median margin, while Panama's median margin decreased by slightly more than 4 per cent, to 17.7 per cent. Honduras has been the biggest loser since the SEM took effect: its median margin halved between the pre-SEM and post-SEM periods, falling from 26.8 per cent to a record low of 13.2 per cent. Finally, Nicaragua, remaining in last position, was actually made worse off since the SEM took effect, with its median margin declining from 17.2 per cent to 12.2 per cent.

Fig. 7.19   Box plots of banana margins of the exporting countries   in the German commodity chain (post-SEM)

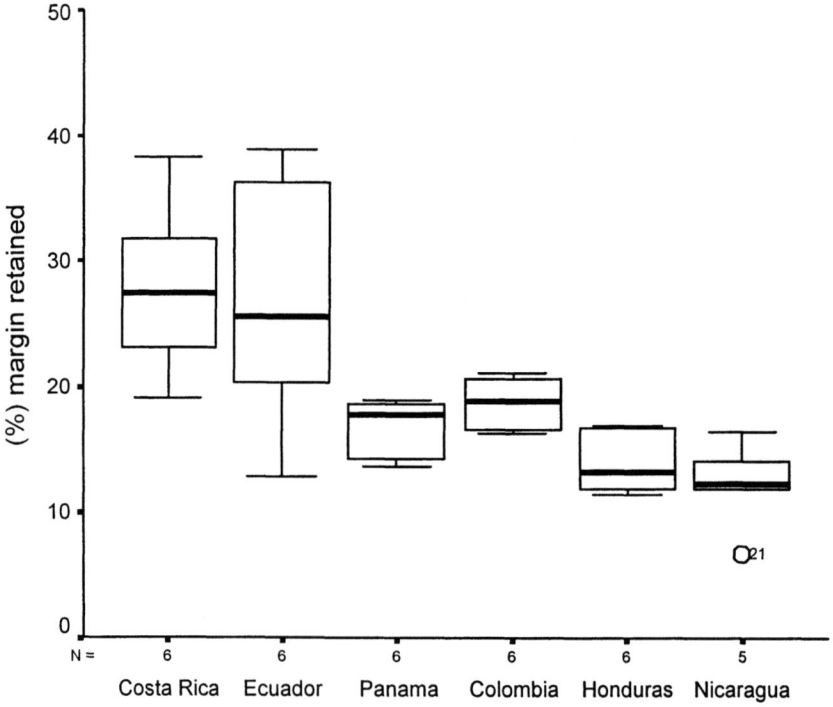

Source: Author's database.

Yet, Ecuador's performance is a notable exception to the direction of change of margins since the SEM took effect: its median share of the commodity chain has actually increased from 19.5 per cent in the pre-SEM period to 25.5 per cent.[50] This further suggests that, there is no simple causal relationship between the retention of surplus and the existence of tariff-quotas. The distinguishing feature of all the other dollar-zone countries is that their bananas are produced, marketed and distributed by US TNCs, while Ecuador's bananas are produced, marketed and distributed by its own TNC, NOBOA. Therefore, the decline in the margin retained by most of the exporting countries might be explained in part by appropriation of some of the margin at the shipping stage by US TNCs in the face of the tariff-quota; a strategy which the Ecuadorian TNC did not need to pursue.

7.4   Isolating the surplus

So far we have demonstrated that although the division of the banana margin between the producer countries and importing EU member states is generally skewed in favour of the EU, countries exporting to the previously protected markets of France and the UK with preferential access retained considerably larger margins than those exporting to Germany. Additionally, although the median shares of the margin retained by most of the countries exporting to Germany declined after the SEM, Ecuador's actually increased, suggesting that the explanation of the decline is linked to the redistribution of value along the commodity chain by US TNCs. But the question remains as to whether the margins retained could be used as proxies for the division of the surplus. Unfortunately, the author was not able to completely decompose the commodity chains for bananas from all countries or under the control of all TNCs because, for reasons of confidentiality, firms were not always able to provide the relevant data. However, several reliable sources did provide some data on the condition that their identities be protected. One source provided sufficient data for comparing the cost structures of one metric ton of "Chiquita" branded bananas from one of Chiquita's Costa Rican plantations to retail outlets in Hamburg (Germany) and New York (United States). Another reliable source provided data from which the author was able to identify the major stages in the commodity chain for "Dole" branded bananas from Costa Rica to The Netherlands. A third source provided data with which the author was able to derive the cost structure of "Fyffes" and "5 Isles" branded bananas from the Eastern Caribbean to the UK. Table 7.1 presents a comparative analysis of these cost structures up to the importation stage in these countries.

Table 7.1   Comparative cost structures for one metric ton of bananas
            (1998 US$)

Cost component	Firm			
	Chiquita (DE)	Chiquita (US)	Dole (NL)	Fyffes (UK)
Farm gate price	148.65	148.65	162.16	327.03
Export cost	106.49	106.49	135.14	258.92
FOB	255.14	255.14	297.30	585.95
Shipping cost	169.19	125.95	267.57	249.19
Margin of shippers	114.05	104.86	127.03	29.73
FOT/FOR	538.38	485.95	691.89	864.86

Source: Author's database.

The following four observations are evident from Table 7.1. First, the
farm gate price is highest for bananas sourced by Fyffes from the Eastern
Caribbean and lowest for bananas sourced by Chiquita for the United States
and German markets. Since these farm gate prices are those actually paid to
farmers, farmers in the Eastern Caribbean effectively receive more than
twice the price paid to farmers in Costa Rica. Second, the cost of preparing
bananas for export (packaging, inland transport, loading and export taxes) is
lowest for Chiquita and highest for Fyffes, whose cost is slightly more than
twice as high as Chiquita's. Third, the shipping cost of bananas is lowest for
Chiquita, whose cost to Germany is only 63 per cent of Dole's cost to The
Netherlands. Finally, while the margins of shippers of both Chiquita and
Dole bananas were in excess of $100 per metric ton, they were considerably
lower for Fyffes' bananas at less than $30 per metric ton. So, clearly,
Chiquita has distinct advantages over its rivals and it strategically exercises
these advantages in such a manner that it incurs the least cost in getting its
bananas into the EU while retaining substantive margins.

    Therefore, considering that there are no major differences in the cost
structures for bananas from other Latin American countries under the direct
control of US TNCs, the preceding analysis of aggregate margins seems
representative of the distribution of surplus along the various banana
commodity chains. Producers of bananas in the Caribbean retain a
considerably larger share of the surplus than do those in Latin America.
Additionally, these data suggest that Chiquita has distinctive advantages in
both shipping and export preparation costs, supporting our earlier
hypothesis of the importance of scale economies in the EU banana business
(Chapters 2 and 3), and hence our choice of c.i.f. over f.o.b. prices in
modelling the welfare effects of trade liberalization.

7.5 Discussion and implications of the division and distribution of margins

This chapter has identified five findings regarding the division and distribution of banana margins along the various commodity chains that warrant further discussion. First, the division of the banana margin along all commodity chains is highly skewed in favour of actors in the importing countries, but to somewhat different degrees, during the pre-SEM period. Importers, wholesalers and retailers in Germany appropriated the largest median share of the banana margin, followed by those in France, while those in the UK appropriated the least. These differences are explained by the differences in the nature of involvement of actors in the respective commodity chains. Since the German commodity chain is the most highly internalized, US TNCs were capable of exercising the most leverage in the redistribution of value to ensure that they captured super normal profits. Firms in the French and British markets, in contrast, were unable to exercise the same degree of leverage, due to their inability to exploit similar economies of common governance. So, in contradiction to the expectations of the neo-classical approach like Borrell and Yang (1990, 1992) that firms in the French and British markets would exercise the most monopoly power, it was in the German market that such market power was optimally exercised. By overemphasizing the potentially pernicious effects of tariff-quota protection and ignoring those due to vertical integration and economies of common governance, neo-classical economists have incorrectly concluded that the French market was the most pernicious in the pre-SEM period, when in reality it was in the German market that producers appear to have been exploited the most.

Second, there were significant differences in the variation in margins retained in the importing countries, with Germany's margins showing the most variability and the UK's the least.[51] This confirms the relative advantages that TNCs operating in a vertically integrated market enjoy over those operating through arm's-length contracts. By increasing the share of the margin retained at the shipping stage in the post-SEM period, TNCs operating along the German commodity chain were able to appropriate more profits outside Germany, as opposed to the wholesale and retail stages inside Germany in the pre-SEM period.

Third, countries exporting bananas to France retained the largest median margin of the commodity chain, while those exporting to Germany retained the least, with those exporting to the UK somewhere in between.[52] This confirms the hypothesis advanced in the conclusion of Chapter 6 – that TNC oligopolists operating in the German market appropriated significantly larger profits as well as revenue along the commodity chain relative to those in other EU member-states.

Fourth, there was a relatively greater degree of dynamism in the reallocation of margins among actors in the British and French commodity chains, compared with the German commodity chain. Most of this dynamism in the former was exercised between actors at the shipping stage and those in the British and French markets, with the margin retained in the exporting countries remaining relatively stable. Therefore, the configuration of the British and French commodity chains is such that exporters to these markets are subjected to the least risk.

Fifth, there was considerable variation in the individual performance of the exporting countries. Among exporters to France, the French DOMs retained the largest median margins, while the dollar-zone countries retained the least, which is largely consistent with neo-classical expectations. However, in the British commodity chain, although on average the Caribbean countries retained the largest margins, it is Ecuador that retained the largest median share of the commodity chain due to the direct *control* over all of its stages by Ecuador's TNC. Finally, in the German commodity chain, the median margin retained by most individual countries was slightly below that for all countries, with the exceptions of Costa Rica and, to a lesser extent, Honduras.

7.6   Conclusion

Like the division of revenue (Chapter 6), the division of the surplus between the exporting countries, the shippers and the importing countries is highly skewed in favour of the importing countries. However, exporters of bananas to the French and British markets were able to retain the largest share of their respective commodity chains while those to the German market retained the least. This confirms our hypothesis (Section 6.4.4) that on average, firms in the German market appropriated considerably larger margins than in other EU member-states. Moreover, there was a considerable degree of flexibility between shippers and actors inside the British and French markets, which was largely absent in the German market. Actors in the former markets retained record low margins in periods of high shipping cost, and higher margins once costs were reduced. This kept the share of the commodity chain retained in the exporting countries relatively stable. In contrast, higher margins at the shipping stage of the German commodity chain reflect increased surplus appropriation by TNCs.

Therefore, to conclude, while the protected banana market in France in the pre-SEM period resulted in larger margins being retained in the DOMs, there was, nevertheless, a considerable degree of monopoly power being exercised in the French market, which resulted in the retention of a disproportionate share of the banana surplus. Yet, the fact that countries exporting to the German market retained an even smaller surplus than those exporting to France indicates the exercise of even more monopoly market power in Germany. This finding will be further supported and discussed in Chapter 8, where we empirically estimate the degree of market power in the French and German markets in both the pre-SEM and post-SEM periods, using econometric methods incorporating co-integration analysis. But our analysis and discussion of firm conduct in the EU banana business so far resonates with Hymer (1970)'s hypothesis of the TNC: as a substitute for the market, which seeks to remove competition and exploit monopoly advantages. Ecuador's exceptional performance in the British market and its improved position in Germany after the SEM is explained by the direct *control* of the marketing and distribution of its bananas by its own TNC, NOBOA.

Notes

[1] It should be noted, though, that data are not available to accommodate a time series analysis of the decompositions of the margins, so neither the changes in the margins over time nor the establishment of causality   is undertaken in this analysis and remains an area for further research.

[2] In light of the fact that during the 1978-82 period, the share of the margin retained in France was remarkably stable, averaging 46.3 per cent. Additionally, although the share of the margin retained among banana exporting countries improved somewhat during 1982-85, that period witnessed a considerable increase in the share of the margin retained in France.

[3] During that period, the French market was controlled almost exclusively by two large co-operatives from the DOMs (which accounted for approximately 66 per cent of the market) and two similar cooperatives from Cameroon and the Ivory Coast (which accounted for approximately 33 per cent). See Chapter 3.

[4] Among the French DOMs, Martinique retained the largest median margin of 29.5 per cent followed by Guadeloupe with 27.9 per cent. There was considerably more variation in the data for Guadeloupe (standard deviation of 8.5) relative to that for Martinique (standard deviation of 6.8).

[5] Among the dollar-zone exporting countries that are major exporters to France, that is, those that command a sizeable share of the market and have exported consistently to France in both the pre-SEM and post-SEM periods. Costa Rica had the largest median share of the margin (16.6 per cent) followed by Colombia (15.0 per cent), with the median share for the remaining dollar-zone countries averaging 12 per cent.

[6] The former French colonies of Madagascar, Ivory Coast and Cameroon retained the next-largest shares of their banana margins, with medians of 21.1 per cent, 18.5 per cent and 18.2 per cent, respectively.

[7] It should be noted, however, that in the case of Honduras the data are for the pre-SEM period only, and comprise a total of 12 observations.

[8] Variability decreased slightly with respect to Guadeloupe's data, with the standard deviation falling from 8.5 to 7.4, but it increased somewhat with respect to Martinique's data, with standard deviation rising from 6.8 to 9.0.

[9] However, there is considerable variation in the Mexican data, with a standard deviation of 6.54 reflecting relative instability in the share of margin retained from one year to the next.

[10] Their shares increased from 50.47 per cent to 54.8 per cent over the 1978-80 period, while the shippers' share of the commodity chain remained relatively stable during that sub-period.

[11] In fact, the share of the margin retained in the UK decreased from 50.4 per cent in 1980 to 47.9 per cent in 1983, while that of the exporting countries increased from 21.5 per cent to 25.1 per cent over the same period.

[12] The share of the banana margin retained in the UK peaked in 1990 at 56.0 per cent, and it was in that same year that the share of the margin retained at the shipping stage reached its minimum level of 21.6 per cent.

[13] Despite the fact that there are outliers at both sides of the distribution and an extreme value on one of the sides.

[14] Its standard deviation of 10.5 was the largest among the dollar-zone banana-exporting countries.

[15] It is worth noting that, for the entire 1978-98 period, all of the retained shares of the British banana margin by Ecuador (21 observations) were above 20 per cent; 17 were above 30 per cent; and 9 were above 40 per cent.

[16] Of the 21 observations for Honduras, 12 recorded margins in excess of 20 per cent and 6 recorded margins between 15 and 20 per cent.

[17] Although Costa Rica's median share was slightly lower than that of Honduras, 7 of its 21 observations recorded margins in excess of 20 per cent, while a further 7 recorded margins between 15 and 20 per cent.

[18] Four of Panama's 21 observations recorded margins above 20 per cent, while 11 recorded margins between 15 and 20 per cent. In Colombia, 3 out of the 21 observations recorded margins above 20 per cent, while 12 recorded margins between 15 and 20 per cent.

[19] Although Surinam and Belize are member-states of the Caribbean Community (CARICOM), they are of course geographically located on the Latin American continent. Banana production conditions in these countries are rather different from those found in the island economies of the Caribbean, and hence in this analysis they are not treated as 'strict' Caribbean countries.

[20] Standard deviation was 4.0. Additionally, of the 21 observations for St. Vincent, 10 recorded margins in excess of 30 per cent, and the remaining 11 all recorded margins in excess of 20 per cent, with 10 of these between 26 and 30 per cent.

[21] Of the 21 observations for Jamaica, 10 recorded margins in excess of 30 per cent, 8 recorded margins between 20 and 30 per cent, 2 recorded margins between 18 and 20 per cent, and there was one record low margin of 12.2 per cent.

[22] Ten of Dominica's 21 observations recorded margins above 30 per cent, while the remaining 11 observations all recorded margins between 26 and 30 per cent.

[23] Eight of St. Lucia's 21 observations recorded margins above 30 per cent, 12 recorded margins between 25 and 30 per cent, and the remaining 1 recorded a margin of 24.0 per cent.

[24] Of Grenada's 21 observations, 9 recorded margins above 30 per cent, 10 recorded margins between 20 and 29 per cent and the remaining 2 recorded margins between 17 and 19 per cent.

[25] Of Cameroon's 20 observations, 4 recorded margins above 30 per cent, 7 recorded margins between 20 and 30 per cent, 8 recorded margins between 10 and 20 per cent, and there was one observation with a margin of 9.6 per cent.

[26] Of Belize's 21 observations, 9 recorded margins between 20 and 30 per cent, 11 recorded margins between 10 and 20 per cent, and one recorded a margin of 30.6 per cent.

[27] Despite Surinam's relatively large median margin, there was considerable variability in the data, with a standard deviation of 8.3, one outlier corresponding to a margin of 36.4 per cent and one extreme value corresponding to a margin of 50.6 per cent. Of the remaining 19 observations, 8 recorded margins between 20 and 30 per cent; and 11 recorded margins between 10 and 20 per cent.

[28] Although the Ivory Coast was the worst performer of all the countries exporting bananas to the UK, a closer examination of the data reveals a less pessimistic picture: of its 19 observations, 4 recorded margins above 30 per cent; 5 recorded margins between 20 and 30 per cent; while the remaining 10 recorded margins between 10 and 20 per cent.

[29] Ecuador's standard deviation in the pre-SEM period was 12.1, compared with 10.5 for the 1978-98 period. Additionally, as shown in the figures below, there is a positive skew associated with Ecuador's distribution of margins in both the pre-SEM period and the entire 1978-98 period, with the tendency to receive larger margins than those received by other dollar-zone exporters on the average.

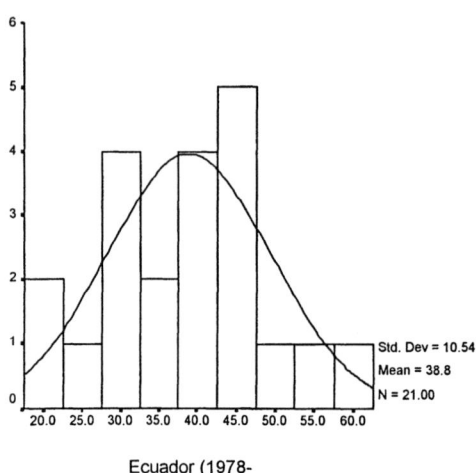

Ecuador (1978-

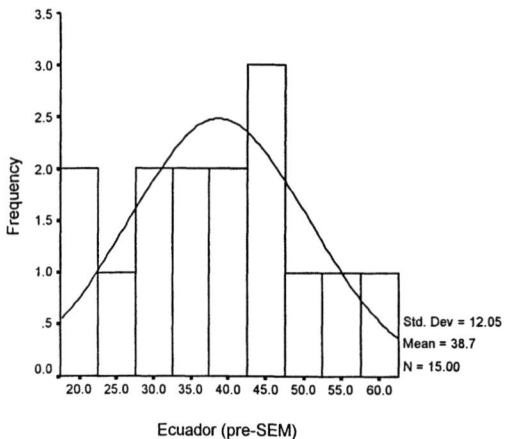

Ecuador (pre-SEM)

[30] Panama's median margin remains virtually unchanged when the two periods are compared.

[31] A comparison of the distributions of Colombia's margins in the pre-SEM and post-SEM periods is shown below. In the pre-SEM period, Colombia recorded margins within the 9-10 per cent interval; there was a negative skew about the

median of 15.5; and the highest recorded margin was in the 19-20 per cent interval. However, in the post-SEM period the lowest margin was in the 19-20 per cent interval, the highest margin was in the 23-24 per cent interval, and there was a slight positive skew about the median of 20.2.

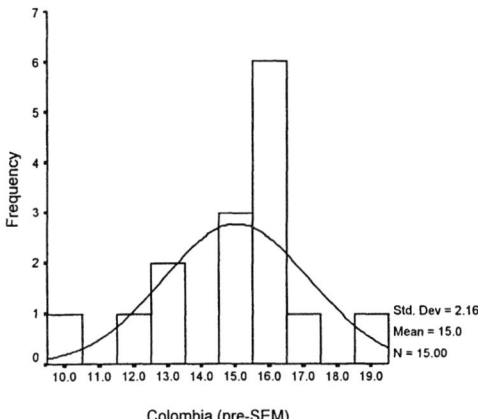

Colombia (pre-SEM)

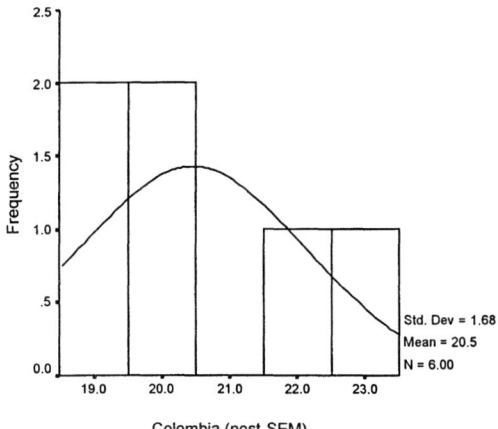

Colombia (post-SEM)

[32] For instance, see Mangold et al. (1996) and the Campaign for Labor Rights (1998) for details.

[33] In the case of Dominica, the decrease was only a fraction of a per cent; for St. Vincent, by 1.5 per cent and for Grenada, slightly more than 5 per cent.

[34] In this regard, size refers to the quantity of bananas under cultivation, and not the area of these islands.

[35] A comparison of the distributions of banana margins for Jamaica and St. Lucia in the pre-SEM and post-SEM periods is presented in the figures below. It is clear that the SEM has shifted the lower-bound (interval) of margins to the right in both cases: Jamaica's lower-bound moved from the 10.5-12.5 interval to the 29.0-30.0 interval; while St. Lucia's lower-bound did not change in any significant way, but both its upper-bound and distribution function shifted to the right.

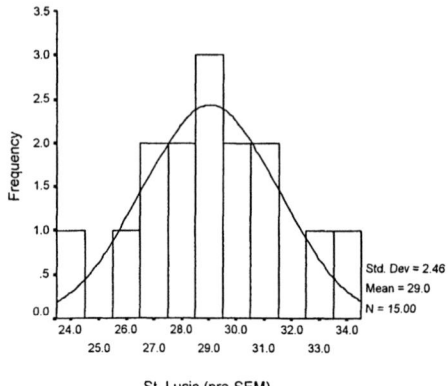

St. Lucia (pre-SEM)

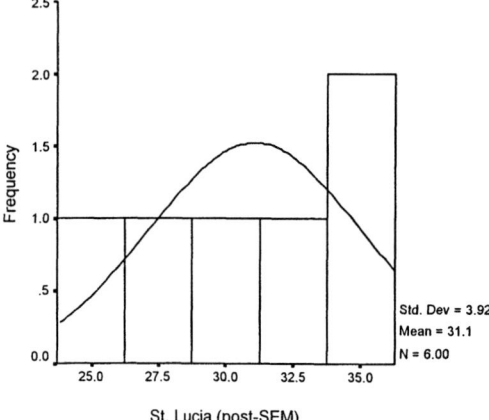

St. Lucia (post-SEM)

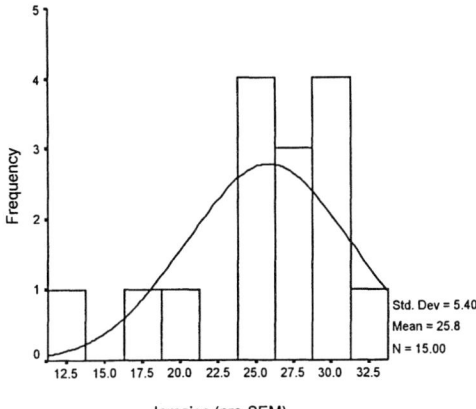

Jamaica (pre-SEM)

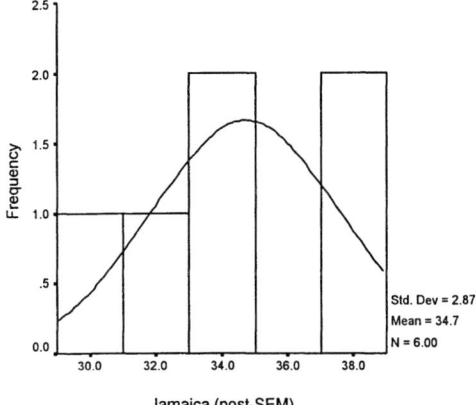

Jamaica (post-SEM)

[36] Specifically, the 12.4 per cent decrease in the share of the banana margin retained in Germany between 1978 and 1985 was accompanied by a 6.5 per cent increase in the margin share of the exporting countries, while 5.9 per cent being appropriated at the shipping stage.

[37] According to World Reefer List (1998), the average size of pure reefer vessels, that is, those with capacity of more than 100,000 cubic feet, has increased constantly over the years and stands at 366,000 cubic feet. Moreover, between 1988 and 1998, the total supply of palletized reefer vessels more than trebled. The major banana TNCs have by no means been left behind: Chiquita owns 16 vessels, all of them having capacity greater than 400,000 cubic feet, while Dole owns 10 vessels, most of which have a capacity larger than 400,000 cubic feet.

[38] Of the 8.0 per cent increase in the share of the banana margin retained in Germany between 1986-92, 3.6 per cent was at the expense of exporting countries and 4.4 per cent was at the expense of shipping. It should also be noted that the largest share of the commodity chain retained in Germany during the entire period 1978-98, 60.7 per cent, was in 1992.

[39] In the pursuit of further technological innovation, in 1992 Chiquita implemented a refrigerated controlled-atmosphere environment – high level of nitrogen and low level of oxygen to retard ripening – in all of its vessels. Subsequently, in 1993 it developed containerization from packing (on plantations) to retail, and in 1994 it implemented a controlled atmosphere environment in refrigerated containers. (Roche, 1998:126).

[40] Of the 9.3 per cent decrease in the share of the margin retained in Germany, most (7.0 per cent) was appropriated by the exporting countries, with only a residual proportion (2.3 per cent) being appropriated at the shipping stage.

[41] Of the 21 observations for Germany, 8 recorded margins in the 40-50 interval, 12 recorded margins in the 50-60 interval and 1 recorded a margin in the 60-plus interval.

[42] It should be noted that Costa Rica's minimum share of the chain retained was 15.3 per cent and the maximum was 43.0 per cent. Of its 21 observations, 4 recorded margins in the 10-20 interval, 5 recorded margins in the 20-30 interval, 11 recorded margins in the 30-40 interval and 1 observation recorded a margin above 40.

[43] Of Honduras' 21 observations, 6 recorded margins in the 10-20 interval, 11 recorded margins in the 20-30 interval, and 4 recorded margins in the 30-40 interval.

[44] Both Ecuador and Panama recorded 21 observations. In the case of Ecuador, 10 observations recorded margins in the 10-20 interval, 9 recorded margins in the 20-30 interval and 2 recorded margins above 30; while for Panama, 10 recorded margins in the 10-20 interval and 11 recorded margins in the 20-30 interval.

[45] Of Colombia's 21 observations, 13 recorded margins in the 10-20 interval and 8 recorded margins in the 20-30 interval.

[46] Of the 14 available observations for Nicaragua, 1 recorded a margin in the 0-10 interval, 11 recorded margins in the 10-20 interval, and 2 recorded margins in the 20-30 interval.

[47] In both these cases, variability has been affected: for Costa Rica there was a slight increase in variability, but for Honduras there was a considerable decline in variability, with the standard deviation falling from 7.5 to 3.8.

[48] Variability improved considerably for Ecuador and marginally for Panama; however, it worsened slightly in the case of Colombia.

[49] Costa Rica's median margin actually declined by approximately 4 per cent in the post-SEM period and the data show decreased variation.

[50] Although there is considerably more variability in the post-SEM data (standard deviation increased from 3.3 to 9.8) and there are fewer observations than in the pre-SEM period.

[51] In the German data there were three outliers, while all observations were within 1.5IQR for France and the UK.

[52] When the entire 1978-98 period is considered, the same general pattern holds among these countries.

8   Oligopoly Market Power and its Implications for Trade Liberalization in the EU's Banana Business

8.1   Introduction

It will be recalled that in Chapter 2 we discussed the neo-classical theory of trade liberalization and how it has been applied for predicting the welfare effects in specific commodities and industries. We then analysed the specific arguments that have been advanced for liberalization of the EU banana trade and came up with two conclusions: (i) the prevailing assumptions of previous studies that the EU banana market is perfectly competitive and/or contestable are not likely to be correct; and (ii) predictions of welfare effects based on such assumptions are not likely to be correct. Additionally, we demonstrated that by introducing changes in the assumptions about the price transmission mechanism, both the direction and magnitude of the overall welfare effects changed considerably.

Against the background of these findings in Chapter 2, we proceeded to undertake a deeper analysis of the empirical evidence about the EU banana market structure and the conduct of firms within it, over time (Chapter 3). We developed three arguments: (i) the EU banana market structure is oligopolistic, with three firms controlling more than 60 per cent of all banana imports; (ii) given the considerable levels of capital investment undertaken by oligopolists and the asset specificity of the commodity, the market is not likely to be contestable; and (iii) firms in the market are associated with a history of anti-competitive conduct, including price discrimination, product differentiation, and huge barriers to entry.

With this in mind, the objective of the present chapter is to measure the degree and direction of market power in two EU member-states, both prior to, and since the implementation of, the SEM. We will then use our knowledge of the market power behaviour obtained in Chapter 9 to simulate the welfare effects of trade liberalization, using a three-period *sequential* oligopoly game. The methodology that is used for measuring market power is a structural econometric model in which the behaviour of firms in a market is assumed to be captured by their conjectural variation parameters. It will be recalled that in Chapter 4, different approaches to modelling oligopoly were discussed and the conjectural variations method isolated as the most useful for this study. In the conjectural variations method, oligopolists are modelled as conjecturing the existence of a relationship between their own output choices and those of their rivals. This method features prominently in the literature on oligopoly models (Pfaffermayr, 1999; Mai and Hwang, 1999; Chiou and Hwang, 1998; Nevo, 1998 and Genesove and Mullin, 1995) have all used this method in recent empirical work. The conjectural variation is the rate of change of rivals' total output with respect to own output (McMillan, 2001:19). Essentially, it uses the responsiveness of price-to-cost determinants under different demand conditions to infer market power (Genesove and Mullin, 1995). Additionally, since our analysis is based on time series data, the Johansen co-integration method is used to establish robust coefficients and the presence of long-run model dynamics.[1] The remainder of the chapter is organized as follows.

Section 8.2 presents the methodology. It begins with an overview of oligopoly models that have been used for measuring market power, discusses the conjectural variations method in some detail and concludes with the specification that is used in this chapter. The data that are used are discussed in Section 8.3. Here, their sources, compilation methodology, assumptions made and limitations are identified. Additionally, a number of statistical tests are performed on those data, particularly the Augmented Dickey-Fuller (ADF) test,[2] to ensure that they reasonably satisfy the specific assumptions of the estimation procedure that is used. Section 8.4 reports the results of these estimations, while their detailed analysis and discussion is presented in Section 8.5. Finally, section 8.6 presents the conclusions.

8.2   Methodology

Conceptually, market power means the wedge (gap) between the price (P) that a firm charges for a good and its marginal cost (MC) of production. This relationship can be captured in the form of the Lerner index (L) as follows:

$$L = \frac{P - MC}{P} \qquad (8.1)$$

Equation 8.1 tells us that a firm enjoys no market power (is a price taker) when $P = MC$, and that it enjoys maximum market power (is a monopolist) when $P - MC \rightarrow P$. Given that the empirical analysis conducted in Chapter 3 confirms that the EU banana market is oligopolistic, it is of interest to determine the value for the Lerner index as well as whether or not, and the extent to which, it is statistically significant from 0 (competition) or 1 (collusion). Moreover, computing the Cournot-Nash equilibrium for specific segments of the EU banana market, as suggested in Chapter 4, will help determine whether the direction of firm behaviour is towards collusion or competition in each case.

8.2.1   Empirical applications of oligopoly – static, dynamic and conjectural variations models

Various models of oligopoly have been used for analysing firm behaviour and measuring the degree of market power in different markets and industries; however, of interest to us are those models that have been used in the food- and trade- related industries. Schroter (1988), Azzam and Pagoulatos (1990) and Stiegert et al. (1993) use different models for estimating market power in the meat industry; while Lopez (1984), Just and Chern (1980) and Bhuyan and Lopez (1997) use other models for estimating market power in the food processing, tomato, and food and tobacco industries, respectively. With regard to export markets for which very few studies have been conducted, the following works are available: Buschena and Perloff (1991), who use a static oligopoly model to analyse market power in the coconut oil export market; Karp and Perloff (1989) and Karp and Perloff (1993), who use dynamic oligopoly models for estimating market power in the rice and coffee markets, respectively; and Deodhar and Sheldon (1995), who use a conjectural variations model to estimate the degree of market power in the banana industry in Germany during the pre-SEM period.

Since marginal cost data are rarely available for individual firms, and even when available, firms tend to treat them with strict confidentiality, the methodological challenge of these studies is to derive an indirect technique for determining the value of the Lerner index (8.1). Therefore, all of these approaches follow a generally similar procedure. First, a general structure is built which takes into consideration all exogenous and endogenous factors that might affect market demand and supply. Second, a residual supply or demand function is derived for the dominant firm or group of firms that are likely to exercise market power. Third, on the assumption that firms maximize profits, the first derivative of the residual demand curve facing each firm is obtained in order to determine its effective (or perceived) marginal revenue. Finally, a functional form for the general structure is chosen which allows for the identification of the market power parameter. In order to further clarify this procedure, the various stages are discussed in some detail for three of the approaches used in the studies cited earlier.

Buschena and Perloff's (1991) model

Buschena and Perloff (1991:1000) estimate the degree of market power exercised by the Philippines in the coconut oil industry following the institutional and legal changes that took place in the early 1970s when the Philippine Coconut Authority took control of all coconut oil refining and export. Prior to this, the Philippine coconut oil industry had been rather competitive, since several firms were involved in almost all aspects of the industry. Additionally, during the period under study (1959-87) the Philippines accounted for approximately 80 per cent of all the world's coconut oil exports, making it the dominant actor in international markets.

Buschena and Perloff's model takes into account several other factors. First, since the 1980s there has been a general tendency for consumers to reduce both the use and types of fat in their diets, switching from saturated to unsaturated fats. Since coconut oil is of the saturated variety, this has led to a reduction in its share of world demand for edible oil exports. Second, the United States, which imports approximately 40 per cent of all world coconut oil exports, granted free entry to coconut oil from the Philippines for the 1921-74 period. Third, there has been a tendency for other major coconut oil-exporting countries to reduce their supplies over time for a number of reasons (Buschena and Perloff, 1991:1001-2). The model is as follows.

The world's market demand curve is:

$$Q = Q(p, Z) \tag{8.2}$$

where Q represents world purchase, p is the real price of this homogeneous product, and Z is a vector of other variables that affect demand. The competitive (price-taking) supply, Q_f, of the fringe is:

$$Q_f = Q_f(p, X) \tag{8.3}$$

where X is a vector of other variables that affect the quantity exported. The residual demand, Q_d, facing the dominant firm is the world demand minus the competitive fringe's supply:

$$Q_d(p,Z,X) = Q(p,Z) - Q_f(p,X) \tag{8.4}$$

The dominant firm maximizes its profits subject to its residual demand. In other words, the profits that the dominant firm can make are constrained by the world competitive supply. Assuming that the dominant firm fully exercises its market power, then its equilibrium condition is determined by equating its marginal revenue (corresponding to its residual demand curve) and its marginal cost (MC). Therefore, the Philippine export equation can be written in the following manner:

$$p(Q_d,Z,X) + \lambda p'(Q_d,Z,X)Q_d = MC$$

$$\Rightarrow p(Q_d,Z,X) = MC - \lambda p'(Q_d,Z,X)Q_d \tag{8.5}$$

where $p(Q_d,Z,X)$ is the inverted residual demand curve (solving equation 8.4 for p as a function of Q_d); $p'(Q_d,Z,X)$ is the first derivative of the residual demand curve with respect to Q_d; and $p(Q_d,Z,X) + \lambda p'(Q_d,Z,X)Q_d$ is its effective marginal revenue, taking into account political and other trade-offs within the decision-making body. λ, which determines the wedge between price and marginal cost, reflects the degree of market power actually exercised.

It has been established theoretically, by Bresnahan (1982), that the oligopoly solution concept (the value for λ) can be identified only if specific functional forms are used for estimating equations (8.2)-(8.5). Specifically, functional forms must be chosen which could cause both a shift in, and a rotation of, the demand curve. A shift of the demand curve alone could arise from either competition or collusion; however, a rotation of the demand curve about the equilibrium point reveals the degree of market power (Bresnahan, 1982:92). Guided by Bresnahan's theoretical finding, Buschena and Perloff estimate the following functional forms for the structural equations (8.2)-(8.5) above. The demand equation (8.2) becomes:

$$Q = \alpha_0 + \alpha_1 p + \alpha_2 Z + \alpha_3 pZ_1 + \varepsilon_1 \tag{8.2*}$$

where Z is a vector of exogenous factors that affect demand, Z_1 is a subset of these factors that enter the equation as cross products with the price, and ε_1 is a normal error term capturing random fluctuations in demand.

The estimated fringe export supply equation (8.3) becomes:

$$Q_f = \beta_0 + \beta_1 p + \beta_2 X + \varepsilon_2 \qquad (8.3^*)$$

where X is a vector of exogenous variables[3] that affect supply and ε_2 is a normal error term capturing random fluctuations in supply. The estimated residual demand facing the Philippines is the difference between equations (8.2*) and (8.3*) or the identity $Q_d \equiv Q - Q_f$. Therefore,

$$Q_d = (\alpha_0 - \beta_0) + (\alpha_1 - \beta_1 + \alpha_3 Z_1) p + \alpha_2 Z - \beta_2 X + (\varepsilon_1 - \varepsilon_2)$$

$$\Rightarrow \quad Q_d = \delta_0 + (\delta_1 + \delta_2 Z_1) p + \delta_3 Z + \delta_4 X + (\varepsilon_1 - \varepsilon_2) \qquad (8.4^*)$$

where the slope of the residual demand curve, $\dfrac{\partial Q_d}{\partial p} = \delta_1 + \delta_2 Z_1$, is negative. Finally, the Philippine marginal cost of producing and exporting coconut oil is:

$$MC = \theta_0 + \theta_1 Q_d + \theta_2 W \qquad (8.6)$$

where W is a vector of exogenous variables that affect the marginal costs of producing and exporting coconut oil.[4] From equations (8.6) and (8.4*), the Philippines' first-order condition for profit maximization (equation 8.5) becomes:

$$p = \theta_0 + \theta_1 Q_d + \theta_2 W - \left[\frac{\lambda}{\delta_1 + \delta_2 Z_1} \right] Q_d + \varepsilon_3 \qquad (8.5^*)$$

The estimates of δ_1 and δ_2 obtained from equations (8.2*) and (8.3*), are used for identifying λ in equation (8.5*).

Lopez and You's (1993) model

Lopez and You (1993) assess the impact of exporters' oligopsony[5] power and government taxation on coffee prices, production, consumption, exports and revenue distribution in Haiti. Their justification for the study arose from three major considerations: first, the Haitian coffee market is characterized by exploitation of farmers by market intermediaries; second, two-thirds of all coffee production is exported through primary intermediaries; and third, the coffee market is subjected to regular government intervention and coffee accounts for a considerable share of total government revenue (Lopez and You, 1993:465-6).

Market participants are aggregated into three groups: producers, domestic consumers and exporters. Their model treats domestic wholesalers, who purchase for re-selling in the local market as price takers, while oligopsony power is derived from the exporter group.

Coffee producers are assumed to be price takers and so their supply function is:

$$Q^s = f(P, Z^s) \qquad (8.7)$$

where Q^s is the total quantity of coffee produced, P is the price received by producers and Z^s is a vector of supply shifters.

Domestic consumers are assumed to be price takers and so their demand function is:

$$Q^d = g(P, Z^d) \qquad (8.8)$$

where Q^d is the quantity of coffee consumed locally and Z^d is a vector of other relevant variables that affect domestic demand.

The residual export supply function is:

$$Q = Q^s - Q^d = h(P, Z^s, Z^d) \qquad (8.9)$$

where Q is total exports. Let q_i denote the quantity of coffee that the ith exporter purchases for export, (i=1,2,...N) where N is the total number of exporters.

An exporter's profit maximization objective is given by:

$$Max\Pi_i = [P_w(1-t) - c - P]q_i \qquad (8.10)$$

where P_w is the f.o.b. price of coffee, t is the government tax on exports and c is the per unit marketing cost.

To maximize profit with respect to q_i, the first order condition is:

$$P_w(1-t) - c - P\left(1 + \frac{\theta_i}{\eta}\right) = 0 \tag{8.11}$$

where $\theta_i = \left(\dfrac{\partial Q}{\partial q_i}\right)\left(\dfrac{q_i}{Q}\right)$ is the conjectural variation elasticity or the perceived market response to changes in the purchases of that exporter, and $\eta = \left(\dfrac{\partial Q}{\partial P}\right)\left(\dfrac{P}{Q}\right)$ is the price elasticity of export supply.

Equation (8.11) implies that each exporter sets coffee purchases such that his net value of marginal product (NVMP) equals his perceived marginal cost (PMCC), or:

$$P_w(1-t) - c = P\left(1 + \frac{\theta_i}{\eta}\right)$$

from which the percentage mark-down, defined in the form of the Lerner index (L), is as follows:

$$L = \frac{(NVMP - P)}{P} \tag{8.12}$$

$$\Rightarrow \quad L = \left[\frac{P_w(1-t) - c - P}{P}\right]$$

$$\Rightarrow L = \frac{\theta}{\eta} \tag{8.13}$$

The choice of the general structure used in this model does not necessitate introducing Bresnahan's theoretical finding, since the Lerner index can be measured directly. Therefore, the authors use double log functional forms for estimations of demand and supply. The estimated supply system uses the sum of eight lags of the coffee price to determine the value for the price coefficient. It is represented as:

$$Log(q_s) = \alpha_0 + \alpha_1 \sum_{k=0}^{7} Log(p_{t-k}) + \alpha_2 Log(p_b) + \alpha_3 Log(p_c) + \alpha_4 Log(w_i)$$

$$+ \alpha_5 \sum_{k=1}^{2} Log(q_{t-k}) + \varepsilon_1 \qquad\qquad (8.14)$$

where $Log(q_s)$ is the estimated quantity supplied, $Log(p_{t-k})$ is the lagged coffee price, $Log(p_b)$ is the price of bean, $Log(p_c)$ is the price of corn, $Log(w_i)$ is a weather index, $Log(q_{t-k})$ is the lagged supply quantity, $\alpha_i (i = 0,1,....5)$, is the estimated coefficient of the ith explanatory variable, and ε_1 is an error term.

The estimated demand system is represented as:

$$Log(q_d) = \beta_0 + \beta_1 Log(p_t) + \beta_2 Log(GDP) + \beta_3 D_{1978} + \varepsilon_2 \qquad (8.15)$$

where $Log(q_d)$ is the estimated quantity demanded, $Log(p_t)$ is the price, $Log(GDP)$ is the gross domestic product, D_{1978} is a dummy variable for 1978, $\beta_i (i = 0,1,...3)$ is the estimated coefficient of the ith explanatory variable, and ε_2 is an error term.

Deodhar and Sheldon's (1995) model

Deodhar and Sheldon (1995) use a structural econometric method to estimate the degree of market imperfection in the German banana market. That study was conducted against the background of the introduction of the new banana import policy for the EU in 1993 (as discussed in Chapter 3), and calls for implementation of a free trade regime justified on the grounds of increasing global welfare (as discussed in Chapter 2). In their model, the market demand function for bananas takes the following form:

$$Q_t = Q(P_t, Z_t) \qquad\qquad (8.16)$$

where Q_t is the total quantity demanded, P_t is the market price, Z_t is a vector of exogenous variables, and t is a time subscript. The simultaneous determination of Q_t and P_t implies that the demand function could be written in inverse form as:

$$P_t = P(Q_t, Z_t) \tag{8.17}$$

At any given time, revenue in the banana industry as a whole is defined as:

$$R_t = P_t Q_t \tag{8.18}$$

Therefore, perceived marginal revenue $MR_t(\lambda)$ is given by the expression:

$$MR_t(\lambda) \equiv P_t + \lambda Q_t \frac{dP_t}{dQ_t} \tag{8.19}$$

where, in equilibrium, λ represents the gap between price and marginal cost, or the extent of market power. It contains an index of the beliefs that each firm has about the others' reactions to setting output choices, or a conjectural variations parameter.

Since, in equilibrium, perceived marginal revenue equals marginal cost, then:

$$P_t + \lambda Q_t \frac{dP_t}{dQ_t} = MC_t \tag{8.20}$$

If firms are engaged in either Bertrand-Nash or competitive behaviour, $\lambda = 0$; if firms are engaged in perfectly collusive behaviour, $\lambda = 1$; otherwise, if firms are engaged in Cournot-Nash behaviour, $0 < \lambda < 1$.

The fact that λ conceptually contains a conjectural variations parameter or the reaction beliefs of one firm about the other's output decisions is derived as follows. Consider a simple duopoly model in which firm 1 expects firm 2 to produce q_2^e units of output and firm 1 itself produces q_1 units of output. The total output that firm 1 expects to be sold in the market is given by $Q = q_1 + q_2^e$. The profit-maximizing problem for firm 1 is:

$$\arg\max_{q_1}[P(Q)q_1 - c_1(q_1)]$$ (8.21)

where $P(Q)$ is the inverse demand function, and $c_1(q_1)$ is firm 1's total cost function.

The first-order condition is:

$$P(Q) + \left[\frac{dP}{dQ}\frac{dQ}{dq_1}\right]q_1 = MC_1(q_1)$$ (8.22)

where $MC_1(q_1)$ is firm 1's marginal cost. If the derivatives are treated as discrete changes, then we can write $dQ = dq_1 + dq_2^e$, so that $\frac{dQ}{dq_1} = [1 + \frac{dq_2^e}{dq_1}]$. In equilibrium, $q_2^e = q_2$, therefore the equilibrium expression (equation 8.22) could be rewritten as:

$$P(Q) + \frac{dP}{dQ}\left[1 + \frac{dq_2}{dq_1}\right]q_1 = MC_1(q_1)$$ (8.23)

From equation (8.23), the term $\frac{dq_2}{dq_1}$ is the conjectural variation parameter of firm 1. It captures how firm 1 believes firm 2 will change its output if firm 1 makes a small change in output. By letting $V = \frac{dq_2}{dq_1}$, and assuming all firms to be symmetric so that they have identical costs and output capacities, for n firms equation (8.23) becomes:

$$P(Q) + \frac{dP}{dQ}\left[\frac{1 + (n-1)V}{n}\right]Q = MC$$ (8.24)

But, since equation (8.24) is essentially the general form of equation (8.20), we could write:

$$\lambda = \left[\frac{1 + (n-1)V}{n}\right]$$ (8.25)

If firms engage in Cournot-Nash behaviour, then $V = 0$, so $\lambda = \dfrac{1}{n}$.

In order to estimate the degree of market power in the German market in the pre-SEM period, Deodhar and Sheldon (1995) used the following econometric model. The demand function is specified in linear form as:

$$Q_t = \alpha_0 + \alpha_1 P_t + \alpha_2 Z_t + \varepsilon_1 \tag{8.26}$$

where Q_t is quantities of bananas sold at retail, P_t is retail prices, Z_t is a vector of exogenous variables affecting demand and ε_1 is an error term, such that $\varepsilon_1 \sim N(\mu, \sigma^2)$. The marginal cost function is specified as:

$$MC_t = \gamma_0 + \gamma_1 W_t + \gamma_2 T \tag{8.27}$$

where W_t is the import prices for bananas, which are assumed to be proxies for the cost of bananas to retailers, and T, a time trend variable, captures reductions in marginal cost due to technological advances in storage. By substituting the marginal cost equation (8.27) into the profit maximizing condition, equation (8.20), the following linear specification is derived:

$$P_t = \gamma_0 + \gamma_1 W_t + \gamma_2 T + \gamma_3 Q_t + \varepsilon_2 \tag{8.28}$$

where $\gamma_3 = -\lambda \left[\dfrac{dP_t}{dQ_t} \right]$, and $\varepsilon_2 \sim N(\mu, \sigma^2)$. If equation (8.26) is differentiated with respect to Q_t, then:

$$\frac{dP_t}{dQ_t} = \frac{1}{\alpha_1} \tag{8.29}$$

$$\Rightarrow \quad \gamma_3 = \frac{-\lambda}{\alpha_1} \tag{8.30}$$

$$\Rightarrow \quad \lambda = -\alpha_1 \gamma_3 \tag{8.31}$$

Since Deodhar and Sheldon assume a technology of fixed marginal cost, the oligopoly solution concept is directly identifiable from the cross products of the coefficients of the relevant parameters in equation (8.31).

However, that would not have been the case if marginal costs were assumed to be variable, in which case the model would need to be adjusted in accordance with Bresnahan (1982)'s theoretical finding. The specification of the demand function actually estimated is:

$$Q_t = \alpha_0 + \alpha_1 P_t + \alpha_2 Z_t + \alpha_3 T + \alpha_4 TT + \varepsilon_1 \qquad (8.32)$$

where Z_t is the German population aged 65 years and older and T and TT are trend and squared trend variables, respectively.

8.2.2   An oligopoly model for the EU banana market

The methodology that is used in this chapter draws heavily on the approaches used by Deodhar and Sheldon (1995) and Buschena and Perloff (1991). However, there are a few differences. First, unlike Deodhar and Sheldon (1995), who make the theoretical assumption of constant marginal costs, this study follows the more general approach of Bresnahan (1982) in which it is assumed that firms enjoy decreasing marginal costs. This theoretical proposition seems justifiable given the importance of economies of scale in the banana business.[6]

Second, Deodhar and Sheldon (1995) use annual data for their econometric analysis, while this study makes use of both annual and monthly data. The superiority of monthly data over annual data derives from the seasonality of demand for bananas in Europe. Since demand for bananas is higher in the winter-spring than in the summer-autumn seasons, firms' conjectures might vary accordingly, and such variations are likely to be better captured in monthly rather than annual data. Additionally, given the limited number of years for which reliable data on world banana trade are available, the accuracy of econometric analysis might be compromised under certain circumstances, due to insufficient degrees of freedom.[7]

Third, while Deodhar and Sheldon (1995) estimate the degree of market power for the German market during the pre-SEM period *only*, this chapter estimates the degree of market power for Germany and France, both prior to and since the implementation of the SEM. A comparative analysis of these markets is then undertaken to determine whether the existence of either free trade (the German case) or protectionism (the French case) has any statistically significant effect on the behaviour of firms. Thus, it will be determined whether firms behave in accordance with the Hwang and Mai (1988) hypothesis of equivalence of tariffs and quotas, or whether the choice of a tariff is always superior, as demonstrated theoretically by Bhagwati (1988).

Fourth, while Deodhar and Sheldon (1995) measure market power only from import to retail,[8] there is the possibility that firms enjoy different levels of market power at various stages in the banana commodity chain. Therefore, in this chapter market power is estimated from import to wholesale, wholesale to retail and import to retail.

Fifth, one of the major problems encountered when working with time series data is that they tend not to be stationary; and it is not clear how Deodhar and Sheldon (1995) have addressed this problem in their model.[9] Therefore, we shall utilize the Johansen co-integration approach in this work. This allows us to estimate error correction models, which in addition to providing more accurate coefficients also capture long-run relationships in the data. Additionally, co-integration is regarded as one method of minimizing multicollinearity, since the variables actually used in the model are difference stationary (Maddala, 1988).

Finally, by estimating the degree of market power both before and since the implementation of the SEM, the chapter will offer an opinion as to whether the introduction of the tariff-quota has promoted competition or rent-seeking behaviour.

In order to empirically determine the degree of market power in an EU member-state, specifications of the following general form are used. The demand function is assumed to take the following linear form:

$$Q_d = \upsilon_0 + \upsilon_1 P_{rw} + \upsilon_2 Z_d + \varepsilon_d \qquad (8.33)$$

where Q_d is quantities of bananas sold at retail (or wholesale) level by firms in a market segment, P_{rw} is the retail (or wholesale) prices of bananas, Z_d is vectors of exogenous factors affecting demand and ε_d is error terms affecting demand, such that $\varepsilon_d \sim N(\mu, \sigma^2)$.

Included in Z_d are population, population over 65 years, income and per capita income. As discussed in Chapter 3, bananas are considered a healthy snack in the diets of especially the very old and this is captured in the population variables. Additionally, several studies have suggested that income or per capita income is likely to affect consumer demand, while bananas tend to be consumed out of choice.[10]

The marginal cost function is assumed to take the following linear form:

$$MC_s = \psi_0 + \psi_1 W_s + \psi_2 T \qquad (8.34)$$

where W_s is import (or wholesale) prices for bananas, which are taken as proxies for the cost of bananas to retailers (or wholesalers); T is a time trend which captures reductions in marginal cost due to technological advances in storage and ripening; and $\psi_i (i = 0,1,2)$ is the coefficient of the estimated parameters. By substituting equation (8.34) into the profit maximizing condition, equation (8.20), marginal cost is rewritten in the following linear form:

$$P_{rw} = \psi_0 + \psi_1 W_s + \psi_2 T + \psi_3 Q_d + \varepsilon_s \qquad (8.35)$$

where $\psi_3 = -\lambda \left[\dfrac{dP_{rw}}{dQ_d} \right]$, and $\varepsilon_s \sim N(\mu, \sigma^2)$. Therefore, in accordance with the specifications presented in equations (8.28-8.30) above, the market power parameter λ is the product of the regression coefficients υ_1 and ψ_3. See Tables A2.1 to A2.3 in Appendix 2 for the proof that this system of equations is identified.

8.3   Data

The data used in all estimations are from the author's database, which was constructed with inputs primarily from the FAO, EUROSTAT, firms trading in the EU banana business, banana exporting countries, the WTO, UNCTAD, industry experts and the European Commission. Monthly banana import, wholesale and retail prices, in national currencies per metric ton or kilogram, were obtained from FAO's secretariat in Rome for the 1970 to 1999 period during fieldwork by the author in 2000. Monthly quantities (in metric tons) and value (000s of ECUs) of bananas imported into individual EU member-states during the 1988-1999 period were obtained by the author from the Comext database of the EUROSTAT office in Luxembourg in 2000. Annual data on banana import quantities and value from 1976 were also obtained from Comext. Other data obtained from EUROSTAT technical databases are income, prices of competing and substitute fruits, and population. See Appendix 2 for results of the statistical tests performed upon them.[11]

Results of the Augmented Dickey Fuller (ADF) tests for order of integration of these data are shown in Tables A2.4 to A2.9 in Appendix 2. If the calculated ADF statistic is greater than the MacKinnon critical values, the variable is integrated at the respective order.[12] We have performed the test at all levels for all variables because the final model uses variables that are all integrated at the same order. As expected, most of these data are not stationary in levels, but are stationary at first or second difference.

8.4   Econometric method, results and analysis

The econometric method used for estimating market power is two-stage least squares (TSLS), consistent with modelling requirements for estimating a simultaneous equation system. In TSLS the reduced form for each endogenous variable is first estimated and the fitted values from these regressions are used in the structural equations. This eliminates any bias from the estimated coefficients that might have otherwise arisen when using ordinary least squares (OLS).[13] The instruments used were wholesale (or import) prices;[14] income, per capita income, population, population over 65 years,[15] and a trend variable T.[16]

In all cases, prior to estimations the following steps were undertaken in turn. First, Johansen co-integration tests were performed on the variables used in each of the supply and demand systems in order to determine the number of co-integrating equations at the 5% level of significance.

Second, the levels regressions (corresponding to the number of co-integrating equations) were estimated and their error terms (residuals) were saved in variables corresponding to the number of co-integrating equations. Details of results in each case are reported in Appendix 2.

Finally, the models were estimated, using the method of differences along with the corresponding vector error correction terms.[17] A measure of the degree of market power was first estimated for the entire period (1970-99), using annual data for each country. This was followed by estimates for the sub-periods before, and since, the implementation of the SEM.

8.4.1   Aggregate market power (1970-99)

The results of the econometric estimations for France and Germany are reported in Tables 8.1 and 8.2, respectively (see also Tables A2.10 to A2.13 in Appendix 2 for respective co-integrating equations).

Using the econometric estimations in Table 8.1, aggregate market power in the French market, λ_{FR}^a, for the period 1970-99 is given by: $\lambda_{FR}^a = -(-2.97)(0.15) = 0.45$.

Using the econometric estimations in Table 8.2, aggregate market power in the German market, λ_{DE}^a, for the period 1970-99 is given by: $\lambda_{DE}^a = -(-1.04)(0.49) = 0.51$.

Table 8.1   Market power from import to retail levels in France

$\Delta Q_{FR} = 1670.75 - 2.97\Delta P_{FR} + 227.74\Delta Y_{FR} - 7.22\Delta Pop65_{FR} + 0.61Ect_{d1}$
          (7.03)   (-5.99)   (0.28)   (-1.08)   (3.03)
R^2 between observed and predicted 0.58
$D_L = 0.752 < D_W = 2.183 > D_U = 2.023$

$\Delta P_{FR} = 66.51 + 0.15\Delta Q_{FR} + 0.87\Delta W_{FR} + 0.99Ect_{s1}$
            (7.30)   (3.35)   (17.69)   (3.16)
R^2 between observed and predicted 0.93
$D_L = 0.894 < D_W = 1.84 > D_U = 1.828$

Note: t-Statistics are shown in parentheses.

Table 8.2   Market power from import to retail levels in Germany

$\Delta Q_{DE} = 1823.87 - 1.04\Delta P_{DE} + 311.52\Delta Y_{DE} - 0.000171\Delta Pop_{DE} + 0.43Ect_{d1}$
          (4.53)   (-4.19)   (5.65)   (3.46)   (1.29)
R^2 between observed and predicted 0.69
$D_L = 0.863 < D_W = 2.011 > D_U = 1.940$

$\Delta P_{DE} = 443.17 + 0.49\Delta Q_{DE} + 1.37\Delta W_{DE} + 1.01Ect_{s1} + 0.18Ect_{s2}$
            (2.34)   (3.08)   (13.77)   (2.74)   (0.77)
R^2 between observed and predicted 0.93
$D_L = 0.894 < D_W = 1.84 > D_U = 1.828$

Note: t-Statistics are shown in parentheses.

On the basis of the results obtained in Tables 8.1 and 8.2, the null hypotheses that the German and French banana markets are perfectly competitive are rejected at the 5% level of significance, since the estimated values of λ are statistically significantly different from 0. The null hypotheses of collusion are also rejected in both cases, at the 5% level of significance, since the estimated values of λ are statistically significantly different from 1. However, the hypotheses that firms are engaged in

Cournot-Nash behaviour cannot be rejected in either case, since the values of the calculated market power parameters approximate to the shares of the market that firms of identical size would command if engaged in oligopolistic interdependence.

It will be recalled from Chapter 3 that two major conglomerates control the marketing of bananas in France, while three firms control the market in Germany. Therefore, the predicted values of λ would suggest that firms in both the German and French markets are engaged in behaviour that is less competitive than the Cournot-Nash outcome. Moreover, it would appear that firms in the German market are far less competitive than those in the French market. The reader will recall when we discussed wholesale-import and retail-wholesale price margins in Chapter 3, we saw that the extent of these margins was greatest for bananas sold in Germany (particularly 'Chiquita' brands). The present econometric results are consistent with those findings.

Below, we shall continue our analysis of market power in the EU banana industry by first exploring the movements in price margins and quantities of banana imports for the periods prior to, and since the implementation of, the SEM. We shall then econometrically estimate the degree of market power.

8.4.2   Market power in the pre-SEM period

Market power in the pre-SEM period was estimated using monthly data covering 1988-93.[18] The results are reported by country and at three different stages when relevant: the import-wholesale stage, the wholesale-retail stage, and the import-retail stage.[19] Where the entire banana commodity chain is vertically integrated, the movements in retail-import margins, in response to quantities, capture the magnitude and direction of market power over time. Where, instead, autonomous firms handle individual stages of the chain, the movements in wholesale-import and retail-wholesale margins, in response to movements in quantities, best capture the direction and magnitude of market power.

If the French banana market is considered to be vertically integrated, market power in that industry should have decreased over time. In fact the quantity and retail-import margins of bananas imported into France declined between January 1988 and June 1993, while the index of real retail-import margins declined from 139 in March 1988 to 91 in June 1993 (Figure 8.1).

However, conceptualizing the French banana market as comprising autonomous firms at the import, wholesale and retail stages reveals a somewhat different picture, as shown in Figures 8.2 and 8.3.

Fig 8.1:   *France – Market power under vertical integration*

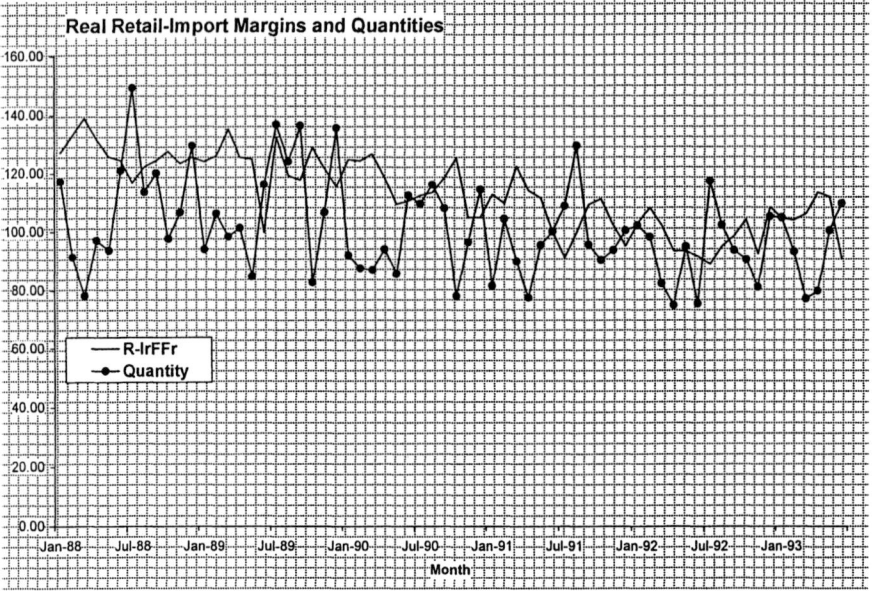

Fig 8.2:   *France – Market power between wholesale and import*

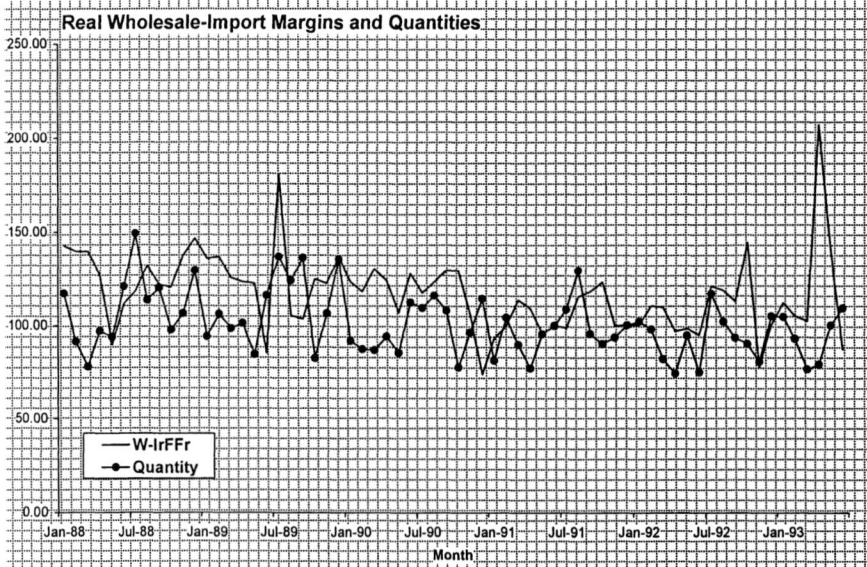

Fig 8.3: France – Market power between retail and wholesale

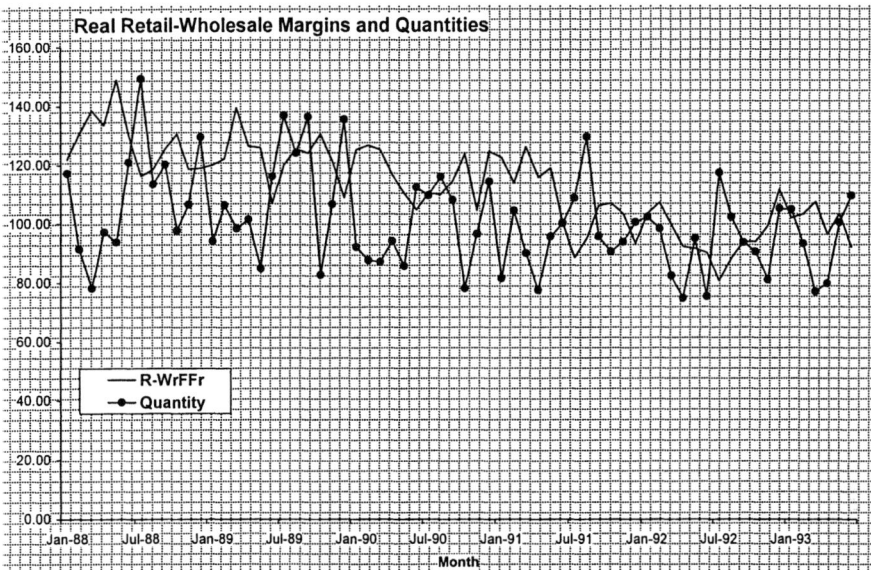

Firms in the French banana market do appear to have exercised considerably higher levels of market power at the wholesale stage (Figure 8.2) than at the retail stage (Figure 8.3). The real index of wholesale-import margins averaged 118 throughout the period, peaking at 207 in April 1993, while the same index for retail-import margins averaged 112 throughout the period, peaking at 149 in May 1988, after which both show a secular decline, falling below the 100 level since June 1991. The econometric estimations of market power at the wholesale stage are shown in Table 8.3 (see also Tables A2.14 and A2.15 in Appendix 2 for the respective co-integrating equations).

From these equations, the market power between wholesale and import, λ_{FR}^{WI}, is $\lambda_{FR}^{WI} = (0.76)(0.67) = 0.51$. This result confirms the hypothesis that although aggregate market power exercised in the French market is somewhat higher (less competitive) than the Cournot-Nash equilibrium, it is at the wholesale stage of the banana chain that firms really exercised their market power in the pre-SEM period.

Table 8.3   Market power from import to wholesale levels in France

---

$\Delta Q_{FR} = -31990.53 + 0.76\Delta P_{FR} + 1.39\Delta\,Pop_{FR} + 2.98\Delta Y_{FR} + 0.88Ect_{d1}$
$\quad\quad\quad\quad (-1.69)\quad\quad\quad (3.11)\quad\quad\quad (1.39)\quad\quad\quad\quad (1.50)\quad\quad (6.84)$

$\quad\quad -3.02\,Ect_{d2} + 0.002Ect_{d3}$
$\quad\quad\quad (-2.09)\quad\quad\quad (0.40)$

$\quad\quad R^2$ between observed and predicted 0.48

$\quad\quad D_L = 1.370 < D_W = 1.96 > D_U = 1.843$

$\Delta P_{FR} = 0.67\Delta Q_{FR} + 0.28\Delta W_{FR} + 0.65Ect_{s1} - 0.02Ect_{s2} + 1.08Ect_{s3}$
$\quad\quad\quad\quad (4.86)\quad\quad (1.97)\quad\quad\quad (4.69)\quad\quad\quad (-1.35)\quad\quad\quad (0.33)$

$\quad\quad R^2$ between observed and predicted 0.68

$\quad\quad D_L = 1.438 < D_W = 1.82 > D_U = 1.767$

Note: t-Statistics are shown in parentheses.

Therefore, to summarize, during the pre-SEM period the banana business in France was most lucrative for wholesale firms and they appear to have exercised the most market power in that industry. Notwithstanding this, the banana business in France as a whole appears to exhibit decreasing profitability over time. This decreasing profitability derives from a reduction in both the margins that firms are capable of commanding as well as the quantities of bananas that are imported.

The German market presents a somewhat different picture when compared with the French market. If the market is conceptualized as being vertically integrated, the movements in the indices of quantity and retail-import margins during the pre-SEM period reveal two distinct features: (i) a marked, secular decline in the quantities of bananas imported over time, and

(ii) a cyclical and slightly increasing trend in real retail-import margins (Figure 8.4). This suggests that in that market, firms tended to increase their market power over time. If, instead, the German banana market is conceptualized as comprising distinct stages under the control of autonomous firms, then a somewhat different picture emerges. Firms operating at the wholesale stage of the chain appear to be least profitable, with their wholesale-import price indices averaging 112. Moreover, their profitability, measured here as their ability to command higher margins, appears to be decreasing over time (Figure 8.5). However, firms operating at the retail stage appear to be the most profitable, with their retail-wholesale price indices averaging 124, and their profitability tending to increase (Figure 8.6).

Fig 8.4:   *Germany – Market power under vertical integration*

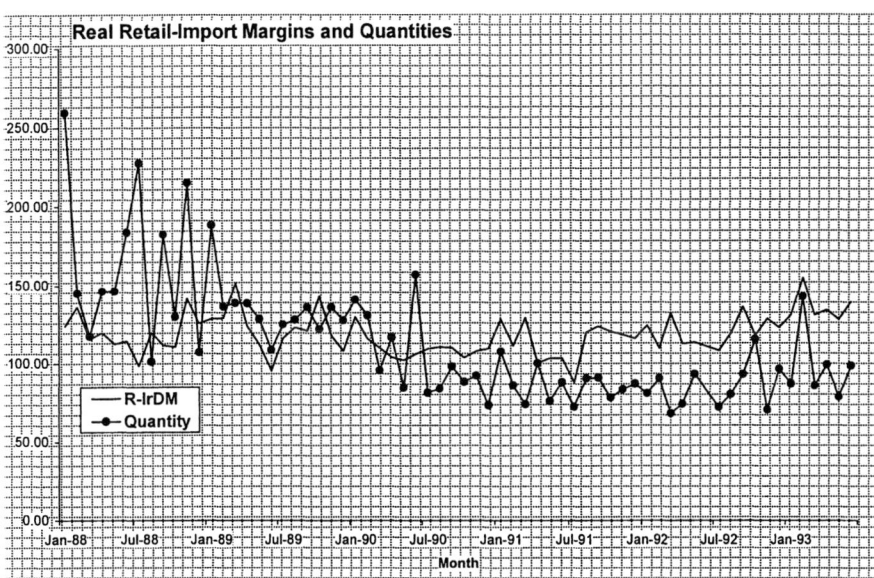

This analysis suggests that firms in the German banana market exploit most of their market power at the retail stage of the chain. But, more importantly, the fact that both the real retail-import and retail-wholesale indices show increasing trends confirms that vertical integration is the dominant form of industrial organization in that market.

Fig 8.5:   *Germany – Market power between wholesale and import*

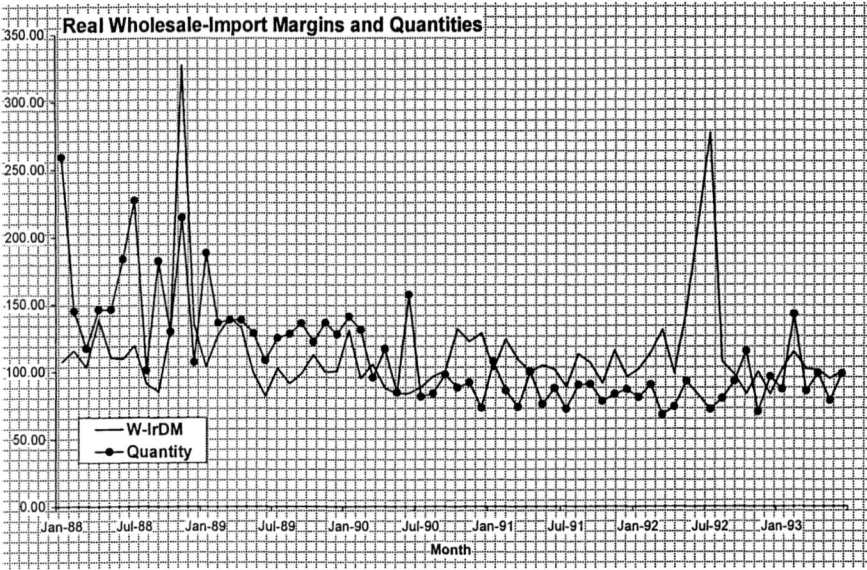

Fig 8.6:   *Germany – Market power between retail and wholesale*

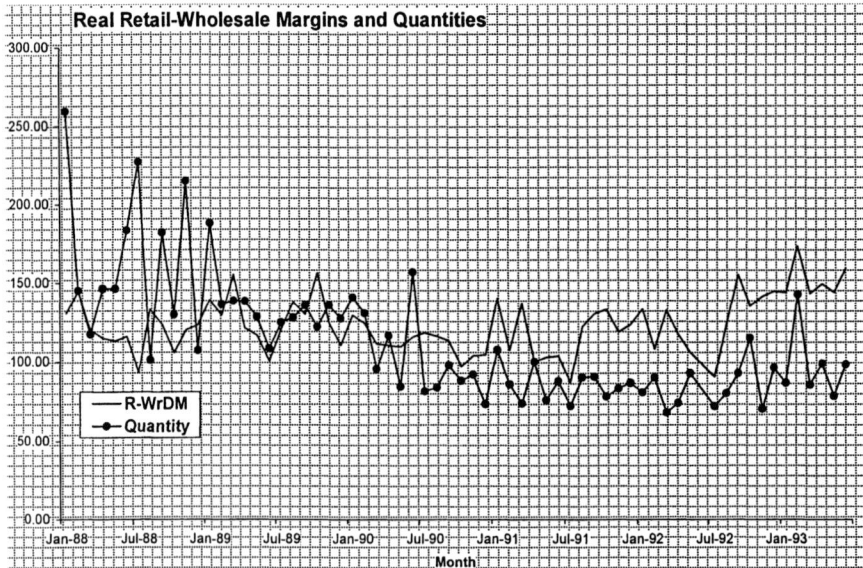

Table 8.4   Market power from retail to wholesale levels in Germany

$\Delta Q_{DE} = 116.16 - 0.76\Delta P_{DE} - 0.2\Delta Pop_{DE} + 27.62\Delta Y_{DE} + 1.11 Ect_{d1}$
    (6.67)   (-4.54)   (-0.94)   (0.40)   (8.94)

    $-3.02\,Ect_{d2}\; +\; 0.002 Ect_{d3}$
        (-2.09)   (0.40)

    R^2 between observed and predicted 0.56

    $D_L = 1.438 < D_W = 1.88 > D_U = 1.767$

$\Delta P_{DE} = 123.60 - 0.60\Delta Q_{DE} + 1.32 Ect_{s1}$
    (19.97)   (-6.38)   (0.75)

    R^2 between observed and predicted 0.63

    $D_L = 1.503 < D_W = 1.67 < D_U = 1.696$

Note: t-Statistics are shown in parentheses.

From Table 8.4, the degree of market power actually exercised in the German market between retail and wholesale, λ_{DE}^{RW}, is given by $\lambda_{DE}^{RW} = (0.76)(0.60) = 0.46$ (see also Tables A2.16 and A2.17 in Appendix 2 for the co-integrating equations). This confirms the hypothesis that, while firms in the German market have generally exercised market power, it is at the retail stage of the chain that such power is fully exercised.[20]

Therefore, to summarize, during the pre-SEM period there were distinct differences in the manner in which market power was exercised in Germany and France. In France, wholesalers appear to have exploited the most market power, but towards the end of that period their ability to do so had diminished considerably. Moreover, there appears to be no statistically significant relationship between the exploitation of market power at the wholesale stage and overall market performance, suggesting that vertical integration has not been the dominant *modus operandi* in that market. In contrast, the trend in the German market reflects increasing market power over time, up to the commencement of the SEM, and a strong relationship between the exploitation of market power at the retail-wholesale and the retail-import stages. This latter result confirms the importance of vertical integration in that market.

8.4.3   Market power in the post-SEM period

The implementation of the SEM was expected to drive up banana prices in Germany, at least to the extent of the 20 per cent tariff set by the

Commission, and to reduce banana prices in France, since firms operating in that market would have been at liberty to import bananas from cheaper sources of supply. Given these assumptions, the expected outcomes were: (i) decline of market power exercised by firms in these markets; and (ii) decreased profits for firms in both the German and French banana markets. This section, therefore, attempts to determine whether, and to what extent, the implementation of the SEM has affected the degree of market power actually exercised by firms.

Looking at the movements of import, wholesale and retail banana prices in France between July 1993 and December 1998 (Figure 8.7), it is evident that the wedge between retail and wholesale prices is considerably larger than that between wholesale and import prices. Consequently, it is assumed that market power is likely to be exercised most at the retail stage and least at the wholesale stage of the banana chain.

Fig. 8.7   France - Banana prices (current FFR/metric ton) post-SEM

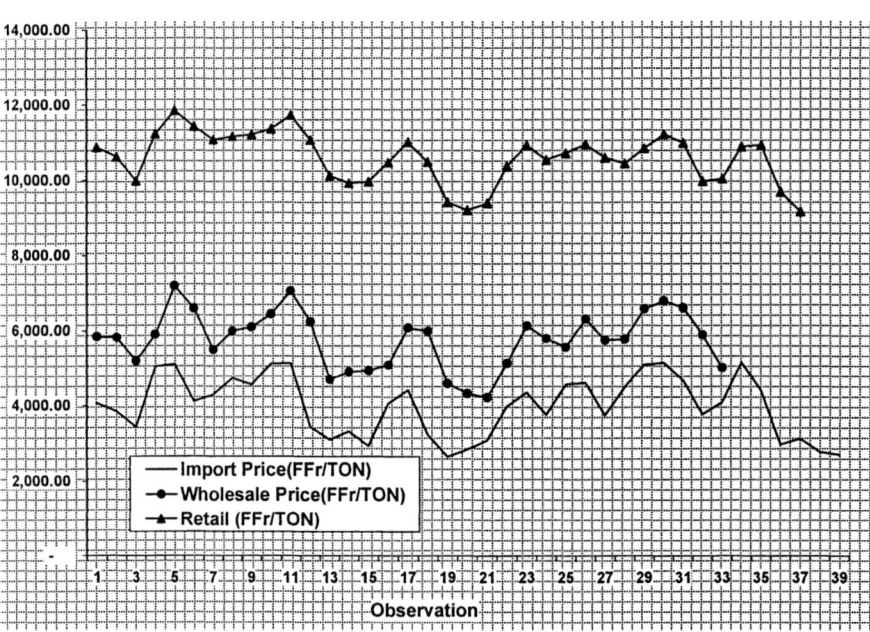

The results of the econometric estimations for the existence of market power between retail and wholesale stages (Table 8.5) show that the degree of market power actually exercised is $\lambda_{FR}^{RW} = -(0.35)(-0.33) = 0.12$ (see also Tables A2.18 and A2.19 in Appendix 2 for the co-integrating equations). Of course, attempts to estimate the degree of market power actually exercised between wholesale and import stages proved futile, since the coefficient of the quantity variable on the supply function was statistically insignificant.[21]

Table 8.5   *Market power from retail to wholesale levels in France (post-SEM)*

$$\Delta Q_{FR} = 0.35\Delta P_{FR} + 0.18\Delta W_{FR} + 1.39\Delta Pop_{FR} + 2988036\Delta Y_{FR}$$
$$\quad (8.74) \qquad (5.06) \qquad\quad (1.69) \qquad\quad (1.50)$$

$$\quad + 0.68 Ect_{d1} + 2.49 Ect_{d2}$$
$$\quad\quad (5.45) \qquad\quad (2.10)$$

R^2 between observed and predicted 0.32

$D_L = 1.404 < D_W = 1.78 < D_U = 1.805$

$$\Delta P_{FR} = 130.98 - 0.33\Delta Q_{FR} - 0.14\Delta W^*_{FR} + 0.95 Ect_{s1}$$
$$\quad\quad (28.97) \quad (-4.22) \quad (-5.57) \qquad (1.09)$$

R^2 between observed and predicted 0.66

$D_L = 1.471 < D_W = 2.24 > D_U = 1.731$

Note: t-Statistics are shown in parentheses.

Movements of banana prices in Germany since the SEM was implemented (Figure 8.8) are strikingly similar to those in Figure 8.7. Whereas prior to implementation of the SEM, firms in France exercised market power most at the wholesale stage, since the SEM took effect, these firms like their German counterparts, have exploited most of their market power at the retail stage.

Again, attempts to estimate the degree of market power exercised between import and wholesale stages proved futile, since the coefficient on the quantity variable obtained from attempting to estimate the supply function was statistically insignificant. The degree of market power actually exercised between retail and wholesale stages, estimated using the results of the econometric equations in Table 8.6, was $\lambda^{RW}_{DE} = -(-0.27)(0.45) = 0.12$ (see also Tables A2.20 and A2.21 in Appendix 2 for the co-integrating equations).

Fig. 8.8   Germany - Banana prices (current DM/metric ton) post-SEM

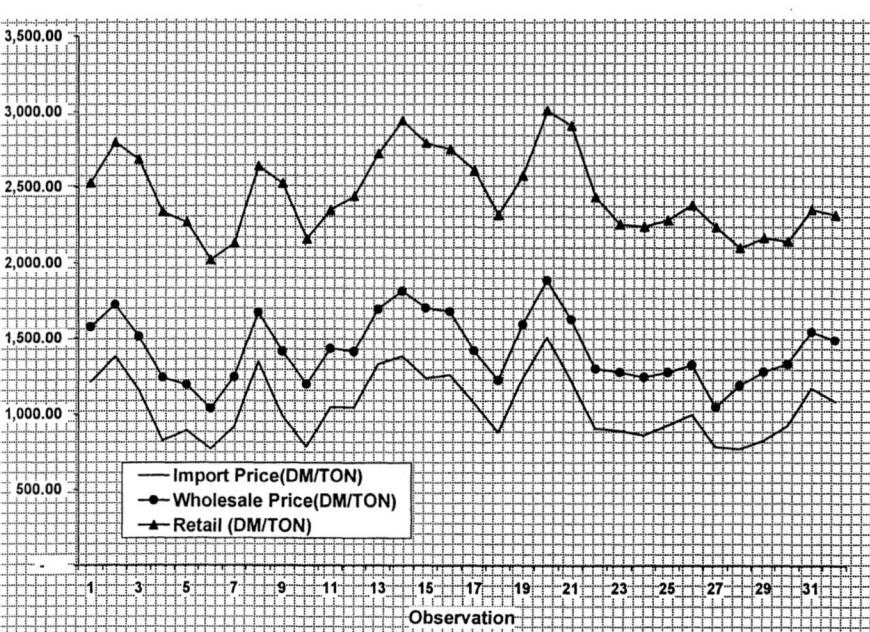

*Table 8.6   Market power from retail to wholesale levels in Germany
(post-SEM)*

$\Delta Q_{DE} = 90.54 - 0.27\Delta P_{DE} - 68.53\Delta Y_{DE} - 0.30\Delta Pop_{DE} + 1.10\ Ect_{d1}$
　　　　(7.94)　　(-2.69)　　　(-0.64)　　　　(-1.16)　　　(6.81)

　　　$+ 12.24 Ect_{d2} + 14.06 Ect_{d3}$
　　　　(1.06)　　　　　(0.32)

R^2 between observed and predicted 0.53

$D_L = 1.379 < D_W = 1.74 < D_U = 1.843$

$\Delta P_{DE} = 0.45\Delta Q_{DE} + 2.23\Delta W_{DE} - 1.47\Delta W^*{}_{DE} + 0.11 Ect_{s1}$
　　　　(3.80)　　　(17.02)　　　(-14.07)　　　(1.92)

R^2 between observed and predicted 0.91

$D_L = 1.471 < D_W = 1.72 < D_U = 1.731$

Note: t-Statistics are shown in parentheses.

These results suggest that the SEM has reduced the degree of market power exercised in the banana industries in both Germany and France, to the extent that profitability is likely to have diminished considerably as these markets might have become more competitive. The fact that the degree of market power actually exercised in both cases is identical is coincidental: in the German case, the conjectural variation elasticity on the quantity variable is larger than that on the price variable, while they are practically identical in the French case. Yet, it does appear that the importance of oligopolistic interdependence remains. Moreover, the SEM appears to have affected the point in the banana commodity chain at which firms appropriate the most profit, with French firms shifting their locus of market power away from the wholesale to the retail stage, possibly in pursuit of vertical integration.

However, while the hypothesis that firms in the German banana market have maintained vertically integrated systems from import to retail cannot be rejected, given the consistent and statistically significant results obtained (Table 8.7 and Tables A2.22 and A2.23 in Appendix 2 for the co-integrating equations), the degree of market power actually exercised in the French market between the retail and import stages could not be identified with any degree of statistical significance.

Table 8.7   Market power from retail to import in Germany (post-SEM)

$\Delta Q_{DE} = 90.40 - 0.33\Delta P_{DE} - 0.12\ \Delta Pop_{DE}\ +1.16\ Ect_{d1}$
$(8.94)\quad (-3.18)\quad\ (-0.27)\qquad\ (6.82)$

$-8.26 Ect_{d2}\ +\ \ 0.01 Ect_{d3}$
$(-0.41)\qquad\ (0.42)$

R^2 between observed and predicted 0.49

$D_L = 1.404 < D_W = 1.59 < D_U = 1.654$

$\Delta P_{DE} = 77.38 - 0.53\Delta Q_{DE} + 0.49\Delta W_{DE} + 0.04\Delta W^*{}_{DE}$
$(3.70)\quad\ (-2.64)\qquad (3.30)\qquad\ (2.72)$

$-105.05 Ect_{s1}\ +\ \ 101.81 Ect_{s2} - 82.43 Ect_{s3}$
$(-0.48)\qquad\quad (0.48)\qquad\quad (-0.48)$

R^2 between observed and predicted 0.67

$D_L = 1.404 < D_W = 1.59 < D_U = 1.802$

Note: t-Statistics are shown in parentheses.

8.4.4   Analytical summary

There are three major findings from this chapter that require further discussion and analysis. First, there has been a marked decline over time in the degree of market power actually exercised by firms in both the French and German banana markets, both of which appear to have become reasonably competitive. Second, while firms in the French market do appear to have strategically changed the stage in the banana chain at which market power is actually exercised, there has been no observed change in the behaviour of German banana firms. Third, whether or not trade in a market is 'free' is not by itself a sufficient condition for predicting the welfare outcomes of consumers and producers; indeed, market structure and firm behaviour do matter as well.

In the pre-SEM period, banana prices were consistently higher in France, where tariffs and quotas existed, than in Germany, where no such barriers existed. Consequently, earlier mainstream works on the EU banana trade (Chapter 2) assumed that liberalization of trade in the commodity implied the best scenario for consumers and producers. Implicit in such a hypothesis was the notion that firms in the German banana market exercised little, if any, market power. Yet, this chapter has shown that not only did firms in the German market possess market power, but that such power was actually exercised to an extent statistically not significantly different from that of French firms. Consequently, the economic welfare which consumers in the German market, and/or producers in the exporting countries, should have enjoyed in the pre-SEM period was being appropriated by German firms as profits, primarily at the retail stage. This finding is consistent with our analysis of the division of revenue and surplus along the respective commodity chains (Chapters 6 and 7).

There is, therefore, overwhelming evidence of the importance of vertical integration as a means of improving operational efficiency of banana firms through enhanced economies of scale and governance. Litvak and Maule (1977) have argued that the oligopolistic market structure of the banana industry that existed in the United States in the 1950s is precisely what TNCs are likely to pursue elsewhere in the absence of legislation to force them to behave otherwise. Prior to the implementation of the Consent Decree in the United States in 1958, two banana TNCs, the United Fruit Company (Chiquita) and Castle and Cooke (Dole) accounted for 89 per cent of that market (Litvak and Maule, 1977:542). When the Consent Decree effectively prevented US banana TNCs from controlling all stages of the commodity chain, TNCs sought to retain their market power through their ownership and control of banana production and transportation outside the

United States as a means of effectively functioning as large vertically integrated operations in the U.S. market (Litvak and Maule, 1977:537). Therefore, the change in strategy of French banana TNCs could be viewed as a means of pursuing vertical integration in order to become more efficient and competitive in light of possible complete liberalization of the EU banana trade.[22]

In light of these findings with respect to two of the major banana-importing countries in the EU, prior to implementation of the SEM, the hypothesis that trade liberalization in and of itself necessarily increases consumer and/or producer welfare is difficult to maintain. On the contrary, it would appear that freeing trade under certain conditions of oligopoly increases monopoly profits, rather than consumer or producer welfare as suggested by previous mainstream studies. Whether or not firms behave in accordance with the expectations of the Hwang and Mai (1988) hypothesis will be further investigated in Chapter 9. However, given that even in a relatively free market firms would attempt to exploit market power if possible, the question of 'who gains' from trade liberalization can only be satisfactorily answered from a decomposition of value added along banana commodity chains, as has been done in Chapters 6 and 7.

8.5   Conclusions

The objective of this chapter has been to determine empirically whether firms in the EU banana market possess market power and, if so, the degree to which such market power has been exercised over time, particularly with the implementation of the SEM, and whether or not the stage in the banana chain where market power is exercised matters.

We have utilized a conjectural variations method for measuring market power based on the works of Deodhar and Sheldon (1995) and Buschena and Perloff (1991). The chapter's contributions to that methodology have been the incorporation of co-integration analysis techniques in the econometric estimations and the use of both monthly and annual data for estimating market power in both the pre-SEM and post-SEM periods. The results are consistent with the findings of Deodhar and Sheldon (1995) with respect to the German market.

In the pre-SEM period, firms in the EU banana market enjoyed considerable degrees of market power, with a tendency for firm behaviour to approach the collusive outcome in the earlier years of the pre-SEM period and to become more competitive since the SEM took effect. An interesting finding of this chapter is the impossibility to predict the likely impact of trade liberalization on the economic welfare of the various economic actors without taking market structure into account. In fact, the chapter finds that although relatively free trade prevailed in the German market prior to implementation of the SEM, firms operating there exploited their market power like those operating in France, where almost total protectionism existed. It is the SEM that reduced the magnitude of market power actually exercised in both Germany and France. Yet, the importance of oligopolistic interdependence prevailing in both markets cannot be underestimated.

It seems that, especially under conditions of open competition, firms in the banana business would attempt to exploit most of their market power at the retail stage of the commodity chain and strive to obtain vertical integration. Therefore, different modes of organization of the banana chain are likely to result in different distributions of revenue, profits and value-added among the various actors, as demonstrated in Chapters 6 and 7.

Notes

[1] Original works on the Johansen Cointegration method can be found in Soren Johansen (1991) "Estimation and Hypothesis Testing of Cointegration Vectors in Gaussian Vector Autoregressive Models," *Econometrica*, 59, 1551–80; and Soren Johansen (1995) *Likelihood-based Inference in Cointegrated Vector Autoregressive Models*. Oxford University Press.

[2] Existing literature and econometric modelling software on time series econometric analysis widely recognize the ADF test for assessing the integrating properties of a time series. The original contribution to this method is found in the work of Dickey and Fuller (1979), who showed that the t-statistic on the estimated coefficient of regressing the first difference of a variable on its one period lagged value does not follow the conventional t-distribution; but a non-standard distribution, for which they estimated critical values for some sample sizes. MacKinnon (1991) has since extended this original work, using larger sample sizes, which makes it possible to calculate the ADF statistic for any sample size.

[3] X includes dummies for the Indonesian Revolution, the Malaysian Unrest and time trends. The time trends are used as proxies for unavailable cost and weather measures (Buschena and Perloff, 1991:1004).

[4] W includes a real plantation wage index, minimum monthly average rainfall, a one-period lag of minimum rainfall and a real ocean freight rate index for grain (Buschena and Perloff, 1991:1004).

[5] Although that study is about oligopsony as opposed to oligopoly, it is nevertheless discussed here because of the strikingly similar approaches to modelling in both,

and the importance of the former in analysing other stages of the banana chain in the EU.

[6] The argument on the importance of scale economies in the banana trade has been developed in Chapter 3 of this thesis.

[7] Nevertheless, annual data are also used for estimating the degree of market power for comparative purposes. The problems that might arise due to insufficient degrees of freedom are linked to the precise specification of the model. See Mukherjee et al. (1998:216-17) for a brief discussion of these.

[8] Arguably, this approach reasonably accurately captures the degree of market power in the German market, given the fact that that market is highly vertically integrated, from import to retail. Nevertheless, since the data on this market suggest that firms exploit market power to varying degrees at different stages of the chain, such variations are better captured by analysing individual segments of the commodity chain.

[9] Careful examination of their demand function suggests that they might have assumed population, price or quantity to be trend-stationary processes, that is, the residuals from the regression of either of these variables on a trend are stationary. This might explain their use of the trend and squared trend variables.

[10] For instance, see McInerney and Peston (1992)

[11] A comprehensive list of all files in the author's database, which have been used for production of this thesis is shown in the *Database* section following the *References* for the thesis.

[12] A variable is integrated at order z (denoted as I(z)) if differencing that variable z times makes it stationary. If the variable does not need to be differenced to be made stationary, then we denote it as I(0), which also means that it is stationary in levels. If it needs to be differenced once to be made stationary, then we denote it as I(1), and so on.

[13] See Mukherjee et al. (1998:442-5) for a detailed explanation and example of this method.

[14] When measuring market power under the assumptions of vertical integration, the wholesale price variable is used as an instrument for import price; however, when measuring market power assuming arm's-length trade takes place at individual stages, the import price variable is used as an instrument for wholesale price.

[15] Bananas are generally considered to be a desirable commodity for those who wish to live healthy lifestyles given their natural composition of vitamins and minerals (see Chapter 3). Therefore, it is reasonable to postulate that as population increases consumption is likely to increase. Whether the sick and very old consider bananas a desirable component of their diets is captured by the slope coefficient of the variable "population 65 and older".

[16] The trend variable captures whether or not reductions in marginal cost due to advances in the technologies of ripening and storage matter, and if so, whether they follow a linear path.

[17] A detailed explanation of this technique is presented in Mukherjee et al. (1998:406-11).

[18] As has been indicated in earlier chapters of the thesis, although the SEM took effect from 1 January 1993, in the case of bananas, the new banana regime only took effect from 1 July 1993. Therefore, the correct period for econometric estimations in the pre-SEM period includes up to June 1993.

[19] Essentially, where firms do not exercise market power at a particular stage in the banana chain, then either the coefficient of the price variable in the demand function, or that on the quantity variable in the supply function, makes no contribution to explaining the variation in the other variables.

[20] Estimation of the degree of market power at the wholesale stage turned out to be statistically insignificant at all levels.

[21] In fact, the estimated supply function in this case turns out to be linear, with variations in wholesale and import prices accounting for 84 per cent of the variation in wholesale-import margins.

[22] In 1993 a new banana company, Cobamar, was established in Martinique under the leadership of Marcel Fabre, who had previously been CEO of Sicabam for 20 years. Under his guidance, a commercial partnership has been developed with Chiquita, and the company presently exports approximately 70,000 metric tons of bananas annually. This lends strength to the hypothesis that the French market is becoming more vertically integrated (Field interviews with industry officials).

9   Welfare Effects of EU Banana Trade Liberalization Under Imperfect Competition

9.1   Introduction

The central questions that have given rise to this study are: (i) whether or not market structure and the nature of the banana are significant factors for explaining trade in the commodity and predicting the welfare effects under liberalization; and (ii) whether or not liberalization is likely to result in a more (or less) progressive division and distribution of revenue and surplus between EU countries on the one hand, and the exporting countries that survive on the other (Chapter 1). We began this work with a discussion of the welfare effects of trade liberalization under perfect competition and demonstrated that both the magnitude and direction of the welfare effects predicted by previous works based upon this assumption are likely to be considerably overestimated at best, and that liberalization can well lead to global welfare losses in the worst case (Chapter 2). Our initial hypothesis that the EU banana market is neither perfectly competitive nor contestable was further investigated in Chapter 3, which showed empirically that not only is the banana market neither perfectly competitive nor contestable, but in addition TNCs are aware that they possess market power and have repeatedly exercised such power to the detriment of EU consumers. Moreover, our application of the concept of a commodity chain for analysing the division and distribution of revenue and surplus between EU member-states and the exporting countries reveals that during the pre-SEM period countries exporting bananas to Germany retained the least revenue and surplus, while those that export to France and the UK retained the most. And, importantly, this trend has been typically maintained since the SEM came into effect (Chapters 6 and 7). Therefore, even if liberalization were to result in an overall increase in global welfare, the division and distribution of its rewards would be such that TNCs would appropriate most of the rewards while the producing countries and consumers would be made worse off. Finally, our application of a conjectural variations model for measuring the degree of market power in the EU banana business reveals the following: (i) the existence of market power in the banana industry is confirmed; (ii) the degree of market power in France and Germany was of

comparable magnitudes in the pre-SEM period; and (iii) although the degree
of market power actually exercised appears to have reduced somewhat since
the SEM took effect, oligopolistic interdependence nevertheless remains
extremely important.

With the preceding in mind, the objective of the present chapter is to
simulate the welfare effects of trade liberalization by taking the imperfectly
competitive nature of the EU banana market into consideration. Simulations
are meant to illustrate the extent to which the welfare and efficiency effects
of liberalization under imperfect competition differ from those under perfect
competition. Specifically, in addition to modelling the welfare and
efficiency losses that are likely to be incurred due to Commission
intervention, we shall isolate those that are likely to arise due to market
failure, that is, super-normal profits enjoyed by oligopolists due to product
differentiation and interdependence.

The remainder of this chapter is structured as follows. Section 9.2 will
present the methodology. A three-period *sequential* oligopoly 'game' will
be constructed based on empirical evidence about price formation and
market structure presented in Chapter 3 and our knowledge of oligopolistic
interdependence among TNCs derived in Chapter 8. The model
specifications that are actually estimated are presented in section 9.3, along
with a brief discussion of the estimation results. In section 9.4 the data used
for performing simulations are described, followed by results of the
simulations in section 9.5. Section 9.6 discusses and analyses the findings in
the context of the hypotheses that were outlined for this chapter, and section
9.7 summarizes the conclusions.

9.2   Methodology

We shall build a three-period *sequential* oligopoly 'game' for simulating the
welfare effects of trade liberalization under imperfect competition as
follows.[1] First, the EU banana market is conceptualized as an oligopoly
comprising a total of four supplier categories, three of which can exercise
some degree of monopoly pricing power on the basis of differentiated
bananas through branding.[2] Additionally, there is a fringe of suppliers who
sell bananas at artificially high prices due to Commission intervention in the
market. Our choice of such a typology is based on the observed differences
in prices that are paid for bananas on the basis of their brands. The reader
will recall that since "Chiquita" is capable of exercising the most monopoly
power, that brand commands its own price category; "Dole", "Del Monte",
and "Onkel Tuca" command the second price category; "Bonita",

"Corbana", "Turbana", "Fyffes" and "Consul" command the third price category; and the remaining brands – "Tropical Eden", "Golden B", "Excel", and "Goldfinger" do not command any significant degree of monopoly power (Chapter 3).

Second, the entire EU banana market, which is assumed to be in a Cournot-Nash equilibrium, is divided among the various supplier categories in accordance with the shares which they command in the various member-states.[3]

Third, while there are limits to the quantities of bananas that could be obtained from each supplier category, the extent of supplier constraint varies tremendously. Chiquita possesses almost unlimited capacity, second-category suppliers possess moderate surplus capacity, third-category suppliers possess slight surplus capacity, and fourth-category suppliers already operate at their capacity limits. Again, the reader will recall that EU banana supply capacity is not evenly distributed among the various exporting sources; but, instead, a disproportionately large share comes from the dollar-zone region, while only a residual supply comes from elsewhere, notably the ACP countries and the EU's overseas territories. Our observation of the supply capacities of the various categories confirms the existence of such a typology (Chapter 3).

Fourth, the persistence of oligopolistic interdependence ensures the stability of *differences* in prices based on brand recognition and loyalty by consumers (see section 9.3).

9.2.1   Sequential oligopoly model for the EU banana market

With the preceding concept in mind, in *structural form*, our model for the EU banana market is as follows. The quantity of bananas supplied to the EU is a function of all its sources of supply, and the quantity supplied by each source is a function of the price it receives as well as the supplies of its rivals.[4]

Our model is based on the proposition that the conjectural variations (or strategic actions) of TNCs and the degree of monopoly power which they enjoy through branding largely determine the overall welfare effects that might be expected from liberalization, and that such strategic actions are based on the knowledge that various supplier categories have of each others' activities, which approximates to perfect information.

The author believes that the near-perfect information assumption is plausible in this case (for the type of information required) since all the major suppliers are transnational in nature, which, of necessity, means that they are bound to publicly disclose information about their assets, liabilities and major investment strategies, among other things.[5] Moreover, the persistence of price differentials among the various banana brands over time implies that firms are indeed engaged in oligopolistic interdependence and would be contented to command a smaller share of the market at a particular price (whether inferior or not) rather than none at all. Firms, therefore, are tacitly aware of each others' market power.

Fig. 9.1   *Extent to which the price of the "Chiquita" brand exceeds those of its competitors*

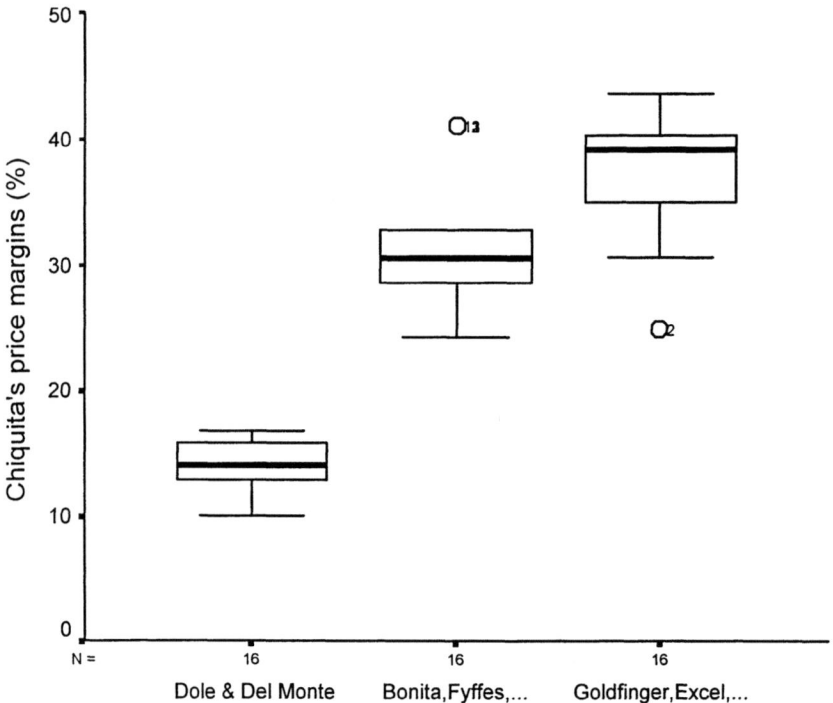

Source: Author's database.

Figure 9.1 shows the extent to which the price of "Chiquita" branded bananas exceeds those of the competition. Two distinctive features are evident from the figure. First, the extent to which the price of "Chiquita" branded bananas exceeds those of the competition is least and most stable for second-class brands ("Dole" and "Del Monte"), with the mean of the distribution practically coincident with the median at slightly more than 14 per cent; and greatest for fourth-class brands ("Goldfinger", "Excel", "Tropical Eden") with a median of slightly more than 39 per cent.

Second, the differences between the medians of second- and third-class brands are considerably larger than those between third- and fourth-class brands. In fact, the figure shows that on more than one occasion there has been an overlap in the margins of third- and fourth-class brands. This further suggests that the real competitive threat to the "Chiquita" brand comes from "Dole" and "Del Monte", with the competitive threats from third-class brands only marginally stronger than those from fourth-class brands. In terms of explanatory power, we expect the relationship between the prices of second-class bananas and the "Chiquita" brand to be the strongest, and those between other brands and the "Chiquita" brand to be the least. Effectively, due to branding, firms in each price category face different demand curves, with "Chiquita" 's demand curve being the least elastic (D_a) and fourth-class brands being the most elastic (D_d) (Figure 9.2).[6]

Fig. 9.2   Demand curves facing banana brands

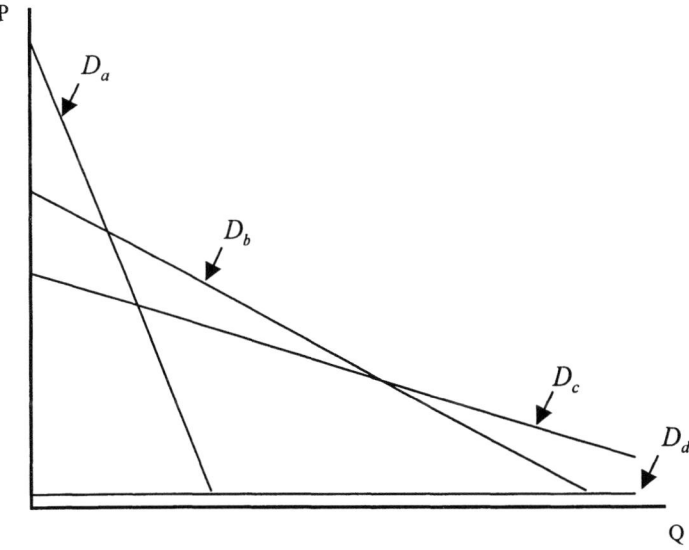

It will be recalled that as far as the neo-classical framework is concerned, the only efficiency distortions in the banana market are likely to arise from the EU's import policy – the existence of a tariff and a quota. Therefore, elimination of these distortions should automatically improve market efficiency (Chapter 2). But, in fact, what we observe here are two types of distortions: those due to intervention by the Commission, and those due to market failure – product differentiation by oligopolists, which results in their ability to charge considerably higher prices for bananas than they should otherwise, whether or not the market is liberalized.

In the simulations performed in section 9.5 we shall therefore seek to answer two additional questions. First, whether or not the efficiency losses that arise from Commission intervention outweigh those that arise because firms exercise market power. Second, whether the elimination of the least-efficient producers (fringe) through liberalization can be justified, given their statistically insignificant share of the market and the persistence of welfare losses due to imperfect competition. We shall now estimate the models that are actually used in the simulations performed in section 9.5.

9.3   Estimation of the model

A major obstacle encountered in conducting this study has been the unavailability of quantity data series that are sufficiently disaggregated by brand to allow estimation of functional forms for the structural relationships presented in equations 9.1 to 9.5 (see endnote 4). This has imposed some limitations on the explanatory power of our model and remains an area for further research if and when such quantity data series become available. The reader will recall that in Chapter 8 we used a conjectural variations method to establish that TNCs engage in strategic quantity-setting behaviour at the *industry* level. With this in mind, we assume that the relative shares of the market by brand, which were obtained through a simple calibration procedure, are reasonably representative of the actual distribution of market shares, at least in the short run.

We have been able to establish the relationships between the various banana brands in the price formation process econometrically, which confirms strategic interdependence through price leadership and the ability of TNCs in each price category to exploit some degree of monopoly power. The econometric models actually estimated and the results obtained are presented and discussed below.

$$\Delta(L\_Dole\_DelMonte) = \alpha_0 + \alpha_1 \Delta(L\_Chiquita) + \varepsilon_1 \qquad (9.13)$$

$$\Delta(L\_Bonita) = \beta_0 + \beta_1 \Delta(L\_Chiquita) + \beta_2 Ect_1 \qquad (9.14)$$

$$\Delta(L\_Tropical\_Eden) = \gamma_0 + \gamma_1\Delta(L\_Chiquita) + \varepsilon_3 \qquad (9.15)$$

In all cases, these models have been estimated using first differences of the logarithms of the original price data, all of which are stationary (see Tables A3.1 and A3.2 in Appendix 3). Therefore, the coefficients are interpreted as elasticities. As an additional measure, the Johansen test for multiple co-integrating vectors was performed on all equations. While no co-integration relationships were found to exist between the variables in equations 9.13 and 9.15, there was one co-integrating vector among the variables in equation 9.14 (see Table A3.3 in Appendix 3). Therefore, models 9.13 and 9.15 were estimated in differences only, while model 9.14 was estimated using the vector error correction method (explained in Chapter 8).

The results in Table 9.1 confirm the importance of interdependence between various TNCs in setting prices – third- and fourth-class banana brands show the most elastic response to changes in price of the premium brand, while second-class banana brands show the least elastic response.

Although the above models appear to adequately explain the price formation process among oligopolists, three alternative hypotheses that seek to determine whether other relationships might explain price-setting behaviour by oligopolists who market third- and fourth-class brands have also been explored. First, whether variations in the price of third-class brands are explained by variations in the price of second-class brands. Second, whether variations in the price of fourth-class brands are explained by variations in the price of second-class brands. Third, whether variations in the price of fourth-class brands are explained by variations in the price of third-class brands. These hypotheses have been explored using the models in equations 9.16 to 9.18 below.

Results initially suggest that price-setting behaviour by oligopolists who market third- and fourth-class banana brands can be explained by prices of second-class banana brands. However, the relationships in Table 9.2 are not as robust as they initially appear to be. Although the slope coefficient of the regression of $\Delta(L\_Bonita)$ against $\Delta(L\_Dole\_DelMonte)$ is significant, the DW statistic of the ADF unit root test on the residuals is only 0.57, suggesting that the error terms are serially correlated.[7] Additionally, with regard to the regression of $\Delta(L\_Tropical\_Eden)$ against $\Delta(L\_Dole\_DelMonte)$, although the slope coefficient is significant the error terms of the regression are only stationary at the level of first differences.[8] Therefore, notwithstanding the initial attractiveness of these results as alternative explanations of price-setting behaviour the model

Table 9.1 Econometric estimates of price relationships between the "Chiquita" brand and other banana brands[1]

	Δ(L_Dole_DelMonte)	Δ(L_Bonita)	Δ(L_Tropical_Eden)
Δ(L Chiquita)	0.94	1.06	1.07
t-statistic	7.82	3.68	4.78
R^2	0.81	0.70	0.62
DW	1.96	1.91	1.86
D_L	0.98	0.98	0.98
D_U	1.54	1.54	1.54
N	16.00	16.00	16.00
Residuals:			
ADF test statistic	-3.73	-3.63	-2.74
1% critical value	-4.07	-4.07	-4.07
5% critical value	-3.12	-3.12	-3.12
10% critical value	-2.70	-2.70	-2.70
Order of integration	I(0)**	I(0)**	I(0)*

Notes: [1] In the case of the relationship between the second-class brands and the "Chiquita" brand, the estimated model including the long-run relationship was:

$$\Delta(L\_Bonita) = 1.06\Delta(L\_Chiquita) + 0.76 E_{ct1}$$
$$\quad (3.68) \qquad\qquad (2.43)$$

**(*) – indicates significant at the 5% (1%) levels, respectively.

estimates in Table 9.1 are superior results.[9] See also Table A3.6 (Appendix 3), which shows that there are no co-integrating relationships between any combination of these variables at the 5% level of significance.

$$\Delta(L\_BONITA) = \delta_0 + \delta_1\Delta(L\_Dole\_DelMonte) + \varepsilon_4 \qquad (9.16)$$

$$\Delta(L\_Tropical\_Eden) = \varphi_0 + \varphi_1\Delta(L\_Dole\_DelMonte) + \varepsilon_5 \qquad (9.17)$$

$$\Delta(L\_Tropical\_Eden) = \lambda_0 + \lambda_1\Delta(L\_Bonita) + \varepsilon_6 \qquad (9.18)$$

Table 9.2 Estimates of alternative relationships between second class banana brands and third and fourth class brands

	$\Delta(L\_Bonita)$	$\Delta(L\_Tropical\_Eden)$
$\Delta(L\_Dole\_DelMonte)$	1.49	1.12
t-statistic	6.97	6.14
R^2	0.78	0.73
DW	2.92	1.68
D$_L$	0.98	0.98
D$_U$	1.54	1.54
N	16.00	16.00
Residuals:		
ADF test statistic	-3.68	-1.95
1% critical value	-4.07	-4.07
5% critical value	-3.12	-3.12
10% critical value	-2.70	-2.70
Order of integration	I(0)**	I(1)**

Note: ** indicates significant at the 5% level.

9.4   Data used in simulations

The base quantity and price data (Table A3.7) and elasticities of demand (Table A3.8) used for performing simulations are for the year 1998. This year was chosen for two reasons: first, because it was the most recent year for which reliable data were available at the time of the field-work (year 2000); second, because it represents a year by which the market should have actually returned to a Cournot-Nash equilibrium following the implementation of the SEM in 1993.

The elasticities of demand used in the model are estimates, which were arrived at through a variety of techniques including industry-level econometric analysis and qualitative evidence about behaviour of firms in the market. As such, they are not rigorous firm-level estimates because of the lack of availability of data at the firm level for such analysis. However, based on our knowledge of industry-level elasticities and their distribution in the EU, these estimates of elasticities reasonably capture actual market situations.

9.5   Simulations

Two sets of simulations are performed, which take into account distortions induced by both the Commission and market failure. In the first set of simulations, monopoly surplus due to imperfect competition and Commission intervention are estimated, assuming that the quantities of bananas supplied in 1998 were optimal – they exhausted EU consumer demand. Gross revenue is the product of the quantity of bananas sold and the prevailing price for each brand; while monopoly surplus due to branding is the product of the quantity of bananas sold and the difference between the prices of branded bananas and the competitive market price, which is taken as the price of fourth-class bananas.[10]

In the second set of simulations, the efficiency and welfare effects are estimated, assuming that liberalization brings about adjustments in quantities of bananas supplied and demanded by firms and consumers, respectively, and that the market eventually resettles to a Cournot-Nash equilibrium after oligopolists have played the three-period sequential game (Figure 9.3) discussed below.

The distinctive feature of this sequential oligopoly 'game' is that, the prevailing strategies of oligopolists and market conditions in period t are carried over into period $t+1$. In the first period, oligopolists pursue a strategy to convince EU consumers, and indeed the Commission, that liberalization is in their own best interest. Therefore, firms are likely to reduce prices by a certain percentage while pursuing the preservation of the oligopolistic structure of the market. This is achieved through price signalling by the dominant TNC, Chiquita. Once Chiquita has reduced its price by a certain percentage, the other oligopolists follow suit, reducing their prices so as to maintain the price differentials between themselves.[11] Since fourth-category suppliers are price takers, any substantive reduction in their price would result in losses and they would be driven out of the market; on the other hand, TNC oligopolists are capable of setting their prices below the free market price since they enjoy superior scale economies. Additionally, since the price of bananas from the fringe is artificially high due to the tariff preference, any significant reduction in price is likely to result in their exit from the market.

Fig. 9.3   *Three-period sequential oligopoly game*

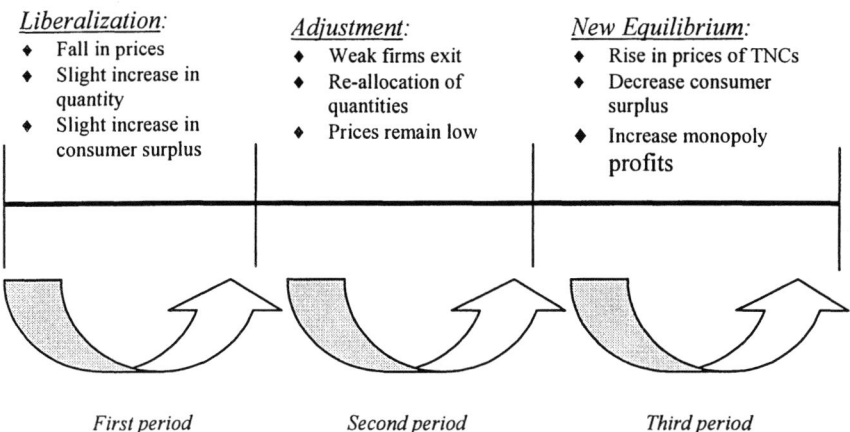

<table>
<tr><td>

Liberalization:
♦ Fall in prices
♦ Slight increase in quantity
♦ Slight increase in consumer surplus
</td><td>

Adjustment:
♦ Weak firms exit
♦ Re-allocation of quantities
♦ Prices remain low
</td><td>

New Equilibrium:
♦ Rise in prices of TNCs
♦ Decrease consumer surplus
♦ Increase monopoly profits
</td></tr>
</table>

        First period   *Second period*   *Third period*

Although we do expect fourth-category suppliers and the fringe to be driven out of the market, the realization of their departure will be in the second period of adjustment due to the investments which these producers would have made during the current cycle. Bananas have a *natural* gestation period of nine months and so any investments (sunk costs) in production from the onset of liberalization would need to be recovered.[12] This chapter argues that both fourth-category suppliers and the fringe would prefer to sell their bananas at a loss rather than have no sales at all, in order to recover some of their fixed and operating costs; however, they would not undertake any investment in new capacity for the following production cycle. TNC oligopolists would then acquire the quantities released by the fringe and fourth-category suppliers in such a manner as to preserve their interdependence, while keeping prices at the levels set during liberalization. Crucially, during the adjustment period oligopolists would like to create trust among EU consumers and the Commission, that liberalization is indeed in their best interest.[13]

During the third period, since banana demand is inelastic, both in terms of income (for high-income countries) and price, once consumer confidence is restored banana prices are likely to increase through price signalling in a manner similar to that during liberalization. We simulate prices returning at least to the levels they were at prior to liberalization; and possibly even higher, since oligopolists could convincingly argue that in real terms banana prices had fallen considerably relative to their pre-liberalization levels. Therefore, when the new Cournot-Nash equilibrium is reached, consumers would buy a smaller variety of bananas at higher prices than before.

9.5.1   Monopoly surplus due to imperfect competition and Commission intervention under optimal quantity supply

Table 9.3 shows the gross revenue and monopoly surplus due to branding for bananas sold in the EU market in 1998. We see that of the nearly $3.0 billion in gross revenue generated by the sale of bananas, approximately $0.8 billion constitutes monopoly surplus due to branding, of which Chiquita alone appropriates 49 per cent, Dole and Del Monte appropriate 48 per cent and third class brands retain the remaining 3 per cent.

Table 9.3   Gross revenue and monopoly surplus due to imperfect competition - branding of bananas (US$)

Brands	Gross revenue	Monopoly surplus due to branding
Chiquita	1,108,527,907	393,890,185
Dole, Del Monte	1,401,346,353	380,435,322
Bonita, Corbana, Turbana, Consul, Fyffes	226,638,503	22,456,297
Goldfinger, Excel, Tropical Eden, Golden B	102,091,103	–
Total	2,838,603,866	796,781,804

Thus, under the assumption of optimal quantity supply most of the monopoly surplus due to branding is appropriated by the US TNCs.

Let us now examine the gross revenue and monopoly surplus due to preferential market access for bananas sold in the EU in 1998 (Table 9.4). Of the nearly $1.0 billion gross revenue generated by these banana sales, approximately $0.5 billion constitutes monopoly surplus due to preferential market access, of which the French marketing firm Pomona Group appropriated 53 per cent and the firms operating in the British market appropriated approximately 47 per cent.

Table 9.4 *Gross revenue and monopoly surplus due to Commission intervention - preferential market access of bananas (US$)*

Brands	Gross revenue	Monopoly surplus due to preferential market
Fyffes, JPs, 5 Isles	462,220,616	239,163,392
Pomona Group	507,083,745	265,653,917
Total	969,304,361	504,817,309

While it is clear that the efficiency of appropriation of monopoly surplus under preferential market access is considerably higher than that due to branding, it should be equally clear that monopoly surplus appropriation due to branding is not insignificant. Yet, while liberalization is likely to eliminate some of the monopoly surplus due to preferential market access, monopoly surplus appropriation due to imperfect competition will remain.

9.5.2 Welfare and efficiency losses under oligopolistic adjustment

The impact of trade liberalization on the prices and quantities of bananas imported by brand is shown in Table 9.5.

Table 9.5 *Quantities of bananas and prices after liberalization*

Brands	Quantity (tons)	Import price (US$/ton)	Retail price (US$/ton)
Chiquita	1,005,676	560.67	1,120.46
Dole, Del Monte	1,504,909	481.84	991.50
Bonita, Corbana, Turbana, Consul, Fyffes	267,314	389.64	804.42
Goldfinger, Excel, Tropical Eden, Golden B	138,324	341.28	724.71
Fyffes, JPs, 5 Isles	29,564	487.87	1,550.98
Pomona Group	247,769	546.95	1,573.21
Others	71,296	386.91	1,069.14

After liberalization (removal of the CET) and a 10 per cent reduction in import prices of dominant oligopolists, we see that Fyffes, JPs and 5 Isles suffer tremendous losses as approximately 90 per cent of the quantity of bananas originally supplied is re-allocated to Chiquita, Dole and Del Monte; the Pomona Group witnesses a 20 per cent decline in the quantity of bananas sold (see Table 9.5). Both these categories of firms prepare to undergo major adjustment or to exit the market altogether, depending on their sources of supply and the flexibility or willingness of these sources to undertake major adjustment.

The welfare effects of liberalization after the first period are shown in Figure 9.4.

Fig. 9.4   *Welfare effects of liberalization after the first period*

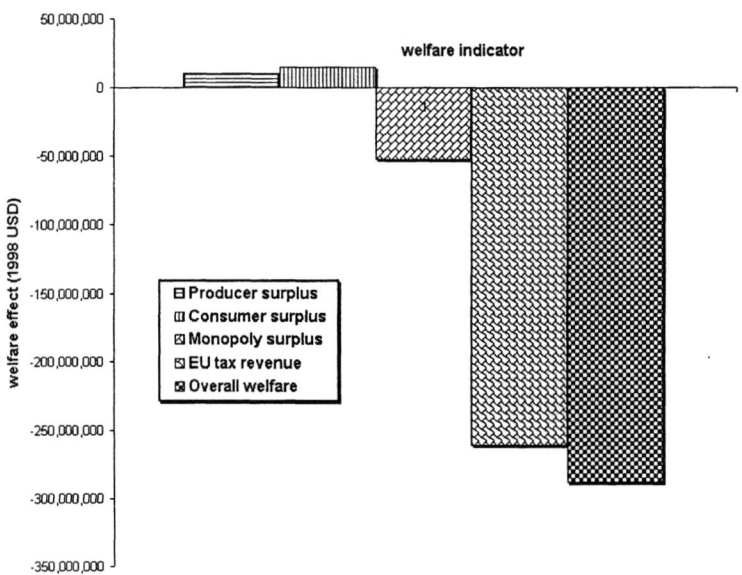

Source: Table A3.9 in Appendix 3.

The increased quantity of bananas sold in the market at lower prices after liberalization results in increased consumer surplus of $14.7 million. As for producer surplus, there are increases but only for those oligopolists who can take advantage of liberalization; thus Fyffes, JPs and 5 Isles jointly suffer producer surplus loss of $1.4 million, while fourth-class banana producers loss $0.7 million. However, in the aggregate producers gain a surplus of $9.6 million.

However, liberalization is likely to result in tremendous costs as well, notably in loss of tax revenue to the EU and the persistence of monopoly surplus due to branding. The sale of increased quantities of bananas in the EU after liberalization will result in the EU's loss of $260 million in tax revenue and consumers being deprived of $52 million in economic welfare due to monopoly surplus retained by oligopolists. Therefore, at the end of the first period, liberalization results in an overall welfare loss of $288 million. Moreover, even if the EU tax revenue is ignored (on the grounds that it should not have existed in the first place), liberalization would still result in an overall welfare loss of $52 million due to monopoly surplus appropriation under imperfect competition.

Since we do not expect there to be any significant welfare differences between the first and second periods, let us now consider the welfare effects after the third period (Figure 9.5). The only major process during the second period is adjustment, which results in the exit of Fyffes, JPs and 5 Isles from the market.[14]

Fig. 9.5   Welfare effects of liberalization after the third period

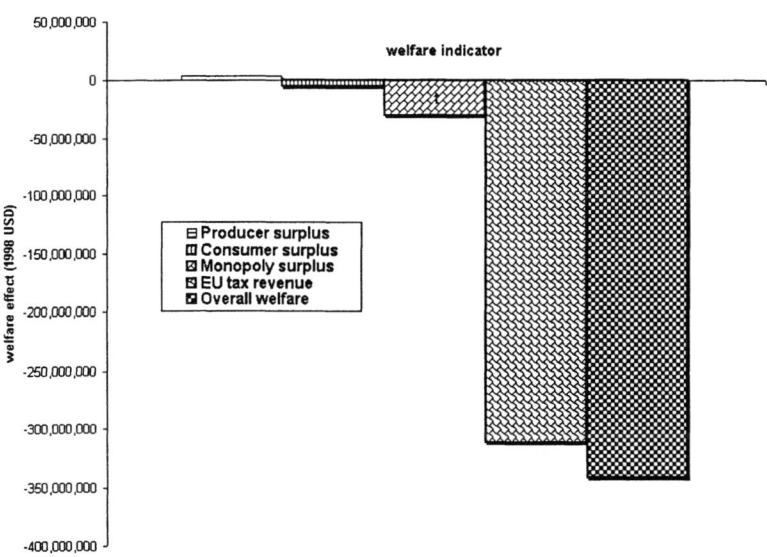

Source: Table A3.10 in Appendix 3.

In the third period, the 10 per cent increase in prices by firms results in a slight decline in the overall quantity of bananas sold in the EU, so consumers lose a surplus of $4.3 million. However, the increase in prices is sufficient to allow some firms a gain in producer surplus of $3.9 million, most of which is appropriated by Chiquita, Dole and Del Monte, although Pomona Group now becomes an important player as well.[15] Yet, any such action by firms will worsen the welfare effects for two reasons. First, the EU would forego tax revenue of $310 million. Second consumers would lose $29.6 million in surplus due to appropriation through imperfect competition by oligopolists. Therefore, at the end of the third period the EU banana market would be subjected to an overall welfare loss of $340 million.

9.5.3   Sensitivity analysis

In performing the preceding simulations we have relied on the fact that oligopolistic interdependence is important in the EU banana industry (Chapter 8), and so the strategy pursued by the industry leader will always be followed by the other oligopolists, since it also represents their dominant strategy. The question that arises, though, is what would be the outcome of the liberalization process if oligopolists pursued alternative strategies? In particular, what if prices were not returned to their pre-liberalization levels at the end of the third period but instead exceeded them? We find that liberalization results in progressive losses in consumer surplus and EU tax revenue concomitant with progressive gains in producer surplus and monopoly surplus due to branding. If oligopolists were to increase prices by 5% more than their pre-liberalization levels, consumers would lose up to $630 million in surplus, while the EU would lose approximately $226 million in tax revenue.[16]

9.6   Discussion and analysis – trade liberalization under imperfect competition

Our major objective in this study has been to determine whether or not the neo-classical framework, which assumes perfectly competitive and contestable markets, is appropriate for predicting the welfare effects of EU-wide banana trade liberalization, and what the implications might be otherwise. We have argued that the market is neither perfectly competitive nor contestable (Chapter 3) and that despite the existence of free trade in Germany and protectionism in France in the pre-SEM period, firms in the markets of both these countries exercised comparable degrees of market power (Chapter 8). Against the background of these arguments we have sought to simulate the welfare effects of trade liberalization, taking the imperfectly competitive behaviour of firms into consideration, that is, monopoly surplus appropriation due to branding and oligopolistic interdependence.

Imperfect competition through branding of bananas results in super-normal profits over and beyond what a firm is likely to enjoy in a perfectly competitive market, while the oligopolistic interdependence of firms serves to preserve their relative prices and market shares. If we assume that EU banana supply just matched demand in 1998, then although consumers were deprived of $0.5 billion in surplus due to Commission intervention, they were, nevertheless deprived of even more surplus, $0.8 billion, due to imperfect competition. Whereas liberalization automatically isolates and eliminates monopoly surplus due to Commission intervention, it cannot eliminate monopoly surplus due to imperfect competition. Super-normal profit appropriation, therefore, is systemic within the market. As long as consumers purchase bananas on the basis of a belief that one particular brand is superior to another, oligopolists will continue to entrench their market power. So, in fact, both the present system and a liberalized one will exploit the EU consumer, the only questions are to what extent, and by which agent – the Commission versus the market. Moreover, as we have shown, the liberalized system might exploit the EU consumer even more, since it will result in the disappearance of some banana brands from the market, concomitant with the appropriation of more surplus by primarily US TNC oligopolists.

What about the producers who are eliminated as a result of liberalization? We have seen that the protected EU firms are the most vulnerable to liberalization, since they obtain their bananas from the higher-cost ACP countries (Chapter 3). We have also seen that the ACP countries, particularly those from the Caribbean, presently retain the largest share of revenue (Chapter 6) and surplus (Chapter 7) along their commodity chains. In contrast, the dollar-zone banana-exporting countries have persistently retained the least. Yet, liberalization will result in the encouragement of banana export production by the latter at the expense of the former, not because it will make the latter better off, but because it will serve as a more efficient mechanism for appropriation of super-normal profits by the US TNCs that control and/or direct the commodity chains of the latter. Therefore, no matter how the game is played, liberalization is pernicious to the EU consumers, the exporting countries that are displaced, as well as those that survive, because monopoly surplus appropriation under perverse oligopoly is systemic. When the outcome of the simulations is compared with internal liberalization (implementation of the SEM) we see that liberalization leads to a game of pure conflict. Although German consumers pay considerably more for bananas than in the pre-SEM period, the trade-off is that ACP countries and EU TNCs enjoy larger monopoly profits.

9.7   Conclusions

Departing from the neo-classical assumptions of a perfectly competitive and contestable EU banana market results in rather different magnitudes and directions of the welfare effects. By treating the banana as a homogeneous commodity and assuming that all are sold in the EU market at the same price, the neo-classical methodology grossly overestimates the gains that might be realized from liberalization, while not even contemplating the existence of super-normal profits due to imperfect competition. However, once the market is conceptualized as an oligopoly in which there is strategic interdependence due to non-contestability, its imperfectly competitive nature emerges and the welfare losses due to imperfect competition can be identified. The contribution of the thesis in this chapter is that the welfare effects of liberalization were estimated by taking the strategic behaviour of TNCs into consideration, and in so doing, we have decomposed the welfare components in a more useful way. We have shown that not only are the welfare losses due to imperfect competition significant, but that they are systemic, making them impossible to eliminate, with or without liberalization.

So, to conclude, while liberalization will definitely isolate and eliminate the market inefficiencies due to Commission intervention, it cannot address the inefficiencies due to imperfect competition. As for the banana-exporting countries, liberalization is not likely to be an ally of either those displaced or those who survive; instead, it is primarily an instrument for more efficient surplus appropriation by the US TNCs and for widening revenue and surplus gaps between the banana-exporting countries and EU member-states.

Notes

[1] Despite the slew of literature on oligopoly models, the practical problem at hand requires construction of a model based on observed behaviour of agents and the dominant strategies they are likely to pursue. As Schmalensee (1988:660) put it, the "Holy Grail of research in oligopoly theory has been the ability to use observable

quantities to predict the intensity of rivalry in markets dominated by a small number of sellers".

[2] Although Farley (1964:14) has found evidence that "price stability tends to be associated with concentration of market share in one brand and more weakly with few brands available in a market.", he did not take oligopolistic interdependence into account in his study, a factor which is likely to make a difference in an oligopolistic market for a commodity like bananas, which are demand price-inelastic.

[3] This assumption derives from our empirical finding in Chapter 8, which showed that firms in both Germany and France are engaged in Cournot-Nash behaviour. Given that similar firms control the market in all EU member-states, we have extended this result to the entire EU.

[4] *Structural form of the Model*

$$Q_a = f(P_a, Q_b, Q_c, Q_d, Q_e, Z_a) \tag{9.1}$$

$$Q_b = f(P_b, Q_a, Q_c, Q_d, Q_e, Z_b) \tag{9.2}$$

$$Q_c = f(P_c, Q_a, Q_b, Q_d, Q_e, Z_c) \tag{9.3}$$

$$Q_d = f(P_d, Q_a, Q_b, Q_c, Q_e, Z_d) \tag{9.4}$$

$$Q_e = f(P_e, Q_a, Q_b, Q_c, Q_d, Z_e) \tag{9.5}$$

$$Q_{EU}^S = f(Q_a, Q_b, Q_c, Q_d, Q_e) \tag{9.6}$$

$$Q_{EU}^D = Q^* \tag{9.7}$$

$$Q_{EU}^D = Q_{EU}^S \tag{9.8}$$

where:

Q_{EU}^S = total quantity of bananas supplied to the EU;

Q_{EU}^D = total quantity of bananas demanded in the EU, Q^*;

Q_a = quantity of bananas supplied by Chiquita at price P_a;

Q_b = quantity of bananas supplied by second-category suppliers at price P_b;

Q_c = quantity of bananas supplied by third-category suppliers at price P_c;

Q_d = quantity of bananas supplied by fourth-category suppliers at price P_d ;

Q_e = quantity of bananas supplied by the fringe at price P_e ; and

Z_i = vectors of exogenous variables affecting supplies of the ith source.

Price P_a , which is exogenous, is set by Chiquita, while the remaining prices are set as follows:

$$P_b = f(P_a, Q_b, Z_b)$$ (9.9)

$$P_c = f(P_a, Q_c, Z_c)$$ (9.10)

$$P_d = f(P_a, Q_d, Z_d)$$ (9.11)

$$P_e = f(Q_e, Z_e)$$ (9.12)

Nested within the $Z_i s$ are all exogenous factors that affect the quantity of bananas supplied to the EU by the ith source. The fact that this system of equations is identified follows from Bresnahan (1982:92)'s theoretical finding, that is, the need for functional forms to be chosen that capture both shifts in, and rotations of, the respective demand and supply schedules. Essentially, it also means deriving the necessary rank and order conditions for identification, following the methodology suggested by Mukherjee et al. (1998:428-34).

[5] In this regard, the reader is referred to the Securities and Exchange Commission (www.sec.gov) where detailed information of this type is available concerning all the major banana TNCs.

[6] The reader is cautioned that we are not purporting to demonstrate any notion of equilibrium in the figure. Demand schedules for various brands have been drawn on the same axes for conservation of space only.

[7] See Table A3.4 in the Appendix 3.

[8] See Table A3.5 in the Appendix 3.

[9] Similarly, regarding equation 9.18, although there was a statistically significant slope coefficient from regressing $\Delta(L\_Tropical\_Eden)$ against $\Delta(L\_Bonita)$ the DW statistic of the regression was 2.88 and the ADF statistic of the residuals was not statistically significant at the 5% level. Therefore, the original models have been retained as superior explanations of price-setting behaviour.

[10] This is clearly a restrictive, but nevertheless useful assumption for performing the simulations. In fact, fourth-class bananas are expected to be sold in the market at a normal economic profit, albeit at a considerably lower level than superior banana brands. The implications, therefore, are that there is likely to be a downward bias in the extent of monopoly surplus due to branding, that is, the estimate of the monopoly surplus is likely to be somewhat lower than it actually ought to be.

[11] It follows from the proposition that oligopolists have been repeatedly playing a *tit-for-tat* game for several decades, a proposition which has been supported by the econometric results in section 9.3. So any reduction in the price of the dominant firm would be seen as a signal for others.

[12] Sunk costs are of particular importance in the banana business, where the specificity of capital is high. Investment by a firm in the cultivation of banana plantations, or the procurement of a reefer fleet, cannot be readily converted for alternative use (see Chapter 3).

[13] One possible strategy for achieving this is for firms to invest in advertising, geared towards convincing consumers that, notwithstanding the disappearance of some brands from the market, they can now enjoy higher quality bananas at lower prices.

[14] We assume that oligopolists increase their import prices by 10 per cent, effectively returning them to their levels before liberalization but without the tariff of 20 per cent.

[15] Pomona Group fails to exit the market largely because its sources of supply, Cameroon and the Ivory Coast, already produce bananas at prices that are comparable to those of the dollar-zone. The increased productivity and competitiveness in these countries stems from increased investment in their plantations by US transnationals, notably Dole.

[16] Of course, oligopolists are not likely to voluntarily undertake further reductions in price (unless adverse market conditions so dictate) since such action would simply lead to losses in profits.

10 Conclusions and Policy Recommendations, Implications for Theory and the Way Forward

10.1   Conclusions and policy recommendations

When the author embarked upon this study, he hoped to address two major questions: (i) whether or not the EU banana market structure and the nature of trade in the banana commodity are significant factors to be taken into consideration when thinking about the welfare effects of liberalized trade, and (ii) how liberalization of the EU banana trade is likely to impact upon the division and distribution of revenue and surplus between EU member-states and their trading partners that survive. In posing these questions, he sought to test the neo-classical doctrine that the EU banana market is perfectly competitive and contestable, and therefore liberalization of trade in the commodity would result in increased efficiency and economic welfare. In order to systematically investigate these questions, he advanced two hypothetical propositions. First, the EU banana market is typified by a transnational oligopolistic structure in which individual TNCs can exercise some degree of monopoly power, through which they appropriate super-normal profits. Second, a combination of the persistence of oligopoly and the nature of trade in the commodity is likely to result in widening of the wealth gap between the producers who survive and individual EU member-states.

From the outset there were methodological challenges, since the prevailing contemporary approaches to conceptualizing international trade in general (Krugman, 1994; Helpman and Krugman 1989; Bhagwati, 1988; Helpman, 1984; Vernon, 1966; Samuelson, 1948) and more specifically the EU banana trade (Borrell and Yang, 1992, 1990; Borrell and Cuthbertson, 1991; Kersten, 1995) hardly capture the complexities of the processes involved. The search for a more representative approach resulted in the espousal of the commodity chain concept (Gereffi, 1999; Dicken, 1998; Mittelman, 1996) as the central unit of analysis. Yet, taken on its own the commodity chain concept was inadequate for the exploration of the hypotheses, since its tools tend to be too descriptive for the tasks that the author sought to accomplish. Therefore, he introduced theories of industrial organization (Bresnahan, 1982; Bresnahan and Schmalensee, 1987; Shapiro,

1989; Schmalensee and Willig, 1989), TNCs (Hymer, 1970, 1976; Teece, 1982, 1993; Casson, 1987; Dunning, 1996, 1993; Pitelis and Sugden, 2000) along with exploratory data analysis and regression analysis for augmentation of the methodology. These tools greatly enhanced the author's ability to analyse the EU banana trade and to articulate fresh perspectives on the questions that were posed.

Since the empirical evidence has been supportive of the hypotheses they have all been retained. Therefore, the present task is to recapitulate the major arguments of this work, interpret the findings in the context of existing knowledge, suggest some policy recommendations and indicate what further research might usefully follow from this work.

10.1.1 Perfect competition and/or contestability versus oligopoly

On the question of perfect competition and/or contestability versus oligopoly, we have argued that the EU banana market is neither perfectly competitive, nor contestable and that the oligopolists who dominate the market continue to exercise statistically significant degrees of market power. This argument is diametrically opposed to the mainstream view that has been popularized by Borrell and Yang (1990, 1992) and others.

We began to develop this argument in Chapter 2, which reviewed the neo-classical approach to estimating the efficiency and welfare effects of trade liberalization. In assuming perfect competition and/or contestability, these works assume that a single retail price was likely to exist throughout the EU if the banana trade was fully liberalized. However, Chapter 2 argued that not only was the latter assumption not likely to be correct, but in addition that it did not capture an important aspect of the nature of trade in bananas. Krugman (1994), Helpman and Krugman (1989), and Dixit and Norman (1980), among others, have emphasized the importance of scale economies in explaining trade. Therefore, the chapter introduced banana c.i.f. prices in EU member-states as a superior choice over f.o.b., since nested within c.i.f. prices are the scale economies in ocean transportation, which are important for explaining trade in bananas. It argued that while it is *theoretically possible* to achieve an overall increase in global efficiency and welfare under liberalization, in practice this *is not* likely to happen since banana retail prices would need to fall to levels below which firms in the market would simply lose money.

The argument was further developed in Chapter 3, which analysed the empirical evidence of the world trade in bananas with particular attention to the structure of the market and the conduct of firms. The analysis demonstrated that world banana trade has been characterized by oligopoly since its inception in the late 1800s and that this form of organization of production and trade has persisted ever since. The argument in the chapter is consistent with the seminal work of Litvak and Maule (1977) regarding the behaviour of US banana TNCs in the US. Moreover, we argued that not only do oligopolists possess market power (Chapter 8) but that they have repeatedly exercised such power in restricting supply, price discrimination, and other forms of anti-competitive conduct (Chapter 3).

Finally, we argued that while one effect of the SEM appears to have been a reduction in the degree of market power actually exercised in EU member-states, oligopolistic interdependence nevertheless remains highly statistically significant (Chapter 8). This suggests that the probability of new firms entering the banana industry is rather small and possibly statistically insignificant. Baumol (1982) and Baumol et al. (1982) have suggested the conditions under which markets are contestable. The EU banana market fails that contestability test. Although the SEM appears to have adversely affected the profitability of Chiquita in the EU banana business since it came into effect, Chiquita nevertheless remains the dominant player and commands significantly larger margins for its bananas than the competition (Chapter 9). Moreover, there is evidence that the present turmoil of Chiquita cannot be explained merely by reduced profitability in the EU, but largely by a series of bad management and conduct decisions undertaken by the firm even before the SEM came into effect (Chapters 3 and 5).

10.1.2   Widening revenue and surplus gaps and EU foreign policy

A major concern of this study has been the question of whether or not the gaps between the shares of revenue and surplus retained by actors in EU member-states and the exporting countries that survive would widen, as a consequence of trade liberalization. Emmerij (2001) has recently presented compelling evidence of how the global gaps have widened between the rich and poor countries of the world since the Second World War.[1] He isolates international trade as one of the instruments through which the gap between the rich and poor countries continues to widen, drawing upon Prebisch (1968)'s original terms of trade argument. The results of our empirical analysis suggest that these gaps are likely to widen if liberalization is fully implemented.

Chapter 6 demonstrated how revenue is divided and distributed between actors in EU member-states and the exporting countries with whom they trade. Specifically, it sought to determine: (i) whether a particular mode of organization of the commodity chain results in a superior division and distribution of revenue; (ii) what impact if any the SEM has had on the division and distribution of revenue; and (iii) whether or not liberalization would affect all commodity chains in a similar manner. Three commodity chains were used for this analysis: German, French and British.

Revenue was most progressively divided and distributed along the French commodity chain and was least so along the German commodity chain, with the division and distribution of revenue along the British commodity chain being between these extremes. Again, this contradicts the mainstream view articulated by Borrell and Yang (1990, 1992), and others. In the pre-SEM period, the median share of revenue retained by actors in Germany was 81.6 per cent and this figure increased to 86.5 per cent in the post-SEM period; for France the corresponding figures were 81.1 per cent and 83.7 per cent, respectively; and for the UK the corresponding figures were 81.4 per cent and 82.9 per cent, respectively.

Therefore, the benefits of free trade in Germany during the pre-SEM period were appropriated by firms operating along that commodity chain and not by the exporting countries. Moreover, since the SEM came into effect firms operating in the German market have increased their share of revenue at the expense of the exporting countries. In contrast, there were only moderate increases in the shares of revenue retained in France and Britain, respectively.

The division and distribution of the surplus (see Chapter 7) reflected a similar pattern to that of revenue. Importers, wholesalers and retailers in Germany appropriated the largest median share of the surplus (54 per cent), while those in the UK appropriated the least (51 per cent); those in France appropriated 53 per cent. Exporting countries along the British commodity chain retained the largest median share (25 per cent) with the least variability, while those along the German commodity chain retained the least (22 per cent); those along the French commodity chain retained 23.5 per cent. The explanation for more efficient revenue and surplus appropriation along the German commodity chain derives from a combination of *control* of all of its stages in the manner suggested by Hymer (1970, 1976) and economies of common governance in the manner suggested by Gereffi (1999).

We have argued that liberalization of the EU banana trade would most likely displace the commodity chains of the least efficient exporting countries, while lending support to the most efficient ones. Yet, the least efficient exporting countries presently retain the largest share of both revenue and surplus along their commodity chains. Therefore, in the absence of any interventions in the EU banana market, liberalization *will* result in the widening of revenue and surplus gaps between EU member-states and the exporting countries that survive. But in its own development policy agenda, the EU has always given primacy to a more progressive division and distribution of global wealth between the rich and poor nations. Certainly, such an outcome from liberalization would be at cross-purposes with the EU's very own policy on development.

10.1.3   Lobbying power and world trade policy

In view of the power of various lobbies, world trade policy might not necessarily be the outcome of diverse interests of *individual nations*, but instead, it might reflect the interests and authority of the most powerful nations, whose interests in turn reflect the strength of their TNCs. Hymer (1970) postulated, based on his seminal work on TNCs, that the coming age of TNCs would present grave social and political problems. He suggested that such problems would arise given the uneven nature of distribution of the benefits of research and the power of TNCs relative to home and host country governments. The EU banana dispute is a concrete example confirming Hymer's postulation. This thesis argued that in the EU banana dispute the US went to great lengths to justify its participation in a WTO Panel and that its involvement was directly related to the vigorous lobbying action of one of its TNCs, Chiquita (Chapter 5).

Prior to the onslaught of Chiquita's vigorous lobbying campaign of both the Democratic and Republican parties, the US government had little interest in EU banana policy. In fact, recognizing the complexity of the EU banana trade and the vulnerability of Caribbean countries, the US government had openly supported preferential access for the Caribbean countries to the EU banana market. The US position began to change in late 1994 after Chiquita made political contributions worth several hundred thousands of dollars, to both the Republican and Democratic parties. Although it was not possible to attach any measure of statistical significance to this, we have shown that some correlation exists between the political contributions made by Chiquita and the severity of action taken by the US government in the WTO against the EU banana import policy (Chapter 5). Interestingly, the finding in that regard confirms Helleiner (1977)'s observation in his discussion of US TNCs and US trade policy: that orthodox theory of international trade fails to address the question of *political sources* of trade policies.

The fact that the actions of individual firms could result in changes in world trade policy makes the multilateral dispute settlement mechanism vulnerable to pernicious manipulation. Therefore, some sort of anti-trust mechanism needs to be introduced into the WTO whereby the claims that are presented before it in dispute settlement could be verified as being legitimate and representative of a particular *country* and not a TNC *per se*. In particular, the nature of involvement of the country presenting the claim in the commodity chain in question needs to be clear. Several WTO panels appear to have been created through lobbying by TNCs, however more research needs to be done to confirm the nature of each individual case.

10.1.4   Liberalization, efficiency and welfare under perverse oligopoly

As far as neo-classical economists are concerned, liberalization – the elimination of government-induced imperfections from a market – automatically improves global efficiency and welfare. So, not surprisingly, in the case of the EU banana market the neo-classical view of the problem has been to simply eliminate the tariff-quota (Chapter 2), which, under perfect competition, results in a single reduced retail price, an increased quantity of bananas consumed, and thus an increase in efficiency and welfare. Despite the important contribution of the NTTs, that scale economies, which lead to imperfectly competitive markets, are a cause of trade, one of the very architects of the NTTs, Paul Krugman, appears to have gone to great lengths to defend unconditional *laissez-faire* (Krugman,1992).

However, a closer examination of the problem reveals that far from being competitive, the EU banana market is oligopolistic and the nature of conduct of oligopolists is such that welfare and efficiency could actually decrease under liberalization.

Oligopolists in the EU banana market face different demand curves with different gradients, which have arisen from their branding of bananas and extensive advertising since the 1960s. Consequently, bananas sold in the EU fall into a particular price class depending on the strength of their brand names. "Chiquita" branded bananas command the highest price class, while brands like "Tropical Eden", "Golden B" and "Goldfinger" command the lowest price class. Moreover, the differences in price classes are stable and statistically significant. "Chiquita" commands a price which, on average, is 39 per cent higher than fourth-class bananas, 31 per cent higher than third-class bananas and 14 per cent higher than second-class bananas (Chapter 9).

Therefore, while EU consumers lose some welfare due to Commission intervention in the market, it is by no means the only sink for welfare loss. In fact, consumers also lose considerably more welfare due to monopoly surplus appropriation by oligopolists, who charge a price based on their degree of market power. The author estimates that whereas EU consumers lose approximately $0.5 billion due to Commission intervention, they lose nearly $0.8 billion due to imperfect competition between oligopolists.

Whereas liberalization will surely result in the elimination of the Commission-induced inefficiencies, those that are induced by failure of the market are systemic, and therefore would persist with or without liberalization. Yet, liberalization would eliminate the high-cost producers, particularly those from the Caribbean, who presently retain the largest shares of revenue and surplus from the commodity chain, while encouraging the low-cost dollar-zone producers who presently retain the least shares of both revenue and surplus. Therefore, it seems that in the presence of perverse oligopoly, liberalization of the EU banana trade is likely to result in widening revenue and surplus gaps between the rich EU member-states and the poorest of the banana exporting countries. Liberalization, then, would promote a more regressive division of wealth among the respective trading nations.

10.1.5   WTO banana precedent: what does it mean for world trade policy?

The WTO banana precedent has effectively broadened the meaning of international trade to include all processes that a physical commodity might be subjected to, even after it has entered a foreign country. This broadening of the meaning of international trade has arisen from the overlapping scopes of applicability of violations under the GATT and the GATS, as interpreted by the Panel in the EU banana dispute (see Chapter 5).

Therefore, world trade policy should now be viewed as being beyond the conventional question of the existence of tariffs and quotas, which restrict or limit the access of physical commodities to a country. Bhagwati (1988), for instance, has placed far too much emphasis on tariffs and quotas as trade-distorting measures without giving due attention to the non-tariff barriers like the expensive 'advance monitoring systems' that Raynolds (1994) has identified, in the case of trade between the US and the Dominican Republic (see Chapter 4). World trade policy needs to address all forms of restrictions, direct or indirect, that in some way might affect access to a physical good by a consumer in the destination market. In the case of bananas, these restrictions include access to transportation, ripening facilities and the conduct of rival firms in destination markets.

Yet, a world trade policy that pays disproportionate attention to the demand side of a commodity chain while espousing indifference to the supply side, is not only pernicious and asymmetric, but is also likely to promote widening of wealth gaps between the producing and consuming countries. We have argued that although consumers in Germany enjoyed the lowest retail price for bananas in the pre-SEM period, this was at the expense of producers along that commodity chain retaining the least revenue and surplus (Chapters 6 and 7). In fact, the extremely low cost of bananas from Latin America is not representative of comparative advantage as such, but instead the unjust exploitation of labour by TNCs. Frank (2002), Campaign for Labor Rights (1998) and Mangold et al. (1996), among others, have all drawn attention to these illicit practices of US TNCs in Latin America and called for improved labour standards.

Therefore, world trade policy, of necessity, *must* address *production conditions* and ensure that illicit practices of TNCs, which constitute their comparative advantage, are treated as anti-competitive, trade-distorting measures, no different from tariffs or quotas.

10.1.6   New meaning to the concept of a commodity

When economists talk about a commodity in international trade, what is it they are really addressing? Clearly, the concept of a commodity, as popularized by Adam Smith and subsequently adopted in the works of David Ricardo and other classical economists, is a far cry from the creature that the WTO seems to have created, based on its ruling in the case of the EU's NBR. Even the neo-classical economists (Heckscher, 1919; Ohlin, 1933; and Samuelson, 1948) seem to have ignored the question of the concept of a commodity that dominated the comparative advantage doctrine and have applied it in developing the concepts of factor endowments, factor abundance and factor intensities. In all of these cases the concept of a commodity is that of a physical good, which is created in its entirety and ready for consumption from its country of production.

While the new trade theorists (Krugman, 1994; Ethier, 1982; Dixit and Norman, 1980) clearly recognized the shortcomings of the assumptions of perfect competition and perfectly competitive markets as the basis for explanation of trade, the models they have proposed nevertheless espouse similar assumptions about the concept of a commodity as did their predecessors. In some ways the literature on intra-industry trade (Grubel and Lloyd, 1975) attempts to address this problem by treating the final commodity as the sum of its individual components from the various locations where they are produced. However, even then components are treated as autonomous commodities to the extent that provisions are continuously being made for their classification and identification in tariffs. But the WTO ruling in the case of the EU banana regime implies re-thinking what economists mean by a commodity in international trade; we need to go beyond the concept that has assumed prominence in the literature so far.

A commodity in international trade needs to be thought of as a physical good embodied within a 'vector' of services, the importance of which changes over space and time. This 'vector' of services might cause a *transformation* of the physical commodity as it moves along its chain or might simply *facilitate* its movement from one location to another. In the case of the EU banana trade, the services 'vector' features prominently at all stages of the commodity chain. During ocean transportation bananas are subjected to two types of services: (i) their physical relocation, and (ii) a controlled cooling process which dictates both their final quality and shelf life after they arrive at the port of destination. Similarly, after their importation into the EU they are again subjected to two types of services: (i) rapid physical relocation to ripening facilities, and (ii) a temperature-controlled ripening process over a period of one week, before being rapidly relocated to retailers. In the WTO Panel's interpretation of the scope of applicability of the GATT and the GATS, any policy that interferes in any way with either the physical movement or value-adding services to the banana constitutes a violation of world trade rules (Chapter 5). Therefore, the services 'vector' becomes a central concept of interest in the explanation of trade in bananas and other similar commodities.

10.1.7   Reflections: why do we need to think differently about trade?

We shall never know with any degree of certainty what inspired the WTO Panel in the EU banana case to adopt such a broad interpretation of the scope of applicability of the GATT and the GATS, to the extent that there is an almost total overlap in the substantive articles (Chapter 5). Perhaps their action was motivated simply by pursuing the path of least resistance to bring about a swift end to a protracted process that had already strained trade relations between the US and the EU. Then again, perhaps they were simply interpreting international trade law in a manner that resulted in consistency of meaning of the relevant articles of the GATT and the GATS. Regardless of what their motive was, the Panel's decision in the EU banana case at the very least calls for some reflections on what economists mean by international trade.

International trade has conventionally meant the exchange of physical commodities between countries; each country specializes in the production of the commodity in which it has a comparative advantage, relative to its trading partner. Both countries are assumed to be made better off by exchanging some of the surplus production. Individual firms cannot affect the process, since their outputs are insignificant relative to that produced nationally, and trade has therefore conventionally meant the exchange of physical goods between countries for mutual gain (Chapter 4).

However, this thesis developed and advanced arguments that demonstrate the need for deeper reflection on what economists mean by trade. We have argued that the dominant players in the EU banana trade are TNCs, which control or govern individual stages and/or the interconnections of the commodity chain (Chapter 3). The value-adding processes to which bananas are subjected along their commodity chains are partly physical and partly intangible, and in many ways, the *intangible* services are more important than the physical ones. Ultimately, the division and distribution of rewards along the commodity chain depends on the extent of involvement of actors at the various stages and between interconnections. Combined with the concept of a commodity that was developed earlier, we advance the hypothesis that international trade is actually the exchange of a physical good and a 'vector' of services from a country where the physical good is initially produced to one where it is finally consumed.

Whether or not, and the extent to which, countries at either end of the commodity chain gain depends on the nature and extent of participation of actors from each country in the commodity chain. In fact, the term 'international' in this instance is misleading and is better substituted with the term 'global', because it is the actors in the global economy who are involved in trade and not nation states *per se*. As for the banana-exporting countries, their option for retaining a larger share of the commodity chain is to integrate forwards along it. Not only would forward integration enable greater control of the commodity chain by the exporting countries, but it would also improve its governance, and hence returns. Ecuador's major TNC, NOBOA, appears to be fully aware of that. For a host of reasons identified in this thesis, TNCs will continue to dominate the transnational banana trade and are likely to acquire complete control if trade is liberalized.

10.1.8   Free trade or protectionism: is that the question?

A distinctive feature of economics as a discipline is that it is a contestation of ideas as advanced by various schools, and the subject of international trade policy has been at the centre of this contest from the very beginning. For the classical and neoclassical economists, free trade is seen as the optimal policy, while the structuralists and neostructuralists have argued that some protectionism is desirable under certain conditions for economic growth and development to take place.[2]

If we think of the industrial revolution as the defining moment in the creation of modern society, then the global economy has been exposed to both free trade and protectionism for over 200 years and there are some lessons which it should have learned. A classical example of the differences between official trade policy of a country and what that country actually practices is found in the US' recent decision to unilaterally impose tariffs on steel imports.[3] Therefore, to paraphrase what one of the author's compatriots has said with regard to economic progress (Lewis, 1955) in the present context, sensible people should not advocate either free trade or protectionism as *the correct* commercial policy, since by now they should have realized that elements of both are desirable at particular stages in the development of nations.

We have argued that although a free market existed in Germany in the pre-SEM period, while the market in France was protected, firms in both countries nevertheless exercised comparable degrees of market power (Chapter 8). Yet, the countries that produced bananas for sale in France retained a disproportionately larger share of both revenue and surplus than those that produced bananas for sale in the German market (Chapters 6 and 7). Similarly, the countries that produced bananas for sale in the protected British market retained a disproportionately larger share of revenue and surplus, relative to those that produced bananas for sale in the German market.

Therefore, if we think of the entire commodity chain of bananas as the entity being traded, then the free market in Germany was pernicious for producer countries along its chain, while the protected markets of France and Britain were beneficial for the producer countries along their chains; however, German consumers appear to have enjoyed the highest welfare.

In a somewhat curious manner, the implementation of the SEM resulted in a reduction in the degree of market power actually exercised in both Germany and France. Germany continues to retain a disproportionately larger share of revenue and surplus than France and Britain. The importance of oligopolistic interdependence in Germany is borne out by the latter observation.

So, to conclude, the question is not whether free trade or protectionism is a superior policy, but instead, it should be: given a particular *commodity chain* and a *development objective*, which of these instruments would be more desirable? If the commodity chain is highly vertically integrated, in which case it is controlled exclusively by TNCs, then a free trade policy in the EU might be good for its citizens but pernicious for the producer countries. If, instead, the commodity chain is loosely vertically integrated, in which case it is only partially controlled by TNCs and the producer countries, then protectionism might benefit the producer countries, but possibly at the expense of reduced welfare for the EU's citizens.

10.2   Implications for theory

The findings in this work present some implications for theory in the following areas: (i) the welfare effects of trade liberalization under perfect versus imperfect competition, (ii) how trade liberalization can affect the division of wealth among nations and (iii) the importance of TNCs and commodity chains in developing a newer theory of trade.

10.2.1   Trade liberalization under perfect versus imperfect competition

What distinguishes this work from existing studies in the subject area is essentially a question of methodology. The mainstream approach to trade liberalization embraces the assumptions of perfect competition and/or contestability of markets, whereas this study has attempted to analyse trade liberalization by taking the imperfectly competitive nature of a market into account. Therefore, not surprisingly, the likely welfare effects have been found to be significantly smaller than existing works have suggested. This finding is not surprising because it is generally accepted in the literature that the consequence of monopoly pricing power in a market is to cause the gradient of the demand function for the commodity to increase (Bresnahan, 1982; Shapiro, 1989; Schmalensee and Willig, 1989).

However, what has been less clear, or has not been explicitly identified in earlier works which recognized the importance of monopoly pricing power (Guyomard et al., 1999; Read, 1994) are the welfare losses due to market-induced distortions, that is, monopoly surplus due to branding.

Unlike welfare losses, which arise in markets due to state intervention and which are readily eliminated through liberalization, those due to branding are systemic and can only be eliminated if the commodity is homogeneous. Future conceptualization of the trade liberalization process, therefore, needs to take the preceding into account.

10.2.2 Trade liberalization and the division of wealth among nations

Conventional trade theory predicts that liberalization will improve the division of wealth among nations. The analysis in this thesis does not support such a theory. In fact, prior to the implementation of the SEM in the EU, the division of the total wealth generated by the banana trade was most progressive between the exporting countries and the EU member-states with protected markets, and least progressive between the exporting countries and Germany, which had a free market at that time. Additionally, while the SEM has improved the division of wealth among trading nations on the whole, the pattern has remained largely unchanged. Therefore, although the type of trade policy might matter for the generation of wealth, other factors need to be considered in order to explain or predict its division among nations.

TNCs are no doubt the dominant players in the global banana trade, and what we have found in this study is that the greater the degree of vertical integration of TNCs along a commodity chain, the least progressive is the division of wealth among the trading nations. Therefore, there is a need to incorporate the commodity chain approach (Gereffi, 1999; Dicken, 1998) and the theory of the TNC (Hymer, 1976; Casson, 1987; Dunning, 1993) into the discussion on trade liberalization and how it affects the division of wealth.

10.2.3 Trade liberalization, TNCs and the commodity chain

The EU banana trade provides a good example of the organization and operation of TNCs in a commodity chain, and the controversies surrounding it have forced us to re-think the concepts of a commodity and that of trade. This study advances the hypothesis of a commodity as a physical good embodied within a 'vector' of services, the nature and importance of which varies over space and time. Where TNCs are concerned, this 'vector' of services might constitute a significant component of the total value-added which transforms and/or modifies the commodity as it traverses its chain.

Where the commodity chain is vertically integrated, global trade itself is better conceptualized as the movement of this commodity from one country to another within an 'insulated container'. The concept of the 'insulated container' emphasizes that the value-adding processes to which the commodity is subjected are not influenced by external actors in any meaningful way, but largely by the TNC.

10.3   Trade liberalization under imperfect competition: the way forward

Departing from the assumption of perfect competition and introducing the concept of a commodity chain for analysing the EU banana trade has led us to results which are significantly different from those of earlier works. We have already discussed all of these, but those that we consider the two most important from a policy standpoint, and their implications for further research, need to be revisited once more.

First, the welfare effects of trade liberalization under imperfect competition are significantly smaller than those under perfect competition, and liberalization cannot eliminate such market-induced distortions. Second, the division of wealth between the exporting countries and EU member-states was most progressive in the protected market and least progressive in the liberalized one, in the pre-SEM period. Yet, even as countries contemplate another round of multilateral trade negotiations their potential gains remain unclear. Upon reflection, the numerous attacks on the WTO since the Seattle Ministerial Conference by activists from both developed and developing countries would suggest at the very least that the experiences of countries with trade liberalization are not in accord with the expectations predicted by conventional theory. Additionally, Maizels (1992:165) has shown that the majority of primary commodities are globally traded in oligopolistic markets (which are dominated by TNCs) and characterized by firm behaviour similar to that which has been identified in the case of bananas.

Therefore, there is a need for further research into trade liberalization in other commodities in a manner that takes the structural characteristics of markets and transnational production systems into account. The elements of such a method have been suggested and applied in this study.

Notes

[1] Emmerij (2001) examined the evolution of gross world product, the average annual rate of growth of GDP and the terms of trade, among others. He showed that the tendency was for agglomeration of global wealth in a select few developed countries and regions.

[2] A recent, fairly comprehensive discussion of elements of the post-Keynesian tradition is found in Deprez and Harvey (1999).

[3] See, for instance, "Trade War Looms over Steel Dispute", *News.bbc.co.uk* (6 March 2002).

Appendix 1

Identification of the supply, demand and retail price system

In order to derive the rank and order conditions for identification of the system of equations 2.1 to 2.4, the author first constructed the coefficient matrix for the system of equations. Then the author constructed $3*3$ matrices with non-zero determinants, from the coefficients of those variables excluded from the equation in question, but included in other equations in the model.

Table A1.1   Coefficient matrix for supply and demand model

Equation	Constant	X	P_1	M	P_2	Q
Supply	ω_0	-1	ω_1	0	0	0
Demand	λ_0	0	0	-1	λ_1	0
Retail price	β_0	0	β_1	0	-1	0
Equilibrium 1	0	-1	0	1	0	0
Equilibrium 2	0	0	0	-1	0	1

Let Z denote the number of *endogenous* variables, and K the number of *exogenous* variables, in the system, respectively. Then, for the system as a whole the number of endogenous and exogenous variables are shown in Table A1.2.

Table A1.2   Endogenous and exogenous variables in the model

Z	K
X, M, P_2, Q	P_1, constant

Derivation of the rank condition for the supply equation

Matrix for which the supply entries have been crossed out as well as all the columns for which there is not a zero coefficient in the supply equation.

$$\begin{pmatrix} -1 & \lambda_1 & 0 \\ 0 & -1 & 0 \\ 1 & 0 & 0 \\ -1 & 0 & 1 \end{pmatrix}$$

Non-zero determinant of reduced $3*3$ matrix.

$$\det \begin{pmatrix} 0 & -1 & 0 \\ 1 & 0 & 0 \\ -1 & 0 & 1 \end{pmatrix}$$

$$= -1 * \begin{vmatrix} 1 & 0 \\ -1 & 1 \end{vmatrix}$$

$$= -1.$$

Derivation of the rank condition for the demand equation

Matrix for which the demand entries have been crossed out as well as all the columns for which there is not a zero coefficient in the demand equation.

$$\begin{pmatrix} -1 & \omega_1 & 0 \\ 0 & \beta_1 & 0 \\ -1 & 0 & 0 \\ 0 & 0 & 1 \end{pmatrix}$$

Non-zero determinant of reduced $3*3$ matrix.

$$\det \begin{pmatrix} 0 & \beta_1 & 0 \\ -1 & 0 & 0 \\ 0 & 0 & 1 \end{pmatrix}$$

$$= \beta_1 * \begin{vmatrix} -1 & 0 \\ 0 & 1 \end{vmatrix}$$

$$= -\beta_1.$$

Derivation of the rank condition for the retail price equation

Matrix for which the retail price entries have been crossed out as well as all the columns for which there is not a zero coefficient in the retail price equation.

$$\begin{pmatrix} -1 & 0 & 0 \\ 0 & -1 & 0 \\ -1 & 1 & 0 \\ 0 & -1 & 1 \end{pmatrix}$$

Non-zero determinant of reduced $3*3$ matrix.

$$\det \begin{pmatrix} 0 & -1 & 0 \\ -1 & 1 & 0 \\ 0 & -1 & 1 \end{pmatrix}$$

$$= 1 * \begin{vmatrix} -1 & 0 \\ 0 & 1 \end{vmatrix}$$

$$= 1.$$

Derivation of the order condition for the demand, supply and retail price system

Let z be the number of *endogenous* variables in each individual equation and k the number of *exogenous* variables in each equation. Then the individual equations are identified if $K - k \geq z - 1$. The values for $K - k$ and $z - 1$ are reported in Table A1.3.

Table A1.3   Order condition for demand, supply and retail price

Equation	K-k	z-1	Result
Demand	1	1	identified
Supply	0	0	identified
Retail price	0	0	identified

Table A1.4   Elasticities of demand and supply

Demand		Supply	
Country	Elasticity	Country	Elasticity
France	-0.4	EU producer territories	1.0
United Kingdom	-0.5	ACP producer countries	1.0
Italy	-1.0	Dollar zone producer countries	3.0
Spain & Portugal	-1.0		
Germany	-0.4		
Other EU Member States	-0.4		
Rest of the World	-1.0		

Source: Borrell and Yang (1990).

Table A1.5a   Prices

Country	Prices ($ per Ton)
US Retail	1060.0
Germany Retail	1550.0
UK Retail	2100.0
France Retail	2200.0
Italy Retail	2640.0
Spain & Portugal Retail	1980.0
Other EU Retail	1705.0
US Import Price	572.0
EU Import Price -dollar zone	668.0
EU Import Price-Jamaica & Windward Isles	712.9
EU Import Price -Guadeloupe & Martinique	992.0
EU Import Price-Cameroon & Cote d'Ivoire	678.6
EU Import Price-Somalia	529.9
EU Import Price -Canary and Madeira	835.8
EU Import Price -Other ACP	663.9

Table A1.5b   Prices

Country	Quantity ('000s metric ton)
France	501.4
UK	393.2
Italy	321.9
Spain & Portugal	431.7
Germany	1051.1
Other EU	334.2
Rest of World	5697.5

Table A1.5c   Exports

Country	Quantity ('000s metric ton)
Guadeloupe and Martinique	298
Jamaica & Eastern Caribbean	300
Cameroon & Cote d'Ivoire	228
Somalia	14
Canary and Madeira	340
Other ACP	53
Rest of World	8314

Table A1.6a   Prices

Country	Prices ($ per metric ton)
US Retail	1080.0
Germany Retail	2270.0
UK Retail	1440.0
France Retail	2150.0
Italy Retail	2070.0
Spain & Portugal Retail	1935.0
Other EU Retail	2474.3
US Import Price	449.0
EU Import Price-dollar zone	1053.0
EU Import Price-Jamaica &Windward Isles	796.5
EU Import Price-Guadeloupe & Martinique	765.0
EU Import Price-Cameroon & Cote d'Ivoire	714.1
EU Import Price-Somalia	604.4
EU Import Price-Canary and Madeira	869.2
EU Import Price-Other ACP	739.6

Table A1.6b   Prices

Country	Quantity ('000s metric ton)
France	484.7
UK	453.4
Italy	223.8
Spain & Portugal	288.4
Germany	900.4
Other EU	735.3
Rest of World	7528

Table A1.6c   Exports

Country	Quantity ('000s metric ton)
Guadeloupe and Martinique	245
Jamaica & Eastern Caribbean	284
Cameroon & Cote d'Ivoire	348
Somalia	22
Canary and Madeira	577
Other ACP	86
Rest of World	9756

Table A1.7   Pre-SEM simulation results

Panel 1 - Impact on importing countries

Quantity ('000s metric ton)

Country	Base Imports	New imports	Change in consumer surplus($)	Change in EU tax ($)
France	501.4	542.0	232,596,020	-1,449,400
UK	393.2	425.6	141,580,739	-9,064,777
Italy	321.9	281.8	-99,184,424	-33,461,316
Spain & Portugal	431.7	447.9	32,558,024	-11,971,447
Germany	1,051.1	1,014.0	-141,153,336	0
Other EU	334.2	323.7	-43,915,829	-41,937,538
Rest of World	5,697.5	5,640.5	-301,967	0

Panel 2 - Impact on exporting countries

Quantity ('000s metric ton)

Country	Base Exports	New Exports	Change in producer surplus ($)	Loss in revenue from exports ($)
Guadeloupe and Martinique	298	203	-79,437,262	-94,561,360
Jamaica & Eastern Caribbean	300	284	-11,159,123	-11,466,507
Cameroon & Cote d'Ivoire	228	227	-899,810	-
Somalia	14	17	2,244,213	-
Canary and Maderia	340	274	-49,496,352	-54,775,583
Other ACP	53	54	575,308	-
Rest of World	8,314	8,563	48,269,421	-

Figure A1.1   Pre-SEM sensitivity of welfare effects to prices

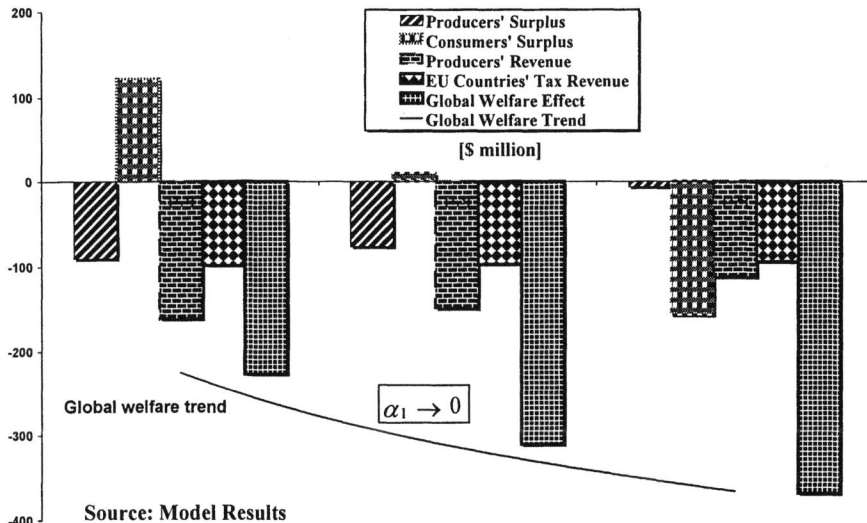

Source: Model Results

Table A1.8   Post-SEM simulation results

Panel 1 - Impact on importing countries

Quantity ('000s metric ton)

Country	Base Imports	New Imports	Change in consumer surplus ($)	Change in EU tax ($)
France	484.7	457.8	-140,535,812	-1,956,549
UK	453.4	431.4	-61,713,125	-10,312,778
Italy	223.8	165.8	-104,442,115	-33,794,470
Spain & Portugal	288.4	217.7	-120,072,677	-2,462,653
Germany	900.4	922.3	125,469,993	-191,149,428
Other EU	735.3	753.2	111,688,945	-152,951,365
Rest of World	7,528.0	7,603.3	406,512	-

Panel 2 - Impact on exporting countries

Quantity ('000s metric ton)

Country	Base Exports	New Exports	Change in producer surplus ($)	Loss in revenue from exports ($)
Guadeloupe and Martinique	298	203	-79,437,262	-94,561,360
Jamaica & Eastern Caribbean	300	284	-11,159,123	-11,466,507
Cameroon & Cote d'Ivoire	228	227	-899,810	-
Somalia	14	17	2,244,213	-
Canary and Maderia	340	274	-49,496,352	-54,775,583
Other ACP	53	54	575,308	-
Rest of World	8,314	8,563	48,269,421	-

Figure A1.2   Post-SEM sensitivity of welfare effects to prices

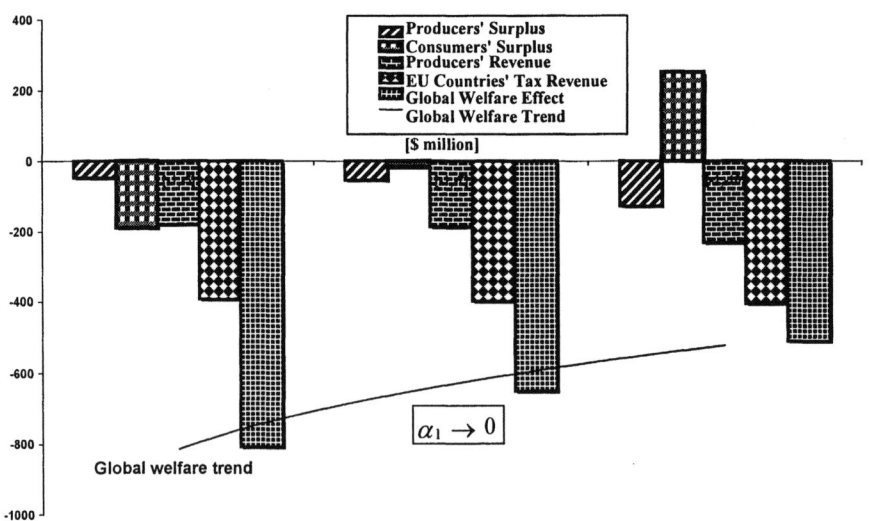

Source: Model Results

Appendix 2

Identification of the demand and supply system

In order to derive the rank and order conditions for identification of the system of equations, the author first rewrote the system of equations in expanded form as follows.

$$Q_d = v_0 + v_1 P_{rw} + v_2 Pop_{65} + v_3 Y_{ecu}$$

$$P_{rw} = \psi_0 + \psi_1 W_s + \psi_2 T + \psi_3 Q_s$$

$$Q_d = Q = Q_s$$

Then, the coefficient matrix (Table A2.1) for this system of equations was derived, and the author constructed 3*3 matrices with non-zero determinants, from the coefficients of those variables excluded from the equation in question, but included in other equations in the model.

Table A2.1   Coefficient matrix for supply and demand model

Equation	Constant	Q_d	P_{rw}	Pop_{65}	Y_{ecu}	W_s	T	Q_s	Q
Demand	v_0	-1	v_1	v_2	v_3	0	0	0	0
Supply	ψ_0	0	-1	0	0	ψ_1	ψ_2	1	0
Equilibrium 1	0	-1	0	0	0	0	0	0	1
Equilibrium 2	0	0	0	0	0	0	0	-1	1

Let M denote the number of *endogenous* variables, and K the number of *exogenous* variables in the system, respectively. Then for the system as a whole the number of endogenous and exogenous variables are shown in Table A2,2.

Table A2.2   Endogenous and exogenous variables in the model

M	K
Q_d, Q_s, Q, P_{rw}	constant, Y_{ecu}, Pop_{65}, W_s, T

Derivation of the rank condition for the supply equation

Matrix for which the supply entries have been crossed out as well as all the columns for which there is not a zero coefficient in the supply equation.

$$\begin{pmatrix} -1 & v_2 & v_3 & 0 \\ -1 & 0 & 0 & 1 \\ 0 & 0 & 0 & 1 \end{pmatrix}$$

Non-zero determinant of reduced 3*3 matrix.

$$\det \begin{pmatrix} v_2 & v_3 & 0 \\ 0 & 0 & 1 \\ 0 & 0 & 1 \end{pmatrix}$$

$$= -v_3 * \begin{vmatrix} v_2 & 0 \\ 0 & 1 \end{vmatrix}$$

$$= -v_2 v_3$$

Derivation of the rank condition for the demand equation

Matrix for which the demand entries have been crossed out as well as all the columns for which there is not a zero coefficient in the demand equation.

$$\begin{pmatrix} \psi_1 & \psi_2 & 1 & 0 \\ 0 & 0 & 0 & 1 \\ 0 & 0 & -1 & 1 \end{pmatrix}$$

Non-zero determinant of reduced 3*3 matrix.

$$\det \begin{pmatrix} \psi_1 & \psi_2 & 1 \\ 0 & 0 & 0 \\ 0 & 0 & -1 \end{pmatrix}$$

$$-\psi_2 * \begin{vmatrix} \psi_1 & 1 \\ 0 & -1 \end{vmatrix}$$

$$= \psi_1 \psi_2$$

Derivation of the order condition for the demand and supply system

Let m be the number of endogenous variables in each individual equation and k the number of exogenous variables in each equation. Then the individual equations are identified if $K - k \geq m - 1$. The values for K-k and m-1 are reported in Table A2.3.

Table A2.3   Order condition for demand and supply system

Equation	K-k	m-1	Result
Demand	2	1	identified
Supply	2	1	identified

Table A2.4   *Results of ADF tests on Germany's annual data (1970-99)*

Variable	ADF test statistics in			Critical Values		Order of integration
	Levels	first difference	second difference	1%	5%	
qty_ton	-2.45529			-3.8067	-3.0199	
		-2.740301		-3.8304	-3.0294	
			-3.128629	-3.8572	-3.0400	I(2)*
ip_dm_ton	-2.56381			-3.8067	-3.0199	
		-4.626018		-3.8304	-3.0294	
			-6.627215	-3.8572	-3.0400	I(1)** I(2)**
wp_dm_ton	-0.67747			-3.8304	-3.0294	
		-4.505846		-3.8572	-3.0400	
			-8.013709	-3.8877	-3.0521	I(1)** I(2)**
rp_dm_ton	-3.19801			-3.8067	-3.0199	
		-6.408466		-3.8304	-3.0294	
			-9.023869	-3.8572	-3.0400	I(0)* I(1)** I(2)**
y_ecu_mn	0.01879			-3.7856	-3.0114	
		-1.971469		-3.8067	-3.0199	
			-3.861370	-3.8304	-3.0294	I(2)*
ypc	0.016757			-3.7856	-3.0114	
		-1.977543		-3.8067	-3.0199	
			-3.876780	-3.8304	-3.0294	I(2)**
population	-4.00458			-4.5743	-3.6920	
		-1.394986		-4.5743	-3.6920	
			-1.838081	-4.6193	-3.7119	I(0)*
population_65+	-5.44598			-4.5348	-3.6746	
		-3.016257		-4.5743	-3.6920	
			-3.132705	-4.6193	-3.7119	I(0)**

Note: * (**) indicates significance at the 5% (1%) levels, respectively.

Table A2.5 **Results of ADF tests on France's annual data (1970-99)**

Variable	ADF test statistics in			Critical Values		Order of integration
	Levels	first difference	second difference	1%	5%	
qty_ton	-0.31089			-3.7667	-3.0038	
		-3.062268		-3.7856	-3.0114	
			-8.743210	-3.8067	-3.0199	I(1)* I(2)**
ip_ffr_ton	-1.87093			-3.6959	-2.9750	
		-3.621426		-3.7076	-2.9798	
			-9.721555	-3.7204	-2.9850	I(1)* I(2)**
wp_ffr_ton	-2.29240			-3.8304	-3.0294	
		-2.320823		-3.8572	-3.0400	
			-6.286815	-3.8877	-3.0521	I(2)**
rp_ffr_ton	-2.58846			-3.8067	-3.0199	
		-1.871974		-3.8304	-3.0294	
			-5.423987	-3.8572	-3.0400	I(2)**
y_ecu_mn	0.309065			-3.6959	-2.9750	
		-2.190621		-3.7076	-2.9798	
			-3.233786	-3.7204	-2.9850	I(2)*
ypc	-1.92589			-3.6852	-2.9705	
		-2.363467		-3.6959	-2.9750	
			-2.986956	-3.7076	-2.9798	I(2)*
population	0.256313			-3.6959	-2.9750	
		-4.399563		-3.7076	-2.9798	
			-3.241303	-3.7204	-2.9850	I(1)** I(2)*
population_65+	-1.17561			-4.3382	-3.5867	
		-2.715811		-4.3552	-3.5943	
			-4.629561	-4.3738	-3.6027	I(2)**

Note: * (**) indicates significance at the 5% (1%) levels, respectively.

Table A2.6   Results of ADF tests on France's monthly data (pre-SEM)

Variable	ADF test statistics in			Critical Values		Order of integration
	Levels	first difference	second difference	1%	5%	
qty_ton	-4.24888			-3.5362	-2.9077	
		-6.118962		-3.5380	-2.9084	
			-7.02563	-3.5398	-2.9092	I(0)** I(1)** I(2)**
ip_ffr_ton	-3.75940			-3.5362	-2.9077	
		-5.969955		-3.5380	-2.9084	
			-7.738516	-3.5398	-2.9092	I(0)** I(1)** I(2)**
wp_ffr_ton	-3.84645			-3.5362	-2.9077	
		-5.974697		-3.5380	-2.9084	
			-7.334736	-3.5398	-2.9092	I(0)** I(1)** I(2)**
rp_ffr_ton	-2.32922			-3.5362	-2.9077	
		-5.293659		-3.5380	-2.9084	
			-7.795057	-3.5398	-2.9092	I(1)** I(2)**
y_ecu_mn	-2.31354			-3.5362	-2.9077	
		-0.169323		-3.5380	-2.9084	
			-4.756041	-3.5398	-2.9092	I(2)**
ypc	-2.12764			-3.5362	-2.9077	
		-0.183138		-3.5380	-2.9084	
			-4.775060	-3.5398	-2.9092	I(2)**
population	0.625251			-3.5362	-2.9077	
		-1.875774		-3.5380	-2.9084	
			-4.529752	-3.5398	-2.9092	I(2)**
population_65+	0.261468			-3.5362	-2.9077	
		-1.697532		-3.5380	-2.9084	
			-4.363739	-3.5398	-2.9092	I(2)**

Note: * (**) indicates significance at the 5% (1%) levels, respectively.

Table A2.7   *Results of ADF tests on France's monthly data (post-SEM)*

Variable	ADF test statistics in			Critical Values		Order of integration
	Levels	first difference	second difference	1%	5%	
qty_ton	-1.25995			-3.5153	-2.8986	
		-6.97796		-3.5153	-2.8986	
			-8.88105	-3.5153	-2.8986	I(1)** I(2)**
ip_ffr_ton	-4.01257			-3.5153	-2.8986	
		-7.185412		-3.5153	-2.8986	
			-8.817009	-3.5153	-2.8986	I(0)** I(1)** I(2)**
wp_ffr_ton	-3.61782			-3.5345	-2.9069	
		-5.367516		-3.5345	-2.9069	
			-7.323058	-3.5345	-2.9069	I(0)** I(1)** I(2)**
rp_ffr_ton	-4.03099			-3.5200	-2.9006	
		-4.959996		-3.5200	-2.9006	
			-6.769087	-3.5200	-2.9006	I(0)** I(1)** I(2)**
y_ecu_mn	1.181846			-3.5153	-2.8986	
		-2.185364		-3.5153	-2.8986	
			-5.163443	-3.5153	-2.8986	I(2)**
ypc	1.006126			-3.5153	-2.8986	
		-2.278547		-3.5153	-2.8986	
			-5.157859	-3.5153	-2.8986	I(2)**
population	-0.06076			-3.5153	-2.8986	
		-2.989635		-3.5153	-2.8986	
			-5.111421	-3.5153	-2.8986	I(1)* I(2)**
population_65+	-2.12479			-3.5297	-2.9048	
		-0.591697		-3.5297	-2.9048	
			-4.667648	-3.5297	-2.9048	I(2)**

Note: * (**) indicates significance at the 5% (1%) levels, respectively.

Table A2.8 *Results of ADF tests on Germany's monthly data (pre-SEM)*

Variable	ADF test statistics in			Critical Values		Order of integration
	Levels	first difference	second difference	1%	5%	
qty_ton	-1.30464			-3.5362	-2.9077	
		-8.813274		-3.5380	-2.9084	
			-11.06152	-3.5398	-2.9092	I(1)** I(2)**
ip_dm_ton	-4.87641			-3.5362	-2.9077	
		-7.237261		-3.5380	-2.9084	
			-7.127285	-3.5398	-2.9092	I(0)** I(1)** I(2)**
wp_dm_ton	-4.22238			-3.5362	-2.9077	
		-6.263305		-3.5380	-2.9084	
			-7.002004	-3.5398	-2.9092	I(0)** I(1)** I(2)**
rp_dm_ton	-3.89626			-3.5362	-2.9077	
		-5.898389		-3.5380	-2.9084	
			-6.718113	-3.5398	-2.9092	I(0)** I(1)** I(2)**
y_ecu_mn	1.350596			-3.5362	-2.9077	
		-4.605498		-3.5380	-2.9084	
			-7.562858	-3.5398	-2.9092	I(1)** I(2)**
ypc	1.176844			-3.5362	-2.9077	
		-4.715822		-3.5380	-2.9084	
			-7.527058	-3.5398	-2.9092	I(1)** I(2)**
population	-2.68120			-4.1083	-3.4812	
		-1.842040		-4.1109	-3.4824	
			-4.597340	-4.1135	-3.4836	I(2)**
population_65+	2.716985			-3.5362	-2.9077	
		0.018036		-3.5380	-2.9084	
			-4.853637	-3.5398	-2.9092	I(2)**

Note: * (**) indicates significance at the 5% (1%) levels, respectively.

Table A2.9   *Results of ADF tests on Germany's monthly data (post-SEM)*

Variable	ADF test statistics in			Critical Values		Order of integration
	Levels	first difference	second difference	1%	5%	
qty_ton	-6.12278			-3.5153	-2.8986	
		-7.239522		-3.5153	-2.8986	
			-10.18966	-3.5153	-2.8986	I(0)** I(1)** I(2)**
ip_dm_ton	-3.95677			-3.5153	-2.8986	
		-6.271598		-3.5153	-2.8986	
			-8.903862	-3.5153	-2.8986	I(0)** I(1)** I(2)**
wp_dm_ton	-3.30078			-3.5312	-2.9055	
		-5.127631		-3.5312	-2.9055	
			-6.940085	-3.5312	-2.9055	I(1)** I(2)**
rp_dm_ton	-3.81861			-3.5239	-2.9023	
		-5.572266		-3.5239	-2.9023	
			-7.198087	-3.5239	-2.9023	I(0)** I(1)** I(2)**
y_ecu_mn	-2.28816			-3.5153	-2.8986	
		-6.146585		-3.5153	-2.8986	
			-8.037201	-3.5153	-2.8986	I(1)** I(2)**
ypc	-2.73882			-3.5297	-2.9048	
		-5.160966		-3.5297	-2.9048	
			-7.395443	-3.5297	-2.9048	I(1)** I(2)**
population	0.079135			-4.0990	-3.4769	
		-2.282368		-4.0990	-3.4769	
			-4.878873	-4.0990	-3.4769	I(2)
population_65+	-2.36517			-3.5297	-2.9048	
		-0.70997		-3.5297	-2.9048	
			-4.825173	-3.5297	-2.9048	I(2)

Note: * (**) indicates significance at the 5% (1%) levels, respectively.

Table A2.10   *Johansen Test for multiple co-integrating vectors and normalized co-integrating equations*

France demand system (annual data)			
Variables: qty_tons, rp_ffr_ton, population, ypc			
H_0	Maximum Eigenvalue	Likelihood Ratio	Critical Value 5%
r=0	0.81	60.64	47.21
r<=1	0.52	29.23	29.68
r<=2	0.41	15.22	15.41
r<=3	0.23	5.04	3.76

L.R. test indicates 1 cointegrating equation at the 5% significance level

ECM_{d1} = qty_tons - 0.71rp_ffr_ton + 0.000151population - 50.84ypc + 510048.70 = 0

SE   (-0.19285)   (0.0011)   (-14.0308)

Table A2.11   Johansen Test for multiple co-integrating vectors and normalized co-integrating equations

France supply system (annual data)
Variables: rp_ffr_ton, qty_tons, ip_ffr_ton, y_ecu

H_0	Maximum Eigenvalue	Likelihood Ratio	Critical Value 5%
r=0	0.74	51.72	47.21
r<=1	0.53	25.99	29.68
r<=2	0.44	11.57	15.41
r<=3	0.02	0.45	3.76

L.R. test indicates 1 co-integrating equation at the 5% significance level
$Ect_{s1} =$ rp_ffr_ton - 4.31qty_tons + 0.86ip_ffr_ton + 0.09y_ecu - 22264.02 = 0
          SE   (4.89689)   (0.96351)   (0.02571)

Table A2.12   Johansen Test for multiple co-integrating vectors and normalized co-integrating equations

German demand system (annual data)
Variables: qty_tons, rp_dm_ton, population, ypc

H_0	Maximum Eigenvalue	Likelihood Ratio	Critical Value 5%
r=0	0.91	71.83	47.21
r<=1	0.68	27.75	29.68
r<=2	0.29	6.30	15.41
r<=3	0.01	0.10	3.76

L.R. test indicates 1 co-integrating equation at the 5% significance level
$Ect_{d1} =$ qty_tons - 1.22rp_dm_ton - 548.67ypc - 0.000438population + 57262.96=0
          SE   (0.23156)   (85.2358)   (8.8E-05)

Table A2.13   Johansen Test for multiple co-integrating vectors and normalized co-integrating equations

German supply system (annual data)
Variables: rp_dm_ton, qty_tons, ip_dm_ton, ypc, wp_dm_ton

H_0	Maximum Eigenvalue	Likelihood Ratio	Critical Value 5%
r=0	0.92	97.33	68.52
r<=1	0.79	49.21	47.21
r<=2	0.44	19.48	29.68
r<=3	0.26	8.34	15.41

L.R. test indicates 2 co-integrating equations at the 5% significance level
$Ect_{s1} =$ rp_dm_ton - 0.38ip_dm_ton - 589.72ypc - 0.60wp_dm_ton + 58158.68 = 0
          SE   (0.41236)   (66.2892)   (0.38543)
$Ect_{s2} =$ qty_tons + 1.54ip_dm_ton - 846.92ypc - 1.11wp_dm_ton + 84192.61 = 0
          SE   (0.23382)   (37.5878)   (0.21855)

Table A2.14   *Johansen Test for multiple co-integrating vectors and normalized co-integrating equations*

France demand system with monthly data (pre-SEM)
Variables: **qty_tons, wp_ffr_ton, population, ypc**

H_0	Maximum Eigenvalue	Likelihood Ratio	Critical Value 5%
r=0	0.38	75.05	47.21
r<=1	0.37	44.94	29.68
r<=2	0.19	16.22	15.41
r<=3	0.04	2.65	3.76

L.R. test indicates 3 co-integrating equations at the 5% significance level

Ect_{d1} =   qty_tons - 0.006626population - 60276.08ypc + 929384.90 = 0
          SE   (0.00575)   (89239.80)

Ect_{d2} =   wp_ffr_ton + 0.003500population + 36871.28ypc -569116.60 = 0
          SE   (0.00065)   (10034.50)

Ect_{d3} =   population + 15317711ypc - 2.08E+08 = 0
          SE   (7737767)

Table A2.15   *Johansen Test for multiple co-integrating vectors and normalized co-integrating equations*

France supply system with monthly data (pre-SEM)
Variables: **wp_ffr_ton, qty_tons, ip_ffr_ton**

H_0	Maximum Eigenvalue	Likelihood Ratio	Critical Value 5%
r=0	0.38	54.04	29.68
r<=1	0.21	24.14	15.41
r<=2	0.14	9.51	3.76

L.R. test indicates 3 co-integrating equations at the 5% significance level

Ect_{s1} =   wp_ffr_ton - 0.06qty_tons - 1.12ip_ffr_ton + 1136.86 = 0
          SE   (0.01575)   (0.11273)

Ect_{s2} =   Wp_ffr_ton - 0.68ip_ffr_ton - 3460.76 = 0
          SE   (0.17966)

Ect_{s3} =   Qty_tons + 7.78ip_ffr_ton - 81502.78 = 0
          SE   (4.01010)

Table A2.16   Johansen Test for multiple co-integrating vectors and normalized co-integrating equations

Germany demand system with monthly data (pre-SEM)
Variables: qty_tons, rp_dm_ton, population, ypc

H_0	Maximum Eigenvalue	Likelihood Ratio	Critical Value 5%
r=0	0.37	54.20	47.21
r<=1	0.26	24.72	29.68
r<=2	0.08	5.56	15.41
r<=3	0.00	0.23	3.76

L.R. test indicates 1 co-integrating equation at the 5% significance level

Ect_{d1} = qty_tons - 117.99rp_dm_ton + 0.100515population + 170.63ypc - 9806680 = 0
SE   (48.19)   (0.07847)   (107.54)

Table A2.17   Johansen Test for multiple co-integrating vectors and normalized co-integrating equations

Germany supply system with monthly data (pre-SEM)
Variables: rp_dm_ton, qty_tons, ip_dm_ton

H_0	Maximum Eigenvalue	Likelihood Ratio	Critical Value 5%
r=0	0.35	32.54	29.68
r<=1	0.07	5.51	15.41
r<=2	0.02	1.27	3.76

L.R. test indicates 1 co-integrating equation at the 5% significance level

Ect_{s1} = rp_dm_ton – 0.000694qty_tons – 1.96ip_dm_ton – 327.41 = 0
SE   (0.00120)   (0.25996)

Table A2.18   Johansen Test for multiple Co-integrating Vectors and Normalized Co-integrating Equations

France demand system with monthly data (post-SEM)
Variables: qty_tons, wp_ffr_ton, population, ypc

H_0	Maximum Eigenvalue	Likelihood Ratio	Critical Value 5%
r=0	0.41	68.50	47.21
r<=1	0.31	34.55	29.68
r<=2	0.12	10.42	15.41
r<=3	0.03	2.04	3.76

L.R. test indicates 2 co-integrating equations at the 5% significance level

Ect_{d1} = qty_tons + 0.12population - 1798405ypc + 10578083 = 0
SE   (0.03537)   (633109)

Ect_{d2} = wp_ffr_ton -0.006population + 112732.3ypc - 769988 = 0
SE   (0.00342)   (61257.4)

Table A2.19 *Johansen Test for multiple co-integrating vectors and normalized co-integrating equations*

France supply system with monthly data (post-SEM)
Variables: wp_ffr_ton, qty_tons, ip_ffr_ton, ypc

H_o	Maximum Eigenvalue	Likelihood Ratio	Critical Value 5%
r=0	0.28	50.27	47.21
r<=1	0.25	29.66	35.65
r<=2	0.16	11.16	15.41
r<=3	0.00	0.19	3.76

L.R. test indicates 1 co-integrating equation at the 5% significance level
Ect_{s1} = wp_ffr_ton - 0.06qty_tons - 1.21ip_ffr_ton - 23403.15ypc + 233362.2 = 0
      SE   (0.02640)   (0.15199)   (12683.10)

Table A2.20 *Johansen Test for multiple co-integrating vectors and normalized co-integrating equations*

Germany demand system with monthly data (post-SEM)
Variables: qty_tons, rp_dm_ton, population, ypc

H_o	Maximum Eigenvalue	Likelihood Ratio	Critical Value 5%
r=0	0.47	97.36	47.21
r<=1	0.39	54.47	29.68
r<=2	0.23	20.99	15.41
r<=3	0.05	3.49	3.76

L.R. test indicates 3 co-integrating equations at the 5% significance level
Ect_{d1} = qty_tons - 39.23ypc - 0.03population + 2718381 = 0
      SE   (48.54)   (0.05)
Ect_{d2} = rp_dm_ton + 2.15ypc + 0.002958population - 265534.30 = 0
      SE   (0.82)   (0.00077)
Ect_{d3} = ypc + 0.000863population - 80306.39 = 0
      SE   (5.1E-05)

Table A2.21   Johansen Test for multiple co-integrating vectors and normalized co-integrating equations

Germany supply system with monthly data (post-SEM)
Variables: rp_dm_ton, qty_tons, wp_dm_ton

H_0	Maximum Eigenvalue	Likelihood Ratio	Critical Value 5%
r=0	0.44	52.83	29.68
r<=1	0.19	14.82	15.41
r<=2	0.01	0.92	3.76

L.R. test indicates 1 co-integrating equation at the 5% significance level
Ect_{s1} =   rp_dm_ton + 0.95wp_dm_ton - 4931.73 = 0
　　　　SE　　　(0.79)

Table A2.22   Johansen Test for multiple co-integrating vectors and normalized co-integrating equations

Germany demand system with monthly data (post-SEM)
Variables: Qty_tons, rp_dm_ton, population, ip_dm_ton

H_0	Maximum Eigenvalue	Likelihood Ratio	Critical Value 5%
r=0	0.52	94.66	47.21
r<=1	0.35	46.02	29.68
r<=2	0.20	17.39	15.41
r<=3	0.04	2.74	3.76

L.R. test indicates 3 co-integrating equations at the 5% significance level
Ect_{d1} =   Qty_tons + 0.02population + 16.27ip_dm_ton - 1745353 = 0
　　　　SE　　　(0.01094)　　　(9.72374)
Ect_{d2} =   rp_dm_ton + 0.000920population - 0.38ip_dm_ton - 77439.57 = 0
　　　　SE　　　(0.00015)　　　(0.13475)
Ect_{d3} =   Population + 1402.14ip_dm_ton - 83887879 = 0
　　　　SE　　　(518.17)

Table A2.23 *Johansen Test for multiple co-integrating vectors and normalized co-integrating equations*

Germany supply system with monthly data (post-SEM)			
Variables:	rp_dm_ton, ip_dm_ton, qty_tons		
H_o	Maximum Eigenvalue	Likelihood Ratio	Critical Value 5%
r=0	0.46	70.22	29.68
r<=1	0.20	26.42	15.41
r<=2	0.14	10.37	3.76

L.R. test indicates 3 co-integrating equations at the 5% significance level

$Ect_{s1} =$ rp_dm_ton - 0.74ip_dm_ton - 0.024qty_tons - 381.75 = 0
          SE   (0.23550)   (0.00716)

$Ect_{s2} =$ rp_dm_ton - 0.028qty_tons - 1292.50 = 0
          SE   (0.01106)

$Ect_{s3} =$ ip_dm_ton - 0.005736qty_tons - 1229.76 = 0
          SE   (0.00794)

Appendix 3

Table A3.1 Base price data set for estimating econometric models

Observation	Chiquita	Dole, Del Monte Onkel Tuca	Bonita, Corbana Turbana, Fyffes Consul	Tropical Eden Golden B, Excel Goldfinger
1	35.00	31.00	27.75	27.75
2	39.00	34.00	31.13	31.25
3	40.50	35.00	34.70	31.00
4	40.50	35.00	31.70	30.00
5	40.50	35.00	31.70	29.00
6	40.50	35.00	31.70	29.00
7	38.50	33.00	28.00	27.00
8	38.50	33.00	28.00	27.00
9	38.50	35.00	31.00	28.50
10	38.50	35.00	31.00	28.50
11	39.50	35.00	31.00	28.50
12	39.50	35.00	31.00	28.50
13	39.50	35.00	31.00	31.00
14	36.50	32.00	28.00	28.00
15	36.50	32.00	28.00	28.00
16	36.50	32.00	28.00	28.00

Table A3.2 Augmented Dickey-Fuller Unit Root Tests on variables and their logarithms

Variable	ADF Test statistics in Levels	first difference	second difference	Critical Values 1%	5%	10%	Order of Integration I(0)	I(1)	I(2)
Bonita	-2.374385			-4.0113	-3.1003	-2.6927	No		
		-5.068541		-4.0681	-3.1222	-2.7042		Yes***	
			-6.141636	-4.1366	-3.1483	-2.7180			Yes***
Chiquita	-1.547578			-4.0113	-3.1003	-2.6927	No		
		-3.331898		-4.0681	-3.1222	-2.7042		Yes**	
			-2.920226	-4.1366	-3.1483	-2.7180			Yes*
Dole_DelMonte	-1.923985			-4.0113	-3.1003	-2.6927	No		
		-3.169341		-4.0681	-3.1222	-2.7042		Yes**	
			-4.041232	-4.1366	-3.1483	-2.7180			Yes**
Tropical_Eden	-2.25193			-4.0113	-3.1003	-2.6927	No		
		-3.618798		-4.0681	-3.1222	-2.7042		Yes**	
			-4.310835	-4.1366	-3.1483	-2.7180			Yes***
L_Bonita	-2.388593			-4.0113	-3.1003	-2.6927	No		
		-4.865591		-4.0681	-3.1222	-2.7042		Yes***	
			-5.960366	-4.1366	-3.1483	-2.7180			Yes***
L_Chiquita	-1.511332			-4.0113	-3.1003	-2.6927	No		
		-3.339028		-4.0681	-3.1222	-2.7042		Yes**	
			-2.946617	-4.1366	-3.1483	-2.7180			Yes*
L_Dole_DelMonte	-1.891164			-4.0113	-3.1003	-2.6927	No		
		-3.165474		-4.0681	-3.1222	-2.7042		Yes**	
			-4.022123	-4.1366	-3.1483	-2.7180			Yes**
L_Tropical_Eden	-2.249809			-4.0113	-3.1003	-2.6927	No		
		-3.589697		-4.0681	-3.1222	-2.7042		Yes**	
			-4.290044	-4.1366	-3.1483	-2.7180			Yes***

Table A3.3 Johansen Test for multiple co-integrating vectors and normalized co-integrating equations

Relationship between Second Class Brands and the Chiquita Brand
Variables: L_Dole_DelMonte, L_Chiquita

H₀	Maximum Eigenvalue	Likelihood Ratio	Critical Value 5%
r=0	0.38	9.26	15.41
r<=1	0.17	2.63	3.76

L.R. test rejects any cointegration at the 5% significance level

Relationship between Third Class Brands and the Chiquita Brand
Variables: L_Bonita, L_Chiquita

H₀	Maximum Eigenvalue	Likelihood Ratio	Critical Value 5%
r=0	0.71	20.71	15.41
r<=1	0.21	3.25	3.76

L.R. test indicates one cointegrating equation at the 5% significance level
Ect1 =   L_Bonita - 0.844689L_Chiquita - 0.323169 = 0
       SE   (0.20435)

Relationship between Fourth Class Brands and the Chiquita Brand
Variables: L_Tropical_Eden, L_Chiquita

H₀	Maximum Eigenvalue	Likelihood Ratio	Critical Value 5%
r=0	0.52	15.06	15.41
r<=1	0.29	4.72	3.76

L.R. test rejects any cointegration at the 5% significance level

Table A3.4 Residuals from regression of $\Delta(L\_Bonita)$ against $\Delta(L\_Dole\_DelMonte)$

ADF Test Statistic	-3.659026	1% Critical Value*	-4.0681
		5% Critical Value	-3.1222
		10% Critical Value	-2.7042

*MacKinnon critical values for rejection of hypothesis of a unit root.

Augmented Dickey-Fuller Test Equation
Dependent Variable: D(L_resid)
Method: Least Squares
Sample(adjusted): 4 16
Included observations: 13 after adjusting endpoints

Variable	Coefficient	Std. Error	t-Statistic	Prob.
L_resid(-1)	-1.617262	0.441993	-3.659026	0.0044
D(L_resid(-1))	0.144115	0.254214	0.566907	0.5833
C	-0.003088	0.007628	-0.404787	0.6942
R-squared	0.796925	Mean dependent var		-0.005028
Adjusted R-squared	0.756311	S.D. dependent var		0.055667
S.E. of regression	0.027480	Akaike info criterion		-4.151538
Sum squared resid	0.007552	Schwarz criterion		-4.021165
Log likelihood	29.98500	F-statistic		19.62150
Durbin-Watson stat	0.569738	Prob(F-statistic)		0.000345

Table A3.5   Residuals from regression of $\Delta(L\_Tropical\_Eden)$
              against $\Delta(L\_Dole\_DelMonte)$

ADF Test Statistic	-3.523239	1% Critical Value*	-4.1366
		5% Critical Value	-3.1483
		10% Critical Value	-2.7180

*MacKinnon critical values for rejection of hypothesis of a unit root.

Augmented Dickey-Fuller Test Equation
Dependent Variable: D(L_resid ,2)
Method: Least Squares
Sample(adjusted): 5 16
Included observations: 12 after adjusting endpoints

Variable	Coefficient	Std. Error	t-Statistic	Prob.
D(L_resid (-1))	-1.831305	0.519779	-3.523239	0.0065
D(L_resid (-1),2)	0.219893	0.289035	0.760784	0.4662
C	0.004500	0.010194	0.441450	0.6693
R-squared	0.764430	Mean dependent var		-0.000648
Adjusted R-squared	0.712081	S.D. dependent var		0.065523
S.E. of regression	0.035159	Akaike info criterion		-3.645582
Sum squared resid	0.011125	Schwarz criterion		-3.524356
Log likelihood	24.87349	F-statistic		14.60258
Durbin-Watson stat	2.131201	Prob(F-statistic)		0.001495

Table A3.6   Johansen Test for multiple co-integrating vectors and
              normalized co-integrating equations

Relationship between Third Class Brands and Second Class Brands
Variables: L_Bonita, L_Dole_DelMonte

H₀	Maximum Eigenvalue	Likelihood Ratio	Critical Value 5%
r=0	0.57	13.73	15.41
r<=1	0.12	1.80	3.76

L.R. test rejects any cointegration at the 5% significance level

Relationship between Fourth Class Brands and Second Class Brands
Variables: L_Tropical_Eden, L_Dole_DelMonte

H₀	Maximum Eigenvalue	Likelihood Ratio	Critical Value 5%
r=0	0.51	14.93	15.41
r<=1	0.30	4.97	3.76

L.R. test rejects any cointegration at the 5% significance level

Relationship between Fourth Class Brands and Third Class Brands
Variables: L_Tropical_Eden, L_Dole_DelMonte

H₀	Maximum Eigenvalue	Likelihood Ratio	Critical Value 5%
r=0	0.38	11.17	15.41
r<=1	0.27	4.38	3.76

L.R. test rejects any cointegration at the 5% significance level

Table A3.7   *Base quantity and price data used for simulations*

Brands	Quantity (TONS)	Import Price ($/TON)	Retail Price ($/TON)
Chiquita	837,600	778.71	1,323.46
Dole, Del Monte	1,196,572	669.22	1,171.13
Bonita, Corbana, Turbana, Consul, Fyffes	239,314	541.16	947.03
Goldfinger, Excel, Tropical Eden, Golden B	119,657	474.00	853.20
Fyffes, JPs, 5 Isles	270,668	677.60	1,761.75
Pomona Group	282,971	759.65	1,792.78
Others	61,515	537.38	1,262.84

Table A3.8   *Elasticities of demand, by brand*

Brands	Elasticities
Chiquita	-0.40
Dole, Del Monte	-0.50
Bonita, Corbana, Turbana, Consul, Fyffes	-0.75
Goldfinger, Excel, Tropical Eden, Golden B	-1.00
Fyffes, JPs, 5 Isles	-0.75
Pomona	-0.75
Others	-1.00

Table A3.9   *Welfare effects of liberalization after the first period game*

Brands	Producer Surplus	Consumer Surplus	EU Tax Revenue	Surplus due to branding	Overall Effect
Chiquita	3,318,618	3,340,544	-99,896,656	-21,082,171	-114,319,666
Dole, Del Monte	5,092,893	5,278,688	-124,477,993	-25,379,186	-139,485,598
Bonita, Corbana, Turbana, Consul, Fyffes	1,212,192	1,235,466	-20,831,057	-2,231,723	-20,615,122
Goldfinger, Excel, Tropical Eden, Golden B	-707,832	742,034	-9,441,385	0	-9,407,183
Fyffes, JPs, 5 Isles	-1,353,519	1,655,672	0	0	302,153
Pomona	1,625,093	1,844,357	0	0	3,469,451
Others	420,486	585,252	-5,517,096	-3,368,868	-7,880,226
Total:	**9,607,932**	**14,682,014**	**-260,164,188**	**-52,061,949**	**-287,936,192**

Table A3.10 Welfare effects of liberalization after the third period game

Brands	Producer Surplus	Consumer Surplus	EU Tax Revenue	Surplus due to branding	Overall Welfare Effect
Chiquita	1,074,718	-1,138,313	-109,162,909	-8,724,262	-117,950,767
Dole, Del Monte	1,670,095	-1,821,420	-134,975,217	-11,068,656	-146,195,198
Bonita, Corbana, Turbana, Consul, Fyffes	406,206	-436,085	-22,020,510	-1,267,030	-23,317,420
Goldfinger, Excel, Tropical Eden, Golden B	245,476	-271,062	-9,845,477	-271,062	-10,142,125
Pomona	887,981	-515,698	-28,874,672	-7,138,027	-35,640,416
Others	-343,896	-160,589	-5,827,571	-1,136,719	-7,468,775
Total:	**3,940,579**	**-4,343,167**	**-310,706,357**	**-29,605,755**	**-340,714,700**

References

Arthur D. Little International (1995) 'Study of the Impact of the Banana CMO on the Banana Industry in the European Union', (20 September).

Arts, K. (2000) *Integrating Human Rights into Development Cooperation: The Case of the Lomé Convention.* Amsterdam: Ph.D. Thesis.

ASEAN (1977) 'Agreement on ASEAN Preferential Arrangements', Jakarta: ASEAN Secretariat.

Azzam, A. M. and E. Pagoulatos (1990) 'Testing Oligopolistic and Oligopsonistic Behaviour: An Application to the US Meat-Packing Industry', *Journal of Agricultural Economics*, 70: 158-62.

Bain, J. (1968) *Industrial Organization, Second Edition.* New York: John Wiley & Sons.

Bain, J. (1956) *Barriers to New Competition.* Cambridge, MA: Harvard University Press.

Banacol.com (2002) 'Banana Consumption in the United States', (February).

Baran, P. A. and P. M. Sweezy (1966) *Monopoly Capital. An Essay on the American Economic and Social Order.* 1968 edition. Harmondsworth: Penguin.

Barlett, D. L. and J. B. Steele (2000) 'How to Become a Top Banana', *Time Magazine* (February 7).

Baumol, W. J. (1982) 'Contestable Markets: An Uprising in the Theory of Industrial Structure', *American Economic Review*, 72: 1-15.

Baumol, W.J.; J. C. Panzar and R. D. Willig (1982) *Contestable Markets and the Theory of Industry Structure.* New York: Harcourt Brace Jovanovich.

Bhagwati, J. N. (1988) *Protectionism.* Cambridge, MA: The MIT Press.

Bhuyan, S. and R. A. Lopez (1997) 'Oligopoly Power in the Food and Tobacco Industries', *American Journal of Agricultural Economics*, 79(3): 1035-43 (August).

Blomström, M. (1994) 'Multinationals and Market Structure in Mexico', in C.R. Frischtak and R.S. Newfarmer (1994) (eds) *Transnational Corporations: Market Structure and Industrial Performance.* United Nations, Transnational Corporations and Management Division, London and New York: Routledge.

Borrell, B. (1994) 'EU Bananarama III', *World Bank Working Paper, No. 1386,* Washington, DC: The World Bank.

Borrell, B. (1996) 'Beyond EU Bananarama 1993: The Story Gets Worse', *Canberra and Sydney, Australia: Centre for International Economics*.

Borrell, B. and M. C. Yang (1992) 'EC Bananarama 1992: The Sequel to The Commission Proposal', World Bank Working Paper No. 958. Washington, DC: The World Bank.

Borrell, B. and M.C. Yang (1990) 'EC Bananarama 1992', World Bank Working Paper No. 523, Washington DC: The World Bank (October).

Borrell, B. and S. Cuthbertson (1991) 'EC Banana Policy 1992', Canberra, Australia: Centre for International Economics.

Boyle, S. E. and R. L. Sorensen (1970) 'Concentration and Mobility: Alternative Measures of Industry Structure', *Journal of Industrial Economics*, 19(1):118-32.

Brander, J. and B. Spencer (1985) 'Export Subsidies and Market Share Rivalry', *Journal of International Economics*, 18: 83-100.

Bresnahan, T. F. (1982) 'The Oligopoly Solution Concept is Identified', *Economics Letters*, 10: 87-92.

Bresnahan, T. F. and R. Schmalensee (1987) "The Empirical Renaissance in Industrial Economics: An Overview", *Journal of Industrial Economics*, 35(4): 371-8.

Buschena, D. E. and J. M. Perloff (1991) "The Creation of Dominant Firm Market Power in the Coconut Oil Export Market", *American Journal of Agricultural Economics*, 73: 1000-8.

Camdessus, M (1999) "International Monetary Fund: Statement by Mr. Michel Camdessus, Managing-Director", WTO Seattle Ministerial Conference, Third Session (30 November).

Campaign for Labor Rights (1998) "Chiquita Exposed: Part 1. Chiquita and Worker Rights", (May 6).

Cantwell, J. (2000) "A Survey of theories of international production", in Pitelis, C. and R. Sugden (eds) *The Nature of the Transnational Firm.* Second Edition. London, UK and New York, US: Routledge.

Casson, Mark (1987) *The Firm and the Market: Studies on Multinational Enterprise and the Scope of the Firm.* Oxford, UK: Basil Blackwell.

Casson, Mark (1986) (ed.) *Multinationals and World Trade: Vertical Integration and the Division of Labour in World Industries.* London: Allen & Unwin.

Caves, R. (1982) *Multinational Enterprise and Economic Analysis.* Cambridge, UK: Cambridge University Press.

Cerjack, H. (2000) Letter to the Minister of Foreign Affairs of Trinidad and Tobago from the Minister of Foreign Relations of Panama, outlining the position of Panama with regards to the WTO banana dispute (March 14).

Chiou, J. R. and H. Hwang (1998) "Tariff, Equivalent Quota and Technology Choice (English Summary)", *Taiwan Economic Review*, 26(3): 319-36.

Chiquita Brands International, Inc. (2000a) *1999 Annual Report and form 10-K*, for fiscal year ended December 31, 1999.

Chiquita Brands International, Inc. (2000b) "Chiquita launches program to combat fad diets and promote healthy eating", November 17.

Coase, R. (1937) "The Nature of the Firm", *Economica*, 4(4): 386-405.

Collins, N. R. and L. E. Preston (1961) "The Size Structure of the Largest Industrial Firms, 1909-1958", *The American Economic Review*, 51: 986-1003.

Compton, J. (1995) "Letter to President Clinton on the initiation of Section 301 Action and threat of WTO action by Michael Kantor" (26 April).

Connor, J.M. and W.F. Mueller (1977) 'The shaping of market structures by multinationals: Brazil, Mexico, and the United States', Staff Paper Series No. 120, Department of Agricultural and Applied Economics, University of Wisconsin-Madison.

Cowling, K. and R. Sugden (1987) *Transnational Monopoly Capitalism*. Brighton: Wheatsheaf.

Davenport, M. and S. Page (1991) *Europe 1992 and the developing world*, London: Overseas Development Institute.

Deodhar, S. Y. and I. M. Sheldon (1995) 'Is Foreign Trade (Im)perfectly Competitive?: An Analysis of the German Market for Banana Imports', *Journal of Agricultural Economics,* 46(3): 336-8 (September).

Deprez, J. and T. Harvey (1999) (eds) *Foundations of International Economics. Post Keynesian Perspectives*. London, UK: Routledge.

Dicken, P. (1998) *Global Shift: transforming the world economy, Third Edition.* London: Paul Chapman Publishing Ltd., Thousand Oaks, CA: SAGE Publications Inc. and New Delhi: SAGE Publications India Pvt Ltd.

Dickey, D.A. and W.A. Fuller (1979) 'Distribution of the Estimators for Autoregressive Time Series with a Unit Root,' *Journal of the American Statistical Association*, 74, 427–431.

Dijkstra, G. (1997) 'Trade Liberalization and Industrial Development: Theory and Evidence from Latin America', ISS General Working paper series No. 255, The Hague: ISS.

Dixit, A. K. and V. Norman (1980) *Theory of International Trade: A Dual, General Equilibrium Approach*. Cambridge: Cambridge University Press.

Dole Food Company, Inc. (2001) *Annual Report and Form 10-K*, for fiscal year ended December 30, 2000.

Dunning, J. H. (1993) *Multinational Enterprises and The Global Economy.* Reading, Massachusetts: Addison-Wesley Publishing Company.

Dunning, J. H. (1996) 'The Nature of Transnational Corporations and Their Activities', in United Nations (eds) *Transnational Corporations and World Development.* London, UK, & Boston, MA: International Thomson Business Press, pp.27-43.

Dunning, J. H. and A. M. Rugman (1985) 'The Influence of Hymer's Dissertation on the Theory of Foreign Direct Investment', University of Reading, Department of Economics, Discussion Papers in International Investment and Business Studies, No. 85 (May).

Dunning, J.H. (1973) 'The Determinants of International Production', *Oxford Economic Papers*, 25: 289-336.

Dunning, J.H. (1979) 'Explaining Changing Patterns of International Production: In Defence of Eclectic Theory', *Oxford Bulletin of Economics and Statistics*, 41: 269-95.

Dunning, J.H. (1980) 'Towards an Eclectic Theory of International Production: Some Empirical Test', *Journal of International Business Studies*, II: 9-31.

Ebrill, L, J Stotsky and R Gropp (1999) 'Revenue Implications of Trade Liberalization', IMF Occasional papers No. 180, Washington, DC: IMF.

Emmerij, L. (2001) 'Widening Global Gaps? : Action or Inaction and the United Nations', Public Lecture Delivered at the Institute of Social Studies, The Hague (8 March).

Engle, R.F. and C.W.J. Granger (1991) (eds) *Long-run Economic Relationships: Readings in Cointegration.* Oxford: Oxford University Press.

Ethier, W. (1982) 'National and International Returns to Scale in the Modern Theory of International Trade', *The American Economic Review*, 72: 389-405.

European Commission (1976) 'Proceeding Under Article 86 of the EEC Treaty (IV/26999-Chiquita)', *Official Journal of the European Communities,* 238-57.

European Commission (1992) 'Setting-up the Internal Market in the Banana Sector', report compiled by a Commission ad hoc 'Bananas' interdepartmental working party to Commission guidelines. Brussels: Commission Working Document SEC(92) 940 final.

European Commission (1994) 'Report on the EC Banana Regime', Brussels: VI/5671/94 (July).

European Commission (1995) 'Report on the Operation of the Banana Regime', Brussels: SEC (95) 1565 Final (11 October).

European Council (1993) 'Council Regulation (EEC) No 404/93 of 13 February 1993 on the Common Organization of the Market in Bananas', *Official Journal of the European Communities*, L047.

European Council (1998) 'Council Regulation (EC) No 1637/98 of 20 July 1998 amending Regulation (EEC) No 404/93 on the Common Organization of the Market in Bananas', *Official Journal of the European Communities*, L210.

European Court of Justice (1993) *Order of the Court of 29 June 1993*, in 'Case C-280/93 R, Federal Republic of Germany v Council of the European Communities', *European Court Reports*.

EUROSTAT (1997) 'Computer Data Files on EU Banana Imports: 1976-96', Luxembourg: Statistical Office of the European Communities.

EUROSTAT (2000) 'Computer Data Files' *Downloaded from Comext Database*, Luxembourg: EUROSTAT (February).

Everling, U. (1996) 'Will Europe Slip on Bananas? The Bananas Judgement of the Court of Justice and National Courts', *Common Market Law Review*, 33: 401-37.

FAO (1986) 'The World Banana Economy 1970-1984: Structure, Performance and Prospects'. Rome: FAO Economic and Social Development Paper 57.

FAO (1997a) 'Banana Diversification: Major Issues and Constraints'. Rome: Committee on Commodity Problems, Intergovernmental Group on Bananas, (1-5 May).

FAO (1997b) 'Banana Statistics', Rome: Committee on Commodity Problems, Intergovernmental Group on Bananas, (1-27 May).

FAO (1999) 'Commodity Market Review 1998-99', Rome: Commodities and Trade Division.

Farley, J.U. (1964) 'Why Does 'Brand Loyalty' Vary over products?', *Journal of Marketing Research*, 9-14.

Federal Register (2001) 'Termination of Action and Monitoring: European Communities' Regime for the Importation, Sale and Distribution of Bananas', Office of the United States Trade Representative (July 6).

Federal Register (1999) 'Implementation of WTO Recommendations Concerning the European Communities' Regime for the Importation, Sale and Distribution of Bananas', Office of the United States Trade Representative (April 19).

Federal Register (1998) 'Implementation of WTO Recommendations Concerning the European Communities' Regime for the Importation, Sale and Distribution of Bananas', Office of the United States Trade Representative (November 10).

Federal Register (1996) 'WTO Dispute Settlement Proceedings Concerning the European Communities' Banana Regime', Office of the United States Trade Representative (April 25).

Federal Register (1995) 'Termination of Investigation; Initiation of New Investigation and Request for Public Comment: European Union Banana Regime', Office of the United States Trade Representative (October 4).

Fitzpatrick, J. and Associates (1990) 'Trade Policy and the EC Banana Market: An Economic Analysis', London: Dole Europe Limited.

FLO and EUROBAN (2000) 'Position Paper on the Proposed Reform of the European Union Banana Import Regime', Fair Trade Labelling Organizations (FLO) and the European Banana Action Network (EUROBAN) (January).

Fonsah, E. and A. Chidebelu (1996) *Economics of Banana Production and Marketing in the Tropics: A case study of Cameroon*. Montreux, London and Washington: Minerva Press.

Frank, D. (2002) 'Our Fruit, Their Labor and Global Reality', *Washingtonpost.com* (June 2).

Fresh Del Monte Produce (2000) *Annual Report and form 10-K*, for fiscal year ended December 31, 1999.

FreshInfo.com (2002) 'Ecuador faces grim allegations', (30 May).

Frischtak, C. R. and R. S. Newfarmer (1994) (ed.) *Transnational Corporations: Market Structure and Industrial Performance*. United Nations, Transnational Corporations and Management Division, London and New York: Routledge.

Frischtak, C. R. and R. S. Newfarmer (1996) 'Market Structure and Industrial Performance', in United Nations (eds) *Transnational Corporations and World Development*. London, UK, & Boston, MA: International Thomson Business Press, pp. 294-324.

Fyffes PLC (2001) 'Fyffes Looks Forward to Better Results in 2001', www.hemscott.com, (21 March).

GATT (1993) 'EEC – Member States' Import Regimes for Bananas: Report of the Panel', DS32/R (3 June).

GATT (1994) 'EEC – Import Regime for Bananas: Report of the Panel', DS38/R (18 January).

Genesove, D. and W. Mullin (1995) 'Validating the Conjectural Variations Method: The Sugar Industry, 1890-1914', Working Paper 95/20, Massachusetts Institute of Technology (October).

Gereffi, G. (1994) 'The Organization of Buyer-Driven Global Commodity Chains: How U.S. Retailers Shape Overseas Production Networks', in G.

Gereffi and M. Korzeniewicz (eds) *Commodity Chains and Global Capitalism.* Westport, Connecticut: Praeger, pp. 95-122.

Gereffi, G. (1995) 'Global Production Systems and Third World Development', in B. Stallings (ed.) *Global Change, Regional Response.* Cambridge: Cambridge University Press, pp.100-42.

Gereffi, G. (1996) 'The Elusive Last Lap in the Quest for Developed-Country Status', in J. H. Mittelman (ed.) *Globalization: Critical Reflections.* Colorado, US and London, UK: Lynne Rienner Publishers, Inc., pp. 53-81.

Gereffi, G. (1999) 'International Trade and Industrial Upgrading in the Apparel Commodity Chain', *Journal of International Economics*, 48: 37-70.

Geroski, P. A. (1982) 'Interpreting a Correlation Between Market Structure and Performance', *Journal of Industrial Economics*, 30(3): 319-26.

Goldfrank, W. L. (1994) 'Fresh Demand: The Consumption of Chilean Produce in the United States', in G. Gereffi and M. Korzeniewicz (eds) *Commodity Chains and Global Capitalism.* Westport, Connecticut: Praeger, 267-79.

Gowan S. (1995) (ed.) *Bananas and Plantains.* London, UK: Chapman & Hall.

Graham, E. (2000) 'Strategic Management and Transnational Firm Behaviour: A Formal Approach', in Pitelis, C. and R. Sugden (eds) *The Nature of the Transnational Firm.* Second Edition. London, UK and New York, US: Routledge.

Gray, H. P. (1996) ' The Role of Transnational Corporations in International Trade', in United Nations (eds) *Transnational Corporations and World Development.* London, UK, and Boston, MA: International Thomson Business Press, pp.250-68.

Grossman, G. and E. Helpman (1991) *Innovation and Growth in the Global Economy.* Cambridge, MA: The MIT Press.

Grubel, H. G. and P. J. Lloyd (1975) *Intra-Industry Trade: The Theory and Measurement of International Trade in Differentiated Products.* London: Macmillan and New York: Halsted.

Guyomard, H., C. Laroche and C. Le-Mouel (1999) 'An Economic Assessment of the Common Market Organization for Bananas in the European Union', *Agricultural Economics*, 20(2): 105-20 (March).

Haberler, G. (1936) *The Theory of International Trade.* London, UK: W. Hodge and Co.

Hallam, D. (1995) 'The World Banana Economy', in S. Gowan (ed.) *Bananas and Plantains.* London, UK: Chapman & Hall (509-33).

Hallam, D. and L. Peston (1997) 'The Political Economy of Europe's Banana Trade', Department of Agricultural and Food Economics, University of Reading, Occasional Paper No. 5 (January).

Heads of State and Government of the Caribbean Community (1999) 'Statement on the United States' Unilateral Imposition of Sanctions Against the European Union Banana Import Marketing Regime' Paramaribo, Suriname (5 March).

Heckscher, E. F. (1919) 'The Effect of Foreign Trade on the Distribution of Income', *Ekonomisk Tidskrift*, pp. 497-512. Reprinted in H. S. Ellis and L. M Metzler (1950) *Readings in the Theory of International Trade.* Homewood Ill.: Irwin, pp. 272-300.

Helleiner, G. K. (1977) 'Transnational Enterprises and the New Political Economy of the U.S. Trade Policy', *Oxford Economic Papers*, 29: 102-16.

Helpman, E. (1981) 'International Trade in the Presence of Product Differentiation, Economies of Scale and Monopolistic Competition: A Chamberlain-Heckscher-Ohlin Approach', *Journal of International Economics*, 11(3): 305-40.

Helpman, E. (1984) 'Increasing Returns, Imperfect Markets and Trade Theory', in R. W. Jones and P. B. Kenen (Eds.) *Handbook of International Economics, Volume 1, International Trade.* Amsterdam: North-Holland, pp. 325-365.

Helpman, E. and P. R. Krugman (1989) *Trade Policy and Market Structure.* Cambridge, MA, and London, UK: The MIT Press.

Helpman, H. and P. R. Krugman (1985) *Market Structure and Foreign Trade.* Cambridge, MA: Harvard University Press.

Hennart, Jean-François (2000) 'Transaction Costs Theory and the Multinational enterprise', in Pitelis, C. and R. Sugden (eds) *The Nature of the Transnational Firm.* Second Edition. London, UK and New York, US: Routledge.

Houtkamp, J. A. (1996) *Tropical Africa's Emergence as a Banana Supplier in the Inter-War Period.* Hampshire, UK: Avebury.

Hwang, H. and C. Mai (1988) 'On the Equivalence of Tariffs and Quotas Under Duopoly', *Journal of International Economics*, 24: 373-80.

Hymer, S. (1970) 'The Efficiency (Contradictions) of Multinational Corporations', *The American Economic Review*, 60(2): 441-8 (May).

Hymer, S. (1976) *The International Operations of National Firms: A Study of Direct Foreign Investment.* Cambridge, MA and London, UK: The MIT Press.

Ietto-Gillies, G. (1992) *International Production. Trends, Theories, Effects.* Polity Press.

Ingco, M D and L A Winters (2001)(eds) 'Agricultural Trade Liberalization in a New Trade Round: Perspectives of Developing Countries and Transition Economies', World Bank Discussion Papers No. 418, Washington, DC: World Bank.

Irish Sunday Independent (2002) 'Fyffes Chief quizzed on Chiquita rumours' (3 March).

Johansen, S. (1991) 'Estimation and Hypothesis Testing of Cointegration Vectors in Gaussian Vector Autoregressive Models,' *Econometrica*, 59, 1551–1580;

Johansen, S. (1995) *Likelihood-based Inference in Cointegrated Vector Autoregressive Models*. Oxford University Press.

Just-Food.com (2002) 'Del Monte Loses Bid to Prevent Dole Foods Marketing Sweet Pineapple' (6 February).

Just, R. E. and W. S. Chern (1980) 'Tomatoes, Technology and Oligopsony', *Bell Journal of Economics*, 11: 584-602.

Karl, K. (2000) 'Signing Ceremony in Cotonou. A New Era of Cooperation', *The Courier*, Special Issue (September).

Karp, L. S. and J. M. Perloff (1989) 'Dynamic Oligopoly in the Rice Export Market', *The Review of Economics and Statistics*, 71: 462-70.

Karp, L. S. and J. M. Perloff (1993) 'A Dynamic Model of Oligopoly in the Coffee Export Market', *American Journal of Agricultural Economics*, 75: 448-57 (May).

Kasteele, A. van de (1998) 'The Banana Chain anno 1998', Amsterdam: Food World R&C (February).

Kersten, L. (1995) 'Impacts of the EU Banana Market Regulation on International Competition, Trade and Welfare', *European Review of Agricultural Economics*, 22(3): 321-35.

Korzeniewicz, R., P. and W. Martin (1994) 'The Global Distribution of Commodity Chains', in G. Gereffi and M. Korzeniewicz (eds) *Commodity Chains and Global Capitalism.* Westport, Connecticut: Praeger, pp. 67-91.

Krugman, P. (1979) 'Increasing Returns, Monopolistic Competition, and International Trade', *Journal of International Economics*, 9: 469-79.

Krugman, P. (1980) 'Scale Economies, Product Differentiation, and the Pattern of Trade', *The American Economic Review*, 70(5): 950-9.

Krugman, P. (1981) 'Intraindustry Specialization and the Gains from Trade', *Journal of Political Economy*, 89: 959-73.

Krugman, P. (1992) 'Does The New Trade Theories Require a New Trade Policy', *The World Economy*, 15(4): 423-41.

Krugman, P. (1994) *Rethinking International Trade,* Cambridge, MA: The MIT Press.

Kuilwijk, K. J. (1996a) 'The EC Banana Saga: Some Reflections on the Rights of EC Importers and Community Public Interest', in K. J. Kuilwijk and R. Wright (eds.) *European Trade and Industry in the 21st Century: Future Directions in EC Law and Policy*. Nexed Editions Academic Publishers and Centre for Critical European Studies, pp. 159-93.

Kuilwijk, K. J. (1996b) 'The Common Market in Bananas: Public Interests versus Individual Rights' in 'The European Court of Justice and the GATT Dilemma' *Critical European Studies*, Series-Volume 1.

Kumm, M. (1998) 'Who is the Final Arbiter of Constitutionality in Europe?', Jean Monnet Working Papers, Harvard: Harvard Law School.

Kwoka, J. E. (Jr.) (1981) 'Does the Choice of Concentration Measure Really Matter?', *Journal of Industrial Economics*, 29(4): 445-52.

Lall, S. (1996) 'Transnational Corporations and Economic Development', in United Nations (eds) *Transnational Corporations and World Development*. London, UK, and Boston, MA: International Thomson Business Press, pp. 44-72.

Lall, S. (1973) 'Transfer-Pricing by Multinational Firms', *Oxford Bulletin of Economics and Statistics*, 35(3): 173-195.

Lancaster, K. (1980) 'Intra-industry Trade Under Perfect Monopolistic Competition', *Journal of International Economics*, 10: 151-75.

Lewis, W. A. (1955) *The Theory of Economic Growth*. London: Allen and Unwin.

Linder, S. B. (1961) *An Essay on Trade and Transformation*. New York: John Wiley and Sons.

Litvak, I. A. and C. J. Maule (1977) 'Transnational Corporations and Vertical Integration: The Banana Case', *Journal of World Trade Law*, 11(6):537-49.

Lopez, R. E. (1984) 'Measuring Oligopoly Power and Production Responses of the Canadian Food Processing Industry', *Journal of Agricultural Economics*, 35: 219-30.

Lopez, R. A. and Z. You (1993) 'The Impact of Oligopsony and Taxation on the Haitian Coffee Economy', *World Development*, 21(3): 465-73.

MacKinnon, J.G. (1991) 'Critical Values for Cointegration Tests,' Chapter 13 in R. F. Engle and C.W.J. Granger (eds) *Long-run Economic Relationships: Readings in Cointegration*. Oxford: Oxford University Press.

Maddala, G. S. (1988) *Introduction to Econometrics*. New York, NY: Macmillan.

Magdoff, H. (1966) *The Age of Imperialism*. 1969 edition. New York: Monthly Review Press.

Mai, C. and H. Hwang (1999) 'Technology Choice under Duopoly', *Pacific Economic Review*, 4(1): 31-42 (February).

Maizels, A. (1992) *Commodities in Crisis: The Commodity Crisis of the 1980s and the Political Economy of International Commodity Politics*. Oxford: Clarendon Press.

Mangold, A., I. Halpern and J. Berman (1996) 'Working for the Yankee Dollar: The Honduran Republic of Chiquita', Council of Hemispheric Affairs, Occasional Paper Volume 1, Number 3.

Marshall, A. (1920) *Principles of Economics, An Introductory Volume, 8th Edition*. London: Macmillan.

Mavroidis, P. C. and W. Zdouc (1998) 'Legal Means to Protect Private Parties' Interests in the WTO: The Case of the EC New Trade Barriers Regulation', *Journal of International Economic Law*, 407-32.

McCorriston, S. and I. M. Sheldon (1996) 'The Effects of Vertical Markets on Trade Policy Reform', *Oxford Economic Papers*, 48:664-72.

McInerney, J. and L. Peston (1992) (eds) 'Fair Trade in Bananas? International Trade Policies in Bananas and Proposals to Alter Existing Policies in Line with the Single European Market', Report No. 239 (December). University of Exeter: Agricultural Economics Unit.

McMillan, J. (2001) *Game Theory in International Economics*. London: Routledge. (First published in 1986 by Harwood Academic Publishers GmbH).

Milner, C. and R. Read (2002) (eds) *Trade Liberalization, Competition and the WTO*. Cheltenham : Edward Elgar.

Mittelman, J. H. (1996) (ed.) *Globalization: Critical Reflections*. Colorado, US and London, UK: Lynne Rienner Publishers, Inc.

Moore, M. (2000) 'Address to the National Press Club', Washington, D.C. (13 April).

Mukherjee, C., H. White and M. Wuyts (1998) *Econometrics and Data Analysis for Developing Countries*. London and New York: Routledge.

Nash, J. (1951) 'Non-Cooperative Games', *Annals of Mathematics*.

Nash, J. (1950) 'The Bargaining Problem', *Econometrica*.

Nath, S. K. (1969) *A Reappraisal of Welfare Economics*, London: Routeledge & Kagan Paul.

Navaretti, G. B.; R. Faini and A. Silberston (1995) *Beyond the Multifibre Arrangement: Third World competition and restructuring Europe's textile industry*. Paris: OECD.

Nevo, A. (1998) 'Identification of the Oligopoly Solution Concept in Differentiated-Products Industry', *Economics Letters*, 59(3): 391-95 (June).

Newfarmer, R. S. and L.C. Marsh (1981) 'Industrial Interdependence and Development: A Study of International Linkages and Industrial Performance in Brazil', report to the US Commission on Trade (July).

Noich, A. (1985) 'European Community Trade Regulations for Bananas and Imports from Developing Countries', *Quarterly Journal of International Agriculture,* 24(1) (January- March).

Nurse, K. and W. Sandiford (1995) *Windward Islands Bananas: Challenges and Options Under the Single European Market*. Kingston, Jamaica: Friedrich Ebert Stiftung (July).

Odlum, G. (2000) 'Statement on Bananas.' Second Annual Meeting of Foreign Ministers of the Caribbean and the Secretary of State of the United States.

Ohlin, B. (1933) *Interregional and International Trade*. Cambridge: Harvard University Press.

Orozco-Santos, M.; J. Farias-Larios; G. Manzo-Sanchez and S. Guzman-Gonzalez (2001) 'Black Sigatoka disease (Mycosphaerella fijiensis Morelet) in Mexico', *Infomusa* 10:1(June).

Peers, S. (1999) 'Banana Split: WTO Law and Preferential Agreements in the EC Legal Order', *European Foreign Affairs Review*, 4(2): 195-214.

Peoples, J. and R. Sugden (2000) 'Divide and rule by transnational corporations', in Pitelis, C. and R. Sugden (eds) *The Nature of the Transnational Firm*. Second Edition. London, UK and New York, US: Routledge.

Pitelis, C. N. and R. Sugden (2000) (eds) *The Nature of the Transnational Firm*. Second Edition. London and New York: Routledge.

Plasschaert, S. (1996) 'Transfer pricing and taxation', in United Nations (1996) (ed.) *Transnational Corporations and World Development.* Routledge, London: International Thomson Business Press, 394-417.

Pfaffermayr, M. (1999) 'Conjectural-Variations Models and Supergames with Price Competition in a Differentiated Product Oligopoly', *Journal of Economics*, 70(3): 309-26.

Posner, M. V. (1961) 'International Trade and Technical Change', *Oxford Economic Papers*, 13: 323-41.

Prebisch, R. (1968) 'Towards a Global Strategy of Development : Report by the Secretary-General of the United Nations Conference on Trade and Development to the Second Session of the Conference, New Delhi', New York: United Nations.

Preville, C. (1997) 'Impacts of the Collapse of the EU's New Banana Regime (1993) on Eastern Caribbean and European Union's welfare', msRP, Institute of Social Studies, The Hague, The Netherlands.

Preville, C. (1999) 'How Will Free Trade Impact on Net Global Economic Welfare?: An Analysis of the EU's Banana Market Structure', Working Paper Series No. 290, Institute of Social Studies, The Hague, The Netherlands.

Pugel, T. A. and I. Walter (1984) 'US Corporate Interests and the Political Economy of trade Policy', Discussion Papers in International Investment and Business Studies, No. 78, University of Reading.

Pugel, T. A. (1978) *International Market Linkages and U.S. Manufacturing.* Cambridge, MA: Ballinger Publishing Company.

Raynolds, L. T. (1994) 'Institutionalizing Flexibility: A Comparative Analysis of Fordist and Post-Fordist Models of Third World Agro-Export Production', in G. Gereffi and M. Korzeniewicz (eds) *Commodity Chains and Global Capitalism.* Westport, Connecticut: Praeger, 143-61.

Read, R. A. (1986) 'The Banana Industry: Oligopoly and Barriers to Entry', in Mark Casson (ed.) *Multinationals and World Trade: Vertical Integration and the Division of Labour in World Industries.* London: Allen & Unwin, 317-42.

Read, R. A. (1994) 'The EC Internal Banana Market: The Issues and Dilemma', *The World Economy,* 17: 219-35.

Read, R. A. (2002) 'The EU-US WTO Banana Trade Dispute and the Evolution of the EU Banana Regime', in C. Milner and R. Read (eds) *Trade Liberalization, Competition and the WTO.* Cheltenham: Edward Elgar.

Ricardo, D. (1817) *On the Principle of Political Economy and Taxation,* Reprinted in Sraffa and Dobb (Eds.) *The Works and Corresponds of David Ricardo, Volume I.* Cambridge: Cambridge University Press.

Roche, J. (1998) *The International Banana Trade.* Cambridge, UK: Woodhead Publishing Limited.

Rugman, A. (1979) *International Diversification and the Multinational Enterprise.* Lexington, MA: Lexington Books.

Samatar, A. I. (1993) 'Structural Adjustment as Development Strategy? : Bananas, Boom and Poverty in Somalia', *Economic Geography,* 69(1): 25-43 (January).

Samuelson, P. A. (1948) 'International Trade and the Equalization of Factor Prices', *Economic Journal,* 58(230): 163-85 (June).

Sandiford, W. (2000) *On the Brink of Decline: Bananas in the Windward Islands.* St. George's, Grenada: Fedon Books.

Schmalensee, R. (1988) 'Industrial Economics: An Overview', *The Economic Journal*, 98: 643-681 (September)

Schmalensee, R. and R. D. Willig (1989) (Eds.) *Handbook of Industrial Organization.* North-Holland, Amsterdam: Elsevier Science Publishers B.V.

Schroeter, J. R. (1988) 'Estimating the Degree of Market Power in the Beef Packing Industry', *The Review of Economics and Statistics*, 70: 158-62.

Shafaeddin, S M (1994) 'The Impact of Trade Liberalization on Export and GDP Growth in Least Developed Countries', UNCTAD Discussion Paper No. 85, Geneva: UNCTAD.

Shapiro, C. (1989) 'Theories of Oligopoly Behavior', in R. Schmalensee and R. D. Willig (Eds.) in *Handbook of Industrial Organization, Volume 1.* North-Holland, Amsterdam: Elsevier Science Publishers B.V.

Smith, A. (1776) *The Wealth of Nations Volume I,* in Ernest Rhys (ed.) (1946) Everyman's Library No. 412. London: J. M. Dent & Sons Ltd.

Smith, A. and A. J. Venables (1988) 'Completing the Internal Market in the European Community: Some Industry Simulations', *European Economic Review*, 32: 1501-25.

Sopisconews.com (2002) 'Comment on the European Commission's Proposal for Allocation of Licenses to Non-traditional Operators', (8 February).

Stallings, B. (1995) (ed.) *Global Change, Regional Response. The New International Context of Development.* Cambridge: Cambridge University Press.

Stevens, C. (1996) 'EU Policy for the Banana Market: The External Impact of Internal Policies', in H. Wallace and W. Wallace (eds) *Policy Making in the European Union.* Oxford: Oxford University Press.

Stiegert, K. W., A. Azzam and B. W. Brorsen (1993) 'Markdown Pricing and Cattle Supply in the Beef Packing Industry', *American Journal of Agricultural Economics*, 75: 549-58 (August).

Stuckey, J. A. (1981) 'Vertical Integration and Joint Ventures in the International Aluminium Industry', Ph.D. dissertation, Harvard University.

Sutton, P. (1997) 'The Banana Regime of the European Union, the Caribbean, and Latin America', *Journal of Inter-American Studies and World Affairs*, 38(2): 5-36.

Talbot, J.M. (1997) 'Where Does Your Coffee Dollar Go?: The Division of Income and Surplus along the Coffee Commodity Chain', *Studies in Comparative International Development*, 32(1): 56-91 (Spring).

Teece, D. J. (1982) 'A Transactions Cost Theory of the Multinational Enterprise', Paper No. 66. Reading, UK: Department of Economics, University of Reading.

Teece, D. J. (1993) 'The Multinational Enterprise: Market Failure and Market Power considerations', in J. Dunning (ed.) *The Theory of Transnational Corporations, Volume 1*, UNLTNC. London: Routeledge, pp. 163-82.

Tradewatch (2002) 'EU Agriculture Council Adopts Proposal', (16 January).

Treaty of Rome (1957) 'Consolidated Version of the Treaty Establishing the European Community', www.europa.int.eu.

US/LEAP (1999) 'Global Banana Crisis Threatens Central American Unions and Wages', Newsletter (December).

USTR (1995) 'United States Will Challenge European Union Banana Import Regime in the World Trade Organization', (27 September).

Vernon, R. (1966) 'International Investment and International Trade in Product Cycle', *Quarterly Journal of Economics*, 80(2): 190-207.

Vernon, R. (1977) *Storm over the Multinationals: The Real Issues.* Cambridge, Massachusetts: Harvard University Press.

Vernon, R. (1994) 'Storm over the Multinationals', in C. R. Frischtak and R. S. Newfarmer (eds) *Transnational Corporations: Market Structure and Industrial Performance*, Vol. 15, UNLTNC, London: Routledge, pp. 63-82.

Viaene, J. and X. Gellynck (1995) 'Structure, conduct and performance of the European food sector', *European Review of Agricultural Economics*, 22(3): 282-95.

Wallace, H. and W. Wallace (1996)(eds) *Policy Making in the European Union.* Oxford: Oxford University Press.

Wolfensohn, J D (1999) 'World Bank: Statement by Mr. James D. Wolfensohn, President', WTO Seattle Ministerial Conference, Third Session (30 November).

World Bank (1985) *Dominican Republic: Economic Prospects and Policies to Renew Growth.* Washington D.C.: World Bank.

World Reefer List (1998) 'Reefer and Freezer Vessels above 50,000 cubic feet', Copenhagen, Denmark: Lauritzen Reefers A/S.

WTO (1997a) *Report of the Panel* in 'European Communities – Regime for the Importation, Sale and Distribution of Bananas – WT/DS27/ECU (May).

WTO (1997b) *Report of the Appellate Body* in 'European Communities –
Regime for the Importation, Sale and Distribution of Bananas – AB-1997-
3', WT/DS27/AB/R (September).

WTO (1999) *Report of the Panel* in 'European Communities – Regime for
the Importation, Sale and Distribution of Bananas – Recourse to Article
21.5 by Ecuador', WT/DS27/RW/ECU (12 April).

WTO (2000) *Status Report by the European Communities: Addendum* in
'European Communities – Regime for the Importation, Sale and
Distribution of Bananas ', WT/DS27/51/Add.7 (March).

WTO (2001) 'Conference ends with agreement on new programme', *Doha
WTO Ministerial 2001: Summary of 14 November.*

Yamin, M. (1991) 'A Reassessment of Hymer's Contribution to the Theory
of the Transnational Corporation', in C. Pitelis and R. Sugden (eds) *The
Nature of the Transnational Firm*. London, UK: Routledge.

Yamin, M. (2000) 'A critical re-evaluation of Hymer's contribution to the
theory of the transnational corporation', in C. Pitelis and R. Sugden (eds)
The Nature of the Transnational Firm. London, UK: Routledge.

Internet sources

The following websites were used by the author throughout the period of
research for either construction of his database, or for materials that have
been referenced in this thesis. Details of citations are given in endnotes
where relevant.

www.access.gpo.gov
www.banacol.com
www.bizjournals.com
www.chiquita.com
www.dole.com
www.europa.eu.int
www.fao.org
www.freshdelmonte.com
www.freshinfo.com
www.fruitnet.com
www.fyffes.com
www.geest-bananas.co.uk

www.hairyape.co.uk
www.hemscott.com
www.ifpri.cgiar.org
www.just-food.com
www.news.bbc.co.uk
www.nyse.com
www.oakleaf-european.co.uk
www.sec.gov
www.sopisconews.com
www.turbana.com
www.usaid.gov
www.usinfo.be
www.ustr.gov
www.washingtonpost.com

Newspapers

The following newspapers were used by the author throughout the period of research for either construction of his database, or for materials that have been referenced in this thesis. Details of citations are given in endnotes where relevant.

Agence Europe
Irish Sunday Independent
Reuters
The International Herald Tribune
The Times
The Wall Street Journal
Tradewatch

Database

(The author has used the files listed below for construction of the database that has been used for production of this thesis).

Banana Link (2000) 'The Banana Industry in Cameroun: A Social and Environmental Disaster Area', *Banana Trade News Bulletin*, No. 19 (February).

Business Wire (2000) 'Dole Food Company Inc. Announces Organizational Changes', *Nyse.com* (31 January).

Business Wire (2000) 'Dole Food Company Inc. Issues first-quarter 2000 Earnings Expectations and Announces Conclusion of Goldman Sachs and Co. Engagement', *Nyse.com* (29 March).

Canary Islands Regional Government (1998) 'Introduction to the Common Market Organisation for Bananas', (March).

Chiquita Brands International, Inc. (1994) 'Annual Report Pursuant to Section 15(d) of the Securities Exchange Act of 1934, for the Fiscal Year Ended December 31, 1993', *Sec.gov* (28 June).

Chiquita Brands International, Inc. (1994) 'Registration statement under the Securities Act of 1993', *Sec.gov* (24 January).

Chiquita Brands International, Inc. (1999) 'Quarterly Report Pursuant to Section 13 or 15(d) of the Securities Exchange Act of 1934', Sec.gov (30 September).

Chiquita Brands International, Inc. (2000) '1999 Annual Report and Form 10-K', 8 February.

Chiquita Brands International, Inc. (2000) 'Quarterly Report pursuant to Section 13 or 15(d) of the Securities Exchange Act of 1934', *Sec.gov* (30 September).

Chiquita Brands International, Inc. (2001) '2000 Annual Report and Form 10-K', 15 February.

De Lombaerde, G. (1997) 'Chiquita's Fruit-drink Supplier Goes Belly-up', *Bizjournals.com* (27 October).

De Lombaerde, G. (1999) 'Lindner Adds Chiquita Stock', *Bizjournals.com* (30 August).

Dole Food Company, Inc. (1995) 'Annual Report Pursuant to Section 13 or 15(d) of the Securities and Exchange Act of 1934, for the Fiscal Year Ended 31 December, 1994', *Sec.gov* (17 March).

Dole Food Company, Inc. (1995) 'Quarterly Report Pursuant to Section 13 or 15(d) of the Securities and Exchange Act of 1934, for the Quarterly Period Ended October 7, 1995', *Sec.gov* (28 December).

Dole Food Company, Inc. (1996) 'Annual Report 1995', (March).

Dole Food Company, Inc. (1997) 'Quarterly Report Pursuant to Section 13 or 15(d) of the Securities and Exchange Act of 1934, for the Quarterly Period Ended October 4, 1997', *Sec.gov* (18 November).

Dole Food Company, Inc. (1998) 'Quarterly Report Pursuant to Section 13 or 15(d) of the Securities and Exchange Act of 1934, for the Quarterly Period Ended October 10, 1998', *Sec.gov* (24 November).

Dole Food Company, Inc. (2000) 'Annual Report Pursuant to Section 13 or 15(d) of the Securities and Exchange Act of 1934, for the Fiscal Year Ended 1 January, 2000', *Sec.gov* (31 March).

Dole Food Company, Inc. (2001) 'Annual Report Pursuant to Section 13 or 15(d) of the Securities and Exchange Act of 1934, for the Fiscal Year Ended 30 December, 2000', *Sec.gov* (30 March).

Dorfman, B. (2001) 'Chiquita Pact Cedes Equity to Senior Debt Holders', *Reuters* (12 November).

Dow Jones and Company Inc. (2000) 'Dole Food sees 1st Quarter Net Exceeding Analysts' Estimates', *Nyse.com* (29 March).

Dow Jones and Company Inc. (2000) 'Dole Issues Rosy Outlook, Says It No Longer Is Considering Sale of Company', *Nyse.com* (29 March).

Dow Jones and Company Inc. (2000) 'Philippine San Miguel, Dole End Talks', *Nyse.com* (2 April).

Dow Jones and Company, Inc. (2001) 'Chiquita Brands Halts Bond Payments, Plans to Restructure Debt', *Nyse.com* (16 January).

European Commission (1997) 'The Common Agricultural Policy. Attitudes of EU Consumers to Fair Trade Bananas', Directorate–General for Agriculture (DGVI).

European Commission (1999) 'European Union Banana Imports: 1988-98', Directorate- General Agriculture (DGVI), Comext (17 May).

EUROSTAT (2000) 'Banana Imports and Intra-trade of EU10-12: 1976-87', *Computer Data Files*.

EUROSTAT (2000) 'Monthly and Annual Banana Imports and Intra-trade of EU12-15: 1988-99', *Computer Data Files*.

EUROSTAT (2000) 'Monthly and Annual Exchange Rates of the ECU to National Currencies 1988-99', *Computer Data Files*.

EUROSTAT (2000) 'Monthly and Annual Exchange Rates of the ECU to the US dollar 1988-99', *Computer Data Files*.

EUROSTAT (2000) 'Population by EU Member State: 1970-99', Computer Data Files.

Fairtrade Foundation (2000) 'Unpeeling the Banana Trade', *Fairtrade.org.uk* (August).

FAO (1998) 'Quarterly Bulletin of Statistics', Vol. 11, No. 3/4.

FAO (1999) 'Banana Information Note', (December).

FAO (1999) 'Projections for Supply and Demand of Bananas to 2005', Committee on Commodity Problems, Intergovernmental Group on Bananas and Tropical Fruits, Gold Coast, Australia (4-8 May).

FAO (1999) 'Quarterly Bulletin of Statistics', Vol. 12, No. 3/4.

FAO (1999) 'The Impact of Banana Supply and Demand Changes on Income, Employment and Food Security', Committee on Commodity Problems, Intergovernmental Group on Bananas and Tropical Fruits, Gold Coast, Australia (4-8 May).

FAO (1999) 'The Market for 'Organic' and 'Fair-Trade' Bananas', Committee on Commodity Problems, Intergovernmental Group on Bananas and Tropical Fruits, Gold Coast, Australia (4-8 May).

FAO (2000) 'EC Banana Supply: 1986-99', *Computer Data Files.*

FAO (2000) 'France – Banana Import Prices (FFR/KG) by month: 1971-99', *Computer Data Files.*

FAO (2000) 'France – Banana Retail Prices (FFR/KG) by month: 1978-99', *Computer Data Files.*

FAO (2000) 'France – Banana Wholesale Prices (FFR/KG) by month: 1978-99', *Computer Data Files.*

FAO (2000) 'Germany – Banana Import Prices (DM/TON) by month: 1971-99', *Computer Data Files.*

FAO (2000) 'Germany – Banana Retail Prices (DM/KG) by month: 1978-98', *Computer Data Files.*

FAO (2000) 'Germany – Banana Wholesale Prices – Chiquita (DM/TON) by month: 1973-98', *Computer Data Files.*

FAO (2000) 'Japan – Average Banana Import Prices (YEN/KG) by month: 1971-98', *Computer Data Files.*

FAO (2000) 'Japan – Average Banana Retail Prices (YEN/KG) by month: 1978-98', *Computer Data Files.*

FAO (2000) 'Japan – Average Banana Wholesale Prices (YEN/KG) by month: 1978- 98', *Computer Data Files.*

FAO (2000) 'United Kingdom – Banana Retail Prices (Pence/Kg) by month: 1973-98', *Computer Data Files.*

FAO (2000) 'United Kingdom – Banana Wholesale Prices – Central America (Pence/K) by month: 1973-98', *Computer Data Files.*

FAO (2000) 'United States – Banana Import Prices (US$/TON) by month: 1971-99', *Computer Data Files.*

FAO (2000) 'United States – Banana Retail Prices (US$/TON) by month: 1973-98', *Computer Data Files.*

FAO (2000) 'United States – Banana Wholesale Prices (US$/TON) by month: 1973- 98', *Computer Data Files.*

FAO (2000) 'World Banana Exports by Countries of Destination: 1988-97', *Computer Data Files.*

FAO (2000) 'World Banana Gross Imports by Country of Origin: 1988-97', *Computer Data Files.*

FAO (2000) 'World Banana Harvest in Hectares: 1971-99', *Computer Data Files.*

FAO (2000) 'World Banana Net Imports: 1973-85', *Computer Data Files.*

FAO (2000) 'World Banana Net Imports: 1986-98', *Computer Data Files.*

FAO (2000) 'World Banana Production (TONS): 1971-99', *Computer Data Files.*

FAO (2000) 'World Banana Yields (KG/Ha): 1971-99', *Computer Data Files.*

FAO (2000) 'World Export Value of Bananas: 1970-98', *Computer Data Files.*

FAO (2000) 'World Export Value of Plantains: 1970-98', *Computer Data Files.*

FAO (2000) 'World Gross Banana Exports: 1973-99', *Computer Data Files.*

FAO (2000) 'World Per Capita Banana Net Imports (KG/Head) by month: 1973-85', *Computer Data Files.*

FAO (2000) 'World Per Capita Banana Net Imports (KG/Head) by month: 1986-99', *Computer Data Files.*

FAO (2000) 'World Plantain Harvest in Hectares: 1971-99', *Computer Data Files.*

FAO (2000) 'World Value of banana imports: 1970-98', *Computer Data Files.*

Fresh Del Monte Produce, Inc. (2000) 'Annual Report pursuant to Section 13 or 15(d) of the Securities and Exchange Act of 1934, for the fiscal year ended 31 December, 1999', *Sec.gov* (27 March).

Fresh Del Monte Produce, Inc. (2001) 'Annual Report pursuant to Section 13 or 15(d) of the Securities and Exchange Act of 1934, for the fiscal year ended 29 December, 2000', *Sec.gov* (07 March).

Hemmer, A. (1996) 'Chiquita will stay in smaller space', *Bizjournals.com* (5 August).

Higgins, M (2000) 'Chiquita top banana with product certification', Environmental News Network, (November 20).

Islam, N. (1990) 'Horticultural Exports of Developing Countries: Past Performances, Future Prospects, and Policy Issues', Research Report 80, International Food Policy Research Institute (April).

Kincaid, V. (1996) 'Chiquita in Line for Major Ruling', *Bizjournals.com* (11 November).

Ngeze, P B (1994) *Bananas and Their Management*. Bukoba, Tanzania: Kagera Writers and Publishers Co-operative Society Ltd.

Olson, R W (2001) 'Chiquita Files Damages Suit Against the European Commission', *Chiquita.com* (25 January).

Preville, C. (2000) 'Distribution of Banana Revenue (French commodity chain)', *Computer data files*.

Preville, C. (2000) 'Distribution of Banana Revenue (German commodity chain)', *Computer data files*.

Preville, C. (2000) 'Distribution of Banana Revenue (British commodity chain)', *Computer data files*.

Preville, C. (2000) 'Distribution of Banana Surplus (French commodity chain)', *Computer data files*.

Preville, C. (2000) 'Distribution of Banana Surplus (German commodity chain)', *Computer data files*.

Preville, C. (2000) 'Distribution of Banana Surplus (British commodity chain)', *Computer data files*.

Preville, C. (2000) 'World Banana Prices', *Computer data files*.

Preville, C. (2000) 'World Banana Exports', *Computer data files*.

Preville, C. (2000) 'World Banana Imports', *Computer data files*.

Preville, C. (2000) 'Pre-SEM Pattern of Trade', *Computer data files*.

Preville, C. (2000) 'Post-SEM Pattern of Trade', *Computer data files*.

Preville, C. (2000) 'Market Power Regressions – FAO – Annually', *Computer data files*.

Preville, C. (2000) 'Market Power Regressions – FAO – Monthly', *Computer data files*.

Preville, C. (2000) 'Firm Market Shares', *Computer data files*.

Preville, C. (2000) 'Firm Market Shares 1992-98', *Computer data files*.

Preville, C. (2000) 'Cost Structure – Chiquita Bananas!', *Computer data files*.

Preville, C. (2000) 'Chiquita's Pattern of Contributions', *Computer data files*.

Preville, C. (2000) 'Banana Brands!', *Computer data files*.

Preville, C. (2000) 'Market Power Regressions – Importing Countries (annually)', *Computer data files*.

Preville, C. (2000) 'Market Power Regressions – Importing Countries (monthly)', *Computer data files*.

Preville, C. (2000) 'Composition of EU trade (1976-87)', *Computer data files.*

Preville, C. (2000) 'Retail Import Margins', *Computer data files.*

Preville, C. (2000) 'Liberalization Oligopoly – base data!', *Computer data files.*

Preville, C. (2000) 'EU Population Structure', *Computer data files.*

Preville, C. (2000) 'US-EU Price Relationship – Model', *Computer data files.*

Preville, C. (2000) 'World Banana Costs of Production', *Computer data files.*

PRNewswire (2001) 'Chiquita Announces Financial Restructuring Initiative', *Nyse.com* (16 January).

Regional Negotiating Machinery (2000) 'International Economic Negotiations. The First Triennium: Challenges Ahead', (March).

Riley, J B (2001) 'Chiquita Announces Second Quarter Results', *Chiquita.com* (24 July).

Sandstrom, W T (2001) 'Chiquita Announces First Quarter Results', *Chiquita.com* (24 April).

US/Guatemala Labor Education Project (1998) 'Guatemala: Conflict on Banana Plantations', *Laborrights.org* (26 March).

Warshaw, S G (2001) 'Chiquita Comments on US-EU Banana Trade Agreement', *Chiquita.com* (11 April).

Watkins, S. (1999) 'Short-selling in Beleaguered Chiquita Stock Still Climbing', *Bizjournals.com* (11 September).

WIBDECO (1998) 'Annual Report 1997', (11 September).

WIBDECO (1999) 'Annual Report 1998', (15 July).

WIBDECO (2000) 'Market Report July: Weeks 27-30', (4 August).

Index

ADF
  discussion of test results, 244
  extensions of original work, 260
  origins of the test, 260
  relevance for model selection, 282
  results of tests on monthly and
    annual data, 310–15
  significance in price relationships,
    269
  tests performed, 231
Appellate Body
  decision against EU banana
    policy, 6
  endorsement of Panel findings,
    143
  scope of applicability of the
    GATS, 144
banana
  as a physical good subject to
    service value added, 3
  commodity chain as the unit of
    analysis, 7
  conceptualization of EU trade in,
    4
  empirical evidence about EU
    trade in, 2
  EU's regime under regulation 404,
    2
  import policies of EU member-
    states, 16-17
  nature of EU trade in, 2-3
  stages in the commodity chain, 20
Borrell, Brent
  assumption of perfect
    competition, 14
  assumptions on super-normal
    profits to ACP countries, 205
  early empirical work on EU
    banana trade, 14

Borrell (cont'd)
  estimate of consumer surplus, 31
  evidence contrary to assumptions,
    27
  evidence contrary to expectations
    of exporting countries, 187
  evidence contrary to expectations
    on monopoly power, 219
  expectations regarding exporting
    countries, 165
  exponent of the neo-classical
    approach to trade
    liberalization, 10
  indifference to market structure,
    11
  influence of work on trade policy,
    31
  neo-classical methodology, 23
  US banana price as world price,
    19
box plots
  of banana revenue for the banana-
    exporting countries, 179, 180,
    181
  of banana revenue in France, 171
  of banana revenue in Germany,
    163
  of banana revenue in the UK, 178
  of margins for the banana-
    exporting countries, 195, 196,
    197, 201, 202, 203, 204, 205,
    210, 214, 215, 216
  of margins in France, 194
  of margins in the UK, 200
  of revenue for banana-exporting
    countries, 164, 165, 166, 167,
    172,173,181, 183, 184
  used for demonstrating division of
    revenue, 158
  used for exploratory data analysis,
    5

Claudius Preville

Admitted to the ISS Ph.D. programme in January 1999 on the basis of:

BSc in Physics and Computer Science (1989)
University of the West Indies,
Bridgetown, Barbados.

MA in Economics of Development (1997)
Institute of Social Studies,
The Hague, The Netherlands.

This Ph.D. thesis has not been submitted to any university for a degree or any other award.